BIG ID[EAS]
GREAT [SOLUTIONS]

*AND THE WORLD-WIDE EXPERIENCE
TO HELP MAKE THEM WORK...FOR YOU*

CMBS *Analyst*™- *The On-Line CMBS Portfolio Analytical Tool*

The CMBS *Analyst* facilitates secondary market activity by enabling traders and investors to analyze projected CMBS performance. Using our existing KPMG *FAST*™ technology, the CMBS *Analyst* offers transaction and portfolio analytics specifically tailored to the CMBS trader/investor, such as:

- *Dial-In accessibility which enables the user to analyze projected CMBS performance on a real-time basis...*

- *Scenario analytics which enables the user to assign prepayment, default, loss and extension assumptions at either the loan or pool level...*

- *Loan level stratifications based on either individual or multiple criteria which may be used for constructing "what if" scenarios...*

- *On-Line access to monthly updates of underlying mortgage loan level and securities information...*

- *Ability to retrieve mortgage loan level and securities information to facilitate internal research and secondary trading...*

- *Report generation capabilities, including price/yield tables, weighted average lives, and duration as well as prepayment lock-out and premium analysis of the mortgage pool...*

- *Underlying modeling capabilities which accommodate different tranche and collateral types, capital structures and/or payment allocations currently in the market (e.g., bond yield maintenance allocation of prepayment charges)...*

- *Ability to interface with other analytical tools for performing collateral sensitivity analysis at the property level.*

KPMG

THE GLOBAL LEADER™

Michael Horn
Partner and National Director - Mortgage and Structured Finance Group
202-467-3236

KPMG Peat Marwick LLP is a U.S. member firm of KPMG International.

The Handbook of Commercial Mortgage-Backed Securities

Edited by

Frank J. Fabozzi
Adjunct Professor of Finance
Yale University
and
Editor
The Journal of Portfolio Management

and

David P. Jacob
Managing Director and
Director of Research and Securitization
Nomura Securities International, Inc.

Published by Frank J. Fabozzi Associates
in conjunction with
Nomura Securities International, Inc.

© 1997 By Frank J. Fabozzi Associates
New Hope, Pennsylvania

This publication is designed to provide accurate and authoritative information in regard to the subject matter covered. It is sold with the understanding that the publisher is not engaged in rendering legal, accounting, or other professional services.

ISBN: 1-883249-11-2

Printed in the United States of America

TABLE OF CONTENTS

CONTRIBUTING AUTHORS

Jesse M. Abraham	Federal Home Loan Mortgage Corporation
John W. Alexander	Price Waterhouse LLP
David Baranick	Price Waterhouse LLP
Manus J. Clancy	The Trepp Group
Michael Constantino, III	The Trepp Group
Patrick Corcoran	Nomura Securities International, Inc.
John N. Dunlevy	Hyperion Capital Management
Joseph L. Ferst	Price Waterhouse LLP
Joseph C. Franzetti	Duff & Phelps Credit Rating Co.
Galia Gichon	Nomura Securities International, Inc.
Keith A. Gollenberg	CIGNA Investment Management
Ted C.H. Hong	Nomura Securities International, Inc.
David P. Jacob	Nomura Securities International, Inc.
Duen-Li Kao	General Motors Investment Management Corp.
Elazar Katz	Commercial Assets, Inc.
Dan Lee	
Laurence H. Lee	Nomura Securities International, Inc.
Alice A. Lustig	Nomura Securities International, Inc.
Jojy Mathew	SS&C
Gregory S. McCauley	Price Waterhouse LLP
J. Zachary Monsma	Fitch Investors Service, L.P.
Michael R. Pfeifer	Wolf & Pfeifer
Janet G. Price	Fitch Investors Service, L.P.
Shahid H. Quraishi	Price Waterhouse LLP
Israel Snow	Price Waterhouse LLP
H. Scott Theobald	Federal Home Loan Mortgage Corporation
Lynn Tong	Nomura Securities International, Inc.

INDEX OF ADVERTISERS

Chapter 1

A Property Market Framework for Bond Investors

Patrick Corcoran, Ph.D.
Vice President
Nomura Securities International, Inc.

INTRODUCTION

The newly emerging market in commercial mortgage-backed securities (CMBS) consists of securities backed by commercial mortgage whole loans and these loans, in turn, are generally secured by first liens on the underlying real estate. These underlying properties could be office buildings, retail shopping malls, or neighborhood shopping centers, industrial warehouses, hotels, or multifamily residential properties. In addition, the real estate collateral might be less traditional property types such as seniors housing, mobile home parks, or factory outlet centers. The purpose of this chapter is to set out a framework for thinking about these different types of real estate and to illustrate and apply the framework principles in each of the major property types.

REAL ESTATE FUNDAMENTALS

As with the fundamentals of individual companies, real estate fundamentals are not locked in stone but depend upon market forces of demand and supply. These can and do change over time, providing rewards for the diligent analyst.

Demand and Supply for Space
At a basic level, the demand for the services of real estate space is a derived demand; that is, it derives from the business and activity of the users of the space. The demand for space will reflect the character of the operating businesses which seek to utilize it.

1

In the case of retail properties, the ultimate support for the property's rental cash flows comes from the sales of goods and services by individual retailers. Thus, demand for a property's space will reflect the aggregate success or failure of various groups of retailers. It will also be influenced by the unique locational characteristics of each individual property. For example, the locational attractiveness of retail properties will depend on local area population densities and income distributions as well as local highway and traffic patterns.

The demand for properties in a particular market can be represented graphically as in Exhibit 1 (top panel). Holding other things unchanged, the demand for space is downward sloping or negatively related to the market rental rate. With the supply of space fixed in the short run, the market rent is determined at point A. These analytical notions can be used to highlight two general characteristics of the demand for space. The first is the cyclical sensitivity of space demands to general conditions in the economy. For example, in a typical recession, apartment and retail properties are generally thought to exhibit the smallest deterioration in performance. Industrial and office properties would be considered moderately sensitive to such a downturn while hotel properties would be considered highly sensitive.

Such generalizations must be made carefully, however; for example, the mid-1980's 40% decline in oil prices caused a very sharp regional downturn in the Southwest in which apartment commercial mortgage delinquencies exceeded those in other real estate sectors.

A second general characteristic of the demand for space is its trend rate of growth. In the office market, for example, about 80% of absorption in the past decade has occurred in suburban markets rather than in downtown markets. In the hotel area, "limited service" hotels have posted higher occupancies than "full service" hotels for the past decade — despite a faster rate of new construction. In other words, demand for their services has grown faster.

An obvious general contributor to strongly rising space demands is new business relocations and population growth such as has been occurring in the Texas markets, the Mountain states, and the Southeast. This has led to rising trends in space demands for apartments, industrial properties, and suburban offices in many of these markets.

Another important factor in shaping trends is shifting demographics. Baby boomers heading into their fifties are more likely to spend money on services including travel and health care rather than goods.

These factors all have important implications for the trend growth in the demand for space. Obviously, differences in trend demand growth have the potential over time to be much more important than temporary cyclical shortfalls in demand. For example, if a market has a vacancy rate of 10% with trend absorption growth of 5% per year, it only requires one year's absorption to reduce the vacancy rate to 5%. If absorption growth were 1% per year, five years would be required. However, because changing trends in demand are difficult to establish and distinguish from cyclical movements, there is a tendency among analysts to be very slow to perceive new trends and to overemphasize the purely cyclical variability in demand.

Exhibit 1: Real Estate Markets: 1980s Overbuilding

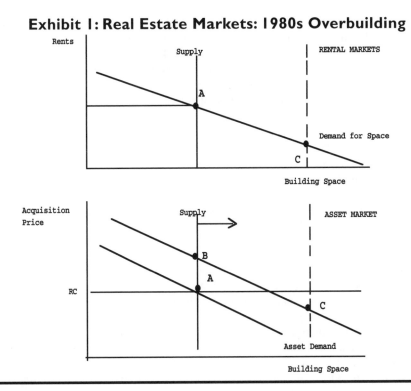

Supply Outlook for Space

Incentives governing new supply and the linkage between real estate and the capital markets are captured in the bottom panel of Exhibit 1. Unlike the top panel, which represents the rental market, the bottom panel represents the asset market.[1] The downward sloping demand curve represents the demand to own real estate as an asset at different property prices. At a point in time, the demand or valuation relationship is influenced by the level of interest rates and attitudes about risk and current and future earnings. With the existing supply of space fixed for the moment, the demand and supply for the asset determine today's market valuation (at point A).

A key indicator of future supply is whether property values are above or below replacement cost, and by how much. If property values are far above replacement cost (B exceeds RC in bottom panel), as occurred in the 1980s, there will be large incentives for excessive new development because the difference between property value and replacement cost is the developer's profit margin. Alternatively, following the overbuilding of the 1980s, today's values remain well below replacement cost in many markets (position C, bottom panel). This means that no new supply is forthcoming because developers' profit margins are negative.

---

[1] For early exposition of this "two market" view, see Patrick J. Corcoran, "Explaining the Commercial Real Estate Market," *Journal of Portfolio Management*, Autumn 1987.

In general, upward shifts in the demand for space tend to be matched by roughly parallel increases in property valuations because the higher rents and net operating income are capitalized into higher values. The resulting parallel increases in rents and property values tends to keep property markets roughly in balance by generating parallel increases in the demand and supply of space.

Exceptions to this tendency highlight episodes or markets that are either very favorable or very unfavorable to real estate investors. A notable example was the 1980's overbuilding boom when the demand to own real estate as an asset rose far more than the demand for space. The dynamics of this episode are captured in Exhibit 1. Excessive optimism about real estate returns shows up as an upward shift in the valuation curve (bottom panel), which is not accompanied by a parallel increase in the demand for space (top panel). The resulting increase in property prices (A to B, bottom panel) creates strong incentives for new development. This in turn increases the outstanding supply of space, thereby ultimately pushing down rents and values (position C, both panels).

Another example was the aftermath of the 1980s overbuilding boom in the first half of the 1990s (see Exhibit 2). Investors who were burned on the downside of the cycle were very slow to price in rising rents and net operating income (NOI) into values even though space markets had been tightening for several years in a row. Thus, the bottom of the cycle and early recovery phase can be as favorable to real estate lenders as the top of the cycle is unfavorable. With space demands rising and supply constrained, rising rents and property values show up in Exhibit 2 as the movement from A to B (top and bottom panel).

In contrast to generally overbuilt markets in the 1980s and their aftermath in the 1990s, "normal" real estate markets exhibit much greater diversity in terms of demand/supply fundamentals. Indeed, in these markets our discussion points to a more general issue for lenders and bond investors. In principle, real estate markets can be favorable either because the demand for space is very strong or because demand is only moderate but new supply is very weak. In practice, however, today's "weak supply" markets are usually yesterday's overbuilding episodes in which investors took a beating. The result is that lenders are prone to avoid these markets like the plague and "weak supply" markets are often bastions of relative value for lenders willing to take contrarian positions. In the context of a large pool or portfolio of commercial mortgage loans (or CMBS), a mix of "strong demand" and contrarian lending is a profitable avenue for diversification because it represents a bet on a different set of real estate fundamentals.

In this context, Exhibits 1 and 2 can represent more general dynamics of local markets or sectors that are strongly in favor and out of favor. If investors' love for a particular market outruns real estate fundamentals (as represented in Exhibit 1), the problems are twofold. Not only are investors "overpaying," but the excessive valuations bring on future new supply which reduces rentals and increases vacancies. This is part of the backdrop of the problems that the retail sector is experiencing in the mid 1990s. The contrary case of an out of favor submarket or sector with excessively pessimistic valuations is represented in Exhibit 2. Here deeply discounted valuations are a barrier to new supply which, combined with modesty growing space demands, turns out very favorably.

Exhibit 2: Real Estate Market: 1990s Aftermath

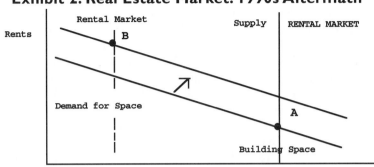

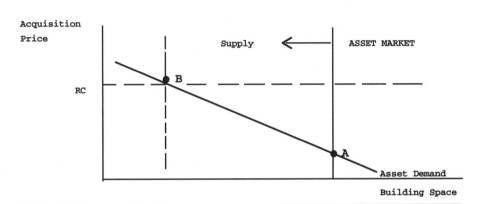

"Quality" Real Estate

The notion of high quality real estate is used in many different ways. Bond investors or lenders should be interested in concepts of quality that limit downside risk relative to alternative investments offering the same expected returns. Often, however, concepts of quality are simply ways of distinguishing between newer, more modern properties and older more obsolescent properties. Alternatively, quality may be a shorthand way of distinguishing between "in favor" and "out of favor" sectors or, even worse, "my properties" and "your properties."

In insurance company circles, high quality real estate often seems to mean properties in the upper third of the rental distribution, defined either in a narrow submarket or perhaps more broadly. This is because the focus is on a list of desirable property amenities, including "dominant" location, which ought to translate into higher rents. The implicit assumption is that this notion of quality will provide superior protection to a downturn in the economy.

Our "two market" view highlights several problems with this approach. First, it ignores the pricing of the properties (as well as loans secured by such properties). In our view, it is not a coincidence that downtown office properties and full service hotels, which insurance companies thought had high quality in the 1980s, ended up as two of the most overbuilt sectors. Secondly, since amenities, including dominant location, must be paid for and maintained, higher rents do not necessarily translate into higher profit margins. A good example is limited service hotels, which have fewer amenities than full service hotels but whose profit margins have been substantially higher (see below) for the past decade. Thirdly, there is not enough focus on the quality of the loan rather than the quality of the real estate. For instance, direct ownership of a hotel may be more risky than a large apartment property, but a 30% loan to value (LTV) hotel loan may be less risky than an 80% apartment loan.

Rating agency concepts of quality target property specific and local market attributes but also focus heavily on debt service coverage ratios based on current NOIs and loan to value ratios. These ratios are used to set subordination requirements necessary for a CMBS to obtain a given credit rating. Because rating agencies are looking specifically at real estate debt, they do a better job than insurance companies in clearly distinguishing between loan quality and real estate quality. If the rating agencies have done their jobs correctly, a AAA-rated bond supported by a pool of retail loans and a AAA-rated bond supported by a pool of office loans should have the same expected losses.

In summary, all notions of real estate quality ultimately hinge on the fundamentals of demand and supply. Analysts often speak and write as though longer term trends and shorter term cyclical movements could be easily ascertained and distinguished from one another. What analysts call "quality," "trend," and "cycle" are in effect averages of history's demand and supply curves. In practice, whether past trends will continue into the future is subject to considerable uncertainty and future trends often fail to follow in the footsteps of past trends. As one poet has put it, "...history is of ages past, unrequited shadows cast."

Our framework points to the following factors as important "real estate quality" issues for bond investors:

(1) current sustainable cash flow, occupancies, and rentals
(2) sensitivity of property performance to the business cycle
(3) likely future growth of demand for space and rents
(4) the relationship between the property values and replacement costs in the property's local market

The next section looks more closely at these issues for each of the major property sectors.

APARTMENT PROPERTY

In the overbuilding boom of the 1980s, apartments suffered fewer imbalances than other property sectors, experienced smaller value declines, and recovered earlier from the downturn. The relative absence of overbuilding likely reflected a smaller allocation to this sector by institutional investors than would be the case today. Demand for apartment units was initially soft in 1991-1992, paralleling general weakness in the economy's recovery from the recession of the early 1990s. However, net absorption of multifamily space picked up very sharply beginning in 1994 and maintained this stronger pace during 1995. Parallel to this pickup, rents have improved and vacancies fallen. Indeed, by late 1995 the national vacancy rate for larger, professionally managed multifamily properties had fallen to about 5%.

In the mid 1990s, apartments were a sought after asset class by institutional investors, reflecting both the appetites of acquisitive REITs and the underweighting of apartments in the real estate portfolios of many pension fund investors. To some extent the increased interest in apartments arises from "repulsion" from other real estate sectors which performed poorly. A positive attribute of apartments is their general resilience in the face of economic downturns. While this seems to have been generally true, the oil-related downturn in Texas in the mid 1990s is a counterexample.

As shown in Exhibit 3, apartment returns averaged better than 12% in 1994-1995 and life insurer loan delinquencies have been on a sharply falling path since late 1991. Some further improvement in loan performance continued during 1995, although at a slower pace than previously. At this point, apartment valuations were approaching parity with replacement costs in many faster growing markets (see below). The "automatic recovery" mechanisms arising from negligible new supply were largely spent. With the resumption of more "normal" markets, investors need to be more focused on long run real estate fundamentals and the balance of rental demand with emerging new supply.

From a regional perspective, the strongest appreciation has been in the more rapidly growing parts of the country (Exhibit 4), which have benefited from a substantial inflow of business relocations. These include the Southeast, the Southwest, and the surging Mountain states. On a five year basis ending in late 1995, the Mountain states were the only region posting positive appreciation because this period covers the downturn in real estate markets in 1990-1991. During 1995, every region in the country posted increases in values including the lagging California market.

Demand and Supply for Space

With the demand for apartment space rebounding in 1994-1995, absorption has been exceeding the supply of new space for the first time in over a decade. As a result, vacancies have generally been declining, and effective rents increasing *pari passu* with the general inflation rate for the first time since the mid 1980s. While a better demand/supply balance across regions has been a common theme in the mid-1990s, a look at regional vacancy rates over a longer period highlights diverse trends in markets (Exhibit 5). For example, vacancy rates in the southern region (including both southwest and southeast) were pushed up by oil-related regional economy weakness in the mid 1980s. Since then, however, favorable longer term absorption trends helped bring the vacancy rate back down. By contrast, the Northeast saw a combination of overbuilding and more modest absorption push up vacancies from their low levels in the mid 1980s.

Exhibit 3: Multifamily Total Rate of Return and Delinquency

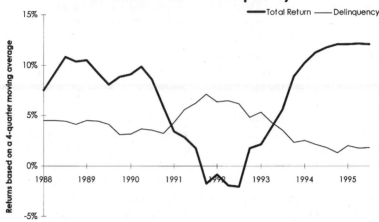

Source: American Council of Life Insurance and NCREIF.

Exhibit 4: Annual Apartment Appreciation Ending Q3'95

	5 Year	3 Year	1 Year
Northeast/Mideast	-3.3	0.9	1.9
East North Central	-2.3	-0.5	2.0
West North Central	—	—	—
Pacific	-5.5	-2.6	2.1
Mountain	1.7	4.7	7.1
Southeast	-1.5	2.2	2.2
Southwest	—	1.2	1.3
Total	-2.6	0.7	2.7

Source: NCREIF.

Exhibit 5: Multifamily Vacancy Rates

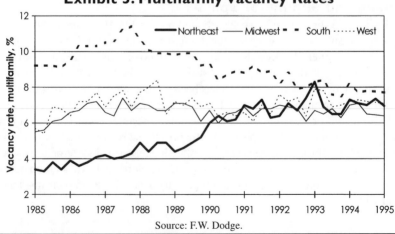

Source: F.W. Dodge.

Exhibit 6: Single Family and Renter Costs
(% of Disposable Income)

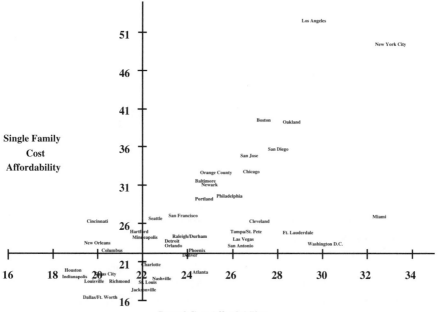

Source: 1995 Study of Housing Costs, E&Y Kenneth Leventhal, Real Estate Group, Ernst & Young LLP.

In general, the mid 1990s has witnessed a resumption of strong space absorption in the south and west — excluding California. The long term tendency of both U.S. residents and immigrants to locate in the sunbelt rather than the frostbelt reflects movement from high cost to low cost centers for conducting business. Historically, regional wage cost advantages for business have always been undergirded by affordable housing for employees. By contrast, a scarcity of affordable housing is a surefire way to create a labor shortage and choke off economic growth. Exhibit 6 shows the cost of single family home ownership on the vertical scale and the cost of apartment renting on the horizontal scale. Both costs are shown relative to area disposable income. Metro areas such as Dallas/Fort Worth and Houston, which continue to experience substantial business relocations, are low cost housing centers — both for single family homes and apartments.

The large cities of the Northeast, by contrast, and California are high cost centers. These metro areas have particularly high costs for single family housing. The cost-driven movement to low cost centers in the south and west is likely to be amplified by the growth of trade with the Pacific Rim and with Latin America.

Exhibit 7: The High Price of High Costs

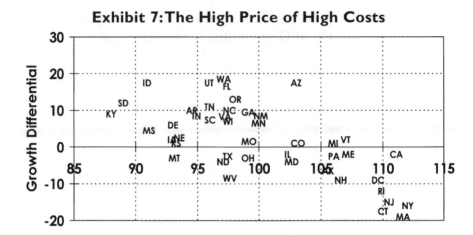

Relative Costs

Source: Regional Financial Associates, Inc.

Low costs of doing business historically have translated into faster growth. Exhibit 7 shows the different states aligned by relative costs (average equals 100) and growth rate differentials (average equals zero) for the three years ending in 1995. The high cost Northeastern states (NJ, CT, MA, NY, RI) and California (CA) are also the low growth states. While rapid new business development will spur demand for other kinds of real estate space, demand for multifamily housing is perhaps the most obvious and predictable beneficiary.

While regional trends affecting multifamily housing seem fairly clear, trends influencing rent-versus-buy choices are mixed to negative. On the one hand, the aging of the baby boomer cohorts and sharp improvement in housing affordability both favor home ownership rather than rental. On the other hand, low inflation rates with correspondingly low ownership returns favor renting. In addition, the increasing segmentation of households has resulted in wide differences in demand for rental space within and across markets. One growing segment of the multifamily market, discussed in the next section, is seniors housing.

Conclusion

The upward momentum in apartment prices beginning in 1994 has resulted from steadily increasing demand and no new supply for several years. In a number of the low cost centers of the south and west, which have been magnets for new business relocations and new business development, property values have risen above replacement cost levels and new development is again occurring. Investors with exposure in these markets are essentially betting on strong continued growth in the demand for space. In other more slowly growing markets, new supply remains constrained by depressed property values. Here, investors' "bets" are a combination of weak supply growth and modest demand growth. Relative to other real estate sectors, however, the apartment markets are further along the road to recovery and generally represent more of a bet on rising demands for space.

SENIORS HOUSING

In its modern format, the seniors housing industry represents a variety of housing options for seniors ranging from congregate care facilities with little in the way of special services to assisted living choices. The surging demand for seniors housing stems from the rising numbers of seniors over age 75 combined with spiraling costs of skilled nursing care and the reduced availability of family support often necessary for continued independent living. These powerful forces have propelled seniors housing to the status of an emerging industry. Interestingly, this has occurred against a public policy backdrop, which has actively impeded the development of noninstitutional options. The prospects of public policy reform lend further impetus to a sector already charged with relative value.

Emerging Market in the 1980s

Early efforts to provide long term care for seniors were primarily those of church groups and the nonprofit sector. The 1980s, however, saw the entry of a variety of "for profit" businesses, which focused on the needs of healthier seniors who could benefit from a range of supportive services catering to their special needs. Congregate services can include common dining services as well as transportation, laundry, social programs and recreational facilities, emergency response systems, and various security features.

Congregate services had been available as early as the 1960s. The additional element in the 1980s was the availability of a variety of additional health and supportive services in assisted living facilities previously unavailable except in nursing homes. This new element paralleled other changes taking place in the health care system. A primary example was the increasing use of outpatient and home health care services, which had previously been available only in hospitals. Assisted living facilities provide a range of additional services for the frail elderly. These units are less likely to include a full kitchen, reflecting a need for greater assistance with meal preparation and the near universal delivery of meals to common dining quarters or residents' rooms. Continuing care retirement communities (CCRCs) offer the complete range of living arrangements from independent living to skilled nursing facilities.

Initial Operating Problems and Overbuilding in the 1980s

Many of the new operators in the 1980s experienced several problems. The first was that many healthy 65- to 75-year old seniors preferred their own independent living arrangements. In addition, congregate facilities that initially attracted younger, healthier seniors were often subsequently unable to hold them because they lacked direct access to supportive and health care services. What emerged, as the market developed, was the ability to allow residents to "age in place"; that is, meet the special needs of seniors by standing ready to offer a different mix of supportive services as their circumstances changed. Indeed, such investments in supportive and health care services which were both flexible and upgradeable to residents' needs became the *sine qua non* of successful operators in the 1980s.

These operating problems were aggravated by the same overbuilding, particularly in the upper income segment, which plagued other sectors of the real estate markets. As supply mushroomed and property values plunged, occupancies appear to have peaked around 1990 and reached their lows in 1992. The decline in property values was amplified by the pullback of lender funds, which helped to drive property cap rates to sky high levels in 1993 (Exhibit 8). As lender funds reentered the sector in 1994-1995, cap rates dropped sharply.

Current Market Conditions Cyclically Favorable

Depressed property values have severely curtailed new supply for the in the first half of the 1990s. During this period, successful operators have been actively acquiring distressed properties and repositioning them with investments in supportive and health care services. Indeed, as of 1994, it appears that about 30% of existing properties represent recent acquisitions and new ownership. Meanwhile, demand for congregate care services has continued to grow strongly. As shown in Exhibit 9, occupancy rates rose sharply by 6% to 93%, on average, at the end of 1993.

Taking into account the impact of repositioned properties, it appears that both demand for space and the "effective supply" have grown rapidly from 1993 to 1995. While end of 1994 figures are not yet available, occupancies likely improved somewhat further in 1994. Looking ahead, we expect demand for congregate care services to continue to grow strongly. Following the burst in acquisition activity from 1992 to 1995, new supply will likely rely more on new development and less on repositioning of older properties.

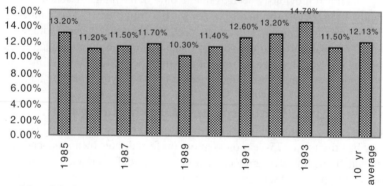

Exhibit 8: Capitalization Rates, Selected Seniors Housing Transactions

Source: Selected Seniors Housing Transactions, 1985-1993 American Seniors Housing Association.

Exhibit 9: Change in Seniors Housing Occupancy Rates, 1992-1993

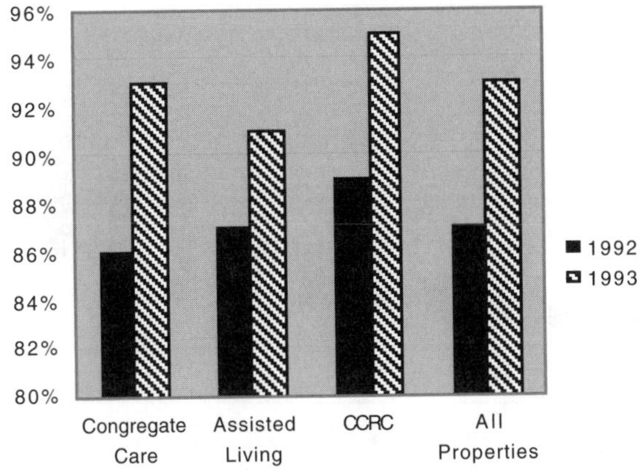

Source: The state of Seniors Housing 1994, American Seniors Housing Association.

Demand for Seniors Housing Services

Unlike nursing homes, seniors housing is largely an industry where residents pay their way with their own money rather than government money. Payment plans generally use a rental fee plus incremental payments for any additional services. In the case of CCRCs, some combination of entrance fee and ongoing rental payment is not uncommon.

Seniors Housing is a Need Driven Product

The demand for seniors housing represents the demand for a mixed bundle of services, which can and will change over time. Prior to the 1980s, many of these services were only available in nursing homes. Both the provision of these services as well as the target market are strongly shaped by seniors' reluctance to move. The predominant "aging in place" model for provision of services, which emerged in the 1980s, appeals to seniors because it reduces the need to move as life conditions change, maximizes the dimensions of independent living, and minimizes costs by customizing assistance to seniors' needs.

Secondly, seniors' reluctance to move shapes the target audience. Many healthy seniors in the 65- to 75-year old age span continue with independent living arrangements usually in communities they have come to know and love. This is most feasible where family support is strong and nearby and where community services cater to the needs of seniors. Indeed, in a recent survey of seniors housing businesses, nearly three-quarters of the respondents believed that "stay at home" services in the community were their greatest competition rather than other seniors housing operators. This suggests that the strongest target audience for seniors housing services may begin at age 75 or so rather than age 65.

Exhibit 10: Actual and Projected Increase in the 70 and Over Population

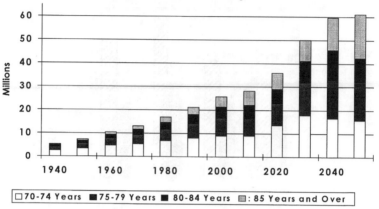

Source: Bureau of Labor Statistics.

Exhibit 11: Distribution of Income of Senior Adults, Age 80 and Over (Thousands of Persons)

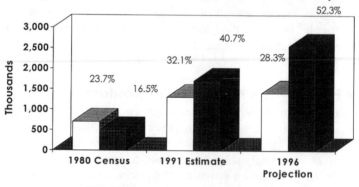

Source: National Planning Data Corporation.

As shown in Exhibit 10, the numbers of seniors in the over 75 age bracket has been increasing rapidly and so have their incomes (Exhibit 11). These factors, combined with reduced family support and rising health care costs, have caused seniors to search for new solutions to old problems. The ability to customize the package of supportive services selected according to the senior's health and the availability of family support allows the selection of an option that both economizes on expensive health care services and builds on the strengths of the senior's resources and capabilities.

While the factors cited above have all contributed to sharply rising demand for seniors housing services, it must be acknowledged that the industry has emerged despite the fairly hostile stance of public policy. The most important provisions in this regard are the coverage of long term skilled nursing care under Medicaid. These provisions have encouraged seniors to transfer assets to their adult children in order to satisfy the "poverty" standards of Medicaid. They are then eligible to obtain Medicaid payments for long term care at public expense. Since the traditional nursing home industry has been the primary recipient of Medicaid long term care outlays, this has discouraged the growth of the seniors' housing industry. Recently, however, a number of states have become concerned about the size of these outlays. For example, a study done for the State of Illinois found expenditures of this kind amounting to $279 million in the year 1993 alone. Such concerns have increased the chances for meaningful reform, which has been supported both by the congregate care and nursing home industries. Needless to say, policy reform carries substantial upside for the assisted living sector.

Investment Focus

There are a number of ways to look at congregate care. These businesses can be viewed as operating companies and also from a real estate perspective. Viewed as operating companies, seniors housing is a management intensive business. Special skills are required in managing both the health care support services and the housing elements and in marketing to a highly conservative audience that is heavily female.

From a real estate perspective, seniors housing can be seen as a kind of multifamily housing, albeit with some differences. The parallel is obviously closest for the independent living, congregate care and assisted living sectors rather than the skilled nursing component. Viewed as housing services, seniors housing clearly exhibits some attractive attributes compared to multifamily. The foremost advantage is stability of cash flows backed by seniors' incomes. These incomes may derive from private retirement pensions and health benefit packages or from seniors' accumulated savings and social security benefits. Relative to the incomes of families who are still working, seniors incomes are recession resistant. In addition, in the hands of experienced operators providing the desired mix of support and health care services, resident turnover is low and this reduces costs. A recent survey derived an average annual resident turnover of 27% (Exhibit 12). This figure is at the low end of the range which might be expected for, say, newer class A suburban garden apartments. The survey also revealed that turnover numbers for top quartile operators (Exhibit 12) were less than half those of bottom quartile operators — again highlighting the value added by the best operators.

While seniors housing exhibits multifamily characteristics, it is multifamily with a difference. The difference is in the investments that must be made by operators for support and health care services and in the expertise required to run a business with these additional specialized elements.

Exhibit 12: Annual Resident Turnover, Seniors Housing

	1st Quartile	Median	4th Quartile
Congregate	16%	23%	30%
Assisted Living	22%	44%	63%
CCRC	23%	38%	58%
All Residences	18%	27%	42%

Source: The State of Seniors Housing, 1994, American Seniors Housing Association.

RETAIL PROPERTY

Like the apartment sector, retail properties experienced relatively modest declines in value in the overbuilding boom of the 1980s. And like apartments, these smaller declines reflected less severe overbuilding compared to the office and hotel sectors. This was fortunate because long run productivity trends in retail, measured as sales per square foot on a same store basis, have been flat. Following the generalized downturn in property markets in 1990-1991, new construction in retail remained tightly constrained for several years while a cyclical rebound in retail sales in 1993-1994 energized retailers' sales productivity. In 1994-1995, however, new construction of retail space picked up sharply, with 1995 construction levels near the historic highs of the 1980s.

As has been the case since the late 1970s, new construction has been concentrated in the stand alone "big boxes" and power centers favored by value retailers and discounters such as Wal-Mart, K-Mart, and Target as well as "category killers" such as Home Depot. Meanwhile, sales productivity growth, which had been running above trend, showed signs of flattening towards the weak long term trend line.

Like the apartment sector, retail properties have been a popular sector for institutional investors in the 1990s. The difference is that the shift to apartments didn't really get going until the 1990s whereas retail was already becoming popular in the late 1980s as insurers and other property managers tried to diversify away from their very heavy exposure to the office market. Investors' affection for retail product, particularly the large regional malls, was evident in the mid 1990s from "cap rates" for large malls around 7.5%, usually ranging 100 to 150 basis points tighter than cap rates on apartment properties. In addition, financing for the desirable regional malls was often available on commercial mortgage loans at spreads around 100 basis points above Treasuries.

Property returns in the late 1980s and early 1990s paralleled performance in the apartment sector (compare Exhibit 13 with Exhibit 12). Double digit returns in the late 1980s faltered and turned negative in 1991-1992. However, in 1993-1995 retail property returns have not been nearly as strong as apartments, reflecting both weaker demands for space and burgeoning new supply. By contrast, still improving loan performance reflects favorable demand and supply fundamentals from 1993 to 1995 — highlighting the lag between today's loan performance and real estate fundamentals.

Exhibit 13: Retail – Total Rate of Return and Delinquency

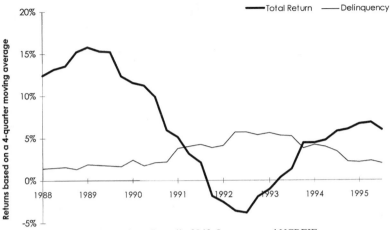

Source: American Council of Life Insurance and NCREIF.

Exhibit 14: Retail Appreciation Rate, Annualized (Q3 1995)

	5 Years	3 Years	1 Year
Northeast	—	-3.1	-2.8
Mideast	-5.2	-4.3	-3.9
East North Central	-3.9	-2.5	-1.2
West North Central	—	0.4	-1.2
Pacific	-5.8	-4.1	-1.3
Mountain	-5.9	-3.2	1.4
Southeast	-3.0	-1.1	-1.1
Southwest	-6.5	-5.3	-5.5
Total	-4.6	-3.0	-2.0

Source: NCREIF.

Regional and Sector Patterns

The regional perspective in retail has interesting similarities and differences from the apartment sector. For one thing, performance is not driven solely from regional growth patterns. The two consistently weak areas over the past years are the Northeast and the Southwest (Exhibit 14). In the slowly growing Northeast, weak performance is mirrored in a shakeout among regional discounters in 1995 with several retailers seeking Chapter 11 protection. In the Southwest, one of the more strongly growing regions, the story is one of excessive development, which outran the region's admittedly stronger growth. This example illustrates the dangers of "falling in love" with a "strong demand" market. In terms of our two market framework, optimistic valuations promote excessive development, which is perfectly capable of outrunning even solid demands for space.

Exhibit 15: Retail Appreciation Rate, Annualized (Q3 1995)

	5 Years	3 Years	1 Year
Super Regional	-4.6	-3.6	-2.9
Regional	-4.9	-2.3	-1.3
Community	-5.1	-3.5	-2.5
Neighborhood	-4.1	-2.4	-1.7
Total	-4.6	-3.0	-2.0

Source: NCREIF.

In the Pacific and Mountain regions, weak five year appreciation rates mirror the depth of the California downturn (Exhibit 14) in the early 1990s. In the Pacific region, the sharply improving momentum in retail properties over the past five years parallels the pattern exhibited in the apartment sector (compare Exhibit 14 to Exhibit 15). The same improving momentum is evident in the Mountain states, which showed more consistent strength in the apartment sector. Finally, over the past five years, the Midwest (consisting of East North Central and the farm-based West North Central) and the Southeast were both stronger than average performers.

From a sectorial perspective (Exhibit 15), five year annualized appreciation rates are very similar for each of the major types of stores, ranging from the very large super regional centers, which draw from a larger trade area, to the smaller neighborhood centers, which cater to a more localized market. This performance highlights the fact that retail goods and services are being marketed through a number of competing "distribution channels." As discussed below, the search for the most cost effective and productive distribution channel has been a recurrent theme among retailers since the early 1980s. When retail property markets are overbuilt, however, each of the major sectors shares in the pain because the size of the retail sales "pie" has not increased. The most recent one year property market declines have been larger for community centers and super regional malls and more modest for the regional and neighborhood store categories.

Space Absorption and New Supply

Data compiled by F.W. Dodge highlight the imbalance in the demand and supply of space between 1989 and 1991 (Exhibit 16). In 1989 and 1990, for example, the overall supply of new space (measured as completions minus removals) amounted to about 100 million square feet. Net absorption of space averaged only about 65 million feet. This shortfall meant that the vacancy rate was rising.

New supply contracted to about 60 million feet in the years 1992-1994 as starts plummeted and the vacancy rate contracted. However, the upsurge of retail starts beginning in 1994 has put upward pressure on vacancy rates. Faster absorption in the years 1992-1994 was tied to a cyclical rebound in retail sales, which as noted above, elevated retailer productivity growth above its stagnant long term trend. However, with moderate and more normal gains in retail sales beginning in 1995, absorption is likely to be well below 1992-1994 levels. With modest absorption combining with stronger new supply, upward pressure on vacancy rates has resumed. The upsurge in starts largely reflects the "big-box" merchandisers and "category killers" who continue to seek to expand market share at the expense of traditional retailers. In such a competitive environment, leasing rate increases will be less than or even with inflation and stronger properties will continue to take market share away from weaker ones.

Trends in Retailing

Traditional department stores lost market share in the 1980s to "discounters" and "category killers." Discounters in particular spearheaded changes in retailing in the 1980s which are often labeled under the term "value retailing." This refers to consumers putting a premium on "value" defined to include a mix of attributes including everyday low prices, convenience of location, warm, helpful salespeople, and well stocked supplies of popular items.

Over the past several years, same store sales per square foot at many department stores have exhibited lackluster growth. Apparel sales, which represent an important, high margin component overall and at the large malls, have been a soft area, particularly women's apparel.

Weakness in the apparel area reflects both increased competitive pressures and softness in demand. Traditional department stores lost apparel market share in the 1980s to specialty stores, often the in-line mall tenants at the large regional malls, as well as discounters. This trend continued into the 1990-1993 period shown in Exhibit 17. In recent years, department stores have redoubled their efforts to take back market share by improving their apparel offerings and more aggressively managing costs.

Exhibit 16: Retail Market Demand and Supply for Space

Retail	1989	1990	1991	1992	1993	1994	1995
Inventory							
Stock (msf)		4,872	4,955	5,014	5,072	5,132	5,219
Percent Change		2.0	1.7	1.2	1.2	1.2	1.7
Additions to Inventory							
Starts (msf)	135.7	117.7	91.1	86.3	103.6	126.1	136.0
Completions (msf)	131.6	132.6	117.6	94.9	93.3	94.7	122.7
Removals (msf)	34.3	35.2	35.2	35.2	35.3	35.5	35.5
Demand for Space							
Net Absorption (msf)	80.0	50.0	53.4	101.2	125.0	100.9	32.2
Vacancy Rate (%)	10.0	10.5	10.9	9.9	8.5	7.6	8.5

Source: F.W. Dodge.

Sears and Federated Department Stores are examples of traditional retailers with improved results in apparel in 1994-1995. At the same time, discounters like Wal-Mart, K-Mart, and Dayton Hudson's Target division, who were winners in the early 1990s (Exhibit 17), continue to seek market share in this higher margin business. These developments have put pressure on the specialty apparel merchants who are the in-line tenants at the large regional malls. These merchants have continued to lose market share just as they did in the early 1990s (Exhibit 17). The result for mall owners has been an increase in tenant turnover and leasing risk. As Milton Cooper, chairman of Kimco Realty, put it: "Today, 50% of the leases signed are to tenants that didn't exist a few years ago."

A number of analysts have argued that the aging of the boomers plays negatively for apparel sales. With fewer women entering the labor force and boomers squarely in middle age, their spending priorities have shifted to areas like travel, technology, and saving for their children's college, their retirement, and their parent's old age. Weakness in apparel sales has been particularly evident in women's apparel. Some mall operators have been shifting footage out of apparel overall into consumer electronics and home related stores. Within apparel, footage devoted to men's apparel has been increasing while space allocated to women's apparel has been decreasing. Despite these efforts, mall owner exposure to apparel remains heavy — around 70% to 80%.

Retail Productivity and Retail Fundamentals

As already noted, new supply of retail space has been concentrated among the discounters and "category killers." Over the past 15 years, discounters such as Wal-Mart and K-Mart have taken market share away from traditional department stores and the mass merchandisers such as J.C. Penney, Sears, and Montgomery Ward. These value retailers prefer "box box" formats because they afford lower occupancy costs and greater roadside visibility and access. These formats include free standing stores, and power centers as well as factory outlet centers. Value retailers have also generated much higher sales volume than their average traditional department store competitors. Thus, the steady stream of new space supplied from this quarter is not a pure example of overbuilding originating with optimistic asset market pricing. Rather, the supply stems from the conviction of value retailers that they have a better "mousetrap," which is able to supplement much of the business of traditional department stores high productivity by virtue of cost efficiencies. At a secondary level, however, capital market optimism has supported retail overbuilding by refusing to recognize the growing risks to the sector generally and particularly for large malls.

A newer development in the area of value retailing is the new supercenter concept, which combines the discount center with a food supermarket store. This store design represents a challenge to community and neighborhood centers in marginal locations or with poorly managed franchises. The basic premise is to use the higher frequency of food shopping to enhance sales at the discount center. While it is too soon to see exactly how this will play out, it may be noted that many of the leading supermarket chains are very efficiently run. It may be safely noted that they do not appear to be in the same position as, for example, traditional department stores in the early 1980s. Nonetheless, the supercenter concept represents a serious challenge to traditional neighborhood and community formats and suggests that a premium should be placed on profitable operators and tenants and strong locations with sufficient size and flexibility to accommodate alternative formats.

Exhibit 17: 1990-93 U.S. Apparel Market by Channel of Distribution the Total U.S. Apparel Market

	Dollars Purchased (mm)			
	1990	1991	1992	1993
Department Store	28,109	27,422	28,776	29,228
Major Chains	16,587	16,733	18,826	19,667
Discount Stores	21,929	22,690	24,423	26,446
Other	9,837	9,277	9,441	9,711
Specialty Stores	21,815	21,759	22,574	23,165
Direct Mail	5,132	6,086	6,890	7,697
Off-Price	6,786	7,216	8,217	8,678
Factory Outlets	3,197	3,352	3,791	4,649
Other	7,621	8,073	8,942	9,443
Total	111,175	113,333	122,439	128,974

	% Dollars Purchased				% Change			
	1990	1991	1992	1993	1990	1991	1992	1993
Department Store	25.3	24.2	23.5	22.7	NA	-2.4	4.9	1.6
Major Chains	14.9	14.8	15.4	15.2	NA	0.9	12.5	4.5
Discount Stores	19.7	20.0	19.9	20.5	NA	3.5	7.6	8.3
Other	8.8	8.2	7.7	7.5	NA	-5.7	1.8	2.9
Specialty Stores	19.6	19.2	18.4	18.0	NA	-0.3	3.7	2.6
Direct Mail	4.6	5.4	5.6	6.0	NA	18.6	13.2	11.7
Off-Price	6.1	6.4	6.7	6.7	NA	6.3	13.9	5.6
Factory Outlets	2.9	3.0	3.1	3.6	NA	4.8	13.1	22.6
Other	6.9	7.1	7.3	7.3	NA	5.9	10.8	5.6
Total	100.0	100.0	100.0	100.0	NA	1.9	8.0	5.3

Source: NPD Data, cited Specialty in Apparel Industry Overview, Josephson Lyon E Ross Incorporated. Catherine DePuy, 10/9/95.

Exhibit 18: Growth in Shopping Center Space per Capital and Sales per Square Foot

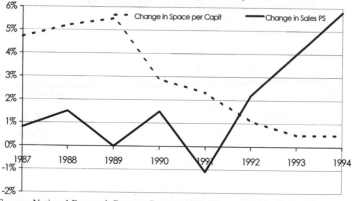

Source: National Research Bureau; Bureau of the Census; and the Balco Company.

As this long-standing competition continues in the second half of the 1990s, there will likely be additional casualties. Witness the bankruptcies of Caldor's, Bradlees, and Jamesway, discounters situated primarily in the Northeast. One of the problems with too much new supply, as we saw in the 1980s, is that it forces property owners of existing facilities to overspend on cap expenditure renovations to keep tenants from running to newly built properties. As long as new supply remains strong, we expect higher than normal renovation outlays generally to hurt operator's bottom line. In the malls, this problem will be amplified by higher than normal tenant turnover for specialty apparel merchants and related tenant improvement charges.

The improved loan performance of retail properties in the past three years reflects reduced supply growth and cyclically improving sales per square foot (see Exhibit 18). Weaker sales and more robust new supply beginning in 1994, however, signal an end to these cyclical productivity gains. However, longer term productivity trends are not encouraging and therein lies the dilemma for investors in retail properties.

Conclusion

Our focus above on competition in apparel highlights some general issues. The headwinds of value retailing will likely continue to push retailers to seek low cost, high productivity distribution channels. At a basic level, the problem with malls' in line space is that it is high cost. In order to justify the higher "all in" rents, retailers' productivity must be correspondingly higher. In the past, the theory of high in line mall rents was that the mall anchors drew the traffic and "cross shopping" opportunities benefitted the in line tenant.

Obviously, the theory doesn't work when the department store anchors take apparel sales away from the specialty apparel in line tenant. This episode highlights part of the risk of being a niche retailer. This suggests that the theory underlying the pricing of in line mall space is wrong and/or incomplete.

Power center tenants in various settings have cut across the traditional categories as well as contributed to their evolution. In the mid-1980s, the typical power center consisted of three or four "big boxes," each 100,000 feet or more. While there are still some power centers in this format, it is much more common in the mid-1990s to see an evolved community/power center anchored by a supermarket and movie theater with several "big box" power tenants. This format obviously requires substantial space that would traditionally have been claimed by a smaller mall. With malls generally experiencing greater stress, this older format has been vulnerable.

In the context of larger community properties, many category killer tenants are under pressure in late 1995.

Looking beyond mid-1990s weakness, the upside for larger community properties rests in the migration of better quality tenants down from the malls. The advantage of community properties for these tenants is lower rents and the opportunity with good operators, for more than commensurate sales productivity. These properties are also more suitable in urban or semiurban settings, which tend to be "understored" areas.

Smaller community/neighborhood centers are often anchored by a supermarket and/or drug store and have the advantage of more stable cash flows. This gives them more long-term stability and generally the smallest downside in 1996.

INDUSTRIAL MARKET

Like apartments and the retail sector, overbuilding in industrial warehouse markets in the 1980s was less severe than the office and hotel sectors and the accompanying declines in property values and deterioration in loan performance were more moderate. Indeed, the warehouse sector seems to have been a sector where the marketplace generally maintained reasonable balance between demand and supply prior to the 1980s. This is often attributed to the relatively short construction lags in the warehouse sector. Our primary focus in this section is on distribution/warehouse facilities, which are "large box" buildings devoted almost exclusively to storage. R&D office refers to light and high tech manufacturing facilities that require office buildout, which can vary in importance. We do not discuss manufacturing/production buildings which primarily feature assembly areas and are largely owned by manufacturers themselves rather than institutional investors.

Relative to the apartment and retail sectors, industrial property markets initially lagged in recovery following the 1990-1991 downturn. Trailing four quarter warehouse returns finally turned positive in early 1994 (Exhibit 19) compared to turning points in early 1993 for retail (Exhibit 13) and mid 1992 for apartments (Exhibit 3). Beginning in 1993, however, industrial property markets experienced a sharp and sustained pickup in demand for space. Strong absorption of warehouse space combined with continuing low new supply to produce steadily rising occupancy rates and firming rents and property values across the country (Exhibit 19). The pickup in industrial markets in the past several years has fueled a sharp turnaround in property returns. As a result, warehouse properties have been much sought after by both pension fund and REIT investors.

The very sharp turnaround in warehouse markets since 1993 has produced a parallel improvement in loan performance (Exhibit 19). Delinquencies on life insurer commercial mortgage loans have fallen from a peak of about 5% to about half that level in the second half of 1995.

The heating up of the industrial property category has been especially pronounced in the nation's suburban markets where modern warehouse and industrial properties are predominantly located and where office absorption trends have also been very powerful. Surging absorption trends in suburban markets have also made themselves felt in R&D/office properties, which have lagged behind warehouse properties because they are near substitutes for office space. However, with both office (see office section below) and warehouse sectors staging strong rebounds in 1995, R&D/office returns have also improved dramatically.

Exhibit 19: Total Rate of Return and Delinquency

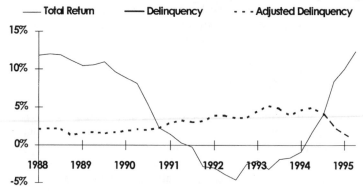

Source: American Council of Life Insurance and NCREIF.

Exhibit 20: U.S. Industrial Construction and Absorption as a Percent of Inventory

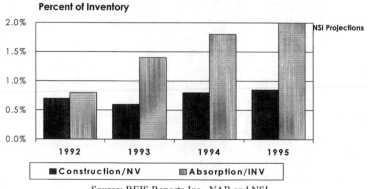

Source: REIS Reports Inc., NAR and NSI.

Exhibit 21: Industrial Appreciation Rate Annualized (Q3 1995)

	Warehouse			R&D/Office
	5 Year	3 Year	1 Year	1 Year
Northeast/Mideast	-6.5	-3.0	2.2	-0.2
East North Central	-5.8	-4.6	0.1	2.0
West North Central	-5.7	-4.1	-4.6	
Pacific	-7.6	-6.0	4.0	0.0
Mountain	-0.6	1.1	6.4	—
Southeast	-5.0	-1.4	3.1	4.3
Southwest	-3.6	-1.0	2.7	
Total	-6.4	-4.3	2.3	0.6

Source: NCREIF.

Exhibit 22: Industrial Vacancy Rates

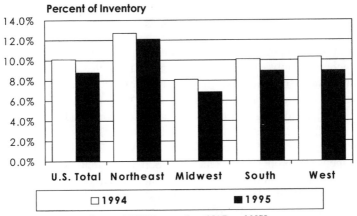

Source: REIS Reports Inc., NAR and NSI.

Regional Patterns in Property Appreciation

For the country as a whole, five-year warehouse appreciation rates are a bit weaker than those in the retail sector and substantially weaker than those in the apartment sector (Exhibit 21). On the other hand, one year appreciation rates (ending in Q3 1995) are about the same as apartments and much stronger than retail, where the appraisal-based NCREIF index has still been declining. These comparisons highlight the strength of the warehouse turnaround in 1995, which, like the apartment sector, has been driven by strong increases in the demand for space accompanied by still limited new supply.

From a regional perspective, the turnaround has been led by strongly growing areas of the country — the Mountain states, the Southeast, and the Southwest. In addition, warehouse markets in the Pacific region, dominated by California, have recently been very strong, paralleling the rebound of California in the apartment and retail markets. While recent measured appreciation in the midwest (East North

Central) has been flat, the midwest still includes the tightest leasing markets in the country (Exhibit 22). Moreover, in the hybrid R&D/office sector, the strongest performing markets — the South and the Midwest (Exhibit 21) — are also the markets with the lowest vacancy rates for warehouse space.

The latter regions include the hot suburban markets of Atlanta, where new construction has emerged in the industrial market parallel to a general tightening of office market conditions. They also include the oil-belt markets (Austin, Dallas, Houston, New Orleans, and San Antonio) where industrial space has generally tightened to the point that speculative developments are appearing in increasing numbers. The latter markets continue to be buoyed by a steady inflow of high-tech business relocations, taking advantage of lower costs and perceived higher quality of life. Finally, they include the industrial markets of the Midwest, which generally exhibit the lowest vacancy rates in the country, and the East-West corridor of suburban Chicago, where big-box industrial space continues to be filled as fast as speculative developers are building it.

Demand

The demand for warehouse space is derived not merely from activity in the local economy geographically adjacent to the property, but rather more broadly from the movement of commerce and goods through a region. The pattern of commerce and trade depends upon the location of manufacturing sites, the availability of transportation technology, and the growth and distribution of world trade. Over the past two decades, manufacturing activity within the U.S. has shifted out of the North-East and Midwest and into the Southeast, South, and West (Exhibit 23). Thus, the turnaround of industrial property markets in the mid-1990s represents a resumption of some of these longer term trends. In today's markets, part of this shifting is coming out of California, which has become a high cost center, and into Oregon, Washington, the Mountain states, and Texas.

Exhibit 23: Increases in Manufacturing Output, 1977 to 1991 (Constant 1987 Dollars, Millions)

Region	Dollars
South East	54,548
Far West	48,154
South West	24,029
New England	16,640
Plains	15,845
Mid East	9,850
Rocky Mountain	6,401
Great Lakes	-9,008

Source: Haver Analytics.

The long term shift to just in time inventory management continues to put a premium on shorter and more reliable delivery times. Sometimes this may necessitate the physical relocation of suppliers, such as occurred in the case of Compaq, the computer manufacturer, headquartered in the Houston suburbs. In other cases, it fosters the connection of modern warehouses to airfreight transportation and airport locations rather than traditional truck and rail. This is especially the case in high-tech industries; where the shipment of expensive, low bulk packages is well suited to airfreight.

Technology and the continued easing of various government regulations continue to allow new efficiencies in warehousing. A recent example is the phasing out of the last of the state regulations governing intrastate hauling. Interstate trucking had been deregulated by the 1980 Federal Motor Carrier Act, which cleared trucking companies to negotiate long-term contracts with manufacturers. The practical effect of eliminating these regulations has been to free manufacturers to dump the large private truck fleets they had built in order to get around the regulations. Further, it created a demand for third-party logistics services which trucking companies have begun to fill. Many large manufacturing concerns have outsourced their shipping and warehousing functions to these third-party vendors, who have taken the economics of distribution and warehousing to a new level.

Conclusion

Like other sectors in commercial real estate, warehouse and industrial properties include some metro markets where demand for space has been growing moderately with no increases in new supply. In many markets discussed above, however, absorption trends are extremely strong so that in some cases new construction has reemerged following the overbuilding of the 1980s. These different metro areas represent different kinds of real estate risk exposures within a favorable setting in the warehouse and industrial sectors. We think that a mix of these exposures serves bond investors well.

OFFICE MARKETS

Office markets, together with hotel properties (see below), are the archetypes of hugely overbuilt markets in the 1980s. While space availability considerations made it easier to overbuild suburban office markets than downtown markets, developers also managed to substantially overbuild downtown markets as well. The lesson here is that zoning restrictions typically prevailing in U.S. markets, lack of available space in urban markets, etc. are not effective "barriers to entry" when property valuations far above replacement cost are signaling new development. The relative weakness of these other "barriers" and the relative strength of market incentives should be borne in mind by investors weighing various arguments about "barriers to entry."

In the 1990s, office markets have been benefiting from resurging demands for space while new supply has been essentially zero for several years after the early 1990s downturn. Following long established patterns, new absorption of space has been concentrated in the suburban markets. As a result, downtown office properties have remained at substantial discounts to replacement cost — creating a market related (and effective) barrier to new supply. Assuming a continuation of modest absorption trends going forward, downtown markets will continue to tighten. In suburban markets, where vacancy rates fell below those in downtown's for the first time in 1994, faster growing demands for space are likely to be accompanied eventually by a pickup in supply. Indeed, in such hot suburban markets as Atlanta and Dallas, this has already occurred.

While office property performance has been weaker than other sectors, declines in prices continue to be moderate. The resulting improvement in total return has produced stronger loan performance at life insurance lenders in the 1992 to 1995 period (Exhibit 24). Within the office category, there are large variations across different markets. Suburban markets likely posted outright price increases in 1993-1995 while downtown markets were in the process of bottoming.

On a regional basis, five year appreciation rates varied between minus 10% and minus 12% per year! (See Exhibit 25.) Obviously, these represent huge cumulative declines across the entire country. This explains why property values remain well below replacement cost in many markets. Over 1995, positive appreciation showed up in the Southeast and Mountain regions. The weakest performance clustered around the lagging urban markets of Los Angeles, Chicago, Dallas, and Houston. Overall, the picture is one of general strength in suburban office markets and of a clear bottoming in most downtown markets with the exception of Los Angeles, Chicago, Dallas, and Houston.

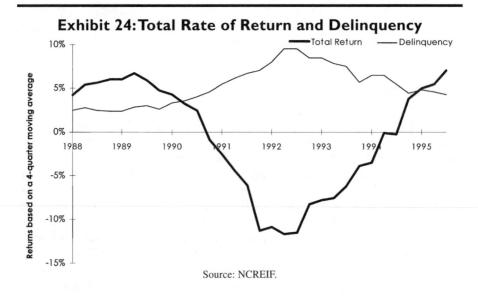

Exhibit 24: Total Rate of Return and Delinquency

Source: NCREIF.

Exhibit 25: Office Appreciation Rate Annualized (Q3 1995)

	5 Year	3 Year	1 Year
Northeast/Mideast	-10.6	-6.5	-0.7
East North Central	-11.7	-9.3	-7.0
West North Central	-11.3	-7.2	-0.7
Pacific	-12.1	-12.0	-4.7
Mountain	-9.8	-6.4	0.5
Southeast	-10.5	-3.2	2.8
Southwest	-10.3	-7.6	-4.3
Total	-11.1	-8.4	-2.5

Source: NCREIF.

Exhibit 26: Changes in Suburban and Downtown Vacancy Rates (June 1993 to June 1995)

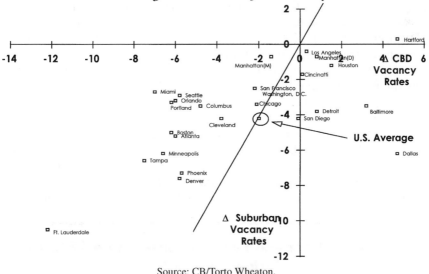

Source: CB/Torto Wheaton.

Trends in Downtown Office Markets

Over the past decade, downtown office markets have accounted for only 20% of space absorption with faster growing suburban markets taking the lion's 80% share. While the pace of downtown absorption varies in the short run, the indications are this modest absorption trend in downtown markets remains in place. This explains a two-year central business district (CBD) vacancy rate decline in 1994-1995 of 2 percentage points while suburban vacancy rates fell 4 percentage points (see U.S. average on Exhibit 26). With resurgent demand in CBD markets and no new supply in the past three years, rents in most CBDs in 1995 have bottomed and are firming. Concessions, including free rent, have all but disappeared. Even the lagging Chicago CBD has seen a pickup of leasing market activity as tenants anticipate rising rents and attempt to lock in lease terms at today's favorable levels. In the flurry of lease rollovers and with ample provision of sublease space, net absorption appears to still be running slightly negative, but rents have definitely firmed.

Some striking indications of a general firming in CBD rental markets appear in a recent survey published by the National Real Estate Index (Exhibit 27). As of the second quarter, this survey showed that, of 56 markets sampled, 27 had seen rent gains of at least 5% in the past twelve months while 22 had seen property price increases of at least 5%. The survey covered apartment, warehouse, and retail markets in addition to CBD office. The downtown office results for rent increases surpassed those for all other property types and results for price increases were nearly as strong as those for the surging apartment sector. Overall, the picture is one of smartly rising rents and property prices in most CBD office markets.

The Korpacz Real Estate Survey reports that CBD class-A properties have been moving quite quickly when put on the market and, as the class-A market has tightened, class-B properties are moving better as well. Investors have generally confined their interest to these higher quality properties so far. Even higher quality CBD property values are still generally at substantial discounts to replacement cost levels, precluding new development. In CBDs dominated by older properties with substantial amounts of functionally obsolete space, the few available class-A properties can find themselves in a "quasi-monopoly" situation which can be quite favorable, especially for bond investors.

In looking at possible CBD office exposure for bond investors, Exhibit 26 can be used to identify metro areas where CBD office absorption has been higher than average. In general, the tremendous diversity of metro areas is very striking, pointing to opportunities side by side with problems. These markets lie to the left of the solid line running from the origin down through the average U.S. market and include such cities as Columbus, Portland, Atlanta, Minneapolis, and Seattle.

Exhibit 27: Rent and Price Increases in Real Estate Markets, June 1995

	Apartments		CBD Office		Warehouse		Retail	
	Prices	Rents	Prices	Rents	Prices	Rents	Prices	Rents
Healthy (5%+)	23	18	22	27	18	21	7	17
Rebounding (2% to 5%)	13	17	17	15	12	13	16	16
Stabilizing (-2% to 2%)	6	11	11	5	13	13	22	14
Declining (-5% to -2%)	3	3	2	4	2	0	2	2
Poor (-5%+)	4	0	0	1	5	3	3	1

Source: National Real Estate Index.

Exhibit 28: Office Space by Downtown and Suburban Location

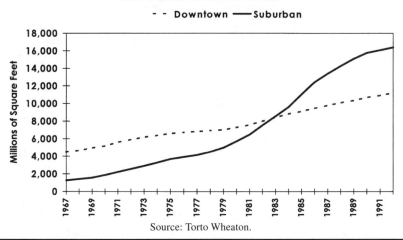

Source: Torto Wheaton.

Trends in Suburban Office Markets

Suburban office markets have benefited from stronger absorption trends, paralleling the development of so-called "edge cities," for the past 25 years. Edge cities have benefited from cheaper costs of doing business, much shorter commuting times for workers — which allows them to pay lower wages, as well as avoidance of many of the problems of large CBDs. As recently as 1968, suburban office space was a mere 20% of downtown space. As shown in Exhibit 28, suburban office growth took off beginning in the late 1970s. The 4 percentage point decline in suburban office vacancy rates in the past two years compared to a 2 percentage point drop for downtown's (Exhibit 26) argues that strong absorption in suburban markets is continuing.

Because of its strong and favorable absorption trends, it's difficult to find suburban office markets where clear caution signals stand out. Two general concerns, however, should be borne in mind. First, in markets where CBD vacancy rates remain very high and absorption trends are only moderate (or worse), the overhang of CBD space will cast a shadow over suburban office markets for some time to come. This is because, even though the CBD space may look uncompetitive today, it will likely be competitive with suburban space at some lower level of rents. This is the situation in Los Angeles and Houston, for example, and may still be an ongoing concern in Chicago.

Second, investors need to be careful going forward about overpaying or lending against overbought valuations in some of the hot suburban office markets, such as Atlanta, where speculative construction is reemerging. More generally, investors need to be aware that relatively low barriers to entry may allow oversupply to develop at some point. Here, monitoring the relationship of valuations to replacement cost should be a prudent yardstick.

In general, however, the clear bottoming of CBD rental markets is highly favorable for suburban office markets. It marks the end of CBD competition with suburban office markets at lower and lower rental rates, a process which diverted absorption back to the struggling CBD markets. The continued strength of suburban office absorption over this period is impressive. Going forward, rising absorption within metro areas should translate more directly than previously into tighter suburban markets.

Suburban office market conditions vary widely. For example, the Texas markets are generally continuing to experience a very substantial inflow of business relocations. This has fueled substantial industrial growth and absorption of newly developed office space in the suburbs of Dallas and Austin, for example, even though the Dallas CBD vacancy rate is the highest among the top 50 markets. Similarly, the Mountain states and the Southeast are generally expected to benefit from continuing strong growth and absorption trends.

At the same time, slower expected growth and absorption trends in the Northeast and California should generally coincide with the continuing development of "edge cities" around the large CBDs. Suburban office markets in Northern Virginia and Northern and Central New Jersey, for example, look particularly promising.

HOTEL MARKET

Hotel markets share with the office property market the distinction of having been hugely overbuilt in the 1980s. In addition, as was the case in the office sector, we can readily identify subsectors within the hotel market where demands to utilize space have grown rapidly and more slowly. In so called full service hotels, which provide a full range of amenities along with core room and food services, demand for rooms has grown at a moderate pace since the late 1970s. On the other hand, a variety of limited service establishments have seen very rapid growth in demand for services during the past 15 years. Another parallel is that new supply is beginning to emerge (as of 1995) in the faster growing limited services sector just as it is in the faster growing market in suburban office. In both cases, this new supply reflects property valuations which are at or above replacement costs. Moreover, constrained new supply in both full service hotels and CBD office derives from deeply discounted valuations relative to replacement costs.

Despite these parallels, there are also differences. For example, 1980s' office overbuilding initially produced higher vacancies in suburban markets. In the hotel market, by contrast, limited service hotels have exhibited higher occupancies since at least the mid 1980s. Another difference is that while office markets were not overbuilt prior to the 1980s, full service hotels were arguably overbuilt before the 1980s boom. Finally, hotels generally have greater sensitivity to business cycle downturns than other real estate and this is particularly true for the full service sector.

The tumultuous decline in hotel prices between the mid 1980s and the early 1990s was widely noted by bank and insurance company lenders and real estate investors generally. Similar to the overbuilt office markets, property values finally bottomed in 1991-1992 at levels hugely discounted to replacement cost. However, with demand for hotel accommodations resurging and construction at a perfectly understandable standstill, occupancies rose steadily beginning in 1992. The years 1994 and 1995 saw the first room rate increases exceeding inflation in more than ten years. With industry operating profits buoyed by these improving fundamentals for more than three years, banks and insurance company lenders nonetheless stayed away, often refusing even to refinance loans already on their books. Beginning in 1995, the much improved condition of the industry has been more widely recognized, resulting in new flows of financing from both Wall Street and traditional lenders.

In this section, we want to distinguish between several different sectors of the hotel market. Full service hotels bore the brunt of the 1980s overbuilding and their values remain at the deepest discounts to replacement cost. As a result, no new development is likely forthcoming any time soon in full service hotels and this constrained supply dominates the industry supply picture. Suite hotels were originally built to serve extended-stay business travelers but have appealed to family leisure travelers as well. Trend demands have been very strong over the past decade. Finally, budget hotels frequented by economy minded leisure travelers have been supported by broad economy trends encouraging families to hold down vacation spending. Suite and budget hotels arguably have lower "barriers to entry" than full service hotels. But they have benefited historically from higher profit margins due to an absence of overbuilding and strongly growing demand for their accommodations.

Improving Loan Performance

Loan performance at insurance companies has been steadily improving since 1992 (Exhibit 29). Since insurance companies having made almost no new hotel loans in the first half of the 1990s, the delinquency numbers correspond to loans originated at 1980s' property values and operating incomes and 1980s' underwriting standards. Hotel delinquencies dipped to 5.2% in late 1995, compared to about 9.2% in 1994. While delinquencies of 1980s vintage loans has improved dramatically, strongly underwritten hotel loans originated in 1993 and 1994 have experienced no problems. This improved loan performance coincided with rising occupancies, room rates, operating incomes, and property values.

According to Hospitality Valuation Services, average hotel property values (including both full service and limited service hotels) rose 16% over 1994 (Exhibit 30), following a 15% increase in 1993 and an 8% increase in 1992. Property value appreciation in 1995 has been supported by a "seachange" in the availability of debt financing. Previously, traditional lenders generally were not even interested in rolling over their existing loans. More recently, investors and lenders are beginning to recognize the industry's hugely improved fundamentals.

Exhibit 29: Hotel Room Prices and Commercial Mortgage Delinquency Rates

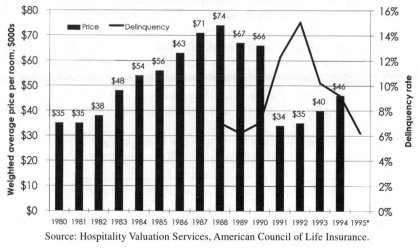

Source: Hospitality Valuation Services, American Council of Life Insurance.

Exhibit 30: Percent Change in Performance Ratios 12 Month Ended July, 1991-1995

	1991	1992	1993	1994	1995
Occupancy	-3.6%	-0.3%	2.5%	2.4%	2.3%
Room Rate	1.2%	0.1%	0.3%	3.6%	4.2%
Supply	3.1%	1.7%	1.1%	1.2%	1.4%
Demand	-0.7%	2.1%	3.5%	3.6%	3.8%

Source: Lodging Outlook, Smith Travel, Research, September 1995.

Demand and Room Rates

Hotel occupancies have been improving for three straight years to 65.2% for the full year 1994, the highest rate posted since 1982. Average room rates in 1994 jumped 4.0% over 1993, the first increase in excess of overall inflation in over a decade. Preliminary 1995 results (Exhibit 30) show continued improvement in occupancies and room demand, but at a somewhat slower pace than increases in 1991-1993. Strongly rising room rates continued in 1995, however, with mid year rates more than 4% above year earlier levels. Strong business travel demands in 1994 propelled the luxury to mid-price market segments generally favored by business travelers to outperform the budget and economy sectors. Business travel has been buoyed by surprisingly strong corporate earnings, which have remained vibrant in 1995 despite slower economic growth. While business travel demands slowed a bit in early 1995, the full service sector, which spans the mid-price to luxury price range, should continue to perform strongly. In addition, results in 1995 point to a relatively strong performance in leisure travel markets generally and Florida destinations in particular.

Exhibit 31: Full Service Hotels – Mix of Business 1993

Room Demand	Percent
Business	46
Tourists	29
Conference	10
Convention	10
Other	5

Source: PKF Trends Report 1994.

Exhibit 32: Gross Operating Profit Ratio to Sales; Full Service Hotels
Full Service: Occupancies, ADRs and Gross Operating Profit (1994)

	Occupancy (%)	ADR ($)	Gross Operating Profit (%)
Luxury	72.8	108	30.5
Upscale	70.8	77	31.8
Midprice	69.8	62	31.6
Economy	67.3	53	23.9

Source: Host Study, Smith Travel Research 1994.

Trends in Full Service Hotels

Full service hotels, which are generally in the luxury to mid-price range, cater predominantly to business travelers as well as to conventions and conferences (Exhibit 31). The common denominator of their business, tourist, and convention traffic is the travelers who is drawn to the higher level of services and amenities provided. In the case of conventions, substantial amounts of public meeting and dining areas are necessary to accommodate these large groups of travelers. While business travel demands have exhibited strong positive trends in recent years, they also are more sensitive to temporary downturns in the economy than the demands of leisure travelers. As already noted, full service properties experienced the largest declines in values in the 1980s' overbuilding boom. Despite sharp increases in values since 1992, these properties today remain in a range between 50% and 65% of replacement cost. Such deep discounts have obviously prevented any new development of full service properties. Combined with strong growth of business travel demands, such constrained supply has pushed up profit margins for full service hotels and the entire industry.

Profit margins for full service hotels have risen four years in a row (Exhibit 32) and are highest for the luxury to mid-price hotels. These margins are measured before deduction of depreciation or debt service expenses, management fees, insurance or property tax payments. In addition to constrained new supply and steadily rising business travel demands, profit margins have been enhanced by ongoing strong improvements in productivity, together with flat to declining hotel employment. Profit margins in 1994 are the highest in at least 15 years. Despite this impressive performance, full service margins remain significantly below limited service profit margins (see below) and below levels where new capital could earn a competitive rate of return. In turn, this suggests that both full service and industry new supply will continue to be tightly constrained, requiring only modest increases in demand to keep full service margins on a rising plane.

Full service occupancy increases over the past several years have been broadly distributed across the various price tiers. In 1994, the largest increase in occupancies occurred in the higher priced luxury/upscale segment and the lower priced economy segment (Exhibit 33). The economy class includes properties that were originally designed to operate within that price range and also less strongly performing properties that have migrated downward to the lower price range. The sharp increase in occupancies for the latter group reflects the much tighter market conditions prevailing in 1994.

Trends in Limited Service Hotels

The term "limited service" refers to several different subsectors within the hotel industry. One common denominator is an absence of food and beverage services and of many of the amenities that are typical of full service hotels. A second common denominator is that these properties have generally had higher occupancies and profit margins than full service hotels over the past decade. Underlying this stronger performance has been faster growing demands for the hotel accommodations, which have more than offset the faster rate of new construction for these properties. A third common feature is a reduced sensitivity to economy downturns, compared to full service properties. Overall, limited service properties have about the same reliance on individual business travelers as full service (Exhibit 34), but they rely significantly more on tourist travelers and less on convention and conference travel.

Exhibit 33: Occupancy Rates by Price Tier
Full Service Hotels

	1993	1994
Luxury/Upscale	70.7	72.1
Midprice	69.3	69.5
Economy	61.7	67.3

Source: Host Study, Smith Travel Research, 1993 and 1994.

Exhibit 34: Limited Service Hotels – Mix of Business 1993

Room Demand	Percent
Business	47
Tourists	41
Conference	3
Convention	1
Other	8

Source: PKF Trends Report 1994.

Exhibit 35: Gross Operating Profit Ratio to Sales
Limited Service Hotels

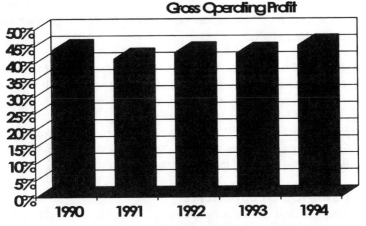

Gross Operating Profit

Limited Service: Occupancies, ADRs and Profit Margins

	Occupancy	ADR	Profit margin
Upscale	77.5%	$66	49.0%
Midpriced	72.5%	$52	46.1%
Economy	70.3%	$45	43.7%
Budget	68.9%	$36	37.7%

Source: Host Report, Smith Travel, 1994.

A final common point is lower barriers to entry compared to full service properties. Lower barriers to entry reflect both lower investment requirements and valuation which has been generally much closer to parity with replacement costs. This last point has a certain irony because in the 1980s it seems to have generated a healthy investor prudence that was obviously lacking in full service hotels.

Exhibit 35 highlights the high and stable profit margins overall for the limited service sector. At about 45% in 1994, the gross profit margin is half again as large as profit margins for full service hotels. In assessing these figures, it should be recalled that capital expenditures are typically significantly lower for limited service properties. Indeed, a recent study suggested that while the "traditional" cap expenditure reserve of 3% per year of total revenues was adequate for limited service properties, something like 6% might be required for full service properties.

Limited Service – Extended-Stay or Suite Hotels The upscale room rate segment of limited service hotels (Exhibit 35 bottom panel) cover extended-stay or suite hotels. In these hotels, each unit consists of a bedroom and living room. Like other limited service facilities, extended-stay properties offer limited public space and services. These properties achieved the highest profit margins in 1994. Suite hotels were originally designed with business travelers in mind, but have been popular with others as well. Today they have about the same mix of individual business travelers and tourist travelers as full service hotels generally. However, there is likely some tendency to downsize in a soft economy which benefits suites relative to full service and which reduces its cyclical sensitivity.

Limited Service — Budget Hotels At the lowest room rates within limited service is the budget hotel sector (Exhibit 36). These are hotels with rooms-only operations and catering very heavily to economy minded leisure travelers. Their heavy dependence on leisure rather than business travelers reduces their sensitivity to the business cycle relative to the full service sector. While budget hotels have lower gross profit margins (Exhibit 36) than other categories of limited service, their cap expenditures are also lower — allowing their net profit margins to remain competitive.

Limited Service Occupancies

As already noted, limited service occupancies have been higher than full service properties for the past decade, reflecting strong demand for their accommodations. In 1994, occupancies continued to rise in all of the limited service price tiers (Exhibit 36). Overall, these increases are larger than those posted in the full service sector (Exhibit 33). Moreover, the largest increase in limited service occupancy is for the upscale segment which corresponds to the extended-stay properties and the budget category.

Conclusion

The 1980s overbuilding boom greatly depressed room rates and property values in the hotel sector. Following a bottom in 1992, however, the industry has been improving sharply in terms of occupancies, room rates, and operating profits — aided by resurging demands for hotel accommodations and historically low new supply. This momentum allowed the industry to post record operating profits of $5.5 billion in 1994 and $8.5 billion in 1995 (Exhibit 37). Indeed, the industry has clearly achieved an overall occupancy which, if maintained, will continue to put upward pressure on both room rates and profits.

Operators of full service properties are benefiting from a virtual absence of new supply, which tends to put upward pressure on occupancies and profits when accompanied by even modestly rising demands. Here, investors will want to deal with superior operators who are "taking a page" from the strategy of limited service operators. The best full service operators are managing their businesses much more aggressively than in the past by insisting on competitive rates of return from food service operations, conference and convention meeting space, and other services. This has led to ongoing productivity gains, reduced hotel employment, and outsourcing of some services such as food catering at conventions.

Limited service hotels, including both extended-stay hotels and budget properties, have benefited from strongly rising demands for their accommodations. Limited service operators have approached the hotel business by shedding ancillary operations, provided in full service hotels, which failed to add value for economy minded leisure travelers or for business travelers for whom ancillary services were unimportant. This has allowed them to achieve higher occupancies and profit margins for the past decade despite a faster rate of new construction in this sector.

SUMMARY

Real estate investment has long been an area plagued by inadequate analysis and a dearth of information. This chapter argues that a relatively simple property market framework has wide applicability to many contemporary real estate problems as we approach the millennium.

Exhibit 36: Occupancy Rates by Price Tier
Limited Service Hotels

	1993	1994
Upscale	71.3	75.8
Midprice/Economy	69.2	70.8
Budget	61.6	68.9

Source: Host Report, Smith Travel, 1993 and 1994, NSI.

Exhibit 37: U.S. Lodging Industry Profitability

Year	Estimated profits ($)
1982	2.5
1983	1.9
1984	1.7
1985	0.1
1986	-0.9
1987	-1.1
1988	-1.3
1989	-2.1
1990	-5.7
1991	-2.8
1992	-0.1
1993	2.4
1994	5.5
1995	8.5

Source: Host Report, Smith Travel 1994; Coopers & Lybrand "Hospitality Directions," August 1995.

Chapter 2

The Whole Loan Commercial Mortgage Market

Galia Gichon
Associate
Nomura Securities International, Inc.

INTRODUCTION

The commercial real estate market is estimated to be valued at $3 trillion. Commercial mortgages, which finance this real estate are estimated to be valued at $1 trillion. While a good portion of real estate is owned debt free, a sizable portion is financed through commercial mortgages (first and second mortgages), lease-backed transactions, and other types of debt. Commercial mortgages are mortgages on income producing properties. This includes multifamily, office buildings, retail properties, mobile home parks, hotels, self-storage, retirement centers, senior housing, even parking lots, golf courses and so on. Commercial mortgages are the raw material from which commercial mortgage-backed securities (CMBS) are created. Therefore, an understanding of the market for commercial mortgages is helpful in understanding the market for CMBS. In this chapter, we discuss the commercial mortgage market, its size and participants, the characteristics of the loans, their historical performance and its current status.

INVESTORS AND LENDING ACTIVITY

While the size of the commercial mortgage market has not changed that much over the last several years (see Exhibit 1), there has been a shift in the holders.

Banks continue to hold the lion's share of outstanding commercial mortgages. As shown in Exhibit 2, banks owned about 39% of the market as of second quarter 1995. Other large holders include life insurance companies, savings and loans associations (S&Ls), pension funds, and the Federal agencies. Traditionally, banks have been one of the main providers of construction loans. Often, following the construction phase, the bank that provided the construction financing makes the permanent loan.

The banks' share of the commercial mortgage market has remained fairly stable over the last several years. However, as shown in Exhibit 3, the S&L's share and the life insurance industry's share have both declined.

A good portion of the decline in the S&L's share is a result of their failure and subsequent seizure and liquidation by the Resolution Trust Company (RTC). Life insurance companies, on the other hand, have been consciously reducing the size of their holdings. Most recently they have been allocating some of their investment to CMBS. This decision is being driven by the attraction of the wider spreads afforded by CMBS, the greater liquidity of CMBS, and the lower NAIC capital requirements for securities compared to whole loans. Exhibit 4 shows the bank and insurance companies with the largest holdings in commercial mortgages.

Exhibit 1: Size of Commercial Mortgage Market

Year	Dollars (Trillions)
1991	1.03
1992	0.98
1993	0.96
1994	0.96
1995	0.98

Source: Federal Reserve.

Exhibit 2: Share of Commercial Mortgage Market
(2nd Quarter 1995)

	Percentage
Banks	39
Life Insurance Companies	20
Savings Institutions	12
Federal Agencies	8
Private Conduits	6
FDIC	1
Others	14

Source: Federal Reserve.

Exhibit 3: Changing Share of Commercial Mortgage Market

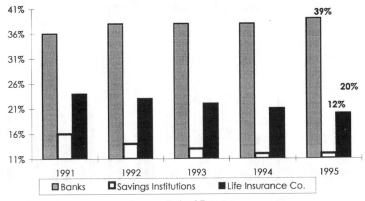

Source: Federal Reserve.

Exhibit 4: Banks and Insurance Companies with Largest Commercial Mortgage Holdings

Banks (as of 12/31/95)	Dollars (Billions)	Percent of Assets
Bank of America	10.17	6
Wells Fargo Bank	9.67	20
Nationsbank (Charlotte)	7.44	9
Citibank	7.17	3
Nationsbank (Atlanta)	5.06	13
First Union NB of Florida	4.66	13
Chemical Bank	4.46	3
First Fidelity Bank	3.93	12
Natwest Bank	3.74	13
Nationsbank of Texas	3.59	7

Insurance Companies (as of 12/31/94)	Dollars (Billions)	Percent of Assets
Teachers Insurance and Annuity, NY	21.01	26
Prudential Insurance, NJ	17.29	10
Metropolitan Life	11.06	8
AETNA Life Insurance, CT	9.79	19
Principal Mutual, IA	9.73	17
Connecticut General Life, CT	8.49	18
Northwestern Mutual, WI	8.36	15
John Hancock Mutual, MA	7.18	14
Equitable Life Insurance, NY	5.09	9
Travelers Insurance, CT	4.90	10

Source: A.M. Best, Sheshunoff Information Services.

Exhibit 5: Insurance Company Commercial Mortgage Commitments by Sector

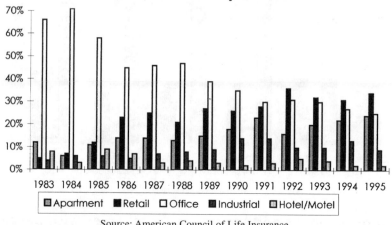

Source: American Council of Life Insurance.

Through the American Council of Life Insurance Companies (ACLI), a great deal of data is available on the industry's participation and performance in the commercial mortgage market. Each quarter, the ACLI publishes a report on delinquencies in the commercial mortgage portfolios of its members. ACLI's membership covers 85% of the assets of insurance companies. The report shows delinquencies by property type and by region of the country. The ACLI also publishes a report on new mortgage commitments, including the rate, debt service coverage ratio (DSCR), and loan-to-value (LTV). During the 1980s, the bulk of life insurance company lending was committed to the office sector as shown in Exhibit 5.

In 1984, commitments to the office sector represented over 70% of total commitments. However, this declined to about 30% by 1995. During this period, commitments to the retail and multifamily sectors increased. Commitments to the hotel sector have always been small, and are almost negligible today. Commercial mortgage lending activity, overall, dramatically declined in 1990 and 1991 as the full force of the real estate crash was felt. As the real estate market began to recover in 1993, lending activity began to pick up, but remains below the peak of the mid-1980s, as seen in Exhibit 6.

YIELD SPREADS

Commercial mortgage spreads over U.S. Treasuries have ranged from over +250 basis points to +75 basis points over the last 13 years (see Exhibit 7). In 1992, spreads reached a peak of +227 basis points as real estate prices were bottoming. (It is likely that loans that were made in the years 1993, 1994, and 1995 will be viewed in years ahead to be of the best vintage as real estate values were low and spreads were wide during this time.)

Since then spreads have generally been tightening as capital returned to the real estate markets. In 1995, spreads fluctuated in a narrow band between +136 basis points and +160 basis points. While these spreads are tighter than several years ago, many lenders find the rates attractive relative to alternative markets. Chapter 17 describes an approach to evaluating the risk-adjusted spread of this market.

LOAN CHARACTERISTICS

Commercial mortgages are usually monthly pay, fixed-rate amortizing loans with maturities ranging from 7 to 30 years. The majority have maturities from 7 to 12 years. They follow a 20- to 30-year amortization schedule and require a balloon payment at maturity. Amortization terms and maturities usually differ by property type.

Exhibit 6: Insurance Company Commercial Mortgage Commitments

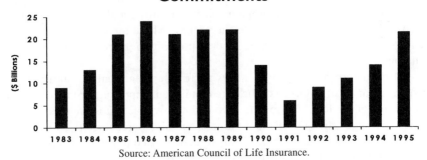

Source: American Council of Life Insurance.

Exhibit 7: Commercial Mortgage Spreads over U.S. Treasury 10 year

Source: Barron's/Levy.

The risk that a borrower may be unable to refinance the mortgage at the balloon date is known as *balloon risk*. This is considered by many to be the greatest risk in commercial mortgages. The amortization of the loan balance, on the other hand, tends to reduce this risk as it represents a built-in deleveraging of the loan. Moreover, some of the newer loans require that if the borrower defaults at the balloon date, the borrower pay a default rate which is set at some onerous spread such as +300 basis points to +500 basis points over Treasuries, and that all excess cash above the debt service payment be used to amortize the loan. Features such as these strongly discourage the borrower from defaulting at the balloon date.

Unlike residential mortgages, commercial mortgages typically have strong prepayment protection. (Chapter 3 discusses commercial mortgage prepayments.) The protection usually consists of a period of lockout followed by a period during which a prepayment penalty is applied. The penalty comes in various forms. Some loans require a yield maintenance penalty which attempts to make the investor, at worst, indifferent to the prepay and possibly better off. The penalty is computed as the positive difference between the present value of the remaining cash flows had the prepayment not occurred and the present value of the cash flows after giving effect to the prepay, where the discount rate used is Treasuries (sometimes plus a spread) corresponding to the remaining term of the cash flows.

In underwriting loans, lenders perform a great deal of qualitative and quantitative analysis. Market studies are conducted, appraisals are made, and the relative risk of the loan is assessed. Two quantitative measures are used: the debt service coverage ratio (DSCR) and the loan-to-value percentage (LTV). DSCR is the ratio of net operating income (NOI) to debt service payment. The greater the DSCR and the lower the LTV, the less risky the loan. A key to conservative underwriting is conservatism in estimating income and value. Various adjustments can be made to income to reflect expected changes and reserves for maintaining the property.

Less conservative underwriters may project growth in income, whereas more conservative underwriters will adjust income downward to reflect market rents, lease rollovers, leasing commissions, tenant improvements, etc. Exhibit 8 shows insurance company DSCRs and LTVs for various property types since 1983.

While DSCRs since 1991 are, on average, higher than in the 1980s, reflecting some conservatism, average LTVs seem to have remained the same. The NAIC model investment law sets targets for insurance companies with respect to LTVs. The regulators want the insurance companies to limit LTV to a maximum of 75%. Of course, the valuation can be somewhat arbitrary. Typically, loans on properties that are considered to have more stable income streams will be underwritten to lower DSCRs and higher LTVs. For example, multifamily properties tend to have the lowest DSCRs whereas hotels tend to have the highest. This conforms with the theory of default risk presented in Chapter 11.

Exhibit 8: DSCRs and LTVs for Various Property Types for Insurance Companies

DSCR

	Apartment	Retail	Office	Industrial	Hotel/Motel
1983	1.23	1.20	1.24	1.23	1.25
1984	1.17	1.26	1.22	1.24	1.47
1985	1.25	1.24	1.22	1.20	1.46
1986	1.34	1.30	1.33	1.27	1.37
1987	1.32	1.26	1.28	1.28	1.50
1988	1.25	1.28	1.27	1.28	1.41
1989	1.24	1.21	1.22	1.23	1.33
1990	1.25	1.22	1.27	1.31	1.33
1991	1.28	1.31	1.50	1.33	1.19
1992	1.40	1.40	1.42	1.36	1.24
1993	1.43	1.48	1.51	1.37	1.28
1994	1.39	1.36	1.40	1.41	1.39
1995	1.49	1.48	1.52	1.42	1.68

LTV

	Apartment	Retail	Office	Industrial	Hotel/Motel
1983	69%	73%	70%	69%	73%
1984	71%	68%	71%	73%	63%
1985	70%	71%	71%	73%	70%
1986	70%	71%	72%	71%	70%
1987	69.4%	72%	74%	71%	69%
1988	78%	81%	82%	75%	77%
1989	74%	74%	75%	73%	71%
1990	72%	72%	72%	71%	74%
1991	69%	70%	69%	68%	62%
1992	72%	68%	77%	73%	78%
1993	73%	70%	80%	74%	86%
1994	69%	68%	76%	74%	75%
1995	70%	68%	68%	73%	66%

Source: American Council of Life Insurance.

Exhibit 9: Commercial Mortgage Delinquencies
(Quarters Ending June 30: 1965-1995)

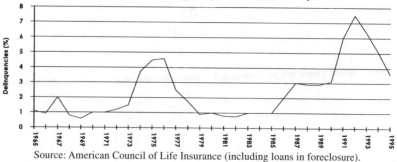

Source: American Council of Life Insurance (including loans in foreclosure).

Exhibit 10: Commercial Mortgage Delinquencies by Property Type

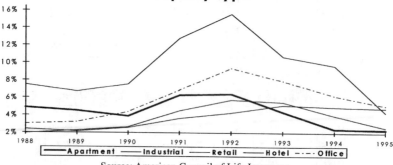

Source: American Council of Life Insurance.

DEFAULTS AND DELINQENCIES

Even with the best underwriting practices, delinquencies and defaults can and have occurred. Exhibit 9 shows the commercial mortgage delinquencies for life insurance companies.

Delinquencies have been steadily declining since the peak in 1992 when they hit 7.5%. While the current level of delinquencies is below the peak reached in 1976, it is still higher than the levels of the 1960s and early 1980s. Delinquency rates have varied by property type. Exhibit 10 shows delinquency by property type since 1988.

Insurance companies had their worst delinquencies in their hotel loans. This is probably why many insurance companies today have a visceral negative reaction to lending on hotels. (As we noted earlier, though, their allocation to this sector has always been very small.)

As of the fourth quarter of 1995, delinquencies on hotels were close to the levels for office properties. Many investors today believe that with conservative under-writing, loans on hotel properties can perform just as well as loans on properties with more stable income streams. With high DSCRs and low LTVs, hotel loans should be able to withstand relatively severe economic climates. Unfortunately for the insurance industry, the DSCRs and LTVs on some of their hotel loans relative to the other property types did not adequately reflect the risk differential as shown in Exhibit 8.

Only a small portion of loans that are delinquent actually end up going through the foreclosure process. As can be seen in Exhibit 11, even at their peak, foreclosure rates were still below 3.5%.

While good underwriting is obviously critical in limiting default, it is worth noting an interesting result from a study published by Mark Snyderman.[1] He found that the year of origination is extremely important in explaining the lifetime performance of a pool of loans. Exhibit 12 shows the lifetime defaults of a large universe of insurance company loans by year of origination.

Exhibit 11: Commercial Mortgage Delinquencies and Foreclosures

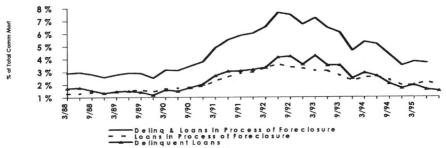

Source: American Council of Life Insurance.

Exhibit 12: Commercial Mortgage Defaults by Year of Origination

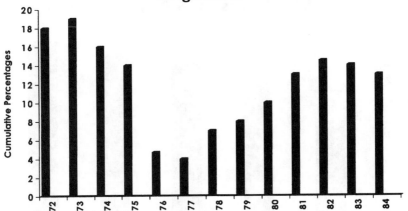

Source: Mark P. Snyderman, "Commercial Mortgages: Default Occurence and Estimated Yield Impact," *Journal of Portfolio Management* (Fall 1991), pp. 82-87.
This copyrighted material is reprinted with permission from Institutional Investor, Inc.
Journal of Portfolio Management, 488 Madison Avenue, New York, NY 10022.

[1] Mark P. Snyderman, "Commercial Mortgages: Default Occurence and Estimated Yield Impact," *Journal of Portfolio Management* (Fall 1991), pp. 82-87.

What is most striking is the contrast between loans originated in 1972 and 1973 versus loans that were originated in 1975 and 1976. Juxtaposing Exhibit 11 and Exhibit 12 provides the key insight, namely that loans that were originated in 1975 and 1976 following the real estate crisis had very low lifetime default rates. This is likely due to the conservatism that takes hold in underwriting following a decline in asset values. One would expect based on this analysis that loans originated in 1992, 1993, and 1994 to be loans with very low lifetime defaults. Perhaps 1995 and 1996 might be excellent performers as well since delinquencies had not yet bottomed.

Investors need to consider not only delinquency and default rates, but also what happens if a loan defaults. How long does it take to foreclose? And, what will the ultimate loss be? It is the combination of the default rate, time to default, and loss severity that will determine the realized yield on the investment. There are several analyses and studies that have addressed these questions. Most of the studies have found the recovery rates to have been from 65% to 75% before expenses and reimbursements. The results show a difference by property type. For example, the ACLI looked at this and found losses to have ranged from 18% for multifamily to 32% for hotels as shown in Exhibit 13.

A number of interesting conclusions were also reached in a 1994 study conducted by Brian Ciochetti and Timothy Riddiough.[2] The main results of their study were as follows:

• The average time from the start of default until the property is transferred to the investor is approximately nine months.

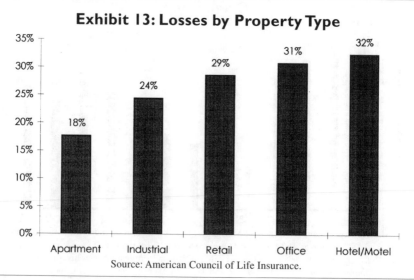

Exhibit 13: Losses by Property Type

Source: American Council of Life Insurance.

[2] Brian A. Ciochetti and Timothy J. Riddiough "Loss Severity and Its Impact on Commercial Mortgages," unpublished manuscript, December 1994.

- When the average delinquency period of about 3.5 months is added, the total average time from delinquency through foreclosure is about 12.5 months. Thus, 12.5 months could serve as a baseline number to be used by analysts for their default scenarios.
- Foreclosure in states where the process has to go through the court system took an average of three months longer than in states where the courts were not involved. (In Exhibit 14 we excerpt from the study the method of foreclosure by state.) In addition, foreclosure time tended to be much shorter in the southwest part of the United States.
- The property value net of foreclosure costs and accrued interest averaged 78% of the outstanding loan balance as of the beginning of the foreclosure process. The recovery rate was 4% higher for states where foreclosure does not go through the courts. In Exhibit 15 we show the reported recovery rates and time to recover by property type.
- Loans that were previously modified had a recovery rate of only 58%.

In a more recent study by Brian Ciochetti, the average recovery rate was found to be 69% including accrued interest.[3] Each of the studies have their own particular measurement problems; nevertheless, they provide investors and the rating agencies some measure to use in stress analysis of commercial mortgages. It is worth noting that the data used in most of these studies covered what was the worst real estate decline in the last 20 years.

CONCLUSION

The lending binge of the 1980s encouraged excessive building. The result was an over supply of real estate and loans which could not be paid. This led to a withdrawal by traditional lenders from the commercial mortgage market. In the early 1990s, very few institutions were willing to finance commercial real estate. Insurance companies limited themselves to rolling over — often with modifications — existing loans in order to avoid going through the expensive foreclosure process. By 1992 and 1993, real estate prices bottomed after, what seemed to be a free fall. In some markets property prices had fallen by as much as 50%. Real estate was selling for less than replacement cost. Gradually traditional lenders returned, although new supply remained mostly non-existent. In 1995, the commercial mortgage market began to revive. However, the trend toward securitization also took hold. Instead of Wall Street simply securitizing existing portfolios of existing or bankrupt lenders, market leaders created relationships with lenders. Loans began to be originated with securitization in mind. This meant loans where the requirements at the origination date were ones which would satisfy the rating agencies and be palatable to investors in fixed income securities. The next chapter covers the origins and market for commercial mortgage-backed securities.

[3] Brian A. Ciochetti,"Loss Characteristics of Commercial Mortgage Foreclosures," unpublished manuscript, February 1996.

Exhibit 14: Credit Events by State Law Convention. Judicial Foreclosure Versus Power of Sales

State	Foreclosure Time
Arizona	PS
California	PS
Colorado	PS
Wash. D.C.	PS
Florida	JD
Georgia	PS
Idaho	PS
Illinois	JD
Indiana	JD
Kansas	JD
Louisiana	JD
Maryland	PS
Michigan	PS
Minnesota	PS
Missouri	PS
North Carolina	PS
New Mexico	JD
New York	JD
Oklahoma	JD
Oregon	PS
South Carolina	JD
Tennessee	PS
Texas	PS
Utah	PS
Virginia	PS
Washington	PS
Wisconsin	PS

State Law	Foreclosure Time	Recovery Rate
Judicial	11.4 months	74.9%
Power of Sale	8.4 months	78.7%

PS = Power of Sale
JD = Judicial Foreclosure

Source: Brian A. Ciochetti, "Loss Characteristics of Commercial Mortgage Foreclosures," unpublished manuscript, February 1996.

Exhibit 15: Foreclosure Time and Recovery Rate by Property Type

Property Type	Foreclosure Time (months)	Recovery Rate (%)
Apartment	8.6	84.8
Hotel	9.8	71.2
Industrial	9.2	79.7
Office	9.3	70.4
Retail	10.1	77.1

Source: Brian A. Ciochetti, "Loss Characteristics of Commercial Mortgage Foreclosures," unpublished manuscript, February 1996.

Chapter **3**

Commercial Mortgage Prepayments

Jesse M. Abraham, Ph.D.
Director, Servicing Division
Federal Home Loan Mortgage Corporation

H. Scott Theobald
Senior Financial Analyst, Finance Division
Federal Home Loan Mortgage Corporation

INTRODUCTION

Prepayments are the primary focus when it comes to the valuation of single-family securities. Virtually all of the market volume is in agency or highly rated private issues which are subject to little or no risk to ultimate repayment of principal. The risk of early retirement of collateral because of mortgage borrower prepayments therefore becomes the key to valuation of those types of securities.

But that is not the case with commercial mortgage-backed securities (CMBS). In this market the prime determinant of pricing is the depth of credit protection required by the rating agencies. That is the case because there are virtually no whole loan issues fully guaranteed by the government (RTC, GNMA) or government sponsored enterprise (FNMA, FHLMC) being done today, while the magnitude of credit risk is much greater than with single-family mortgages.

We appreciate the comments of our colleagues in Freddie Mac's Financial Research department, and of Mark Buono of Goldman Sachs. George Wisniewski assisted in the early stages of this research. The opinions expressed in the paper reflect only those of the authors and not of other employees or the Board of Directors of the Federal Home Loan Mortgage Corporation.

It is also true that contract features of commercial mortgages lend themselves to greater predictability of prepayment behavior than 30-year single-family mortgages: typically there are prepayment disincentives immediately after funding, which discourage early payments, together with short maturities of only 5, 10, or 15 years that together reduce the uncertainty about the timing of prepayments. Still, any payment uncertainty in an investment needs to be understood and priced. And with commercial pools composed of generally fewer loans than single-family passthroughs, the behavior of each individual loan takes on added importance.

In this chapter, we present prepayment data from a sample of multifamily mortgages, and review the issues that differentiate commercial mortgage activity from single-family behavior. The relative importance of theoretical issues for valuation are then brought out through the discussion of a prepayment model estimated with the sample presented earlier.

We assume the reader is familiar with single-family prepayment issues. Therefore, we start in the first section pointing out reasons why single-family experience is not directly transferable to the CMBS market. The second section confronts the data with our now increased sensitivity to features of commercial mortgages. The final section presents a prepayment model and estimation results.

HOW COMMERCIAL DIFFERS FROM SINGLE-FAMILY

An assumption that CMBS and MBS pools of similar vintage should behave in a like manner would be convenient, but inaccurate. Despite gross similarities between these two mortgage instruments, they have markedly different contract features. In addition, the personal incentives of mortgagors are different between (largely) owner-occupied 1-4 unit dwellings and investor-owned, multi-unit rental businesses.

This simple point is driven home by Exhibit 1, which reports conditional and cumulative prepayments for Freddie Mac's single-family and multifamily mortgage loans originated in 1984. For one thing, the average coupons are different, with an average multifamily coupon of 13.41%, and 13.10% for the single-family. The left two columns show that most of the single-family loans prepaid in 1986-87; conditional rates were lower during the subsequent four years, rising again in the refinancing boom of 1992-1993. In contrast, in the right-hand columns multifamily loans did not really get started until some 40% prepaid in 1989, and another 20% the next year, followed by successively smaller conditional rates, even as interest rates crashed in 1992-93, before turning up in 1994.

A useful starting place for investigating the source of these differences is the virtual identity commonly cited in single-family analysis to decompose dollars of prepayments into four components:

total prepayments = relocations – assumptions + curtailments + refinances

Exhibit 1: Comparative Conditional and Cumulative Prepayment Rates (%) Multifamily and Single-family 1984 Originations

Year	Single-family Conditional	Cumulative	Multifamily Conditional	Cumulative
1985	15.7	15.7	1.0	1.0
1986	51.3	58.9	1.7	2.7
1987	36.9	74.1	0.0	2.7
1988	18.2	78.8	6.5	9.0
1989	14.8	81.9	34.6	39.9
1990	13.8	84.4	36.3	60.1
1991	19.3	87.4	29.7	70.1
1992	26.7	90.8	22.1	75.1
1993	24.2	93.0	14.0	77.4
1994	21.1	94.5	39.5	83.1

In single-family prepayment behavior, relocation is important because home sales typically lead to mortgage termination, except when assumptions occur as is allowed with FHA loans securitized by Ginnie Mae. Curtailments, or partial prepayments, are quite small in magnitude but need to be accounted for. The research emphasis is appropriately put on refinances, which are the greatest source of volatility in prepayment behavior.[1]

Commercial loans, if anything, exhibit an even greater sensitivity to refinances. Curtailments are virtually nonexistent (less than 1% of principal in our dataset), as borrowers look to maximize leverage rather than make extra principal payments. In addition, there is a lower frequency of sales in commercial than in single-family properties, including assumptions, as performing real estate is a valuable asset for both its cash flow and for its use as collateral to obtain increased financing.

The conditions which motivate and ultimately enable borrowers to accomplish a refinance require quite different modeling between these two markets. Below we discuss five sources of potential difference between single-family and CMBS loan behavior: the optimization rule; the degree of ruthlessness; the metric for measuring loan quality; extension risk; and, call protection provisions.

The Optimization Rule

In idiosyncratic ways, households seek to manage their portfolio of assets — human capital, physical capital, financial assets, and real estate — to maximize their utility. The impact of maximizing the return on one, e.g. health and well-being, may be only tangentially related to the management of another, such as finances. Some connec-

---

[1] An accessible explanation of each component is provided in Gregg N. Patruno, "Mortgage Prepayments: A New Model for a New Era," Chapter 9 in Frank J. Fabozzi (ed.), *Handbook of Mortgage-Backed Securities* (Chicago: Probus Publishing, 1995).

tions, such as seeking the best job to maximize the return on education and housing, are widely recognized. But sorting through this problem is very complex, it suffers from incomplete data and promises little reward.[2]

The problem is much more straightforward with a commercial property owner who is expected to be a wealth maximizer, and who in every period is looking to increase his portfolio's expected return. An owner's decisions regarding any given loan may be made for financial reasons that are specific to that property, but could also go beyond that one property to his entire portfolio. In addition, there exist a wider variety of financial options available to a commercial borrower than to a single-family borrower, making terms that are familiar to the single-family borrower like "refinance" and "default" too crude to capture the richness of the choices faced by a commercial property owner.

An example of portfolio concerns would be an owner who has cross-collateral agreements from one property to another, or other covenants that restrict his ability to maximize the profit from each property as a separate entity. Reputation effects could well come into play when it comes to capital improvements or a default decision.

That "refinance" is too crude a term for commercial property owners becomes clear when one considers the importance of the preferred degree of leverage to maximize a return-on-equity. Should the property appreciate in value, a refinance (or a second mortgage) lets the owner take money out to fund other investments. But the ability to do that depends upon current interest rates and market liquidity. Tax code changes at the national and local levels — which change periodically for commercial property — can affect whether an owner prefers ordinary income or capital gains, which in turn would drive a "hold or sell" strategy. Whether the investor receives current cash flow or future income can be managed, at least in the short term, by varying capital expenditures.

While conceptually important, fully addressing these issues is beyond the scope of current data and research. The model discussed later will assume that in refinancing borrowers seek to minimize the expected value of payments necessary to retire their outstanding obligation, anticipating that they will continue to own the property for the foreseeable future.

Degree of Ruthlessness

A now commonplace framework for analyzing single-family mortgage behavior is options pricing, in which a borrower is seen to be issued, in addition to a fully amortizing loan, a put option which may be exercised when the property value falls below the par mortgage value, and a call option which may be exercised when the market value of current mortgage payments exceeds the par mortgage value. Clearly, the focus here is on the call option.

---

[2] A good discussion of this issue is provided in Wayne Archer, David C. Ling, and Gary A. McGill, "The Effect of Income and Collateral Constraints on Residential Mortgage Terminations," *Regional Science and Urban Economics,* forthcoming.

Exhibit 2: The Probability of Prepayment
for Single-Family and Commercial Mortgages

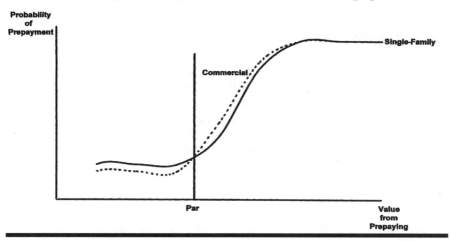

Essential to the application of the option pricing formula is the ruthless exercise of an option given the right circumstances. This does not necessarily mean that the option is exercised immediately upon entering "into the money," only that there is a clear set of rules the holder "ruthlessly" follows to maximize wealth.[3]

The elegance of the application of a pure option pricing solution is belied by observed experience: mortgage holders of a single vintage and coupon never act in concert. Capturing the heterogeneity of borrower experience (and hence behavior) without violating the theoretical insights from the options framework becomes a challenge as soon as the model becomes tested empirically.

Commercial investors should be expected to more ruthlessly exercise wealth maximization options than owner-occupants. This point is illustrated in Exhibit 2, which plots the probability of prepayment against the value from prepaying. The familiar "S" shape arises because single-family loans will have an irreducible prepayment rate from relocations, even when the market value of the mortgage is below par. As interest rates decline and the market value rises, the probability of single-family prepayment rises rapidly, then asymptotes towards 100%. In contrast, we should expect the commercial loan to have a lower autonomous rate, because of fewer relocations. As mortgage rates decline, the probability of refinance should increase faster with commercial mortgages than with single-family mortgages.

Since real world data are net of investor portfolio concerns, and the variety of other possible influences mentioned earlier, estimation results could be

---

[3] This methodology is followed in James B. Kau, Donald C. Keenan, Walter J. Muller III, and James F. Epperson, "Pricing Commercial Mortgages and Their Mortgage-Backed Securities," *Journal of Real Estate Finance and Economics*, 3, 1990, pp. 333-356; and Sheridan Titman and Walter Torous, "Valuing Commercial Mortgages: An Empirical Investigation of the Contingent-Claims Approach to Pricing Risky Debt," *Journal of Finance* (June 1989), pp 345-373.

more equivocal than this discussion suggests. Still, one would expect the theoretical differences between owner-occupants and investors should be born out in the data.

Loan Quality Metric

In the single-family prepayment literature it is widely recognized that models need to include measures of loan quality. In part, this is because loan defaults in investor pools become prepayments. But more importantly, researchers recognize that current investor guidelines require positive equity to refinance a loan. During the 1992-93 bond rally, when interest rates dropped considerably and many borrowers failed to refinance, it became abundantly clear that the likelihood of prepayment is highly correlated with the credit quality of the outstanding loans. The sensitivity of loans that remain in a pool to house price changes is critical for anticipating prepayments.

A reliable measure of loan quality for single-family loans is the loan-to-value (LTV) ratio, so it is used as an explicit threshold for approval for refinancing, with investors such as Freddie Mac requiring refinances to be no greater than 90% LTV. Appropriately, virtually all simulation models that project prepayments therefore include house price appreciation as a key determining "state" variable.

Measuring the credit quality of a commercial property is much more complex than with single-family properties. Not only are there no good measures of property value trends, but it is almost impossible to measure *quality* along a single axis, since a property's cash flow and equity are both important, as well as possibly a host of qualitative factors.

Unlike in the earlier discussion on portfolio effects, in this area we have attempted to reflect this complexity in the modeling work below. The quality measure used for individual properties is a measure of cash flow, the debt coverage ratio (DCR). It is calculated as a property's net operating income — less expenses — divided by debt service payments.[4] A DCR of 1.00 will be close to default, since the cash flow is then only just enough to cover debt service, while a property generating a 1.50 DCR is in good shape, and positioned to be able to absorb several adverse shocks to its cash flow before potentially becoming a problem.

Extension Risk

Single-family loans are typically fully amortizing, over 15- to 30-years, with no penalty assessed should a borrower choose to pay off part, or all, of the loan early. In contrast, commercial loans are typically balloons, may or may not amortize, and almost certainly carry provisions which limit prepayments.

---

[4] A cash flow model of property performance is motivated, developed, and analyzed in Jesse M. Abraham, "On the use of a Cash Flow Time Series to Measure Property Performance," forthcoming in the *Journal of Real Estate Research*. This model is used as the basis for a credit model of multifamily performance in Jesse M. Abraham, "Credit Risk in Commercial Real Estate Lending," Mimeograph, December 1993.

The risk that a borrower will be unable, or unwilling, to refinance a loan when a balloon payment is due is termed *balloon risk* or *extension risk*. At the end of the contracted term the loan technically becomes "in default" and could be taken over by the lender.[5] Only credit-impaired loans will fall in this category, since no borrower with positive equity would welcome this loss of control. However, lenders are rarely eager to become landlords. Industry practice is to engage in workouts or loan modifications, in the hope of avoiding a borrower's milking the property before being forced out, as well as avoiding the deadweight costs of foreclosure proceedings. With loan securitization, investors with different credit exposures can have conflicting interests in how impaired loans should be resolved. Therefore these structures include explicit agreements covering the rights and obligations of all investors, the servicer, and the special servicer.

The financial implications of this practice — and in particular the effect on loan payoffs — are a challenge to evaluate and model. In this chapter, we only examine prepayments during the contract term, since the incentives of both the mortgagor and mortgagee change considerably after the balloon date.

Investor Call Protection

Another feature that is common with commercial, but infrequent in single-family, loans is terms discouraging early prepayment. These could be as modest as a 1% fee, but often are much more complex and costly for a period of time right after origination. Our data cover the gamut from absolute *lockouts* that prohibit prepayments during an initial period, to so called *yield maintenance agreements* (YM) which are less legally restrictive, but meant to have the same effect.

A single YM formula is now commonly used by insurance companies, Freddie Mac, and Fannie Mae. The objective is to remove the borrower's incentive to prepay prior to a designated date by imposing a fee roughly equal to the savings from the (presumably) new lower mortgage rate. It is the present value, over the remainder of the YM period, of the difference between the note rate and a U.S. Treasury yield at prepayment, multiplied by the principal amount to be prepaid.

Our data also include some loans with an even simpler structure. The penalty follows a 5-4-3-2-1 pattern for the first five years of a mortgage. A prepayment in the first year after origination would precipitate a 5% fee, in the second year a 4% fee, etc.

It should be noted that the incentive to prepay is not eliminated, only reduced with these fees. A borrower might be willing to pay the fee if he thought interest rates were going to rise from their current levels, and be much higher after the yield maintenance period was over. Alternatively, it may be well worthwhile to incur some added costs towards the end of the YM period, if low mortgages rates are available to be locked in for an extended period of a new mortgage.

---

[5] Single-family loans can also be restructured, but restructurings occur at a much lower frequency than with commercial properties. Additionally, workout processes at the agencies are not important to single-family passthrough holders since investors get paid off 120 days into a delinquency.

A LOOK AT THE DATA

There are very little data publicly available with which to fashion expectations about commercial loan behavior. The highest volume issuer of CMBS securities, the Resolution Trust Corporation (RTC), conveniently separates its securities by property type. However, their loans are of uncertain credit quality, have unknown prepayment disincentive features, and uncertain extension provisions. Freddie Mac and Fannie Mae factors are another potential source of data, but their total volume to date has been limited. Compared to single-family, loan defaults will have a significant impact on security prepayments, while origination credit quality is not part of the disclosure package.

The data presented here provide one of the first publicly available, systematic reviews of commercial prepayment experience. Before proceeding directly to the modeling, it is helpful to understand the characteristics of this data, and to see the extent to which the data confirm or refute expectations in the market.

Freddie Mac has been in the multifamily market since 1973. However, purchase volume did not become significant until the end of 1983 with the introduction of Plan A and Plan B programs, and in 1989, Plan C. Plan A purchases included a wide variety of contract structures and (now) suffer from incomplete data. The data summarized here are from 7,769 Plan B and C loans originated between 1984 and 1990. Plan Bs are fixed rate, level payment, with 10- or 15-year terms with 15- to 30-year amortization and 4.5-year lockouts; they comprise 87% of the sample. Plan C loans have 5- to 15-year terms, with 30-year amortization, and various prepayment disincentive features. In each year, DCR at origination ranged from just over 1.00 to over 2.00.

Interest Rate Effects

For a given economic environment, one would expect high coupon mortgages to prepay faster than low coupon mortgages. This standard behavior is confirmed in Exhibit 3, which shows Freddie Mac's cumulative multifamily prepayment rates, by origination year, through 1994. For each origination book, coupons less than the sample median were assigned to the low-rate category, while loans with coupons greater than the median were assigned to the high-rate category. The rates reported for each category are the first and third quartile values, respectively.

Looking at the data across origination years, we note that the 1984 and 1985 books have distinctly higher coupons than the remaining books, and they appropriately have prepaid more completely to date. Within origination years, with the exception of the 1988 and 1990 books, more loans have prepaid in the high-rate category than in the low-rate category. Note there is less difference in spread (55 basis points) between the categories in the 1988 book than any of the other books. The 1990 book is not yet completely out of the yield maintenance period.

Exhibit 3: Cumulative Multifamily Prepayment Rates
High and Low Coupons Through 1994

Origination	Low Coupon		High Coupon	
Year	Median Coupon	Prepayment Rate	Median Coupon	Prepayment Rate
1984	13.02	82.4	13.75	83.8
1985	11.62	64.1	12.47	78.8
1986	10.38	48.7	11.03	57.2
1987	9.91	24.7	10.82	34.9
1988	10.74	20.9	11.29	14.9
1989	9.72	13.2	10.69	17.0
1990	9.97	11.8	10.73	10.5

Credit Quality Effects

As discussed in the first section, the credit quality of the collateral securing the loan is important to the ability to obtain funds to refinance, or equivalently, the ability to maximize the leverage of the property. Exhibit 4 shows prepayments for the 1984 and 1985 books broken into four ranges of origination debt coverage ratio. Higher rates of debt coverage at origination, which ought to be correlated with higher ongoing coverage levels, exhibit higher rates of refinancing. (Note that refinancings here do not include loan defaults.)

There is likely a similar story of credit quality behind the Exhibit 5 data, which show that for the 1985 and 1986 books, California loans prepaid at faster rates than New York/New Jersey mortgages. The strong California market in the late-1980s provided plenty of liquidity and opportunities to refinance or sell; the ailing Northeast market battered property values, reducing owners' ability to find new funds, and drove some owners towards assumptions. (This regional breakout used the 1985 and 1986 books since they had the heaviest volume.)

Both Exhibits 4 and 5 look like hockey sticks, illustrating the potent impact of prepayment restrictions. Prepays are virtually nonexistent during the first 4.5 years of the mortgages.

THE PREPAYMENT MODEL

In this section we summarize both the theoretical features and the results of a regression model we have developed. Details of variable construction and model estimation are reported elsewhere.[6]

---

[6] See Jesse M. Abraham and H. Scott Theobald, "A Simple Prepayment Model of Commercial Mortgages," Mimeograph, August 1995.

Exhibit 4: Cumulative Prepayment Rates
by Origination DCR
1984 Originations

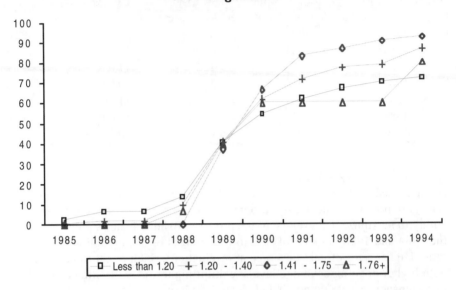

Cumulative Prepayment Rates by Origination DCR
1985 Originations

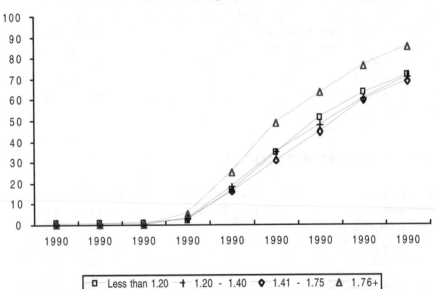

Exhibit 5: Cumulative Prepayment Rates by Property State
1985 Originations

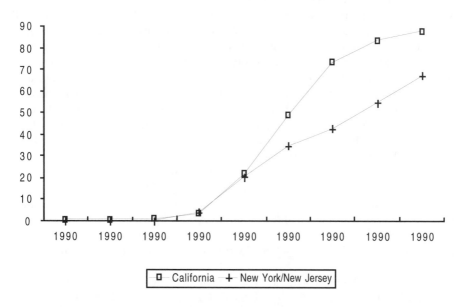

Cumulative Prepayment Rates by Property State
1986 Originations

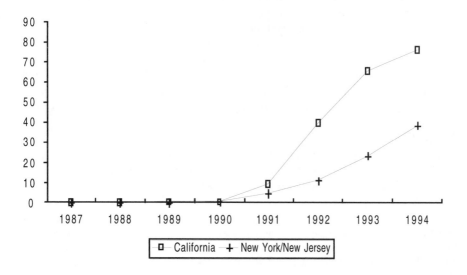

The possibility of an event of significance to a mortgage loan is the result of environment risks that develop over time from four potential sources: market, property, borrower and contract.[7] By *market risk* we mean changes in financial markets, federal tax policy, and other variables that are national in scope and affect all financial markets. In our model, these are captured through interest rate changes. Beyond macroeconomic uncertainty, there are risks specific to *property* markets such as cash flow and valuation volatility, which we represent through changes in property income and expense, and local vacancy rates. *Management actions* also play a part in property-specific realization of this type of risk. The financial circumstances of the borrower — the borrower's portfolio position and strategies or reputation — can evolve in a way that affects the exercise of the mortgage call and put options. And finally, features of the lending *contract* can mitigate or create risks in tandem with the stochastic influences.

A model of borrower behavior is necessary to bring order to this sea of stochastic events to explain mortgage prepayments. A useful framework comes from option pricing theory. Our conceptual view of prepayment of a commercial mortgage is of a borrower exercising a call option: if the expected present value of an available new source of funds, net of contractual constraints (lockouts) or prepayment fees, is lower than on the existing obligation, the borrower will refinance and terminate the existing contract.[8]

Commercial borrowers face contractual and market constraints which limit their opportunities to pay in full before the end of a loan's term. This suggests thinking of the prepayment action as the result of two related, but still behaviorally separate states. First, borrowers may be "eligible" or "not eligible" to prepay. Second, the financial incentives may or may not exist for a prepayment.[9] The conditions under which these two criteria are met are considered next.

The fundamental risks identified above are mapped into the behavioral concepts of the option model in Exhibit 6. There is little to say about borrower risk as regards the prepayment option — it is more important in exercise of the default option than in the prepayment option — so that line is left blank. But the other entries indicate how the fundamental risks identified above affect the two prepayment concepts that are useful to measure, and become important in our empirical results used below.

Eligibility

Not all loans, at any given point in time, are candidates for a refinance. To the extent one can segment existing borrowers into eligible and ineligible borrowers, an estimation model will have improved discriminatory powers.

---

[7] A similar characterization of risks is discussed in the Appendix to Jesse M. Abraham, "On the Use of a Cash Flow Time Series to Measure Property Performance," *Journal of Real Estate Research*, forthcoming.

[8] See Patric H. Hendershott and Robert Van Order, "Pricing Mortgages: An Interpretation of the Models and Results," *Journal of Financial Services Research*, Volume 1, 1987, pp. 77-111 for a good overview of this approach.

[9] The empirical approach followed here was originally developed in Chester Foster and Robert Van Order, "FHA Terminations: A Prelude to Rational Mortgage Pricing," *AREUEA Journal*, 13(2), 1985, pp. 24-36.

Exhibit 6: Translation of Environment Risks into Eligibility and Willingness

	Eligibility	Willingness
Market risk	Level of refinance debt service relative to origination Prospective lender DCR standards	Borrower payback period requirements
Property and management risk	Property's current NOI	Appreciation permits re-leveraging
Borrower and portfolio risk	—	—
Mortgage contract features	Lockout forestalls early prepayment	Yield maintenance and prepayment fees affect loan-specific incentives

A loan's eligibility to be prepaid depends on the current borrower's ability both to escape from the existing contract and to obtain financing for a new contract. Canceling the existing contract may not be an option if the contract is written with a lockout provision.[10]

A prepayment is also possible only if a lender, which could include the current mortgagee, is willing to provide new financing. Reasonably, lenders require a borrower to have positive equity and a healthy cash flow to be eligible for mortgage funds. While minimum equity and debt service levels may vary from one lender to another, too little equity, or too low a DCR, together with certain property characteristics, can make it virtually impossible for an owner to refinance (without putting more money into the property). The ability of a property to satisfy those lenders' conditions changes over time from movements in local housing markets, as well as the national capital markets. Lender standards can also change over time, such as loosening in a period of excess supply of capital (mid-1980s), toughening in a credit crunch (early 1990s), or loosening when new lenders enter the market (the entry of conduits in 1993).

The model presented below measures credit quality using cash flow rather than equity, making our credit threshold a constant debt coverage. In our favored specification, a borrower needs to achieve a DCR in excess of 1.20 using the refinance rate. That is, using our loan level data, in each period during our estimation, a property's prospective debt coverage ratio is compared against the threshold: DCRs exceeding the threshold are deemed "eligible." The prospective DCR is calculated by dividing the property's updated net operating income by the debt service of the outstanding loan balance at refinance rates. Thus eligibility becomes determined both by property-specific cash flow conditions as well as market trends.

---

[10] Some loans in our sample are affected by this, but in practice lockouts have since been replaced with yield maintenance provisions.

An example of the effect of imposing the eligibility criteria in our estimation for the 1984 and 1989 high-coupon books is shown in Exhibit 7. The clear bar shows the percentage of original loans outstanding at the beginning of each exposure year; the shaded bar shows what happens to eligibility. The 1984 book is subject to lockouts, so all loans remain ineligible until 1988. As they emerge from lockout, most, but not all, benefit from the roughly 350 basis point drop in interest rates since origination.

With the 1989 book, with yield maintenance provisions, loans become eligible to refinance much earlier. A relatively low percentage of loans are eligible early on because 78% of the book's originations (compared to 58% of 1984's originations) started with a DCR at or below 1.20. As interest rates declined, and the debt service of the prospective refinanced loan declined, increasing numbers of loans became eligible, while few actually prepaid because of yield maintenance provisions.

Willingness

Not all eligible borrowers will be have incentive to prepay. What we have termed borrower "willingness" to prepay is sensitivity to changes over time in market conditions, property risk, and initial contract features, as indicated in Exhibit 6. The most straightforward way to see this is to calculate the value of PREPAY in the equation below, which is the market value of the existing payment obligation relative to the book value of the existing obligation:

$$PREPAY = (MVUPB - TRNSCOST - PREPFEE)/UPB$$

where

MVUPB = the present value of the principal and interest payments, plus the balloon, of the outstanding mortgage, discounted at the current market (mortgage) rate.

TRNSCOST = the transactions costs of originating a new loan. We assume they are a fixed 2.5% of the outstanding loan balance. However, at the balloon date, transactions costs are not discretionary to the borrower (unless the property is sold), so they should not act as a disincentive to payoff of the loan at that time. What makes transactions costs important is the extent to which they are accelerated from the balloon date. Therefore, in our calculations this variable is set equal to zero at the balloon date, with a 2.5% cost increased in proportion to the time value of refinancing early (with the one-year Treasury bond rate).

PREPFEE = the prepayment fees specific to each loan program. In the Freddie Mac programs, there were no fees to pay off the loan during the last six months of the term. Prior to that, there was a 1% fee, a yield maintenance provision, or a lockout.

UPB = the modeled unpaid principal balance of the loan.

Exhibit 7: Original and Eligible Loans Outstanding
1984 Originations – High Coupon

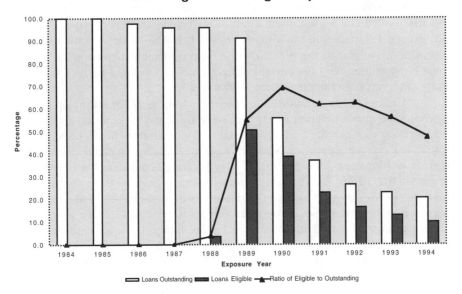

Original and Eligible Loans Outstanding
1989 Originations – High Coupon

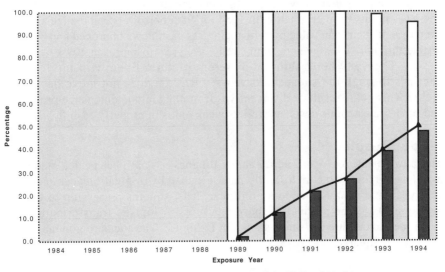

If there is no change in interest rates, the PREPAY variable will remain generally below 1.0 because of the fixed costs associated with a refinance transaction. As interest rates rise, MVUPB falls in value since the same cash flow is now discounted at a higher interest rate. Conversely, as rates decline, PREPAY will exceed 1.0, indicating that the borrower is in-the-money for the refinance option. In other words, the present value from refinancing exceeds the present value of remaining with the current obligation. The variable PREPAY will generally have values in the range from 0.80 to 1.30.

Crucial to the calculation of PREPAY are the assumptions one makes regarding the current market mortgage rate and the payback period required by the borrower to make the transaction viable. Two extremes are defined by borrower views of the current risks and rewards of utilizing financial leverage. An aggressive borrower, seeking to maximize leverage, considers the new loan to be only a substitute for (roughly) the remaining term of the existing loan, financed for the shortest term and with the cheapest source of funds around. A conservative borrower, seeking to minimize leverage, considers the new loan to be a mechanism for retiring the existing loan, financed for a longer term and with a more expensive source of funds. Our empirical testing slightly favored the short term view, with those equations being the source of the results we report later.

The value of the PREPAY variable — averaged across all eligible loans in our sample — is shown for the high-coupon 1984 and 1989 books in Exhibit 8. The horizontal line at a value of 1.0 occurs when the market value, net of transactions costs, equals the book value, putting values exceeding one in the money to prepay. The top panel shows that with a decline in the 10-year Treasury rate of 350 basis points from origination in 1984 to 1988, borrowers can realize a gain of over 10% of their loan value by refinancing. As cash flows improved and declined further through 1993, the gain from a refinance grew to approach 20%.

The 1989 book shows a different picture. Even with interest rate declines through the subsequent years, PREPAY does not move decisively higher. This is the result of disincentives from the yield maintenance provisions and other transactions costs, as well as weak gains in property cash flows.

Model Results

These two measures — eligibility and willingness — have been calculated using loan level Freddie Mac multifamily data, grouped by origination year and exposure year. We then estimated a nonlinear, least squares regression to explain prepayments as the product of these measures. A logistic transformation was performed to capture the shape shown in Exhibit 2. The standard goodness of fit measure, R squared, was 0.75.[11]

---

[11] For a full explanation of what was done, see Abraham and Theobald, "A Simple Prepayment Model of Commercial Mortgages."

Exhibit 8: Value of PREPAY Variable
1984 Originations – High Coupon

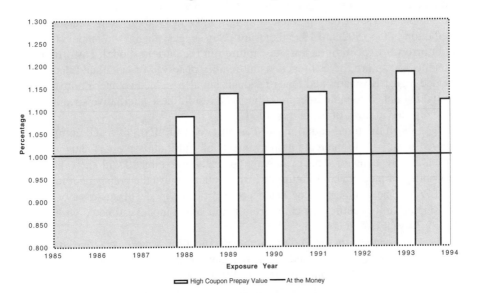

Value of PREPAY Variable
1989 Originations – High Coupon

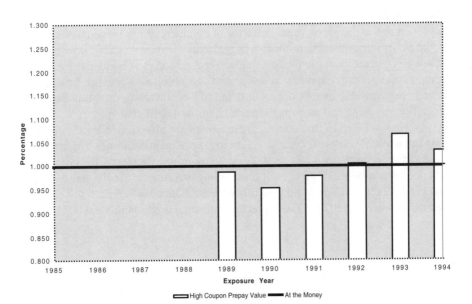

The fitted values for the 1984 and 1989 high-coupon book years are shown in Exhibit 9. Actual prepayments are shown with bars, and fitted values are illustrated with the line. These fits are consistent with those observed for the other book years in our sample data set. Under prediction in the 1989 and 1990 exposure years and over prediction in the 1992 and 1993 exposure years suggest changes in lender standards and borrower expectations not yet captured in the current model. Unfortunately, attempts to capture these impacts using readily observed or calculated data series yielded higher R squares and lower residuals but also yielded counterintuitive coefficients that defied reliable interpretation. As a result, these alternative specifications were rejected in favor of the current model.

With the fitted equation, we can now return to Exhibit 2 and compare the derived sensitivity to interest rate movements of multifamily prepayments with single-family prepayments. This is shown graphically in Exhibit 10 with the value of the probability of prepayment for eligible loans plotted against the prepayment incentive, (PREPAY). The commercial coefficients come from the model discussed above, while the single-family coefficients come from the identical model estimated with single-family 30-year fixed-rate loans.[12]

We can see that the commercial specification is more sensitive to interest rates than the single-family model. The relevant range along the horizontal axis goes from being out of the money by 10% (0.90) to being in the money by up to 30% (1.30). Multifamily goes from being similar to single-family when both are out of the money, to a prepayment rate of nearly 60% versus less than 40% when both are in the money by 30%.

Conclusion

When it comes to the prepayment behavior of commercial mortgage-backed securities, investors currently rely on dealer judgements that CMBSs are "slow prepays" because of contract restrictions. That qualitative assessment is borne out by comparing the cumulative prepayment data reported in Exhibit 1. There are little data or research yet available to support more detailed hypotheses or quantitative assessments. The reasoning and modeling reported here start to fill that void.

We have shown that contract restrictions are effective in limiting prepayments in the early years of a commercial mortgage. Conditional rates can then accelerate sharply when the contract restrictions are removed. However, the eligibility to refinance for a number of loans will remain impaired due to credit quality. Falling interest rates help, but do not remove this problem. Once loans breech the eligibility threshold, however, they have faster prepayments than single-family loans.

---

[12] See Chester Foster and Robert Van Order, "Estimating Prepayments," *Secondary Mortgage Markets*, (Winter 1990/91), pp. 24-26,

Exhibit 9: Incremental Prepayment Rates
High Coupon Originations

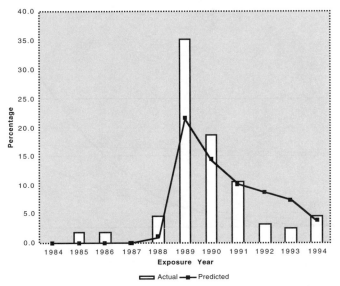

1984   Originations

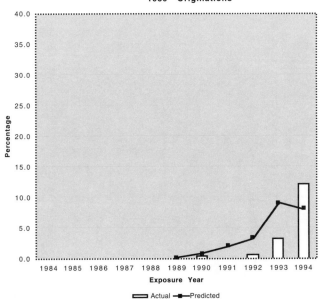

1989   Originations

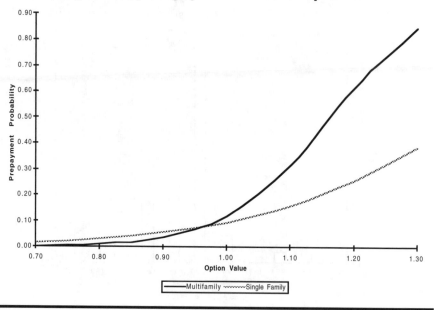

Exhibit 10: Fitted Graph of Multifamily versus Single-family Prepayment Probability Curves

Chapter *4*

The Commercial Mortgage-Backed Securities Market

Alice A. Lustig
Associate
Nomura Securities International, Inc.

INTRODUCTION

Chapter 2 covered the commercial mortgage market. This chapter introduces the market for commercial mortgage-backed securities (CMBS). These securities are receiving greater attention from fixed-income investors as a potential asset class and are being added to portfolios as an alternative to corporate bonds, residential mortgage-backed securities, and other asset-backed securities. This new-found focus is not only because of the need for higher yield, but because many investors believe that this market is relatively cheap and has reached a critical mass which portends greater liquidity. In this chapter we review the growth of this market, types of transactions, and the participants. We also analyze the elements of a CMBS transaction and discuss the performance of the CMBS market to date. Later chapters cover in greater detail the variety of structures and several approaches to valuation.

Evolution of the CMBS Market

CMBS are bonds or other debt instruments that are collateralized by loans secured by commercial real estate. Unlike their residential counterparts, the defining element for commercial mortgages is that the real estate is income producing property which is managed for an economic profit.

Portions of this chapter were taken from David P. Jacob and Kimbell R. Duncan "Commercial Mortgage Backed Securities: An Emerging Market," Nomura Securities International, January 1994.

As of the end of 1992 there were over $1 trillion in commercial mortgages outstanding in the US of which less than 3% had been securitized. In comparison, the residential mortgage market had $3.1 trillion outstanding with approximately $1.5 trillion securitized. As of the end of 1995, 6.5% of the commercial mortgage market was trading in securitized form.

CMBS were slower to develop than residential MBS for a number of reasons. First, commercial mortgage borrowers had traditionally sought financing from banks, thrift institutions, and insurance companies, and the abundance of capital available from these sources in the late 1980s gave them no cause to do otherwise. Second, unlike residential mortgages, commercial mortgages lacked the consistent underwriting standards, agency backing, and uniform loan documentation that would lend themselves easily to securitization. The third reason is that the lack of historical data on loan performance was particularly unpalatable to traditional fixed income investors. While the publicly traded securities market is distinguished by its free flow of information, the commercial real estate market has historically been characterized by its air of secrecy and scant information flow. Even if securities transactions had been attempted, given the excessive leveraging of commercial real estate properties prevalent during this period, they would never have gained acceptable treatment from the rating agencies.

The beginning of the CMBS market, however, was a natural outgrowth of conditions that existed at the end of the 1980s. The easy credit, overleveraging, and the ensuing overbuilding boom of this period were the very factors that set the stage for the introduction of securitization to the commercial real estate market in the early 1990s. The real estate depression had forced the repricing of real estate to reflect fundamentals, and a more conservative approach to leveraging, which were key prerequisites for bringing together the real estate and fixed income markets. By the early 1990s, traditional lenders, such as thrifts, banks and insurance companies, had virtually disappeared from the commercial mortgage market. They had come under regulatory constraints following the real estate market crisis of the late 1980s, which reduced their participation in the primary commercial mortgage market. Even borrowers with strong credit and reasonably leveraged properties had difficulty finding new financing when balloon payments came due. Many had no choice but to seek alternative sources of capital.

A large number of commercial real estate assets and mortgages fell into the hands of the Resolution Trust Company (RTC) and the Federal Deposit Insurance Corporation (FDIC). These agencies were forced to seek alternative and more liquid means to dispose of billions of dollars worth of commercial real estate loans. Securitization aided this process by providing an outlet for real estate investment which offered investors the ability to diversify their exposure, target specific risk/return levels, and enhance their liquidity.

At the same time, the low-yield environment of the early 1990s, and the fall of the junk bond market spurred many investors to seek new higher-yielding, undervalued investment vehicles. CMBS, because of their novelty, feeble information flow, and perceived risk, initially traded at enormous spreads, thereby filling this gap.

Exhibit I: CMBS Issuance

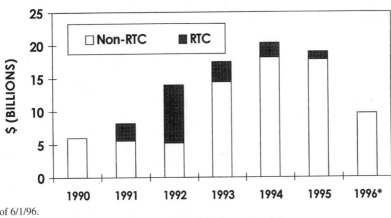

* As of 6/1/96.

Source: Nomura Securities International, Inc.

The growth in the non-agency residential MBS market had in many ways primed the market for CMBS. The development of the market for non-agency MBS and other types of asset backed securities in the mid-to-late 1980s had triggered the creation of new structural and technological advancements, that could be applied to commercial mortgage cash flows as well. More importantly, MBS had created buyers for subordinate tranche securities, which are key pieces of the puzzle in senior-subordinated securities transactions.

CMBS issuance has grown dramatically in recent years. As seen in Exhibit 1, the first major gains in issuance in 1992 were due to RTC transactions. The first RTC multifamily securitization was done in August 1991 (RTC 91-M1) and the first non-multifamily commercial securitization was completed in February 1992 (RTC 92-C1). By July 1993, the RTC had securitized close to $14 billion in performing commercial mortgages. The RTC finished its job and shut its doors at the end of 1995, after securitizing more than $16.89 billion of performing and $977.5 million of non-performing commercial mortgages. This liquidation forced the markets to confront the issues of securitization. The establishment of underwriting standards, rating criteria, valuation techniques, and more standardized securities structures paved the way for further growth in commercial mortgage securitization.

As the RTC issuance wound down, non-RTC issuance replaced it. Non-RTC CMBS issuance can be classified in a number of ways. One is the securitization of seasoned or existing loans versus the securitization of new loans, particularly those designed with securitization in mind. The securitization of existing loan portfolios is somewhat akin to RTC transactions, in that the loans were made at a time when real estate values were elevated, underwriting was based on projections, and information requirements were minimal. The securitization of existing loan portfolios consists of both performing and nonperforming loans. (The characteristics of nonperforming loans and their securitization is somewhat different from that of performing loans and is discussed later.) Insurance companies, and more recently some pension funds, have used securitization as a means of liquefying their portfolios and, as we will discuss later, targeting the risk exposure that best suits their portfolio needs.

Some of the largest deals in the market have been portfolio securitizations. Of the top 10 deals in 1994, two, totaling $2.3 billion, were portfolio deals. The second largest deal of 1995 ($963 million) was Merrill Lynch Mortgage Investors, Inc. 1995-C2, the securitization of a portion of Provident Life Insurance Company's portfolio. The largest CMBS deal to date was SASCO 96-CFL, which was the securitization of the Confederation Life Insurance Company portfolio. The transaction was $1.95 billion, consisting of 564 loans backed by 604 properties. Confederation Life went out of business in 1994 largely due to a decline in the value of its commercial mortgages and equity real estate. About 95% of the loans were originated prior to 1992.

While there have been some very large portfolio securitizations, ultimately this source of securitization will dry up as all those that want to follow this route come to market. The growth area for securitization is coming from newly originated mortgages. In 1995 more than half the CMBS issuance was backed by newly originated loans. New loans arise from old loans that are maturing, loans that traditional lenders do not want to roll over, loans that the borrower wants to refinance, and the financing of real estate acquisitions or the addition of leverage.

Deals backed by newly originated loans can be divided into multi-borrower versus single borrower deals. In the multi-borrower deal category there have been two main types of transactions: small loan deals and MegaDeals^{SM}. The small loan deals consist of loans originated by securities firms directly or through conduit programs. In a conduit program, the securities firm uses partners to originate the loans and then accumulates the loans on its balance sheet until a sufficient size and diversity is aggregated. Conduit issuance has grown dramatically in 1993 and 1994, as shown in Exhibit 2. Recently some securities firms have been forming their own conduit origination programs.

Exhibit 2: Conduit CMBS as a Percentage of New Issuance: 1992 - Q1 1996

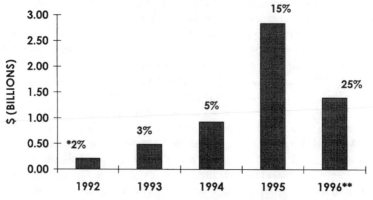

*percentage of total CMBS issuance ** 1st quarter 1996
Source: Nomura Securities International, Inc.

Exhibit 3: CMBS Deals by Property Type — Mixed Format Dominates

Property Type Distribution: 1993 (First Three Quarters)

Property Type	Percent
Mixed	38
Multifamily	25
Retail	18
Seniors Housing	2
Industrial	1
Mobile	4
Office	4
Agency Multifamily (FNMA, FHLMC)	3
Hotel	5

Property Type Distribution: 1995 (First Three Quarters)

Property Type	Percent
Mixed	61
Multifamily	8
Retail	17
Foreign Mixed	4
Office	1
Agency Multifamily (FNMA, FHLMC)	8
Hotel	1

Source: Nomura Securities International, Inc.

The MegaDeal^{SM}, which was created by Nomura Securities, is a deal consisting of 8 to 10 large, low loan-to-value loans, originated directly by the securities firm for securitization. As of the first quarter of 1996, five MegaDeals^{SM}, totaling $3.4 billion, have been brought to market.

While the majority of deals done today are multi-borrower, there are still a few that are single borrower; some are backed by REIT portfolios and some are just smaller sized deals. This format is becoming less common.

Also becoming less common today are deals backed by a single property type. With the exception of multifamily deals, the majority of multi-borrower deals have a variety of property types in the deal, as shown in Exhibit 3.

COMPONENTS OF A CMBS TRANSACTION

To securitize a mortgage or portfolio of mortgages, first a bankruptcy-remote issuing vehicle is usually established. The mortgages are assigned to this entity, most commonly a *special purpose entity* (SPE), whose sole activity is owning and managing the pledged collateral. This is to ensure that, come what may, the mortgaged property is pledged to the trust until the principal amount is repaid in full. No prior liens may be imposed, nor may the properties be accessed by any other creditors of the borrower should the borrower go into bankruptcy. In order to qualify as an SPE, an issuer would have to meet specific criteria including:

- It must not engage in any other activity other than owning and managing the pledged collateral;
- It should be restricted from incurring additional debt (except under special circumstances);
- It should be restricted from engaging in a merger, consolidation, or asset transfer with another entity (except under special circumstances); and
- It should have at least one independent director.

A servicer and a trustee are then appointed, although in some cases, one entity may carry out both these roles. The servicer's responsibility is to oversee the collection of principal and interest from the borrower. This may be an easy task, as in the case of a transaction backed by a single performing mortgage, or it may be far more involved if, for instance, the deal is backed by a pool of hundreds of non- or sub-performing mortgages acquired from the RTC. In the latter case, the servicer may be called upon to advance delinquent cash flows, restructure loan terms, or to liquidate those assets that are in default. In such cases, an issuer may choose to employ a "special servicer" — one with considerable experience with the specific property type — to oversee the servicing function. These two roles, that of the "master" servicer, and the "special" servicer may be carried out by the same entity, or by two separate entities. Choosing a servicer that has the appropriate experience and capabilities is critical to the transaction. It is often the case, too, that the servicer of a transaction also purchases the junior-most tranche of that transaction. This is considered a plus from a credit standpoint, and may influence more favorable treatment from the rating agencies. The rationale is that if the servicer is in the first-loss position, it will have greater incentive to better manage the portfolio (i.e. work out delinquent loans, liquidate REO at favorable rates, etc.).

The servicer forwards its collections, plus any necessary advances (minus a servicing fee, which averages about 6 to 9 basis points) to the trustee. The trustee holds the mortgage loan documents in trust for the benefit of the security holders, is responsible for periodic reporting to security holders, and plays the central role in the distribution of funds throughout the transaction. In the event that a servicer fails to make a required advance, the trustee is usually required to do so. The trustee must also oversee and allocate cash from any reserve funds, which are included in some transactions. The trustee, or its designated paying agent, makes payments from the distribution account to security holders according to the payment rules of the structure. In the event that title to a mortgaged property is acquired through foreclosure, the deed is issued to the trustee on behalf of the security holders, and the trustee manages the sale of the property. Exhibit 4 illustrates the interaction of these entities within a CMBS transaction.

CREDIT ENHANCEMENT

The primary credit risk of a commercial mortgage-backed security derives from the underlying loans. Several forms of credit enhancement have been used to improve the quality of the bonds that are issued. The forms of credit enhancement that have been used in the securitization of commercial mortgages are subordination, overcollateralization, reserve funds, corporate guarantees, letters of credit, cross-collateralization, and cross-defaulting.

Subordination

Subordination is the process of disproportionately allocating credit risk amongst two or more classes of securities backed by the same collateral. In its simplest form, the *senior/subordinated structure* (*A/B structure*), two classes of securities are collateralized by a pool of mortgages with the junior, or B, class providing credit enhancement for the other. The subordinated class is in the *first loss position* — it is required to absorb 100% of losses experienced on the collateral until cumulative losses reduce the balance of the subordinated class to zero. The greater the size of the subordinated class, the greater the credit enhancement. A typical requirement for this structure is that all principal be used to pay the most senior class first (sequential structure). This is particularly the case in the event of recoveries that result from foreclosures. This provides additional protection to the senior class.

Exhibit 4: CMBS Transaction Structure

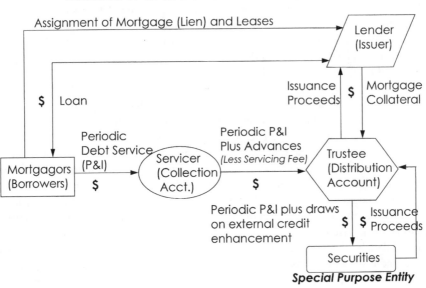

Exhibit 5: Collateral and Credit Tranching
CMBS Spreads/DSCR/LTV

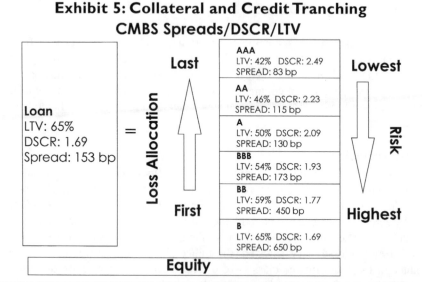

Utilizing subordination, it is possible to create highly rated securities from collateral of lower quality. As shown in Exhibit 5, it is possible to transfer credit losses disproportionately amongst several classes of securities. This is called *credit tranching* and is analogous to the tranching or reallocation of prepayment risk in CMOs and REMICs backed by residential mortgages. Classes are tranched sequentially with respect to loss position — a class does not experience any losses until the balances of the more junior classes are reduced to zero. What the senior subordination effectively does is lower the loan-to-value (LTV) ratio, and increase the effective coverage to the most senior classes. There can be any number of credit tranches. In this example the underlying loan is $65 million and has a 65% LTV (so that the property is assumed to be worth $100 million).

Six classes of bonds are created, with their respective sizes shown in Exhibit 5. As a result of the subordination the most senior class has an effective LTV of 42%. What this means is that this bond class will not suffer credit losses unless the value of the property declines by 58%. The goal of the credit support from the issuer's perspective is to maximize the proceeds from the bond classes. This is accomplished by maximizing the size and duration of the most senior classes and minimizing the size and duration of the most junior classes. However, as discussed later when we cover the rating process, the sizes of each of the classes is dictated by the rating agencies.

From the investor's point of view, credit tranching provides an opportunity to optimize the risk/return profile. Losses are realized first by the equity in the transaction and then by the most junior class of bonds. In this way the junior class is really in the second loss position. As discussed in Chapter 16 these securities are often viewed as alternatives to equity real estate. Today, subordination is by far the most prevalent form of credit enhancement.

Over Collateralization

Another way to improve the credit quality of a CMBS transaction is by issuing fewer bonds or equivalently posting additional collateral. This is analogous to the issuer buying back the subordinated class. Only borrowers that do not need to maximize leverage will elect this form of credit enhancement.

Reserve Funds

Some issuers of less-than-perfect collateral, such as the RTC, have made use of reserve funds either exclusively, but more usually in combination with subordination. Reserve funds are usually established with an initial cash deposit by the issuer and may be required to grow over time to some required level. Reserve funds are the most liquid form of credit enhancement, but are expensive and inefficient. The reserve funds are usually invested in highly liquid short-term government securities.

Corporate Guarantees and Letters of Credit

Guarantees may be provided by the issuer or a third party in an amount equal to the required level of credit enhancement. The guarantor is obligated to cover losses due to delinquencies and foreclosures up to the amount of the guarantee. Similarly, a letter of credit (LOC) obligates the provider to cover losses. Usually commercial mortgages are non-recourse loans, that is, they are secured only by the properties and their cash flows. In the case of guaranteed transactions, limited recourse is extended to the guarantor, who may be affiliated with the borrower.

Both corporate guarantees and LOCs are external sources of credit support, whereas subordination and reserve funds are set up within the structure and rely solely on the credit quality of the collateral. Third-party credit enhancement introduces credit risk not related to the collateral.

Cross-Collateralization

For single-issuer, multiple-loan transactions, cross-collateralization and cross defaulting may be used to further enhance the credit quality of the collateral. *Cross-collateralization* is a mechanism whereby the properties that collateralize the individual loans are pledged against every loan. In a situation where the cash flow from a particular property is not sufficient to meet the debt service on its loan, cash flow in excess of debt service from the other properties is used to pay the debt service on the income deficient property. In this way, the NOI of the pool of properties is available to meet the collective debt service on all of the loans. Consequently, an individual loan cannot become delinquent as long as there is sufficient cash flow from all of the properties to cover its shortfall.

Cross-defaulting is an extension of cross-collateralization. It allows all loans to be put into default and therefore allows for foreclosure of the properties, if any one of the loans is in default. In this way, an investor will not suffer a loss of principal as long as the net proceeds from all of the properties exceeds the principal balance of the loans. *Cross-collateralization and cross defaulting are powerful credit enhancement mechanisms which greatly reduce the risk of a CMBS transaction.*

THE ROLE OF THE RATING AGENCY

In this section we review the rating process and the role played by the rating agencies. Of the four rating agencies some play a more involved role in the CMBS market than others. On the whole, each agency differs in their rating process with a few similarities. After performing qualitative, quantitative, and structural analysis of a transaction, the rating agencies will assign ratings to the bond classes in a CMBS transaction, and establish criteria necessary for a class to achieve a particular rating.

Rating agencies assign ratings on debt and other securitized transactions based on the likelihood of timely payment of interest and principal. In the view of the rating agencies, a triple-A rating for a class of CMBS is equivalent to a triple-A rating for a corporate issue with regard to credit risk to the investor.[1] Because of the real estate crisis of the early 1990s and the lack of a comprehensive set of data, the agencies have been careful to establish very conservative criteria for rating CMBS. We recognize that each agency has its own approach, nonetheless, we try to capture the essence of the process overall.

As mentioned earlier, one of the barriers to the development of the CMBS market has been the lack of loan performance data. While there are limited sources of commercial loan performance data, a common source used by the rating agencies (notably S&P and Fitch) is the American Council of Life Insurance (ACLI). The ACLI collects data from member life insurance companies and reports delinquency and foreclosure results quarterly. Reporting companies hold about 85% of the total commercial mortgages held by U.S. life insurers. This universe of loans currently represents approximately 18% of the commercial mortgage market in terms of principal outstanding.

The ACLI has collected data on an aggregate basis going back to 1965 and by property type since 1988. Since 1965, delinquencies have ranged from about 0.5% in the late 1960s to a high of 7.53% in the middle of 1992. Cyclical peaks occurred in 1976 and 1992 and cyclical troughs occurred in 1969 and 1981.

The usefulness of this data by itself is limited since it does not provide information regarding either cumulative defaults or losses resulting from foreclosures on a static universe of loans which are necessary to develop expectations regarding potential losses on commercial mortgages.

The rating agencies and others have analyzed portfolios of loans to estimate actual cumulative default and loss severity experience. For example, Mark Snyderman found in a study of a universe of 7,205 loans originated by life insur-

---

[1] It is important to note that the rating agencies evaluate credit risk not prepayment risk.

ance companies between 1972 and 1984 that the average cumulative default rate was 12.1% through 1989.[2] Fitch Investors Service analyzed a static universe of 1,524 loans ($15.3 billion) originated by major life insurance companies from 1984 to 1987.[3] Through year-end 1991, the average cumulative default rate was 14%. Furthermore, Fitch estimated that, since many loans were restructured rather than foreclosed, the true cumulative default rate was probably closer to 20%. Fitch also estimated that for the remaining life of the loans an additional 10% would default. Thus, they projected total lifetime defaults to be about 30% (conservatively). As a comparison, cumulative default rates for corporate securities rated single-B have been in the range of 30% to 40%.

The Fitch study was performed on a universe of loans that was originated over a very narrow time span. In contrast, the Snyderman study highlights the importance of the market environment in which loans are originated (see Exhibit 12 in Chapter 2). For example, loans originated in 1976 and 1977 following a real estate recession during 1974-1975 experienced much lower default rates than loans originated during periods of growth. Fitch hypothesizes that default rates vary according to when loans are originated since underwriting standards change during the course of a real estate cycle. Therefore, the current environment of tightening underwriting standards and lower-leveraged financing should result in the superior future performance of loans originated in recent years; these changes should encourage investors to discount past performance data when projecting future performance.

The Snyderman study also analyzes losses on asset sales resulting from foreclosure. It estimates a loss rate of 32% for those loans originated from 1972 to 1984. Fitch cites loss severity results from several other studies which give varying pictures of loss experience. For example, from a study of mid-west life insurance companies' portfolios, an average loss severity of 21% on foreclosed properties is reported. Fitch qualifies those results by noting that life insurance companies often keep the worst quality properties on their books rather than trying to sell them. Thus, loss severity results based on this universe tend to be underestimated. At the other extreme, Fitch quotes a Freddie Mac report that maintains that, when the costs of foreclosure are taken into account, losses averaged 60% on foreclosed multifamily loans. Other data cited showed losses from 25% to 57.5%.

When rating specific transactions, the rating agencies adjust their expectations of defaults and loss severity to reflect the differences between the collateral of the transaction being rated and the universe of loans upon which their studies were performed. For example, S&P utilizes a default model that incorporates loan characteristics such as interest rate, term, and property type which are then used to determine conditional probabilities of default. Incorporating these expectations, they then require sufficient credit enhancement such that the securities experience

---

[2] Mark P. Snyderman, "Commercial Mortgages: Default Occurrence and Estimated Yield Impact," *Journal of Portfolio Management* (Fall 1991), pp. 82-87.
[3] Ron J. Wechsler, Janet P. Forst, Harvey M. Lederman, "Commercial Mortgage Stress Test," Fitch Investors Service, June 8, 1992.

zero losses in scenarios which are defined by some assumed probabilities of default and loss severity on the collateral.

For example, Fitch defines an "A" -level recession scenario as one in which a benchmark universe of loans experiences 30% cumulative defaults. Applying a loss severity of 45%, they expect losses of 13.5% over the life of the loans in such a scenario. Consequently, an "A"-rated security backed by this benchmark universe of loans would require sufficient credit enhancement such that it experiences no losses in the event that the collateral experiences losses of up to 13.5%.

Studies of historical loan performance data provide the foundation for the rating process. Such studies are instrumental in helping the rating agencies form expectations regarding potential defaults and losses on commercial mortgages. However, as noted above, they adjust their expectations according to the unique characteristics of each transaction. It is the review of these characteristics and the conclusions drawn regarding the impact such characteristics have on expected losses (and, hence, credit enhancement levels) about which investors and issuers alike are most concerned. Although the rating agencies differ to some degree in their methodologies, generally each reviews the qualitative and quantitative characteristics of the collateral, the security structure and legal considerations.

Qualitative Review

Unlike residential mortgages or many asset-backed securities, where default behavior can be reasonably modeled to reflect consumer behavior, commercial mortgages are debt instruments that finance businesses. Hence, in their qualitative reviews, the rating agencies concentrate on the characteristics that most influence real estate performance: property type, location, borrower quality, tenant quality, lease terms, property management, property seasoning, construction quality, insurance coverage and environmental liability.

Property Type The risks associated with each property type are obviously very different. Hotels, nursing homes, shopping centers, apartment buildings, office properties, warehouses, etc. are all diverse businesses with different operating margins, cost structures, regulatory constraints, and so on. The fact that these businesses perform differently is borne out by the ACLI loan performance data we have already discussed and the Russell-NCREIF property performance indices. Since the timely payment of principal and interest on the debt is dependent upon the availability of sufficient income being generated from underlying properties, the rating agencies review the economics for the property types which collateralize the loans in the same way that they consider the economics of the industry in which a borrowing company belongs when rating a corporate debt transaction.

Multifamily properties, for example, derive most of their income from tenant rents. Since expenses are largely unrelated to levels of occupancy, property managers try to maximize occupancy. Leases usually have terms of one year or less so that projections of revenue are based upon some assumed rate of vacancy in the future. As expected, borrowers and underwriters tend to be more optimistic in their assumptions, whereas the rating agencies look to the demographics and economic prospects of the region in which the property is located when analyzing occupancy assumptions. Expenses consist of management fees, real estate taxes, insurance premiums, repair and maintenance costs, and other miscellaneous costs (e.g. security, landscaping, etc.). Multifamily properties benefit from tenant diversity which protects against economic downturns. Also, apartment tenants are less inclined to demand the latest technological improvements which might be critical in the office or industrial market. In general, multifamily properties are considered to be less risky than most other types.

When evaluating securities backed by loans on retail properties, the rating agencies are most concerned with the mix of tenants, the quality of the location, and the economic viability of the tenants' business. Unlike apartments where there are many tenants, shopping centers will usually have an anchor tenant who serves as the primary draw to the property and then 10 to 20 specialty stores which serve to diversify the lines of business supporting the property. Income is derived from leases which are usually 3 to 5 years in term. While appearance is very important to shopping center properties, technological obsolescence is not usually a big risk factor. Successful properties generally dominate their local regions, have diverse mixes of tenants, and have good management teams which focus on cost containment and customer services. When analyzing tenant leases on retail properties, care should be given to tenant improvements, leasing commissions, and above average rents.

Office properties present a different set of operational parameters. Their leases tend to be very long relative to other property types — extending as long as 20 years. Consequently, it is important that tenants be contractually responsible for operating expenses (including capital expenses). Also, because of the length of the leases, the credit quality of the tenants becomes a much more important factor in the debt analysis. In many cases, the rating of securities backed by loans on office properties may be tied to the credit rating of the dominant tenant. Although leases will generally extend beyond the maturity of the loans, the rating agencies consider the risk of re-tenanting in the case of tenant default. Office properties need their infrastructures to be kept technologically updated in order to remain competitive and, as a result, the rating agencies may require reserves for future enhancements. Superior office properties are those with quality tenants, state-of-the-art infrastructures, and strong management teams.

Hotels are generally considered to be the most risky type of property. They are clearly different — providing services to short-term guests is a large part of their business operations. Revenues come largely from room rents, although meeting rooms, restaurants, and other "extras" contribute significantly to revenues, particularly at luxury hotels. Small increases in occupancy rates or room prices go a long way to improving profitability due to considerable fixed costs. However, unlike apartments, offices or shopping centers, expenses do increase as occupancy increases; as a result, maximizing occupancy does not always correspond to maximizing long-term profits. Because the performance of hotels depends largely upon the active management of operations, the rating agencies place particular emphasis on the quality of the property management teams. In fact, many pooling and servicing agreements contain provisions that in the case of poor performance, the management may be replaced at the discretion of the bondholders. Well-managed properties with competitive positions in their regions present attractive collateral for commercial mortgages.

Location The local economics in which properties operate can have considerable influence on their performance. The rating agencies study demographic data including population and household formation trends, the dominant types of industry in an area, and even climate to estimate future demand for a particular property type within a local economy. They analyze the impact of infrastructures such as educational facilities, health care facilities, recreational attractions, and transportation links. The local political climate is reviewed with emphasis on tax laws, zoning restrictions, and laws governing landlord/tenant rights.

The value of geographic diversity is demonstrated by the ACLI loan performance data (see Exhibit 6) which exhibit very different results across regional economies for loans backed by similar property types. Transactions with properties distributed among many regional economies are rewarded since this diversity helps insulate the performance of the collateral from a downturn in a particular region. (However, large investors may be able to take advantage of higher yields offered by single property transactions and manage their risk through portfolio diversification.)

Borrower Quality Bad character is virtually insurmountable. In transactions with a small number of borrowers, a review of the borrowers' credit histories is performed to determine creditworthiness. While CMBS structures are designed to minimize the impact borrowers have on the credit quality of the securities, borrower quality is still an important consideration when projecting future loan performance. Oftentimes CMBS deals backed by REIT properties are favored just for this reason. Investors feel more secure with the public company as a borrower.

Tenant Quality Since property income is derived from rents, the ability of tenants to meet their obligations according to their leases is an important consideration in determining the value of most property types. Although "tenant quality" is less applicable to hotels and multifamily properties, the number of rooms/apartments, occupancy rates, and average incomes of the "tenants" are important in determining the quality of these properties. On the other hand, the rating agencies review more closely the tenant profiles of retail and office properties since the numbers of tenants are usually much smaller and the lengths of leases much longer. Tenant review focuses on (1) the number of tenants, (2) the space occupied by each tenant. and (3) the credit quality of the dominant tenants.

In some cases, the rating of CMBS backed by loans on properties with one tenant or a dominant tenant may be tied to the rating of that tenant (particularly in cases when the lease payments of the dominant tenant fully cover the debt service on the loans).

Exhibit 6: ACLI Delinquency Data by Region and Property Type

	Retail (%)	Apartment (%)	Office (%)	Hotel (%)	All (%)
New England	0.62	1.02	4.49		1.25
Mid-Atlantic	2.95	0.53	4.21	19.33	2.47
South-Atlantic	1.28	1.48	2.06	0.73	0.90
North Central	0.86	1.42	2.77	4.13	0.92
South Central	0.85	0.99	2.39	0.55	0.63
Mountain	2.54	0.05	1.32	1.08	0.90
Pacific	3.96	0.57	4.48	6.46	1.58

Source: American Council of Life Insurance

Lease Terms Cash flow is derived from leases and property value is derived from cash flow. Hence, the rating agencies review tenant leases to determine the sustainability of cash flows. Important lease terms are:

• Rental rates
• Expiration schedules
• Rent escalation provisions
• Percentage agreements
• Expense payment provisions
• Renewal and cancellation options
• Tenant improvement rent provisions

For properties that have small numbers of tenants, particularly retail and office properties, the lease expiration schedules are scrutinized by the rating agencies to determine their impact on cash flows. In addition, the rating agencies will "mark-to-mark" lease terms such that projected cash flows reflect current market rents. As an example, consider the following lease expiration schedule where GLA is the gross leasable area for the property and rents are expressed in units of dollars per square foot per year.

Expire Year	Number of Leases	Percent GLA	Cumulative Percent GLA	Annual Rent	Market Rent
1996	4	16.73	16.73	$14	$10
1997	7	50.74	67.47	$15	$9
1998	0	0	67.47	N/A	N/A
1999	3	18.14	85.61	$6	$10
Vacant		14.39	100.0	N/A	$10

In this example, a significant percentage of leases whose rents are currently above market expire in the first two years. In particular, leases on nearly 51% of the gross leasable area expire in 1997 and the rents on these leases will decline by 40% when renegotiated. In addition, leases whose rents are currently at a discount to market rents will not roll over until 1999. In situations like this, the rating agencies would adjust their income projections to reflect the negative impact of the lease expiration schedule.

The rating agencies and lenders prefer leases that extend beyond the maturity of the loans; borrowers/owners prefer shorter expiration schedules in the anticipation of increasing rents.

When evaluating retail properties, emphasis is placed on the mix of tenants and the economic viability of their businesses. Leases are usually 3 to 5 years in duration and may contain percent agreements whereby a portion of rent may be tied to sales thus making the cash flows on the properties more sensitive to economic conditions. Shopping centers usually have an anchor tenant who serves as the draw to the property. The rating agencies pay particular attention to the credit quality of the anchor and the terms of its lease. Renewal options at fixed rent levels are frequently written into leases and are extended at a cost to the landlord. Hence, leases containing such provisions usually carry higher rental rates.

Tenant quality is most important for office properties since these leases tend to be much longer than those of other property types. It is also important that tenants be contractually responsible for operating expenses.

Environmental Liability The rating agencies require environmental reports to be performed on each property. Of particular concern are properties that are, or have been, the site of manufacturing, industrial, or disposal activities. Environmental damage may cause a loss in value and potentially result in substantial clean-up costs. Also, under the laws of certain states, failure to remedy an environmental violation which poses an imminent or substantial endangerment of public health may give rise to a lien on the property which is senior to the lien of an existing mortgage. This would obviously affect the value of securities backed by such mortgaged properties.

In addition, it is unclear whether bondholders could potentially be liable for costs related to the clean-up of environmental problems on underlying properties according to current U.S. law. Under the Comprehensive Environmental Response, Compensation and Liability Act of 1980 (CERCLA), a secured lender could be liable as current owner for the cost of environmental clean-up if it had participated in the management of operations. Hence, it is possible that, if a lender were to take title to a contaminated property, it could incur liability. In certain circumstances, lenders may choose not to foreclose on contaminated properties to avoid incurring liability for remedial actions.

However, although the risks appear daunting, the rating agencies require thorough environmental reviews to be performed on each property and take the risk of future liability into account when assigning a rating. In fact, if a property is not free of environmental problems, it is not eligible as collateral for a rated transaction unless reserves have been established within the security structure to cover the costs of clean-up.

Quantitative Review

Whereas qualitative reviews focus on the characteristics of the underlying properties and their impact on property value, quantitative reviews are concerned with the income being generated by the properties. More specifically, the rating agencies review the debt service coverage and loan-to-value ratios on each of the loans.

Debt Service Debt investors are most concerned about the timely payment of principal and interest on their securities. The ultimate source of these cash flows is the net operating income (NOI) of the properties collateralizing the loans. NOI is defined as gross annual revenues less operating expenses before federal income taxes and excluding depreciation. NOI is what is available to meet debt obligations. Properties that cannot generate sufficient cash flow to cover debt payments will default. The rating agencies review the calculation of NOI and test the revenue and expense components for reasonableness. Prior year financial statements are used but the rating agencies determine whether the past performance is useful in projecting future potential. They may adjust projected NOI for special events such that it represents income from stabilized operations. For example, they "mark to market" rents on all leases in projecting income. The rating agencies often make adjustments to the NOI such that it differs from the underwriter's NOI.

An important measure of the credit worthiness of commercial mortgages is the debt service coverage ratio (DSCR). The DSCR is equal to the NOI from the underlying properties divided by the annual cost of debt service (both principal and interest payments) on the loans. As such, the DSCR measures a borrower's ability to meet periodic debt payments. Therefore, the higher the DSCR, the more creditworthy a loan.

After making adjustments to NOI, the rating agencies require certain minimum DSCRs for various property types in order to achieve specific ratings on securities. Exhibit 7 contains indicative minimum DSCRs required for various rating classes on 20-year fixed-rate amortizing securities collateralized by loans on "good" quality properties. The required DSCRs for various property types differ reflecting the relative risk of the underlying businesses.

Minimum required DSCRs are adjusted upwards to reflect the results of the rating agencies' reviews of the qualitative characteristics of the collateral, the security structure and the legal documentation. It is therefore possible that two structures backed by the same property type, for example, have different required DSCRs due to one structure introducing more risk than the other.

Loan-to-Value Another measure frequently used to indicate the relative safety of collateralized debt is the loan-to-value (LTV) ratio. The LTV is equal to the loan amount divided by the appraised value of the properties. This is an important measure of the leverage within a transaction and the degree of protection in the event of foreclosure and liquidation. Similar to residential transactions, it quantifies the amount of equity "buffer" in the transaction. Relative to residential mortgages, however, commercial mortgages today tend to be much less leveraged — LTVs below 50% are common.

The poor performance of Freddie Mac's multifamily loan portfolio, as highlighted by the Fitch analysis of loss severity, illustrates the leverage/loss-severity relationship. The lower the LTV, the more creditworthy a loan.

The rating agencies set maximum LTVs for each property type in order to award various ratings. These different LTV levels are meant to correspond to the default rates and the loss severity that the security is designed to withstand (which vary by rating class) since the rate of loss that can be realized on the sale of properties before bondholders experience loss of principal is approximately equal to 1 minus the LTV.

Several points should be noted regarding LTV. First, while the loan amount is known with certainty, estimating the market value of the underlying property is largely subjective. Original cost is obviously not useful. Replacement cost is not used because many properties are valued well below replacement cost in today's market. Recent sale prices of similar properties and actual appraisals are typically used.

The rating agencies determine property values by capitalizing the adjusted net operating income by an assumed market rate of return — called the *capitalization rate*, or just the "cap rate." (Herein lies the link between DSCR and LTV. NOI produces debt service coverage and NOI determines value.) The cap rate is analogous to the yield of a property and is higher for property types that exhibit greater uncertainty of business operations. Capitalization rates nationally are currently between 8% and 12% for most property types (Exhibit 8).

Exhibit 7: Indicative Minimum DSCRs

Multifamily

	AAA	AA	A	BBB	BB	B
LTV	45%	50%	55%	60%	70%	75%
DSCR	2.00	1.80	1.60	1.50	1.30	1.20

Retail

	AAA	AA	A	BBB	BB	B
LTV	40%	45%	50%	55%	65%	75%
DSCR	2.25	2.00	1.80	1.60	1.40	1.30

Office

	AAA	AA	A	BBB	BB	B
LTV	35%	40%	45%	50%	60%	70%
DSCR	2.40	2.10	1.90	1.70	1.60	1.50

Hotel

	AAA	AA	A	BBB	BB	B
LTV	30%	40%	50%	60%	65%	70%
DSCR	2.85	2.60	2.20	1.90	1.75	1.40

Nursing

	AAA	AA	A	BBB	BB	B
LTV	35%	45%	55%	60%	65%	70%
DSCR	2.15	2.00	1.90	1.80	1.65	1.50

Source: Nomura Securities International, Inc.

Exhibit 8: Capitalization Rates by Property Type

| | Industrial | | Retail | | | Office | | | |
	Warehouse	R&D	Regional	Power	Community	CBD	Suburban	Apart.	Hotels
Q1/92									
Q2/92	9.5		7.5	10.0	8.6	8.8	9.9	8.7	12.0
Q3/92	9.5	10.3	7.7	9.5	9.5	9.6	10.2	8.9	12.1
Q4/92	9.4	10.0	7.6	9.5	9.5	9.6	10.3	9.1	11.4
Q1/93	9.7	10.5	7.9	9.6	10.0	9.7	10.3	9.1	11.7
Q2/93	9.5	10.1	7.7	9.4	9.8	10.3	10.5	8.9	11.6
Q3/93	9.4	10.4	7.9	9.3	9.6	10.4	10.6	8.9	11.6
Q4/93	9.5	9.9	7.7	9.6	9.7	9.9	10.2	8.8	11.1
Q1/94	9.6	10.3	7.9	9.7	9.8	10.2	10.0	8.8	11.4
Q2/94	9.3	10.4	7.7	9.1	9.8	9.7	9.9	8.8	11.1
Q3/94	9.4	10.4	7.7	9.3	9.8	9.8	9.9	8.8	10.8
Q4/94	9.2	10.2	8.0	9.2	9.6	9.8	9.5	8.7	11.5
Q1/95	9.4	10.1	8.2	9.4	9.7	9.7	9.8	9.0	11.2
Q2/95	9.2	9.6	7.9	9.4	9.5	9.2	9.2	8.9	10.9
Q3/95	8.9	9.9	8.0	9.3	9.4	9.4	9.2	8.8	10.6
Q4/95	9.0	9.6	8.2	9.3	9.2	9.6	9.2	8.8	10.4
Q1/96	9.0	9.7	8.5	9.4	9.4	9.5	9.3	8.8	10.4

Source: Real Estate Research Corp.

As the capital markets become a primary source of financing, it is anticipated that capitalization rates will become more volatile as they track returns available on financial assets. This will result in greater volatility in property values.

It is important to note that, in the past, appraisals performed by commercial lenders were the result of applying cap rates to NOI projections that incorporated optimistic assumptions regarding future occupancy rates and rent levels. In contrast, the rating agencies determine property values by applying cap rates to adjusted NOI projections, assuming current occupancy rates and market rent levels.

If there is a large number of properties, the rating agencies may rely on appraisals performed by one or more independent, accredited Members of the Appraisal Institute (M.A.I.). Such appraisals are usually the result of three approaches to valuation: cost of replacement, recent sales of similar properties, and income valuation. In the event that they rely on third party appraisals, rating agencies review the methods employed by the appraisers to test for reasonableness and consistency with their own underwriting procedures. In general, however, the rating agencies prefer not to rely on third party appraisals.

Security Structure Review

Not all risks associated with commercial mortgages are related to the performance of the underlying properties. The structures of the loans and their interaction with the structure of the securities can introduce the risk that timely payments are not made to investors. The rating agencies review the payment structures of the loans and the securities, the form of credit enhancement being used, the servicer of the loans and the trustee for possible introductions of risk.

Payment Structures

Loans on commercial real estate can vary widely with respect to the method of principal repayment and the way in which interest rates are determined. The rating agencies view the risk of various repayment methods differently. Also, they treat floating-rate loans more conservatively than loans carrying fixed rates. They require that the security structure addresses the risks associated with various loan structures.

There are two main repayment mechanisms employed in the commercial mortgage market. Loans can either be amortizing, paying principal and interest each period, or they can pay only interest each period with principal being repaid in one lump sum (balloon) at maturity. Borrowers prefer longer maturity loans with balloon payments and lenders/investors prefer shorter, amortizing loans. When the collateral underlying the securities are balloon loans, the risk to the investor is greater than when the collateral consists of amortizing loans. This is because there is a risk that the borrower may not be able to refinance its debt in a timely manner at maturity. Hence, with balloon mortgages, the rating agencies are concerned with "extension risk" or the possibility that the borrower does not make the balloon payment on the due date.[4]

Fitch Investor Services has described several approaches that could be used to provide investors with considerable comfort that refinancing will take place before the maturity of securities backed by balloon mortgages. For a single tranche security structure, where the security and the loans mature at the same time, Fitch suggests that the borrowers should be required to prepare items that lenders require (such as new appraisals, engineering reports, and environmental studies) nine months prior to maturity. Moreover, six months prior to maturity, borrowers should be required to have arranged alternative financing or to have obtained signed sales contracts for the underlying properties. Fitch suggests that, if either requirement is not met, all cash flows, net of scheduled debt service, be used to amortize the debt and, in addition, mortgage rates be increased. These features are called "demand notes" and "rate step-ups," respectively. In combination, these requirements provide strong incentive for borrowers to make scheduled balloon payments.

An alternative is to structure the securities so that the final maturity of the securities is beyond the maturity of the loans. In this structure, the targeted maturity of the securities is set prior to the final maturity and corresponding to the maturity of the loans. In the event that the borrower does not make the balloon payment on time, the servicer would be required to make advances to the security holders during this tail period in which foreclosure and liquidation takes place.

Also, with balloon mortgages, the expiration schedule of leases has added importance. If a high percentage of leases expires near the maturity of the loan, the

---

[4] For more information on the different types of balloon risk, see Chapter 6.

refinancing risk of the loan is greater. Hence the rating agencies prefer to see leases which expire well beyond the maturity of the loans.

Loans which carry floating or adjustable interest rates are more risky since, as interest rates increase, the cost of debt service increases and, therefore, the DSCR drops. In order to achieve high credit ratings on securities backed by these loans, the rating agencies require that the loans have caps or that issuers purchase interest rate caps from an external counterpart with a credit rating no less than one rating class below the rating on the highest rated security in a transaction. The rating agencies require that minimum DSCR levels are achieved when the interest rates reach their maximum implied by the caps. In cases where the underlying loans have caps, the securities must have corresponding caps. If the underlying loans are uncapped and an issuer has purchased caps, the securities may or may not be capped.

The rating agencies further determine if there is risk introduced by the interaction of the loan structures with the security structures. For example, the rating agencies penalize transactions where interest rates on the collateral are tied to a different index than that which is used to determine the interest rates carried by the securities (known as basis risk).[5]

Servicers

By assuring timely payment of principal and interest through foreclosure and liquidation and by scrutinizing the borrowers' performances of their obligations, servicers provide a very important level of protection to investors. Therefore, the rating agencies require that an experienced, well-capitalized servicer is in place. In many cases, a back-up servicer is also required to be appointed from the beginning to ensure that a smooth transition can be made if the primary servicer is unable to perform its duties.

Because of the importance of the servicer, the rating agencies conduct a thorough review of both the primary and back-up servicers. They look to see that the historical experience, operations, recovery rates, and financial conditions are of the highest quality. If the servicers are not of the highest quality, the rating agencies may require the issuer to hire a master servicer to perform such duties.[6]

Trustee

The trustee holds the mortgage loan documents in trust for the benefit of the security holders. In the event that a servicer fails to make a required advance, the trustee is usually required to do so. On each distribution date, the trustee sends to each investor a statement describing the distribution and the status of the collateral. The trustee or designated paying agent makes payments from the distribution account to security holders according to the payment rules of the structure. In the event that title to a mortgaged property is acquired through foreclosure, the deed is issued to the trustee on behalf of the security investors and the trustee manages the sale of the properties. The rating agencies review the experience and financial condition of the trustee in the same way they review the servicers.

---

[5] For more information on basis risk, see Chapter 13.
[6] For more information on the qualities of an experienced servicer, see Chapter 5.

Legal Consideration

The rating agencies review all relevant legal documentation including trust indentures, pooling and servicing agreements, prospectus supplements or private placement memoranda, and any other agreements with "outside" entities such as interest rate cap providers. They establish the status of each lien on the underlying properties. In addition, they review the validity of the proposed structure and the distribution of cash flows as planned by the issuer.[7]

Also, in order to assign a credit rating, the rating agencies require the issuing vehicle to be "bankruptcy remote." A vehicle which meets this requirement and is most often employed in the securitization of commercial mortgages is the special purpose corporation entity, which was discussed earlier.

In addition, the rating agencies require that a transaction be insulated from the insolvency of borrowers, property managers, and others. In general, there may be no liens on the properties senior to the mortgages which collateralize the securities. And, in the case of entities other than the SPC, the rating agencies assume that they go bankrupt to test the ability of the transactions to withstand such events.

While the criteria outlined are generally incorporated in the process of rating all commercial mortgage transactions, the methods of evaluating transactions backed by pools of loans on many properties versus those backed by a loan on a single property are different. With single-property transactions, the rating agencies focus heavily on the economic viability of the property, management, etc. On transactions backed by pools of loans with many properties, the rating agencies may focus on the aggregate loan characteristics if the loans were underwritten using uniform standards and the number of loans is large enough. For example, if there are a large number of properties in a transaction, the rating agencies are unlikely to perform site inspections on each property or to perform their own appraisals. Rather, they emphasize the underwriting criteria of the loan originator and inspect a representative sample of the properties. The larger the number of properties in a transaction the more likely the rating agencies will rely on statistical inference in quantifying risks.

Each agency has its own approach. In some transactions, tranches wind up with split ratings. When the tranche receives the same rating from two or more agencies, the investor is getting the benefit of the more conservative agency.

S&P published a thorough description of its criteria in Credit Review dated March 8, 1993. Fitch published its default study results and rating criteria in a special release titled *Commercial Mortgage Stress Test* dated June 8, 1992. Duff & Phelps has recently updated its guidelines in *The Rating of Commercial Real Estate Securities* which it published in May 1993. Moody's recently published its rating guidelines in *Commercial Mortgage-Backed Securities: A Review of Moody's Rating Approach* in November 1993.

---

[7] For more information on the legal consideration of CMBS, see Chapter 19.

Each of the four rating agencies has participated in this market to varying degrees. Exhibit 9 represents the dollar volume of CMBS each of the agencies has rated in 1993, 1994, and 1995. Standard and Poor's has consistently rated the largest volume of deals, although Fitch has been a close and gaining second. Moody's has played the smallest role in this market.

STRUCTURES

Typical Sequential Deal

Exhibit 10 is a graphic depiction of a typical CMBS deal structure. The collateral for this deal consisted of 10 balloon loans totaling $747.79 million. The weighted average coupon of the loans was 8.4%, the weighted average LTV was 62%, and the weighted average DSCR was 1.69x. The property type breakdown was as follows: 50% hotel, 31% retail, 14% office, and 5% industrial.

The loans are aggregated into a pool, and tranched into a senior/subordinated structure. As principal payments come in, they are directed first to the AAA class until it is paid off. Payments then are used to pay off the AA, and then the A, and then all the way down through to the B and unrated classes as each successive tranche receives its principal balance in full. While this is the most common type of paydown schedule, several issuers recently have introduced "pro-rata" structures, whereby the senior and subordinated classes are receiving principal simultaneously.

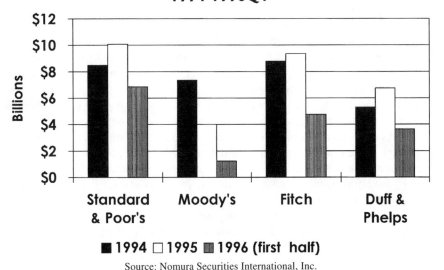

Exhibit 9: Volume of CMBS Rated by Each Rating Agency, 1994-1996Q1

■ 1994 □ 1995 ▦ 1996 (first half)

Source: Nomura Securities International, Inc.

Exhibit 10: Typical Sequential CMBS Structure

Approximate Percent of Total	Approximate Credit Support				
19.4%	33.0%	**Class A-1A**	$150.0	(AAA/AAA/AAA)	**Class CS-1** $150.0 (Notional) (n/a/AAA/AAA)
45.5%	33.0%	**Class A-1B**	$352.0	(AAA/AAA/AAA)	
					Class CS-2 $516.8 (Notional) (n/a/AAA/AAA)
1.0%	32.0%	**Class A-1C**	$7.5	(AAA/n/a/AAA)	
5.8%	26.0%	**Class A-2**	$45.0	(n/a/AA/AA)	
6.8%	19.0%	**Class A-3**	$52.4	(n/a/A/A)	
6.3%	12.5%	**Class A-4**	$48.7	(n/a/BBB/BBB)	
1.5%	11.0%	**Class A-5**	$11.2	(n/a/BBB-/BBB-)	
6.3%	4.5%	**Class B-1**	$48.7	(n/a/BB/BB)	
4.4%	0.0%	**Class B-2**	$33.7	(n/a/B/B)	

▭ Public Certificates   Rating Agencies: (S&P, DCR, Fitch)
▭ Private Certificates S-1 and B-2H classes are not listed

In this particular deal, coupon strips (also known as IOs or interest-only strips) are sliced off the A class certificates, which reduce the coupon payment to class A bondholders.[8] This is done in order to price the bonds closer to par. These interest-only securities are priced at a deep discount and carry no principal balance. In return, coupon strip investors receive narrow "strips" (in this case, 1.28% and 1.05% for CS-1 and CS-2, respectively) of the interest that comes off the notional balance of the underlying bond classes.

In some structures, loans may be separated into two or more groups, and separate bond classes are created which each draw on cash flows from one of the groups. This is sometimes done in cases in which fixed- and floating-rate loans are combined into one deal, or in which floating-rate loans float off different indices. It may also be done to reduce or to concentrate exposure of one of the bond classes to a particular set of cash flows within the deal for purposes such as loans or property type concentration. Such structures are referred to as *multi-towered*.

As is common in many senior/subordinated structured transactions, the investment grade classes are publicly offered, while the non-investment grade tranches are offered by SEC 144A registration. The subordination levels, as determined by the rating agencies, reflect the quality of the collateral, as well as the structural strength of the transaction.

The certificate cash flows will depend on the number, size, and terms of the loans that collateralize the deal. The size and timing of the cash flows from the collat-

---

[8] For more information on CMBS IO Strips, see Chapter 8.

eral will correspond exactly to those of the bonds. Exhibits 11 and 12 provide a visual representation of principal cash flows for the collateral and deal, respectively. It is helpful to look at such representations to see how the loans are amortizing, to identify critical points, such as balloon dates within the life of the deal, and to examine which bonds may have particular exposure to particular loans. For instance, if an investor had a view that loan #8 would default on its balloon payment, he would be inclined to buy a class which receives most of its cash flows before that balloon date.

As we see in Exhibit 11, most of the loans have balloon or bullet payments due in year 10. There is some amortization up front, but most of the principal cash flows come in the form of balloons. More fully amortizing loans will extend the cash flows out more evenly, whereas more balloon loans and bullets will create large aggregated principal paydowns.

Deals Backed by Nonperforming Loans

As U.S. real estate fundamentals continue to improve, and the real estate crisis of the late 1980s recedes further and further into the past, most of new issuance in the U.S. is coming from newly originated loans, in the form of conduits deals and Mega-Deals^{SM}. However, the real estate crisis was not exclusive to the U.S., and much of the rest of the world was slower to recognize losses. What this means is that new portfolios of non-or sub-performing loans may be headed to the U.S. from overseas. Therefore it is important to take a look at yet another type of deal, nonperforming CMBS, that have had considerable success in liquidating distressed real estate assets in the U.S.

Nonperforming CMBS are securities backed by pools of distressed commercial assets. Distressed collateral includes, but is not limited to:

• Loans with less than 1.15X DSCR.
• Loans with LTVs of 85% or greater.
• Loans more than 60 days past due, loans in default, foreclosure, or bankruptcy.
• REO properties.

Note that it is the *loans*, not the properties, that are nonperforming or subperforming. The majority of properties are income producing, but for any number of reasons are unable to cover debt service. Cash flow on these deals comes from interest and principal payments on the loans, and return on asset disposition.

Over the past several years, 15 major deals backed by distressed commercial collateral have come to market. Of these, some are RTC-issued, and the remainder are private deals issued by real estate management companies or funds.

Most nonperforming deals have been private placements or SEC 144A registered, allowing for greater disclosure of property level information to investors. Total issuance of nonperforming CMBS is $3.5 billion, and the average deal size was $236 million. The value of the securities issued, however, is usually dwarfed by the book value of the underlying mortgages. Typically, the dollar amount of the securities may represent only about 30% to 45% of the principal value of the loans. This is because conservative recovery estimates on the properties, and because the issuer (or servicer) may retain a large equity stake in the deal, which is subordinate to the securities.

The RTC has played a major role in the securitization of nonperforming assets, both as an issuer of securities and as a supplier of collateral for the rest of the nonperforming CMBS market. The RTC-N series is collateralized by pools of nonperforming and subperforming RTC mortgages, as well as REO, and many of the privately issued deals in the market are collateralized by nonperforming loans and REO acquired from the RTC.

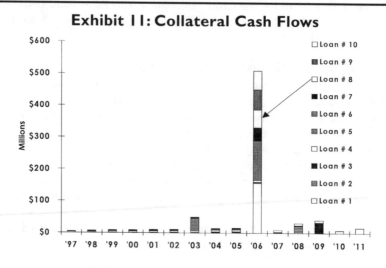

Exhibit 11: Collateral Cash Flows

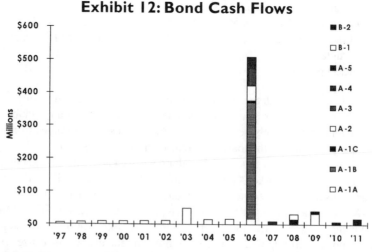

Exhibit 12: Bond Cash Flows

RTC deals will typically have stronger representations, and are guaranteed against breach of representation by the full faith and credit of the U.S. government and therefore warrant lower reserves. They are able to make representations regarding delinquent taxes, and environmental problems (i.e., the RTC will either fix the problems, or buy back the property from the trust). These representations may or may not apply to loans purchased from the RTC and incorporated into non-RTC issued deals, depending on the terms of the purchase from the RTC. Privately issued deals backed by non-RTC properties, however, must set aside significant reserves for delinquent taxes, environmental clean-ups, as well as legal fees.

Common to most nonperforming deals are two forms of reserve accounts: an interest reserve account and an asset reserve account. The interest reserve is in place to cover interest cash flow shortfalls, for a set period of time. The asset reserve account may be directed to a variety of uses, such as payment of deferred maintenance costs, payment of delinquent real estate taxes, payment of leasing commissions or legal costs, repair of environmental problems, or funding of loan commitments. The amount of the reserves will depend on the quality of the assets, and the structure of the deal. In RTC deals, however, reserves are significantly lower, because of the strong representations, and the RTC's government guarantee.

Most nonperforming deals contain a structure whereby all cash flow, other than direct costs of operations and taxes, is paid to amortize debt, with no returns to equity until all debt is retired. In addition, in subordinated deal structures, there are often provisions that prohibit payment of interest or principal to the junior classes until certain principal paydown requirements for the senior classes are met.

Rating agencies look more favorably upon nonperforming deals in which a significant equity stake is either purchased by the servicer or retained by the issuer. This provides an incentive to the issuer or servicer to dispose of assets more quickly and with fewer losses. Release provisions may be included, which stipulate that assets can only be sold off above previously agreed upon prices to prevent below-market liquidation of assets.

Asset quality runs the gamut. Higher quality assets do not automatically translate into strong performance for the bonds; however, seriously distressed collateral may adversely impact the deal. As with standard CMBS, geographic concentration is a negative. One further consideration for nonperforming deals is the percentage of the properties located in states which require judicial procedures to foreclose on properties. Nonjudicial foreclosure may take up to 60 days, with costs totaling approximately $5,000 to $6,000. Judicial foreclosure, on the other hand, can take up to two years, and ranges in cost from about 25% to 100% of the outstanding loan balance.

The strength of the special servicer is one of the most, if not the single most, important factor in determining the quality of a nonperforming CMBS deal. This is because, unlike in standard CMBS deals, the bulk of the assets are earmarked for foreclosure and/or liquidation, which is the sole responsibility of the special servicer. For this reason, most nonperforming CMBS structures provide incentive-based compensation to the special servicer — in the form of fee deferral or ownership interest — in order to maximize recovery values and returns on the pool. Another favored incentive is to allow the servicer to receive higher compensation once the rated debt is retired.

Nonperforming CMBS are measured by *derived investment value* (DIV), instead of DSCR. DIV is an estimate of the net present value of the proceeds from the disposition of the distressed collateral and the time periods over which the amounts are recoverable. Rating agencies use this number to provide quantitative measures of the portfolio, such as LTV. However, the ways in which DIV is calculated can be enormously subjective. Since each agency and each analyst may have a different view as to the recoverable amount and the time required for disposition, DIVs may vary widely.

Performance has been solid, primarily because of the structural strength of these deals. Several nonperforming CMBS deals have been upgraded, and, in fact, there have been proportionally more upgrades among nonperforming CMBS than there have been among the CMBS market as a whole due to the strong credit enhancement requirements. What is particularly noteworthy about nonperforming CMBS, however, is the unpredictability of the cash flows. Unlike in performing mortgages, prepayments and extensions have little to do with interest rate movements. Principal pays down as assets are disposed of, which has more to do with the strength of the servicer than with any desire on the part of the equity holder to refinance. The likelihood of unanticipated extensions necessitates the significant interest reserves mentioned earlier. In most cases, however, the opposite situation occurs, as in the case of RTC 1993-N1. Issued in March of 1993, this deal was scheduled to mature in ten years. By June 1994, the entire deal had paid off.

THE BUYERS OF CMBS

Exhibit 13 is a rough estimate of the CMBS customer base. Typically, insurance companies have targeted the BBB level, while banks and pension funds have stayed in the AAA range. Private pension funds are currently restricted to AAA CMBS due to the ERISA guidelines which apply to private pension funds. Industry groups, however, are working to relax ERISA guidelines to extend to all CMBS of investment grade quality. Should the changes come to pass, pension funds will begin to venture down the credit curve.

Traditional real estate investors, such as real estate funds and investment advisors, have capitalized on their expertise by investing in the higher yielding subordinated classes, or "B-pieces."

CMBS PERFORMANCE

Returns

Investment grade CMBS have outperformed comparably rated corporate bonds for the last several years. The excess return has come from both a relative *tightening* in the spread, as shown in Exhibit 17, as well as the extra income from CMBS. Exhibits 14 and 15 compare the recent total returns from CMBS to those from comparably rated corporates and non-investment grade sectors.

Spreads

Exhibit 16 shows CMBS spreads on a quarterly basis since March 1994. In the high yield sector CMBS had been outperforming corporates; however in the first quarter of 1996, high yield corporate spreads tightened considerably relative to CMBS (Exhibit 18), and as a result, high yield CMBS underperformed corporates.

Exhibit 13: The Buyers of CMBS

Buyer	Percentage
Insurance Companies	47
Money Managers*	28
RE Funds	3
Pension Funds	2
Investment Advisors	5
Banks	16

* Purchasing on behalf of Insurance Companies, Pension Funds, and Mutual Funds.
Source: Nomura Securities International, Inc.

Exhibit 14: CMBS Total Rate of Return versus Lehman Corporate Index Total Return

	AAA	AA	A	BBB
First quarter 1996	0.18%	0.22%	0.22%	0.17%
Fourth quarter 1995 to first quarter 1996	0.38	0.68	0.65	1.39
First quarter 1995 to first quarter 1996	1.46	1.55	1.26	2.58

Source: Nomura Securities International, Inc./Bloomberg

Exhibit 15: CMBS Total Rate of Return versus Merrill Lynch High Yield Index

	BB	B
First quarter 1996	-1.52%	-3.24%
Fourth quarter 1995 to first quarter 1996	0.33	1.38
First quarter 1995 to first quarter 1996	2.09	5.82

Source: Nomura Securities International, Inc./Bloomberg

Exhibit 16: CMBS Spreads

	AAA	AA	A	BBB	BB	B
March 1994	90	120	155	210	435	675
June 1994	85	115	155	210	415	625
September 1994	85	110	140	190	410	630
December 1994	85	110	133	190	425	650
March 1995	80	110	133	190	423	633
June 1995	75	110	133	190	423	633
September 1995	75	110	133	190	423	633
December 1995	80	115	140	190	450	675
March 1996	80	115	140	190	450	675

Source: Nomura Securities International, Inc.

Exhibit 17: Difference Between CMBS Spreads and Corporate Spreads: Investment Grade

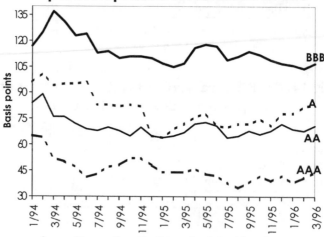

Source: Nomura Securities International, Inc./Bloomberg

Exhibit 18: Difference Between CMBS Spreads and Corporate Spreads: High Yield

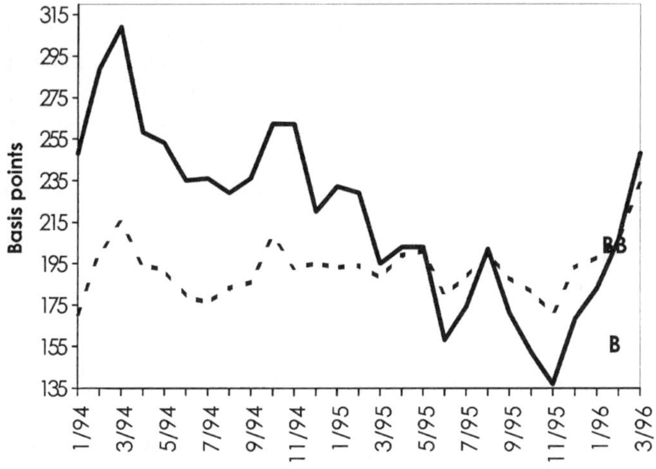

Source: Nomura Securities International, Inc./Bloomberg

Credit

The rating agencies provide ongoing surveillance for the deals they rate, publish annual reviews of most deals, and issue upgrades and downgrades in response to deteriorating or improving credit quality. In 1994 and 1995 15 deals were upgraded and 27 were downgraded. While eroding credit quality for properties has been the cause for downgrades, improving property performance has not been a significant cause for upgrades. The primary criteria for upgrades of CMBS have been amortization of principal balance, rather than improved property performance.

What is particularly notable among deals that have been upgraded is the preponderance of nonperforming deals (5 out of 15). This is indicative of the structural integrity of this deal type, improving real estate fundamentals, as well as the efforts of the special servicers in liquidating the assets. Also notable are the number of deals backed by lesser known property types such as industrial, nursing home, and senior housing. Because of the perceived risks of these property types, deals are often underwritten to include greater amounts of amortization than those backed by more standard property types such as multifamily or retail.

What is immediately apparent about downgrades is that more than half have been tenant credit-dependent deals. These are deals in which the credit rating of the deal is dependent on the credit rating of a single (or, in some cases, multiple) large, corporate tenant(s), and may be secured by lease payments, as well as the actual properties themselves. In 1995, there were many credit downgrades of retail companies — most notably Kmart — due to the softening in that sector. As a result, although the mortgages on the properties themselves may still be performing, these deals experienced downgrades.

As was discussed earlier, borrower character is among the most critical qualitative aspects of CMBS transactions. Its importance was brought into the spotlight in August of 1994 when two deals backed by loans to the same borrower blew up. The deals, DLJ, 1991-MF1 and 93-MF2, were backed by apartment complexes owned by a single borrower. It was later determined that the borrower had made questionable representations to the underwriter regarding the cash flows from the properties. DLJ ultimately stepped up and took the hit, bailing out investors, it is rumored, to the tune of 80 cents on the dollar.

RTC deals and deals backed by RTC properties are equally represented in both upgrades and downgrades. This is to be expected not only because of their inherent volatility and diverse property quality, but also simply because of sheer volume, they represent a significant percentage of the market.

OUTLOOK AND CONCLUSION

The first half of the 1990s has seen significant growth, maturation, and innovation in the CMBS market. Launched initially as a solution to the real estate crisis of the late 1980s, CMBS have evolved into a viable and thriving means of real estate finance. For real estate borrowers the CMBS market represents easier access to capital markets. For fixed income investors, it represents superior returns relative to corporate bonds, and more stable and better call-protected cash flows than residential MBS.

Going forward we expect to see an increased rate of growth, as traditional real estate lenders, such as insurance companies and pension funds, begin to downsize their direct whole loan and real estate holdings and allocate a greater percentage of their investment funds to CMBS. In addition we expect to see a greater flow of deals coming from European portfolios and from the liquidation of Japanese-held real estate assets.

Information flow will continue to be a critical factor for both the primary and secondary markets. Servicers are an increasingly important source of timely, accurate, and easily accessible information about CMBS deals. This enhanced information flow, often available via fax, dial-up, on-line, or internet, will be one of the most significant factors adding liquidity to the market. In addition, several companies, such as Intex, Wall Street Analytics, KPMG, Peat Marwick, and Trepp, are marketing databases with property-level quantitative and qualitative information on public deals. Having access to deal cash flows on a market-wide basis will also be a *sine qua non* for increasing liquidity in CMBS.

This chapter should serve as a basic approach to CMBS. The truth be told, the market is as complex and diverse as the two product areas from which it derives — fixed income securities and commercial real estate.

Chapter **5**

The Role of the Servicer

Galia Gichon
Associate
Nomura Securities International, Inc.

INTRODUCTION

The servicer plays a very crucial role in a commercial mortgage-backed securitization (CMBS). In this chapter, we describe the responsibilities of the servicer, the attributes of a strong commercial mortgage servicer, and some of the conflicts of interest that can arise.

The responsibilities of the servicer for any CMBS deal are described in detail in the Pooling and Servicing (P&S) agreement. The typical statement found in a P&S agreement is that *"The Servicer shall service and administer the mortgage loans on behalf of the trust fund solely in the best interests of, and for the benefit of, the certificate holders with care, skill, prudence, and diligence which is customary of prudent institutional commercial mortgage lenders and servicers"*. Thus, the servicer acts as a fiduciary with respect to the certificate holders in a CMBS transaction and is held to the prudent expert standard.

While the term servicer is used generically, in fact, some of the functions may be split. There may also be several servicers associated with a loan or a deal. The *special servicer* refers to the servicer that has the responsibility for managing loans that have or are about to go into default. If there is a special servicer, it is usually an entity not associated with the servicer carrying out the functions associated with the performing loans. A *subservicer* is a servicer who has been hired by either the regular servicer or the special servicer to provide some specific part of the servicing function. The *master servicer* is like the general contractor who hires subservicers, but has the overall responsibility for the servicing function.

The author would like to thank ABN AMRO, LaSalle National Bank, and Pacific Mutual Life Insurance Company for contributing the remittance report and collateral summary.

Exhibit 1: Top Commercial Mortgage Servicers

Commercial Loan Servicers and Master Servicers	Commercial Mortgage Portfolio (Billion)	CMBS Portfolio (Billion)	Fitch Rating	S&P Rating
Amresco Management, Inc.	$13.50	$9.50	Acceptable	Undisclosed
Banc One Management & Consulting	$4.42	$2.53	Acceptable	Above Average
Bankers Trust	$7.74	$7.74	Acceptable	Above Average
Boatmen's National Mortgage Inc.	$2.14	$1.93	Acceptable	Average
Fleet Management & Recovery Corp.	$4.30	$1.90	Acceptable	Undisclosed
GE Capital Asset Management	$8.20	$5.30	N/R	Strong
Midland Loan Services*	$12.00	$9.00	Acceptable	Above Average
Pacific Mutual Life Insurance Co.	$4.10		N/R	Strong
Wells Fargo	$3.70	$1.20	Acceptable	N/R

*Includes an RTC and Lehman Brother deal as of first quarter 1996.

The servicing business is dominated by several large players. Consolidation of the industry is expected to continue since there are clearly economies and benefits from diversification in being larger. Exhibit 1 lists the top servicers in the commercial mortgage industry. Servicers earn a fee based on the outstanding balance of the loans. Typical fees range from 6 to 9 basis points.[1] In addition, many servicers today are buying the first loss piece, therefore their fee may be adjusted to reflect the purchase price. Servicers vary by quality and are assigned a grade by the rating agencies.

FUNCTIONS OF THE SERVICER

The main functions of the servicer are collection, disbursement, monitoring, preparation of reports, advancing through liquidation, and management of the default/foreclosure process (including loan modification, workouts, and restructurings).

Collection & Disbursement

The servicer is required to make a reasonable effort to collect all payments required under the terms of the mortgage loan. These would include the principal and interest payments, prepayment and yield maintenance penalties, late payment penalties, default penalties, payments to reserve accounts, proceeds from liquidations and insurance claims, and payments for insurance, taxes, etc.

---

[1] This is an average range of fees on current CMBS deals. Older deals usually have higher fees, anywhere from 9 to 15 basis points. If a deal has a very high fee, there is another explanation behind it.

Exhibit 2: Lockbox structure

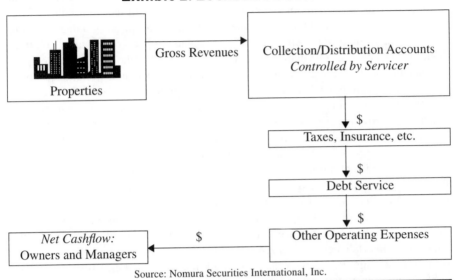

Source: Nomura Securities International, Inc.

A well structured deal should have a lockbox arrangement (see Exhibit 2). In a lockbox arrangement, all the revenues from the property go into the servicer's collection account. Sometimes a distinction is made between a hard lock box and a modified lockbox. In the case of a hard lockbox, the tenants are required to *directly* deposit their rental payments into an escrow account in the trustee's name for the benefit of the certificate holders.[2] In contrast, with a modified lockbox, the *property manager* collects the rent and *deposits* it into the servicer's collection account. While the modified lockbox arrangement is inferior, it still serves as a protection to the lender.

The servicer pays out taxes, insurance premiums, and debt service payments (via the trustee[3]). The borrower is also paid from this account, but not until he certifies that all operating expenses that have been outstanding have been paid.

The servicer insures that the priority of payment outlined in the prospectus is adhered to. It is the servicer's responsibility to keep track of the certificate holders. This is important in order to insure that remittance reports are mailed to the appropriate parties. The Pooling and Servicing agreement dictates that the servicer has the right to deduct its servicing fee from all the cash flow coming in; however, any expenses incurred by the servicer as a result of performing its regular duties are not reimbursed from the incoming cash flow.

Monitoring

One of the most important roles that the servicer plays is monitoring the status of the real estate and the mortgage loans. The condition of the real estate is relevant for all

---

[2] In the case of hotels, credit card payments go directly into the collection account.
[3] See Chapter 4 for a diagram showing the relationship between the servicer and the trustee.

bondholders regardless of the rating category. Even the most senior bond classes can be affected by the uncertain timing of cash flow in the event of recoveries due to foreclosures. Bondholders need to be informed both at the inception of a deal and kept informed on an ongoing basis as to the performance of the real estate. Investors should have access to information that could affect the likelihood of their receiving their payments before the problem shows up as a delinquency in the remittance report.

At inception, deals consisting of newly originated loans tend to have much better information than older deals since, typically, this is now a requirement of many lenders. In particular, if these loans are being originated with expectation of being securitized, information generally comes in the form of several years of audited financial statements, rent rolls, appraisals, etc. Without this, the rating agencies will not be willing to award high ratings to the bond classes. On the other hand, deals such as RTC deals, which were originated when underwriting requirements were more lenient, tend to have less information available even at inception.

After inception the quality and quantity of information made available to investors and rating agencies are a function of what was originally required by the lender. Most loans that closed in 1994 and 1995 have required the borrower to provide to the servicer monthly rent rolls, unaudited quarterly financial statements, and audited annual financial statements. How this information makes its way from the property owner to the bond investor is evolving as the market develops. Once a loan is closed, the servicer is usually the only link to the borrower.

The rating agencies also benefit from the servicer monitoring deals. All of the rating agencies now employ full time surveillance departments for the sole purpose of tracking the real estate collateral on CMBS deals already issued. The primary source for obtaining the updated real estate information is the servicer for that particular deal. The rating agencies are constantly monitoring their rated deals for the purpose of upgrades or downgrades and once a year, they publish a report updating investors on the status of that deal. This report is distributed in printed form and summarized through Bloomberg Financial Markets.

Bloomberg has started to keep track of the property performance on CMBS deals by displaying updated DSCR and occupancy numbers, which are supplied by the servicer on that deal. If an investor is interested in buying or trading these bonds, he can retrieve the structure of the bond and the updated property type information in just a few minutes.

Culturally, real estate owners are not used to the idea of full disclosure, but those that are now involved in borrowing in the public capital markets are getting used to the idea. CMBS deals backed by loans to REITs tend to have good ongoing information. This is because REITs are required to file with the SEC certain reports on their real estate properties. These reports include the 8Q (quarterly financial statements), the 10K (annual financial statements), and the 8K (a report used for declaring any significant events happening in the company).[4] Over time as the market for

---

[4] This partially accounts for why REIT deals trade tighter. Of course, the other reason is that they are viewed as having greater access to capital than traditional real estate borrowers.

CMBS matures, it is expected that deals for which good and timely information are readily available will trade with greater liquidity and be priced at tighter spreads to Treasuries.

In addition to monitoring the real estate and the mortgage loan, the servicer must ensure that insurance policies are kept in force and that tax payments are made. Insurance coverage usually includes fire, casualty, general liability, business interruption, and if applicable, flood and earthquake insurance. If the borrower fails to maintain the policies, the servicer is required to obtain insurance.

The servicer is usually required to have properties inspected on some regular basis (more frequently if mortgage payments are delinquent). In some cases, updated appraisals could be required, in particular when extensions are granted. Many P&S agreements implement "appraisal reduction amounts" in the case of a balloon extension. This is a required updated appraisal that could possibly reduce the current principal balance, thereby affecting the most junior tranche. The servicer has an obligation to notify the special servicer as soon as it becomes aware of a decline in the performance of any property which might ultimately lead to a default. Many loans have provisions that dictate a change in management if the DSCR dips below a certain level.

Reporting

A big part of the servicer's job is the dissemination of information through reports to certificate holders, the trustee, government agencies, and rating agencies. On each distribution date, the servicer sends to each certificate holder[5] (with copies to the underwriter and trustee) a *remittance report* which shows information about the current distribution. There are no set standards for what is included in a remittance report. We have seen a wide variety of reports, some of which show a minimal amount of typewritten information, and others which are computer generated and supply more details.

In our view, a remittance report should at a minimum contain the following:

For each class:

1. the interest payment due, the available funds, and any interest shortfall[6]
2. the principal payment that is due and the amount of available funds
3. the principal and interest advances
4. balances before and after current month distribution (in dollar and factor form)

---

[5] One of the problems that has developed is that the servicer via the trustee typically sends the report to the registered certificate holder. Since certificates are usually not in the investor's name, but in the name of the depository institution holding the certificates, the investors have not been receiving these reports. Newer P&S agreements are requiring that the trustee work with the underwriter to pass these remittance reports on to the beneficial certificate holders.
[6] An issue that arises with interest shortfall is compensating interest. If interest shortfall does occur, the servicer may not always be required to pay the full amount of interest and principal due to the certificate holders.

    5. allocation of losses

    6. current and previous pass-through-through rate

    7. allocation of prepayment principal

    8. allocation of yield maintenance penalties

    9. allocation of penalty payments

    10. allocation of default rate payments

For each loan:

    1. the interest payment that is due and current note rate (if loan is at cap rate, it should be stated and if the loan is a floating-rate note, the LIBOR rate should also be stated)

    2. the principal payment that is due

    3. principal prepayments

    4. original and current balance

    5. original and current loan value[7]

    6. total available funds

    7. yield maintenance premiums

    8. late payment penalties

    9. beginning interest shortfall and ending interest shortfall

    10. delinquency information: 1 month, 2 months, 3+ months, in foreclosure

    11. REO information: principal balance, book value, recovery date and proceeds, realized losses

    12. servicer compensation

    13. servicer advances

For each property:

    1. current and previous NOI unaudited quarterly and audited annually[8]

    2. current and previous occupancy percentages

    3. current and previous DSCR

    4. reserve account: required amount versus actual funding

    5. material events affecting property; for example, major tenant vacating

    In Exhibit 3 we show a sample of a typical remittance report. The first three pages are an example of the remittance report submitted by the trustee. These pages represent the bond structure and loan status. The last two pages are a summary of the collateral. The collateral summary is provided by the servicer.

---

[7] This is done because if a loan with many properties prepays only some of the properties, the loan value will be affected as well.

[8] If there is more than one property within a loan and the properties are cross-collateralized or cross defaulted, the properties need not be listed individually. For more details on this topic, "Pitfalls in Calculating NOI," Nomura Securities International Inc., 1995.

Exhibit 3: Sample Remittance Report and Collateral Summary

ABN AMRO
LaSalle National Bank

Administrator:
Name and Phone #
135 S. LaSalle Street Suite 200
Chicago, IL 60603

Nomura Asset Securities Corporation
(Pacific Mutual Life Insurance Company)
Commercial Mortgage Pass-Through Certificates
Deal Name
ABN AMRO Acct.:

Statement Date:
Payment Date:
Prior Payment:
Record Date:

WAC: 7.50000%
WAMM: 351

Class CUSIP	Original Face Value Per $1,000	Opening Balance Per $1,000	Principal Payment Per $1,000	Principal Adj. or Loss Per $1,000	Negative Amortization Per $1,000	Closing Balance Per $1,000	Interest Payment Per $1,000	Interest Adjustment Per $1,000	Pass Through Rate* Next Rate**
A-1	100,000,000.00	99,315,125.34	78,494.98	0.00	0.00	99,236,630.37	620,719.53	0.00	7.36500%
555555AA5	1000.000000	993.151253	0.784950	0.000000	0.000000	992.366304	6.207195	0.000000	7.36500%
						Total P&I Payment	699,214.51		

* Interest Paid minus Interest Adjustment minus Deferred Interest equals Accrual.
** Estimated

Pool Summary

Loan ID	Opening Balance	Principal Remittance	Closing Balance	Note Rate (%)	Scheduled Interest	Loan Paid Through
000000001	49,657,563	39,247	49,618,315	7.5000%	310,604	Dec-95
000000002	49,657,563	39,247	49,618,315	7.5000%	310,604	Dec-95
Total	99,315,125	78,495	99,236,630		621,207	

Delinquency Summary

Loan ID	One Month		Two Months		Three Months		In Foreclosure	
	Number	Balance	Number	Balance	Number	Balance	Number	Balance
Loan #1	0	0.00	0	0.00	0	0.00	0	0.00
Loan #2								
Total								

Exhibit 3 (Continued)

ABN AMRO	Nomura Asset Securities Corporation	Statement Date:
LaSalle National Bank	(Pacific Mutual Life Insurance Company)	Payment Date:
	Commercial Mortgage Pass-Through Certificates	Prior Payment:
Administrator:	Deal Name	Record Date:
Name and Phone #	ABN AMRO Acct.:	
135 S. LaSalle Street Suite 200		
Chicago, IL 60603		

Summary of REO Property

Loan Number	Loan Name	Principal Value	Book Value	Date of Final REcovery	Amount of Proceeds	Aggregate Other REvenues Collected	
						Current	Next
					W/Ave Net Mortgage Rate	7.5000%	7.5000%
							0.00

Book value of real estate acquired through foreclosure or grant of deed in lieu of foreclosure

Note: Foreclosure and REO Totals are included in the Appropriate Delinquency Aging Category.

Dist-ribution Date	Delinquencies & REOs									Prepayments			Rates & Maturity		
	Delinq 1 Month		Delinq 2 Months		Delinq 3+ Months		Foreclosure		Balance of REOs	Begin Pool Balance (#)	Prepayment $ (# of Payoffs)	Sched Prin.	Next Weighted Avg		WAMM
	#	Balance	#	Balance	#	Balance	#	Balance					Coupon	Remit	
12/4/95	0	0.00% 0.00%	0	0.00% 0.00%	0	0.00% 0.00%	0	0.00% 0.00%	0 0.00%	99,315,125 2	0.00 0	78,495	7.500%	7.365%	351
11/4/95	0	0.00% 0.00%	0	0.00% 0.00%	0	0.00% 0.00%	0	0.00% 0.00%	0 0.00%	99,393,133 2	0.00 0	78,007	7.500%	7.365%	352
10/4/95	0	0.00% 0.00%	0	0.00% 0.00%	0	0.00% 0.00%	0	0.00% 0.00%	0 0.00%	99,470,656 2	0.00 0	77,523	7.500%	7.365%	353
9/4/95	0	0.00% 0.00%	0	0.00% 0.00%	0	0.00% 0.00%	0	0.00% 0.00%	0 0.00%	99,547,697 2	0.00 0	77,041	7.500%	7.365%	354
8/4/95	0	0.00% 0.00%	0	0.00% 0.00%	0	0.00% 0.00%	0	0.00% 0.00%	0 0.00%	99,624,260 2	0.00 0	76,563	7.500%	7.365%	355

Exhibit 3 (Continued)

ABN AMRO
LaSalle National Bank

Administrator:
Name and Phone #
135 S. LaSalle Street Suite 200
Chicago, IL 60603

Nomura Asset Securities Corporation
(Pacific Mutual Life Insurance Company)
Commercial Mortgage Pass-Through Certificates
Deal Name
ABN AMRO Acct::

Statement Date:
Payment Date:
Prior Payment:
Record Date:

| Dist-ribution | Delinquencies & REOs | | | | | Prepayments | | Sched Prin. | Rates & Maturity | | WAMM |
| | Delinq 1 Month | Delinq 2 Months | Delinq 3+ Months | Foreclosure | Balance of | Begin Pool Balance (#) | Prepayment $ (# of Payoffs) | | Next Weighted Avg | | |
									Coupon	Remit	
7/4/95	0 0.00%	0 0.00%	0 0.00%	0 0.00%	0 0.00%	99,700,347 2	0.00 0	76,087	7.500%	7.365%	356
6/4/95	0 0.00%	0 0.00%	0 0.00%	0 0.00%	0 0.00%	99,775,962 2	0.00 0	75,615	7.500%	7.365%	357
5/4/95	0 0.00%	0 0.00%	0 0.00%	0 0.00%	0 0.00%	99,851,107 2	0.00 0	75,145	7.500%	7.365%	358
4/4/95	0 0.00%	0 0.00%	0 0.00%	0 0.00%	0 0.00%	99,925,785 2	0.00 0	74,678	7.500%	7.365%	359
3/4/95	0 0.00%	0 0.00%	0 0.00%	0 0.00%	0 0.00%	100,000,000 2	0.00 0	74,215	7.500%	7.365%	360

Note: Foreclosure and REO Totals are included in the Appropriate Delinquency Aging Category.

Exhibit 3 (Continued)
Sample Deal • Quarterly Collateral Summary • Quarter Ended March 31, 1996

Property	City	State	Total Revenues*	Total Expenses Before Mgt Fees*	Cash Flow Available for Debt Service	Mgt Fees*	Funded Reserves**	Debt Service***	Derived DSCR****	Adjusted Derived DSCR*****	Occupancy****** Rate	Date
Borrower A												
Property 1	Phoenix	AZ	$507,234	$157,445	$349,789	$25,269					96%	Mar-96
Property 2	San Diego	CA	277,507	110,416	$167,091	13,826					97%	Mar-96
Property 3	San Diego	CA	310,105	83,063	$227,042	15,483					97%	Mar-96
Property 4	San Diego	CA	414,312	127,771	$286,541	20,694					87%	Mar-96
Property 5	San Diego	CA	234,630	80,440	$154,190	11,663					93%	Mar-96
Property 6	San Diego	CA	908,803	288,105	$620,698	45,325					92%	Mar-96
Total / Aver			$2,652,591	$847,240	$1,805,351	$132,260	$0	$1,103,487	1.64	1.52	94%	
Borrower B												
Property 1	Tucson	AZ	$1,368,422	$824,838	$543,584	$54,737					93%	Mar-96
Property 2	Tucson	AZ	1,673,523	1,122,254	$551,269	66,540					75%	Mar-96
Property 3	Tucson	AZ	2,828,579	1,846,690	$981,889	113,184					79%	Mar-96
Property 4	Tucson	AZ	1,561,650	968,593	$593,057	62,466					86%	Mar-96
Total / Aver			$7,432,174	$4,762,375	$2,669,799	$296,927	$299,137	$942,998	2.83	2.20	83%	
Borrower C												
Property 1	Phoenix	AZ	$7,256,481	$2,414,685	4,841,796	$206,457					99%	Mar-96
Property 2	Tucson	AZ	$3,169,630	$1,513,316	1,656,314	$89,984					96%	Mar-96
Property 3	Denver	CO	4,325,255	1,414,483	2,910,772	129,466					99%	Mar-96
Property 4	Denver	CO	4,952,623	1,829,017	3,123,606	163,219					99%	Mar-96
Total / Aver			$19,703,989	$7,171,501	12,532,488	$589,126	$384,254	$4,455,856	2.81	2.59	98%	

* The information in this report is based on borrower supplied data and is not necessarily presented in accordance with generally accepted accounting principles (GAAP). The Servicer makes no representation as to its accuracy.

** Adjusted Derived Debt Service Coverage Ratio (ADDSCR) represents, for a specific quarter, i) revenues ii) less the sum of operating expenses plus Management Fees plus funded reserves iii) divided by scheduled principal and interest paid by borrower.

*** The aggregate ADDSCR is based on cumulative quarterly amounts for Cash Flow Available for Debt Service, Funded Reserves, Management Fees and Debt Service.

**** Occupancy information is as disclosed in the QCSR for respective quarters. Refer to QCSR's for effective dates of occupancy information as provided by the respective borrowers.

***** Calculated after deducting Management Fees and Funded Reserves.

****** The occupancy information is the most current information available, as provided by the Borrower.

Exhibit 3 (Continued)

Sample Deal • Quarterly Collateral Report • Summary Information*

	Adjusted Derived DSCR* Most Recent Four Quarters Ending					Occupancy** Most Recent Four Quarters Ending				
	Mar-96	Dec-95	Sep-95	Jun-95	Aggregate (4)	Mar-96	Dec-95	Sep-95	Jun-95	Average
Borrower A	1.52	1.53	1.52	1.49	1.52	94%	91%	88%	85%	93%
Borrower B	2.20	2.19	2.25	2.15	2.20	83%	80%	77%	74%	82%
Borrower C	2.59	2.50	2.50	2.54	2.53	98%	95%	92%	89%	97%
Aggregate Derived DSCR	2.10	2.07	2.09	2.06	2.08					

* The information in this report is based on borrower supplied data and is not necessarily presented in accordance with generally accepted accounting principles (GAAP). The Servicer makes no representation as to its accuracy.

**Adjusted Derived Debt Service Coverage Ratio (ADDSCR) represents, for a specific quarter, i) revenues ii) less the sum of operating expenses plus Management Fees plus funded reserves iii) divided by scheduled principal and interest paid by borrower

In addition to reporting to certificate holders, the servicer has other reporting responsibilities. The servicer usually is required to send to the trustee, following the distribution to certificate holders, a statement showing the status of the collection account showing deposits and withdrawals. Also, on an annual basis, the servicer must send a statement of compliance. It is the servicer's responsibility to retain an accounting firm to annually audit the servicer's procedures. The servicer is obligated to file reports that are required by governmental agencies such as the SEC and IRS. In addition to these reporting requirements, the servicer is required to provide information to the rating agencies. Rating agencies normally receive copies of the information sent to the certificate holders and the trustees.

Advancing

One of the most important functions of the servicer is to act as a source of liquidity in the structure. Because of the possibility of late payments and foreclosure, payments on the underlying mortgages may not be made on time, even if the full amount is eventually recovered. With respect to each distribution date, the servicer is required to advance monthly payments of unpaid principal (other than balloon) and interest, unless the servicer determines that such an advance will not be recoverable. A problem that has risen lately is the determination of recoverability. It is usually not clearly defined whose role it is to determine if an advance would be recoverable. Advancing is usually required through foreclosure. Through this mechanism, the certificate holders receive uninterrupted payments assuming that the servicer determines that it will be able to recover its advances from the liquidation proceeds or insurance. It should be clear that the advancing feature is not a source of credit support, but only liquidity.

In the event that the servicer determines that an advance amount would not be recoverable, the servicer would deliver a notice to the trustee with evidence such as an updated appraisal, recent financial statements, etc.

In addition to advancing principal and interest, the servicer is required to advance other expenses such as taxes, insurance payments, and similar items that if not paid could become liens against the property. The servicer is also required to advance the expenses involved in the foreclosure process.

Recently, we are seeing deals in which the servicer does not advance principal and interest payments to the most junior outstanding class. This is because if the servicer is advancing to the junior class, there is less money available for the senior class in a foreclosure. If advances are made, the junior class would be getting paid interest even if the property were not doing well.

Foreclosing, Loan Workout, and Loan Modification

If a loan runs into trouble, the servicer is empowered to make certain decisions. For example, the servicer may waive late payment charges, or penalty interest in connection with a delinquent monthly payment or balloon payment. The servicer makes enforcement decisions that may affect bondholders. For example, the servicer can waive default penalties or modify coupon terms of the loan that affect cash inflows.[9] In the event that a default is foreseen or has occurred, and the servicer determines that a modification, waiver, or amendment of the terms of the loan is reasonably likely to produce a greater recovery on a present value basis than liquidation, the servicer may accept a modification. Some of these modifications may require the approval of the certificate holders. Many P&S agreements restrict the modifications that a servicer can make in the event of a default. This is for the protection of the bondholder.

The single most important modification that the servicer can make is in the event of a default of a balloon payment. In this situation, the servicer may have the right to grant an extension of the maturity of the loan. There may be a restriction on the amount of time that the servicer may extend the maturity of the balloon loan. For example, the first balloon extension may be granted for a period of 12 months. After that, the servicer may have the right to extend the maturity for no more than three successive times for a total of 36 months. There are also restrictions that may be imposed on the servicer before granting a balloon extension. These restrictions include the fulfillment of certain requirements such as obtaining current property appraisals or approval from the operating advisor or directing holders. The servicer is responsible for any workout of a loan that is delinquent.[10] When no satisfactory arrangement can be made for collection of delinquent payments, the servicer will either foreclose or sell the loan. The servicer will then manage the foreclosure process, look after the REO including finding an independent contractor to operate and manage the property, and oversee final disposition.

ATTRIBUTES OF A QUALIFIED SERVICER

As can be seen from this extensive list of responsibilities, the servicer is a key part of the CMBS structure and acts as a watchdog for the investor. Therefore, the best deals will have the most qualified servicers. The rating agencies review servicers' capabilities, experience, strengths, and weaknesses etc. The following are some of the key attributes that are considered in their review. The first should be the financial strength of the servicer. The financial position of a servicer will indicate its ability to make advances. The servicer needs to demonstrate sufficient sources of liquidity (either internal or from a parent), adequate capital, and diversification of income sources.

The second area to be reviewed should be the servicer's administrative capabilities and experience. This would include an evaluation of its capabilities in all the areas discussed above. Experience in a variety of property types is important and systems for tracking loan performance and collections are critical.

---

[9] Modification of the coupon can have severe consequences on bond classes that receive a weighted average coupon instead of a fixed coupon. In better deals loan coupons can be modified but do not adversely affect WAC bonds or IOs. The WAC is computed based on original coupon and interest shortfalls borne by the subordinate bonds regardless of a WAC or fixed coupon.

[10] Once a loan becomes non-performing it is often turned over to a special servicer.

The third area is a review of management and the organization. Experienced management and staff are needed to anticipate potential problems. A stable, experienced, and adequate sized staff are important so that continuity of oversight is maintained.

As more CMBS deals are entering the market, the bid for a servicer has become more competitive. Servicing fees are becoming lower and lower. This is of some concern since servicers might begin to cut corners in order to maintain their profitability.

If the servicer fails to perform his duties such as make required advances, deposit funds on a timely basis, etc. the servicer will be considered in default and can be terminated by the trustee. In this situation, the trustee will temporarily take over the servicer's duties until a successor servicer can be found. When a replacement servicer is found, the appointment is subject to the approval of the rating agencies.

REPRESENTATIONS AND WARRANTIES

Typically, servicers are required to make certain representations and warranties with respect to the transaction. They need to state that their fees are reasonable and are solely for the servicing function that they are providing. They need to indicate that they have examined and will continue to examine subservicer agreements for compliance with the original P&S agreement. The servicer needs to state that it is licensed and authorized to perform its duties, that there are no conflicts that will affect its performance, and no pending litigations that will affect performance.

POTENTIAL CONFLICTS OF INTEREST

As stated in the pooling and servicing agreement, the servicer is required to act in the sole interest of the certificate holders. While this may sound like a straightforward directive, in reality it is fraught with conflict. First, since the servicer earns a fee as long as the deal is outstanding, the servicer has an interest in not foreclosing. This may be in direct conflict with the bondholder who wants to be sure of recovering principal. If the servicer does not foreclose in a timely manner, the property can continue to decline in value, and the bondholder can receive less than invested from the liquidation proceeds.[11] (Recall that the servicer is entitled to recover advances and earn interest ahead of all the bondholders.) In order to reduce this risk, some deals require certificate holder approval after the initial extension period and updated appraisals are ordered. As a last resort, the servicer can usually be replaced by a majority vote of the certificate holders.

---

[11] This appears to have happened in a recent deal, LB Multifamily Mortgage Trust 1991-4. In this situation the gross proceeds upon disposition of REO was about 60% of the scheduled principal balances Moreover, net proceeds after reimbursement to the servicer for advances and expenses averaged only 20%.

In a multi-class deal, the interests of the senior classes are not always aligned with those of the junior classes. While all parties would like to receive the maximum proceeds, a path that might lead to the maximum proceeds to the senior buyer will not necessarily maximize the proceeds to a junior class. For example, when an extension is granted at a balloon default, the junior class may be happy because it continues to receive coupon and the borrower has been given a chance to work things out. The senior class, depending upon the LTV, might prefer a quick foreclosure.

The conflict can be even greater when the servicer has an equity interest in the transaction as owner of a class.[12] Even though this provides some benefit to bondholders since the servicer in this case has a financial incentive to maximize proceeds, the servicer has an incentive to delay foreclosure if it owns the junior class or accelerate foreclosure if it owns a senior class.

The best way to avoid conflict is for the servicer to be guided by the principle of maximizing the total proceeds on a present value basis. In this way the servicer will not bias its decision in favor of a particular class of securities. As we mentioned earlier, a protection bondholders have is that they can vote to remove the servicer. Some deals allow certificate holders to dismiss and replace the servicer at will, while others require material cause. Some transactions do not allow the servicer to vote on loan modification issues if the servicer is the owner of a bond class. Also, newer deals prevent a bond class from receiving advances if the bond is owned by the servicer.

CONCLUSION

The servicer in a CMBS deal plays a very active role. The functions that are performed are critical to the smooth performance of the deal. Investors rely on the servicer's judgment to look after their interests. For this reason only experienced and well financed servicers should be used.

---

[12] It is usually the special servicer who manages the foreclosure process and may take a position in a junior class.

Chapter **6**

Structural Considerations Impacting CMBS

John N. Dunlevy, CFA, CPA
Director and Senior Portfolio Manager
Hyperion Capital Management

INTRODUCTION

Commercial mortgage-backed securities (CMBS) are a rapidly growing segment of the fixed-income market. This growth has been spurred by the ability of Wall Street to securitize real estate and loans of real estate, and transform equity into real estate investment trusts (REITs) and debt into CMBS (see Exhibit 1). This chapter will focus on the structural considerations impacting CMBS investments. There are five basic types of CMBS transactions; however, we will concentrate on the three types of CMBS deals which are greatly impacted by structure.

BASIC CMBS STRUCTURE

A CMBS transaction is formed when an issuer places commercial loans into a trust which then issues classes of bonds backed by the interest and principal of the underlying mortgages. The basic building block of the CMBS transaction is a commercial loan which was originated either to finance a commercial purchase or to refinance a prior mortgage obligation.

   Many types of commercial loans can be either sold by the originator as a commercial whole loan or structured into a CMBS transaction (see Exhibit 2). The whole loan market, which is largely dominated by insurance companies and banks, is focused on loans between $10 and $50 million issued on traditional property types (multifamily, retail, office, and industrial). CMBS transactions, on the other hand, can involve loans of virtually any size (from conduit loans as small as $1 million to single property transactions as large as $200 million) and/or property type.

Exhibit 1: Transformation of Real Estate and Real Estate Loans

	Equity	Debt
Private	Direct Investments Commingled Funds	Whole Loans
Public	REITs	CMBS

The CMBS transaction structure takes shape when the owner of the commercial loans has a potential transaction "sized" by the rating agencies. This sizing will determine the necessary level of credit enhancement to achieve a desired rating level. For example, if certain *debt service coverage* (DSC) and *loan-to-value* (LTV) ratios are needed, and these ratios cannot be met at the loan level, then subordination is used to achieve these levels. In Exhibit 3, a simple example demonstrates how a CMBS transaction can be structured to meet the rating agencies required DSC and LTV ratios. For example, Duff & Phelps requires a 1.51× coverage to achieve a single-A rating on a regional mall deal. Since that level cannot be obtained at the collateral level (coverage of 1.25×) a CMBS structure with 17.2% subordination is created.

Paydown Priority

The rating agencies will require that the CMBS transaction be retired sequentially with the highest rated bonds paying off first. Therefore, any return of principal caused by amortization, prepayment, or default will be used to repay the highest rated tranche.

Interest on principal outstanding will be paid to all tranches. In the event of a delinquency resulting in insufficient cash to make all scheduled payments, the transaction's servicer will advance both principal and interest. Advancing will continue from the servicer for as long as these amounts are deemed recoverable.

Losses arising from loan defaults will be charged against the principal balance of the lowest rated CMBS bond tranche outstanding. The total loss charged will include the amount previously advanced as well as the actual loss incurred in the sale of the loan's underlying property.

Finally, the investor must be sure to understand the cash flow priority of any prepayment penalties and/or yield maintenance provisions, as this can impact a particular bond's average life and overall yield.

Structural Call Protection

The degree of call protection available to a CMBS investor is a function of the following two characteristics:

1. call protection available at loan level
2. call protection afforded from the actual CMBS structure

Exhibit 2: Commercial Loan Disposition after Origination

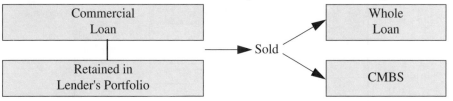

Exhibit 3: How a CMBS Transaction can be Structured to Satisfy Required DSC and LTV Ratios of Duff & Phelps

Loan Information	
Assume $100 million Regional mall loan	DSC 1.25×* LTV 75%*
Market value	$133.3 million
Debt service	$10.0 million
NOI	$12.5 million

CMBS Structure	Required Subordination (%)*	Tranche Size	Tranche LTV (%)	Tranche DSC
AAA	31.4	68.6	51.5	1.82×
AA	23.3	8.1	57.5	1.63×
A	17.2	6.1	62.1	1.51×
BBB	12.0	5.2	66.0	1.42×
BB	6.6	5.4	70.1	1.34×
B	2.6	4.0	73.1	1.28×
NR	0.0	2.6	75.0	1.25×
		100.0		

* Source: Duff & Phelps.

At the commercial loan level, call protection can take the following form:

1. prepayment lockout
2. prepayment penalty
3. yield maintenance penalties

The strongest type of prepayment protection is prepayment lockout. A lockout is a contractual agreement that prohibits all prepayments during the period of the lockout.

Exhibit 4: Sequence of Principal Paydowns

	CMBS Structure	Principal Paydowns
↑	AAA	
	AA	
	A	
	BBB	
	BB	
	B	↓
Losses	NR	

Prepayment penalties are predetermined penalties which must be paid by the borrower if the borrower wishes to refinance. For example, 5-4-3-2-1 is a common prepayment penalty structure. That is, if the borrower wishes to prepay during the first year, he must pay a 5% penalty for a total of $105 rather than $100 (which is the norm in the residential market). Likewise, during the second year, a 4% penalty would apply, etc.

Yield maintenance penalties, in their simplest terms, are designed to make investors indifferent as to the timing of prepayments. The yield maintenance provision makes it uneconomical to refinance solely to get a lower mortgage rate. The simplest and most restrictive form of yield maintenance (Treasury flat yield maintenance) penalizes the borrower based on the difference between the mortgage coupon and the prevailing Treasury rate.

The other type of call protection available in CMBS transactions is structural. That is, because the CMBS bond structures are sequential-pay (by rating) the AA-rated tranche cannot paydown until the AAA is completely retired, and the AA-rated bonds must be paid off before the A-rated bonds, etc. (see Exhibit 4). However, as mentioned earlier, principal losses due to defaults are impacted from the bottom of the structure upward.

Balloon Maturity Provisions

Many commercial loans backing CMBS transactions are balloon loans which require substantial principal payment on the final maturity date. Although many investors like the "bullet bond-like" paydown of the balloon maturities, it does present difficulties from a structural standpoint. That is, if the deal is structured to completely paydown on a specified date, an event of default will occur if any delays occur. However, how such delays impact CMBS investors is dependent on the bond type (premium, par or discount) and whether or not the servicer will advance to a particular tranche after the balloon default. Another concern for CMBS investors in multi-tranche transactions is the fact that all loans must be refinanced to pay off the most senior bond holders. Therefore, the balloon risk of the most senior tranche (i.e., AAA) may be equivalent to that of the most junior bond class (i.e., B).

Exhibit 5: Types of CMBS Balloon Provisions

Method	Description	Examples
Time matched	Balloon maturity and bond maturity are the same	CMBS deals pre-RTC
Internal tail	Balloon maturity and bond maturity same but provisions for refinancing begin 1 to 2 years prior to maturity	DLJ 1992 and 1993 "M" series
External tail	Balloon maturity occurs before bond maturity	Most 1995 conduit deals and secured REIT debt transactions

Currently, there are three types of structural provisions that can be present in CMBS transactions. The provisions are summarized in Exhibit 5.

The first provision — *time matched method* — is no longer used in CMBS transactions because it often results in actual defaults upon balloon maturity. This method was common prior to the real estate recession which began in the late 1980s. Prior to this national real estate downturn, extension risk was not a primary concern for traditional lenders (i.e., insurance companies and banks). However, the real estate recession caused a rapid decline in property values which in turn caused many loans to be non-refinanceable under the original loan terms. Many of these deals did contain default rate provisions. That is, an extension could be granted in exchange for an increase in the interest rate. Further, many deals of this type also had a "cash-trap" mechanism which captured all excess cash flow and used it to paydown debt.

The second type of balloon loan provision is the *internal tail*. The internal tail requires the borrower to provide ongoing evidence of its efforts to refinance the loan. For example, the following procedures would have to be undertaken within one year of the balloon date:

• appraisals on all properties
• Phase I environmental reports
• engineering reports

Finally, within six months prior to balloon maturity, the borrower must obtain a refinancing commitment.

The third type of balloon loan provision is the *external tail*. This method is preferred by the major rating agencies since it gives the borrower the most time to arrange refinancing while avoiding default on the bond obligations. The external tail method, as shown in Exhibit 6, sets the maturity date of the CMBS issue longer than that of the underlying loans. The difference between these two dates acts as a buffer to arrange loan refinancing. Further, the CMBS investor does not suffer an interruption in cash flow during this period since the servicer advances any missing interest and scheduled principal (but not the balloon payment).

Evaluating The Timing of Cash flows

Similar to mortgage-backed and asset-backed securities, CMBS structures can experience principal amortization throughout the life of the underlying loans.

Exhibit 6: External Tail Time Line

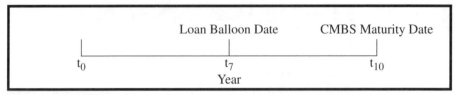

As shown in Exhibit 7, the investor must evaluate CMBS cash flows occurring across the varying principal payment windows. The traditional evaluation uses yield to maturity to evaluate a bond's relative attractiveness. However, yield to maturity assumes each cash flow received over the life of a security can be reinvested at a constant rate. This implies that the yield curve also remains unchanged or flat over time. The "flat" scenario is highly unlikely over extended periods of time. When, for example, the yield curve is steep, the actual total return to maturity should be less than the yield to maturity for amortizing classes.

This is the case because in a steep yield curve environment it is not possible to reinvest at a yield to maturity level without sharply increasing duration. Therefore, a better way to evaluate these securities is to use the bond's *Z-spread*. Z-spread refers to the bond's option-adjusted spread (OAS) at a zero interest rate volatility. Z-spread allows the investor to quantify the cost of the amortization period, and achieve an apples-to-apples comparison between a bullet bond and an amortizing security.

Another key component in evaluating a security's overall attractiveness is the bond's default-adjusted yield. This calculation can only be performed after the necessary time and resources have been committed to building a default model. The recently announced Equitable Real Estate/Hyperion Capital joint venture has built such a model. The key elements to building such a model are as follows:

- 20+ years experience captured with regard to all *actual whole loan experience*

- Database of actual *NOI volatility* by: property type, geographic location, and point in real estate cycle

- Generation of 1,000 interest rate and NOI paths to estimate foreclosure frequency

- Ability to use actual experience as RTC servicer to generate loss severity estimates by: property type and state

- Ability to estimate losses and calculate yield impact on tranches by overlying deal structure

- Ability to calculate standard deviation of defaults and estimate confidence intervals

- Ability to calculate above on a loan-by-loan basis rather than using simplifying assumptions

Exhibit 7: Diagram of Principal Payment Windows

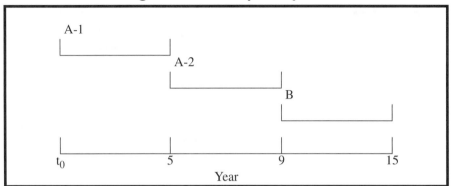

Servicer's Role

The servicer on a CMBS deal can play a key role in the overall success of the transaction. The key responsibilities of the servicer are:

- collect monthly loan payments
- keep records relating to payments
- maintain property escrows (taxes and insurance)
- monitor condition of underlying properties
- prepare reports for trustee
- transfer collected funds to trustee for payment

There are different types of servicers, and their roles can vary from deal to deal. In general, we will discuss three types of servicers: the sub-servicer; the master servicer; and the special servicer. These different servicers are highlighted in Exhibit 8.

The *sub-servicer* is usually the originator of the loan in a conduit deal who has decided to sell the loan but retain the servicing. All payments and property information will then be sent by the sub-servicer to the *master servicer*. The master servicer oversees the deal and makes sure the servicing agreements are maintained. In addition, the master servicer must facilitate the timely payment of interest and principal. That is, when a loan goes into default, the master servicer has the responsibility to provide for servicing advances. This role is critical to the success of a deal; therefore, it is important for an investor to be comfortable with both the financial strength and the overall experience of the master servicer.

A *special servicer* also plays a vital role within a CMBS transaction. The special servicer is usually engaged whenever a loan becomes more than 60 days past due. The special servicer usually has the following powers:

- extend the loan
- make loan modifications
- restructure the loan
- foreclose on the loan and sell the property

Exhibit 8: Types of Servicers

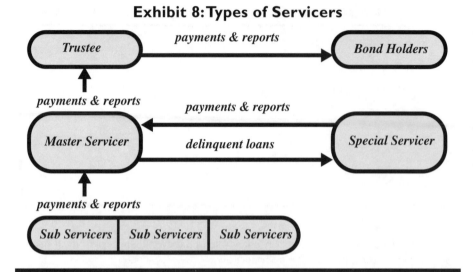

The special servicer is important to subordinated buyers because the timing of the loss can significantly impact the loss severity, which in turn can greatly impact subordinated returns. Therefore, first loss investors usually want to either control the appointment of the special servicer or perform the role themselves.

DIFFERENT TYPES OF CMBS DEALS

Exhibit 9 shows the five types of CMBS deal structures. The first three types — liquidating trusts, multi-property single borrower, and multi-property conduit — will be discussed in detail in this section. These three deal types, which allow investors to focus more attention on structural aspects, have been the focus of most fixed-income money manager's CMBS activity. The latter two deal types — multi-property non-conduit and single-property single borrower — have been the focus of real estate money manager activity within CMBS. The recently announced Equitable Real Estate/Hyperion Capital joint venture will combine the structural skills (Hyperion) necessary to invest in the first three deal types with the real estate skills (Equitable) necessary to invest in the later two deal types.

Liquidating Trusts (Non-Performing CMBS)

A small but interesting segment of the CMBS market is the non-performing or liquidating trusts. This segment, as the name implies, represents CMBS deals backed by non-performing mortgage loans. This market segment contains several structural nuances which must be analyzed when deciding upon the relative attractiveness of a particular bond tranche. Some of the features are discussed below.

Exhibit 9: CMBS Deal Structures

	Liquidating Trusts (Non-Performing)	Multi-Property Single-Borrower	Multi-Property Conduit	Multi Property Non-Conduit	Single-Property Single-Borrower
Sample deals	-RTC N-Series -Lennar -SKW -Kearny Street	-Belaire -Factory Stores	-Nomura -Megadeal -DLJ Conduit	-RTC C-Series -New England	-Danbury Mall -Freehold Mall
Key risks	Structural	Structural/Credit	Structural/Credit	Credit	Credit
Loan age	Seasoned	New	New	Seasoned	New
Available ratings	AA-B	AAA-NR	AAA-NR	AAA-B	AAA-NR

Fast Pay Structure The so-called *fast-pay* structure requires that all cash flows from both asset sales and ongoing debt service, after bond interest payments, be used to retire the most senior bond class outstanding. The fast pay structure prevents the equity holder from receiving any cash flow until all bond classes are retired. Since equity holders are highly sensitive to internal rate of return (i.e., they want to retire the bond classes quickly), the bondholder's interests are aligned with those of the equity holder.

Over Collateralization Liquidating trusts are structured so that the debt obligations (bond classes) are less than the actual receivables outstanding (loan note amount). This creates a level of over collateralization which can be used to offer discounted payoffs in order to accelerate the retirement of the bond classes. As an example, the first non-performing CMBS transaction — RTC 1992-N1 — had the following attributes:

- Estimated market value: $155.3 million (DIV)
- Bond classes issued: $110.0 million
- Original loan balances: $345.8 million
- Equity contribution: $61.8 million

These transactions have proven to work well since structurally the acquisition price or derived investment value (DIV) is often 60% or less of the current balance of the mortgage collateral. In this case the DIV was 45% of the original loan balances ($155.3/$345.8), while the bond classes issued were only 71% of the estimated market value or DIV.

Servicer Flexibility Liquidating trust structures generally allow the servicer maximum flexibility to liquidate the pool's underlying assets. Non-performing loans are generally grouped into three categories: performing, sub-performing, and real estate owned (REO).

As shown in Exhibit 10, the servicer (who is often also the transaction's equity holder) will work to carry out an asset disposition strategy which was designed at the deal's inception. The servicer's ability to dispose of property is paramount to maximizing value for bondholders. To help ensure that bondholder values are maximized, incentives are built in for the servicer.

Exhibit 10: Asset Disposition Strategy by Servicer

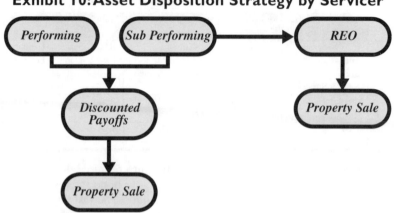

Generally, the servicer can use one of two disposal strategies: discounted pay-offs or take title of a property through foreclosure, then sell the property from REO. The method employed is a function of where the loans are currently situated. That is, if a high percentage of loans are already in REO, the investor will expect a shorter average life and less potential extension risk. Deals with a higher percentage of performing loans are expected to have longer average lives and more extension risk.

Furthermore, performing loans can only be liquidated using the discounted payoff method, as they have the right to continue through the maturity of the loan. The sub-performing loans can be liquidated either by using the discounted payoff method or by initiating foreclosure proceedings. Foreclosure can be a difficult and expensive undertaking, but when it is successful and the title to the property is obtained, the trust can then liquidate the underlying property to retire the mortgage debt.

Reserve Funds Another important structural feature found in liquidating trust trans-actions are reserve funds. Reserve funds are necessary in these transactions since it is difficult to project the timing of asset dispositions and their resulting cash flows. These reserve funds are established at the time of closing and are used to protect bondholders. The two common types of reserve funds are summarized in Exhibit 11.

Usually the asset expenditure reserve can be used to back up the liquidity reserve and make interest payments in the event of interest shortfalls to the invest-ment-grade bonds. However, the asset expenditure reserve is not used to accelerate bond class paydown after the investment-grade bonds are retired.

Required Principal Payments Non-performing CMBS are structured with relatively short average lives that receive cash flows from some loans while others are being dis-posed of. Therefore, the deal will be structured to achieve certain principal pay-down targets. In the event these targets are not achieved, often the fixed rate coupon is scheduled at a preset date (i.e., increased from 10% to 12%). This motivates the bor-rower not to allow extension on the lower rated bond classes.

Exhibit 11: Types of Reserve Funds

	Liquidity	Asset Expenditure
Purpose	Cash flow used to prevent interest short-falls to investment-grade bonds	Cash flow used to pay taxes, legal fees and property maintenance
Used for Acceleration	Yes	No

Single-Borrower/Multi-Property Deals

The second type of CMBS deal which contains important structural considerations is the single-borrower/multi-property transaction. The following are important structural features which are often contained in these deals:

- cross-collateralization and cross-default feature
- property release provisions
- lock-box mechanism
- cash-trap features

Each of these features are discussed below.

Cross Collateralization and Cross-Default Cross-collateralization is a mechanism whereby the properties that collateralize the individual loans are pledged against each loan. Cross-default, on the other hand, allows the lender to call each loan within the pool, when any one defaults. Thus, by tying the properties together, the cash flow is available to meet the collective debt on all the loans. Therefore, from a credit stand-point, an individual loan should not become delinquent as long as there is sufficient excess cash flow available from the pool to cover this shortfall.

Exhibits 12 and 13 show a simplified example of the power of the cross-collateralization cross-default mechanism. In our example, we assume that all properties have the same debt service coverage (DSC) ratio and loan-to-value (LTV) ratio, except for one distressed loan. In Exhibit 12, we calculate the breakeven DSC ratio possible before a default would be likely to occur.

For example, if a single loan pool had a DSC ratio of 1.30x (that is, it can cover debt service by 1.30 times), then the coverage ratio could decline by 23% before a breakeven level is reached. A further decline could lead to a loan default. However, if the same loan was within a pool of five cross-collateralized, cross-defaulted loans it could experience a complete loss of cash flow (100%) and a second loan could also experience a 15% decline in the cash flow before a similar breakeven point is reached. As can be seen from Exhibit 12, the stronger the overall DSC of the pool and the larger the overall pool, the greater the cushion against a single distressed loan. Similarly, Exhibit 13 shows the buffer of protection available on cross-collateralized, cross-defaulted pools by LTV.

As shown in Exhibits 12 and 13, a five loan pool with an initial LTV of 75% could have a single distressed loan decline in value to zero and have a second loan decline in value by 25% before a zero equity position in the pool is reached.

Exhibit 12: Breakeven DSC Ratio

Number of Properties	DSC Ratio (%)				
	1.15 ×	1.25 ×	1.30 ×	1.35 ×	1.50 ×
1	13	20	23	26	33
3	39	60	69	78	100
5	65	100	115	130	167
10	130	200	230	259	333
15	196	300	345	389	500

Exhibit 13: Breakeven LTV Ratio

Number of Properties	LTV Ratio (%)				
	90%	80%	75%	70%	60%
1	10	20	25	30	40
3	30	60	75	90	120
5	50	100	125	150	200
10	100	200	250	300	400
15	150	300	375	450	600

Property Release Provisions Another structural feature often present in single-borrower/multi-property transactions is property release mechanisms. The investor should be concerned about the ability of the lender to prepay or otherwise remove the stronger properties from the pool. Various property release provisions will protect the investor against this risk. These provisions usually take the following form:

- If any properties are sold, the borrower must retire *125% of the initial allocatable mortgage amount*;
- Resulting *DSC ratios cannot be lower than before sale*; and,
- No collateral substitutions are permitted.

These property release provisions are important in order to maintain adequate structural protection in single-borrower transactions. Again, these provisions are to protect the investor from the borrower stripping the pool of its best properties.

Lock-Box Structures Another structural feature often found in single-borrower transactions is the lock-box mechanism. The lock-box mechanism gives the trustee control over the gross revenues of the properties. (See Exhibit 14.)

Just as the cash flow of a CMBS deal flows through a waterfall payment mechanism, the property cash flow in a lock-box structure flow through a waterfall. As shown in Exhibit 14, the owner only has claim to excess cash flow after taxes, insurance, debt service, operating expenses, and property reserves. Likewise, management fees are often subordinate to debt service and operating expenses. The intent of the lock-box structure is not only to insure payment of debt service but also to provide a strong incentive for owners and property managers to operate the properties efficiently since they have a subordinate claim on cash flow.

Exhibit 14: Lock-Box Structure

```
┌──────────────────────┐        ┌──────────────────────────┐
│   Property Revenue    │──────▶│ Collection Account (Trustee)│
└──────────────────────┘        └──────────────────────────┘
                                              │
                                              ▼
                                 ┌──────────────────────────┐
                                 │     Taxes and Insurance     │
                                 └──────────────────────────┘
                                              │
                                              ▼
                                 ┌──────────────────────────┐
                                 │        Debt Service         │
                                 └──────────────────────────┘
                                              │
                                              ▼
                                 ┌──────────────────────────┐
                                 │     Operating Expenses      │
                                 └──────────────────────────┘
                                              │
                                              ▼
                                 ┌──────────────────────────┐
                                 │      Property Reserves      │
                                 └──────────────────────────┘
                                              │
┌──────────────────────┐                      │
│    Property Owner     │◀─────────────────────┘
└──────────────────────┘
```

Cash-Trap Feature Another structural feature sometimes found in single-bor-
rower/multi-property transactions is the "cash-trap." The cash-trap is the CMBS
equivalent of "early amortization" within the asset-backed market. The intent is to
penalize the borrower for something he/she has failed to do by amortizing the
CMBS debt ahead of schedule. In the process, the cash-trap prevents the borrower
from receiving excess cash flow. The most common triggers — which would
cause all of the excess cash flow to be trapped for debt reduction — are:

- Failure to maintain pre-determined DSC ratio
- Failure to maintain required minimum debt ratings
- Failure to maintain adequate property reserves

The cash-trap feature works particularly well with a lock-box structure,
since the trustee can easily "trap" all of the deal's excess cash. Cash-trap features
have not been that common in recent deals (i.e., 1995 vintage) since borrowers
have had more funding options (i.e., traditional lenders have returned and REITs
which issue this type of debt have recently used unsecured debt issuance).

Multi-Borrower/Conduit Deals

Another growing segment of the CMBS is conduit-originated transactions. Conduits are commercial-lending entities that are established for the sole purpose of generating collateral to securitize. Most Wall Street houses have established conduits to originate collateral to be used in CMBS transactions. Some important factors when analyzing conduit deals are: origination standards, number of originators, pool diversification, and degree of loan standardization. Each of these considerations will be further discussed below.

Origination Standards A key consideration in analyzing a conduit CMBS product is understanding how the loans were originated. This analysis must address the following standards:

- Key DSC and LTV ratios
- Cash flow assumptions used in underwriting
- Standards for property reserves
- Method of arriving at appraised values
- Loan terms offered (i.e., amortizing/balloon and call protection terms)
- Geographic and property type diversification
- Timing of loan originations (i.e., month and year of origination)

Analyzing the origination standards are important in understanding how the loans were originated.

Number of Originators Many conduit deals have had more than one originator. This is usually done to speed up the funding period and to accumulate a larger critical mass. Most analysts agree that a minimum issue size of $100 to $125 million is desirable to effectively price a CMBS deal (given the fixed expenses of issuance). However, because multiple lenders may have originated the product, the investor has to get comfortable with the fact that a different lender underwrote the loans in a consistent manner. This can usually only be determined by carefully analyzing the mortgage loan files. It is for this reason that most investors prefer conduit deals originated by a single entity.

Pool Diversification Another important factor to consider in conduit-originated deals is the diversification of the underlying loans. That is, how geographically and numerically diversified are the loans? Most investors like to see loan originations across several states without any major loan concentrations. One recent conduit deal had a single loan which comprised nearly 15% of the pool. A concentration such as this or a group of similar loans could severely impact the default-adjusted yields of the underlying securities.

Furthermore, the rating agencies have recently given lower overall levels of credit-enhancement to deals which contain diversification across property types. The theory being that because one cannot predict which property type will enjoy the best performance going forward, it is better to be adequately diversified.

Degree of Loan Standardization It is important to analyze just how "cookie-cutter" a particular mortgage pool is. The higher the homogeneity, the greater the comfort that investors can look to the deal's structural features. For example, if a deal has a large concentration of 10-year balloon maturities with seven years of prepayment lockout, then the deal will usually appeal to crossover corporate buyers. Moreover, a highly standardized deal will more easily accept tranches such as bond-IOs (interest only strips). However, a deal which enjoys a high degree of standardization with regard to loan terms may not appeal to below investment-grade buyers. This is because the rating agencies have tended only to upgrade deals due to retirement of debt or deleveraging. In the example above, the balloon term usually implies interest only (i.e., no debt amortization), while the long lockout period would prevent voluntary prepayments. Thus, the below investment-grade bonds would not be candidates for upgrade.

SUMMARY

This chapter has focused on the structural considerations impacting MBS investments. We first looked at the basic CMBS structure: paydown priority, structural call protection, balloon maturity provisions, cash flows, and servicers' role. We then discussed the different types of CMBS deals focusing on three types: liquidating trusts, single-borrower/multi-property deals, and multi-borrower/conduit deals.

Chapter 7

The Effects of Prepayment Restrictions on the Bond Structures of CMBS

Manus J. Clancy
Vice President
The Trepp Group

Michael Constantino, III
Associate
The Trepp Group

INTRODUCTION

Since the issuance of the first collateralized mortgage obligation, the challenge of securitizing pools of residential mortgages has been providing greater average life predictability to investors eager to reduce prepayment exposure. In the pursuit of alleviating call risk, bond structures for traditional CMOs have become increasingly complex. Seemingly, with each new issue have come more intricate principal repayment rules and diverse bond types, all aimed at meeting the average life demands of the marketplace and providing greater prepayment certainty. These complexities have been conspicuously absent from the bond structures that have emerged from the securitization of commercial mortgages. The reason is vested in a key difference between residential and commercial mortgages: residential mortgages may be prepaid at any time while commercial mortgages are often written with significant prepayment

139

restrictions. Since commercial loans themselves mitigate prepayment exposure, the need to manage prepayment risk at the security level is greatly reduced. The result has been issues with far fewer tranches and simpler principal paydown rules for commercial mortgage-backed securities as well as bond structures whose primary concern is managing credit risk.

These differences would seem to provide welcome relief to an industry that has spent countless hours modeling complicated payment rules. However, since the prepayment restrictions on commercial mortgages are not perfect deterrents to prepayments, they cannot be overlooked. As a result, the modeling of commercial mortgage-backed securities has certainly proven no easier than analyzing traditional collateralized mortgage obligations backed by residential mortgages. Specifically, two elements of commercial mortgage-backed securities have replaced complicated principal distribution rules in making the analysis process arduous and time consuming. First, due to a lack of standardization in the commercial mortgage market, prepayment restrictions can vary dramatically from loan to loan, making the modeling of collateral cashflows difficult. Second, many prepayment restrictions come in the form of fees that must be remitted to the lender with a mortgage prepayment. The intent of these charges has been to limit or remove the incentive for the borrower to prepay and provide lenders some protection from reinvestment risk. In order to transfer this protection to bondholders, these fees must be passed through. The rules governing the distribution of the fees in commercial mortgage-backed securities have been almost as complicated as those for distributing principal in traditional collateralized mortgage obligations.

This chapter will examine the prepayment restrictions embedded in commercial mortgages and their effect on the bond structures of commercial mortgage-backed securities. First, the differences between bond structures of traditional collateralized mortgage obligations (i.e. those backed by residential mortgages) and commercial mortgage-backed securities will be reviewed. Second, the various types of prepayment restrictions will be described; it will be demonstrated that similar prepayment restrictions can, in fact, be vastly different from loan to loan. Third, a number of different commercial mortgage-backed securities will be examined to show how the distributions of prepayment penalties can differ substantially. Finally, it will be demonstrated that the prepayment penalty distribution method can have a significant effect on the yield of a security.

COMPARING BOND STRUCTURES

Clearly, there are substantial differences between the bond structures that have emerged from issues backed by residential mortgages and those of deals backed by commercial mortgages. For traditional collateralized mortgage obligations in which prepayment or "call" risk has been the dominant concern, the structures have relied heavily on "horizontal" slicing and dicing: carving out different tranche types to meet certain average life demands by the marketplace and providing more prepayment stability. This involves using payment rules to allocate principal in different directions over time. The result has often been 30 or 40 tranche issues with PACs, TACs, VADMs, accrual bonds, and so forth. For agency-backed CMOs, horizontal slicing has been the only structuring tool necessary since there is no credit risk at the bond level. For traditional CMOs backed by whole loans in which both prepayment risk and credit risk are concerns, issuers must combine horizontal tranching to alleviate call risk with "vertical" credit support structuring. This has meant carving out senior tranches, mezzanine tranches, and subordinated tranches to isolate the risks arising from mortgage defaults and delinquencies. Exhibit 1 shows the differences between agency-backed CMOs and whole loan-backed CMOs.

The bond structures of commercial-backed CMOs use vertical slicing almost exclusively. By stipulating prepayment conditions, lenders have greatly altered the nature of call risk associated with commercial mortgage lending. The result has been issues where credit risk has been the principle focus of attention. There is no need for PAC bonds (bonds which return predictable payment streams over a range of prepayment speeds) in commercial mortgage-backed structures or any other tranche types whose goal is to alleviate prepayment risk. Exhibit 2 shows the structure of a typical commercial mortgage-backed security.

Exhibit 1: Principal Distribution for Agency and Whole-Loan CMOs
Agency CMO

A-1 PAC	A-2 PAC	A-3 PAC	A-4 PAC	A-5 Companion	A-7 Companion	A-1	A-2	A-3	A-4
				A-6 Companion					

Whole-loan CMO

A-1 PAC	A-2 PAC	A-3 PAC	A-4 PAC	A-5 Companion	A-7 Companion	A-1	A-2	A-3	A-4
				A-6 Companion					

Subordinated Class B-1

Subordinated Class B-2

Subordinated Class B-3

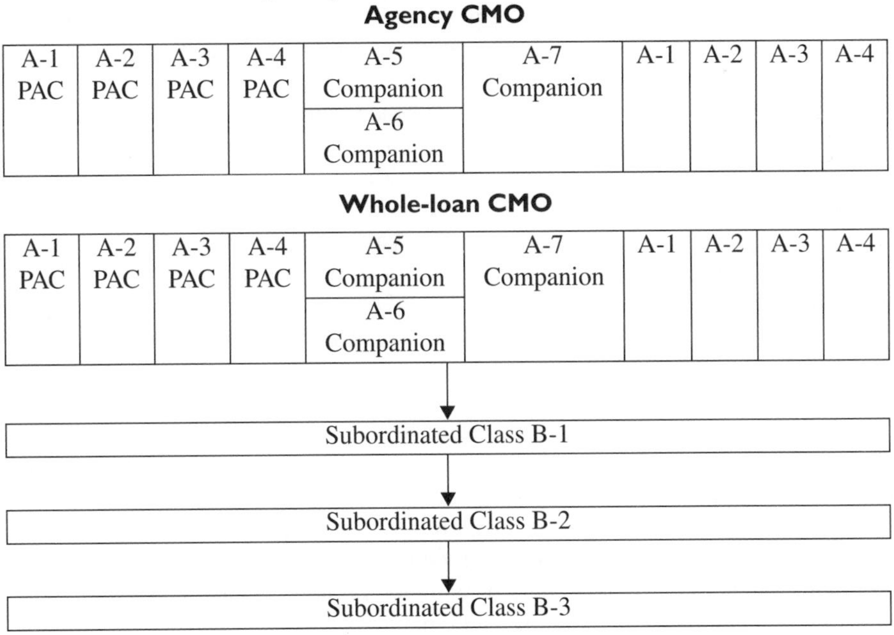

Exhibit 2: Principal Distribution
for Commercial Mortgage-Backed Securities

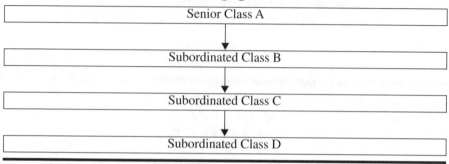

PREPAYMENT RESTRICTIONS

There are a number of different types of prepayment restrictions that are written into loan documents. Those clauses that prevent prepayments altogether are called *prepayment lockouts*. Penalties that cause borrowers to pay a fixed percentage in addition to the prepayment itself are generally known as *prepayment premiums*, while fees that are intended to reimburse the lender for income forgone as a result of a prepayment are referred to as *yield maintenance charges*. Within a particular issue, loans can be found containing each type of prepayment restriction. Further complicating matters, the three types of restrictions may all be applied to a single mortgage. If that is not enough, the methods for calculating prepayment premiums and yield maintenance charges can vary from one mortgage to another.

Prepayment lockouts are very straightforward. The borrower is prohibited from prepaying the loan voluntarily until a certain date. The length of a prepayment lockout can differ greatly from loan to loan.

Prepayment premiums require the borrower to pay a certain percent of the prepayment in addition to the prepayment itself. For instance, the lender may require a 5% charge to accompany any prepayment. A prepayment premium may be used in conjunction with a prepayment lockout: the loan may, for example, prohibit prepayments in the first five years and require a 5% premium on any prepayment thereafter. The penalty percentage may also diminish over time. The loan may prohibit prepayments during the first five years, require a 5% penalty in year six, a 4% penalty in year seven, and so on.

A yield maintenance charge is intended to insure that in the event a borrower voluntarily prepays, the lender will not be adversely affected. The sum of the prepayment and yield maintenance charge reinvested to the maturity date of the original security should return roughly the same flows to the lender as the original security. Unfortunately, due to the lack of standardization in the commercial mortgage market, underwriters of commercial loans have created a plethora of different methods for calculating yield maintenance charges.

The calculation of the yield maintenance charge typically works as follows. The present value of the future flows that would have occurred had the prepayment not taken place is calculated. The discount rate to present value the flows is usually the yield on a Treasury or Treasury index with the same maturity as the loan being prepaid. The amount of the prepayment is subtracted from the present value to give the yield maintenance charge. From the lender's point of view, the series of flows should be roughly identical. The lender can invest the prepayment and yield maintenance charge at a yield on a Treasury of similar maturity and collect the same flows that would have been collected had the prepayment not taken place. This type of yield maintenance calculation is a "discounted" charge.

There are many variations to this type of particular yield maintenance calculation. Some issues, for example, call for a spread to be added to the Treasury yield when calculating the present value. This has the effect of reducing the yield maintenance charge. Other calculations call for the discount rate to be the yield on a Treasury with a maturity comparable to the remaining average life, rather than the maturity, of the loan being prepaid. There are many different types of discounted yield maintenance charges and, as a result, careful consideration must be given to modeling these fees.

In addition to discounted yield maintenance charges, issues will, from time to time, call for calculations that are not the result of present values. For these types of penalties, the charge is the difference between interest flows that would have been realized assuming no prepayment and interest flows assuming the same amortization of principal but with interest calculated at a rate equal to the yield (plus a spread, perhaps) on a Treasury with a maturity similar to that of the loan being prepaid.

Yield maintenance charges are more effective prepayment deterrents than prepayment premiums. Interest rates and yield maintenance charges are inversely proportional: as rates fall, the charges increase. Borrowers may have little or no incentive to refinance. (In certain real estate environments borrowers may still prepay loans with yield maintenance premiums in order to take more cash from the property.) Conversely, with prepayment premiums, if interest rates drop by more than a certain amount the borrower may look to refinance. The amount rates have to drop is a function of the maturity of the loan being prepaid, the costs of refinancing, and the "cash out" potential.

All three prepayment restrictions can be used together on a single loan. For example, a loan may have a lockout period followed by a period where the charge is the greater of a fixed percentage or a calculated yield maintenance charge. Lastly, certain loans permit prepayments "in whole or in part" while others permit prepayments only in full. For those loans that allow full or partial prepayments, the type of the prepayment may determine the calculation method of the prepayment penalty.

The loans collateralizing a commercial mortgage-backed security are rarely homogeneous when it comes to prepayment restrictions. Merrill Lynch Mortgage Investors, Inc. Mortgage Pass-Through Certificates Series 1995-C2 illustrates this point. The issue was collateralized by 367 loans backed by a combination of retail properties, multifamily properties, warehouse/industrial properties, commercial properties, medical office properties, and hospitality properties. Of the 367 loans, 267 require some sort of prepayment penalty (13 of which have lockout periods prior to the period during which the mortgage may be prepaid with a prepayment penalty), while the remainder allow for prepayments "without material restriction." Of the 254 loans with prepayment penalties alone, there exists significant differentiation between the type of fee: 170 loans have yield maintenance charges, 49 have a prepayment premium which declines over time, and 35 have prepayment premiums that are fixed at either 1% or 2%. Further complicating matters, of those loans with yield maintenance charges, 59 use a discounted method while 111 use a non-discounted method. Exhibit 3 illustrates the breakdown of these prepayment restrictions.

Due to the fact that over 25% of the loans may prepay voluntarily without restriction, one must make a prepayment assumption for those particular loans. In a falling rate (and/or favorable real estate) environment, these mortgages without prepayment prohibitions will likely prepay, leaving the issue with a portfolio of loans increasingly unlikely to prepay. This can cause the bonds to become more call protected over time and expected average lives may actually increase as the deal seasons. In this particular issue, given the high number of loans with fixed prepayment penalties, this phenomenon may be offset by the number of loans that become "in the money" as rates fall. (In a falling interest rate environment, the issue may also experience "credit drift." If the loans that are prepaying are predominantly those of the highest credit quality, the issue may see its aggregate LTV and its aggregate debt service coverage ratio fall. This can have significant effects on the performance of the securities.)

By contrast, Kidder, Peabody Acceptance Corporation I Commercial Mortgage Pass-Through Certificates, Series 1993-C1 is completely homogeneous when it comes to mortgage prepayment restrictions. In this issue, no voluntary prepayments can take place before August 1998 for all loans. Beyond that date yield maintenance charges apply.

Exhibit 3: Breakdown of Prepayment Restrictions for Merrill Lynch, 1995-C2

No restriction	100 loans
Lockouts followed by Penalties	13 loans
Declining Prepayment Premiums	49 loans
Fixed Prepayment Premiums	35 loans
Discounted Yield Maintenance Premium	59 loans
Non-discounted Yield Maintenance Premium	111 loans
Total	367 loans

The argument put forth earlier in this chapter stated that one of the elements making the analysis of commercial mortgage-backed securities so difficult is the fact that there are so many variations of prepayment restrictions. Thus far, the focus of this chapter has been pointing out the different types of prepayment restrictions. The next step will be to demonstrate why the existence of such differences makes the modeling process so tricky. To do this, the steps that must be taken to produce a simple cash flow will be described.

For simplicity purposes, the assumption will be that the goal is to produce a cash flow for a commercial mortgage-backed security given a static interest rate environment. First, the collateral cash flow generation model must be written so that mortgages are categorized according to prepayment condition. This is necessary since the prepayment assumption is so closely tied to the prepayment restrictions embedded in the loan. The model must be able to re-categorize loans in each period of the analysis since loans may switch over time from having one type of prepayment restriction to another.

Next, the model must be able to generate each of the different prepayment penalties. From an execution point of view, this can be accomplished in one of two ways. One option is to define a set of variables for each loan and have those values feed a routine in the model that produces the prepayment penalty. Just as interest rate, balance, and remaining term are used to calculate scheduled principal and interest, new variables are required to project prepayment penalties. The number of variables that must be established is not insignificant. Some of the data that must be provided include prepayment lockout date; a vector of prepayment premiums and dates corresponding to that vector; yield maintenance charge method; the index or Treasury to use when calculating the yield maintenance charge; first and last date to calculate yield maintenance; and whether yield maintenance charges are added to or applied instead of (given certain conditions) prepayment premiums. The list could go on and on. If a model is set up in this manner, one problem exists. The routines themselves cannot reflect all the subtleties of the various methods of calculating prepayment penalties without allowing for an extraordinary number of variables. Therefore, individuals modeling commercial mortgage-backed securities for the purpose of purchase must choose between providing heaps of data while writing a sophisticated prepayment penalty calculator and providing less data while ignoring some of the more complicated elements of prepayment penalties. The second option is to establish a more flexible model in which a separate prepayment "rule" must be written for each loan. While a model set up in this manner allows for the analysis of every nuance related to the calculation of a prepayment penalty, the process of writing a rule for each mortgage can be mind numbing.

After the model has been set up to segregate mortgages and calculate prepayment penalties, the assumptions for generating the collateral cash flows can be provided. This, too, requires that the model be flexible. It must be able to handle different prepayment assumptions for those mortgages that have no prepayment restrictions, those that call for prepayment premiums, and those that have yield maintenance charges.

Pulling all of this together, a complete CMBS model must be able to:

- Determine whether the loan has any prepayment restriction.
- Generate a prepayment assumption for those mortgages without prepayment restrictions (unfortunately, unlike with residential loans, a different assumption will likely have to be made for each mortgage).
- Determine whether those mortgages with prepayment premiums are "in the money."
- Select a prepayment assumption for those mortgages with prepayment premiums that are in the money.
- Calculate the prepayment premiums (and for reasons that will become clear later, segregate those premiums from yield maintenance charges).
- Determine whether the yield maintenance charges are "perfect" or "imperfect" prepayment deterrents (imperfect charges being ones that may not completely deter the mortgagor from prepaying).
- Choose a prepayment assumption for those loans with yield maintenance charges but which may still prepay.
- Calculate the yield maintenance charges.

The focus of the analysis can then, thankfully, turn to providing default assumptions and modeling bond payment rules. Reviewing all this, there can be little doubt that prepayment restrictions add considerable complexity to the modeling process.

DISTRIBUTIONS OF PREPAYMENT CHARGES

The second part of the original argument stated that the process of modeling commercial mortgage-backed securities is further complicated by the intricacies of the rules governing the distribution of prepayment penalties. Specifically, there are three structuring techniques employed that add layers of difficulty to analyzing commercial issues. First, any prepayment penalties, though collected with monthly payments, are often distributed separately and independently from mortgage principal and interest receipts. This means two or more sets of payment rules must be written for each issue. Because issues are structured this way, these penalties may not be available to provide additional protection against losses associated with delinquent or defaulted mortgage loans. Second, there is seemingly no end to the number of ways underwriters can distribute the penalties. Underwriters have utilized these monies as an additional way to segment flows and the rules for their distribution can differ from those attributable to principal and interest. Third, although prepayment premiums and yield maintenance charges both constitute an additional fee paid by the borrower, some issues distribute the two separately while others combine the fees. This means writing three sets of payment rules rather than two. (Whether these fees are always collectible is subject to debate, but that is an entirely different discussion altogether).

A frequent characteristic of commercial mortgage-backed securities is that prepayment penalties are often distributed separately from mortgage principal and interest. There are two elements that make future cash flows of mortgages unpredictable. One is the ability of the borrower to make debt service payments (credit risk) and the other is the likelihood that the borrower will prepay (call risk). To distinguish between the two, most issues collect the *available distribution amount* — defined as scheduled principal, prepayments, interest, servicer advances, recoveries, etc. — and prepayment penalties, separately. The available distribution amount is allocated according to a set of priorities; those tranches that receive principal and interest first are shielded from the adverse effects resulting from shortfalls in available cash. Independently, the prepayment penalties are collected and distributed according to their own set of priorities; the securities that have first stake to the prepayment penalties are shielded from the reinvestment risk associated with early retirement of principal.

Because an issue is collateralized by many mortgages, both types of risk may occur simultaneously: one loan may be defaulting while another is prepaying with a premium (incidentally, loans that default may also be contractually liable to pay a prepayment penalty when foreclosed upon). Since the available distribution amount is segregated from prepayment penalties, the losses arising from one mortgage are not reduced by the presence of a prepayment penalty on another. Asset Securitization Corporation Commercial Mortgage Pass-Through Certificates, Series 1995-MD IV illustrates this point. It has a specific distribution for "Available Funds" which specifically excludes prepayment premiums. Separately, the issue distributes prepayment premiums.

Prepayment penalties, aside from being segregated from the available funds, are segmented by a set of payment rules that may be different from the distribution of the available distribution amount. Similar to the allocation of the principal distribution amount, prepayment premiums and yield maintenance charges are allocated to designated tranches. The order of this distribution does not by any means have to mirror the allocation of available funds. In fact, as the traditional CMO market has illustrated, there are no limits to the combinations that may be used to segregate funds.

For example, FannieMae 1994-M4 aggregates prepayment premiums and yield maintenance charges and distributes them according to the following payment priority. Fifty percent of all prepayment penalties collected are distributed sequentially to Classes A, B, C, and D. The remaining 50% is distributed simultaneously to the interest only or N Class. An issue may have prepayment penalties on 100% of the mortgages, yet the holder of a tranche may receive no benefit from the penalties. In effect, there exists a prepayment deterrent, but reinvestment risk still exists. This particular example demonstrates the importance of examining the prospectus language closely. A quick peek at the documents reveals prepayment penalties on the loans, and one might assume some protection against prepayments and reinvestment risk. However, closer inspection indicates that while the loans may have prepayment penalties not all tranches may get reimbursed for any reinvestment risk. Due to their position on the distribution pecking order, the B, C, and D tranches may get little or no compensation for their share of the call risk (although those tranches may benefit if purchased at a discount). Exhibit 4 illustrates how prepayment penalties are distributed for FannieMae 1994-M4.

Exhibit 4: Distribution of Prepayment Penalties
for Fannie Mae 1994-M4

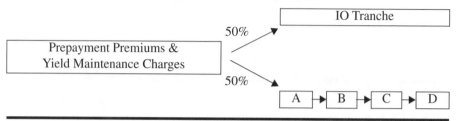

In Nomura 1994-C3, prepayment premiums and yield maintenance charges are similarly aggregated. However, the penalties are distributed in an entirely different manner. In this issue, the structure has attempted to capture the essence of the yield maintenance charge that exists at the loan level and recreate it at the bond level. Specifically, all penalties collected are distributed to certificate holders sequentially, in order of seniority. However, instead of giving all of the fees to the most senior tranche until that tranche is retired (which some issues do), the distribution assigned to the senior tranche and all subsequent tranches is capped. The cap is essentially a security level yield maintenance charge. The calculation of the cap takes the total cash flows anticipated to be received absent the prepayment and discounts them at a rate equal to a coupon on the bond in question plus a spread. From that amount is subtracted the amount of the prepayment that goes to the class for which the cap is being calculated. From that total is subtracted the present value of the total cash flows that are anticipated to be received after the prepayment, discounting at a rate equal to a Treasury yield plus a spread. With this form of calculation, a limit is placed on the amount a tranche may be compensated for reinvestment risk. By comparing FannieMae 1994-M4 to Nomura 1994-C3, one can easily see how diverse these distribution patterns can be and how difficult some may be to calculate when projecting cash flows or performing price/yield analyses.

FannieMae 1994-M3 adds yet another wrinkle to the modeling process. This issue distributes prepayment premiums and yield maintenance charges separately according to different allocation rules. (It was mentioned earlier that it is important that any model aggregate prepayment premiums separately from yield maintenance charges — this is why.) Fifty percent of all prepayment premiums collected are distributed to the A and B Classes in the same ratio that prepaid principal is distributed to such classes and the remaining 50% is distributed to the Interest Only Class. Yield maintenance charges, conversely, are allocated to the A and B classes in an amount equal to the product of a fraction and the yield maintenance charge collected and the remainder goes to the IO class. The numerator of the fraction is the rate on the A and B certificates less the discount rate used in the calculations of the yield maintenance charge. The denominator is the mortgage interest rate of the loan being prepaid less the discount rate. If the discount rate is greater than the rate of the A and B certificates, the yield maintenance charge is allocated to the interest only certificates.

Exhibit 5: Relationship Between Yield and Distribution
of Prepayment Penalties

Sequential Tranche A		Yield assuming penalty allocation		
Purchase Price	Average Life @ 10 CPR	0%	50%	100%
95	10.25	9.36	9.47	9.57
100	10.25	8.56	8.67	8.77
105	10.25	7.82	7.92	8.02

WAC IO Tranche		Yield assuming penalty allocation		
Purchase Price	Average Life @ 10 CPR	0%	50%	100%
6	11.44	8.76	10.32	11.65
7	11.44	5.67	7.31	8.70
8	11.44	3.19	4.90	6.34

The previous examples demonstrate some of the complex calculations that must be performed in order to effectively generate cash flows for commercial mortgage-backed securities.

YIELD CONSIDERATIONS

The distribution of prepayment penalties within an issue can have a significant effect on the yield of a particular tranche. To illustrate this point, a hypothetical commercial mortgage-backed security was constructed. The issue was modeled assuming four classes of bonds. Classes A, B, and C represented standard senior and subordinated tranches. The fourth tranche was an IO whose notional balance was the sum of the balances of Classes A and B. Interest on the IO was calculated as the spread between the weighted average rate on the collateral and the coupons on Classes A and B. The collateral for this hypothetical issue consisted of a single balloon loan with a maturity of 15 years and an amortization term of 30 years. In generating the cash flows it was assumed that a prepayment lockout existed for the first eight years. Thereafter, prepayments could take place with the payment of a premium equal to 6% in year nine stepping down to 1.5%.

Price/yield calculations were done assuming prepayments would take place at 10% CPR. The A and IO Classes were isolated to see the effect on yield of paying 0, 50, or 100 percent of the prepayment premiums to the tranche. The results are shown in Exhibit 5. Not surprisingly, the yield on a class increases significantly when the class is given all or part of the prepayment penalty.

CONCLUSION

For those who may have thought the evolution of the mortgage-backed securities industry toward the securitization of commercial mortgages meant less complicated bond structures and less time staring at the computer monitor, easier days are not forthcoming. The combination of having to calculate prepayment penalties and learning how to distribute these penalties has proven to be a difficult task (not to mention the issues surrounding credit risk). Furthermore, those who believe quick and dirty analyses would be sufficient for the analysis of these instruments must think again. The failure to model commercial mortgage-backed securities correctly can cause the projected return of the security to differ significantly from the actual return.

Chapter 8

An Investor's Perspective on Commercial Mortgage-Backed Coupon Strips

Keith A. Gollenberg, CFA
Vice President
CIGNA Investment Management

INTRODUCTION

Although most investors despise coupon strips, or interest only strips (IOs) as they are commonly called, I would venture to say almost all investors have in the past bought an IO — anybody bought a premium bond lately? A premium bond is a par bond plus an IO. For example, if an underlying mortgage loan pool has an 11% weighted average coupon, or WAC (after all trustee, servicing and other fees), and par bonds can sell at a 9% yield, then there is 2% of additional interest. In this example the issuer has three options:

- issue a par priced bond with a coupon of 9%, and choose to retain the excess interest of 2%,
- issue a premium priced bond with a coupon of 11%, or
- issue a par priced bond with a coupon of 9%, and issue an IO bond with a coupon of 2%.

Since premium bonds are comprised of a par bond plus an IO, investors must therefore understand how to price an IO.

I view buying IOs like financial bungee jumping — if you do not know what you are doing, you can get badly hurt. But if you take the time to learn and understand the nuances, you can obtain an excellent return. My objective in this chapter is to help demystify IOs by explaining the factors which affect the returns of an IO, and the framework that can be used to price an IO.

PRICING AN IO

The price and return of a commercial mortgage-backed security IO are primarily affected by three options that are embedded in every commercial mortgage-backed security (CMBS):

- the borrower's prepayment option (or call option),
- the borrower's default option (or put option), and
- the servicer's restructuring option.

Higher option values mean lower IO returns.

As we examine these three options, it will become clear that the value of each option depends upon four factors:

- the terms and call protection of the individual loans in the pool,
- the financial margins and underwriting standards of the individual loans in the pool,
- the overall structure of the CMBS, and
- the structure of the IO certificate.

PREPAYMENT (CALL) OPTION PRICING

Residential IO Versus a CMBS IO

The prepayment option value is highest when the borrower can prepay at par, and lowest when the borrower cannot prepay at all. This means that a residential IO has a high prepayment option cost since residential borrowers can prepay their loans at par, at any time. Since residential borrowers prepay when rates go down, a residential IOs performance is directly linked to interest rate movements. Therein lies the dilemma for a residential IO — anybody willing to make bets on movements and volatility of interest rates?

Unlike a residential IO, a CMBS IO is generally less sensitive to interest rate movements, and therefore has a lower prepayment option cost. This is because the underlying mortgage loans usually have some sort of call protection for all, or a significant portion, of the loan term. There are typically three types of call protection that are used on the underlying commercial loans:

• lockouts,
• fixed-percentage prepayment fees, and
• yield-maintenance prepayment fees.

One or a combination of all three can be used to protect a loan from prepayment. Each type of call protection is calculated differently, which means that each one provides a different type of call protection to the IO.

Bullet Proof Versus Partial Protection

The strongest call protection to the IO holder is a lockout for the entire term of the loans, because in this case the IO holder is assured its cash flow no matter which way interest rates happen to move. On the contrary, yield maintenance provides great call protection in a static or downward rate environment, but yield maintenance provides no protection against prepayments in an upward rate environment.

For example, let's assume the following:

• an investor buys an IO on day one for $100,
• the underlying loan pool consists of one loan that can be prepaid at any time for a yield-maintenance prepayment fee, calculated using a discount factor of Treasury plus 50 basis points.
• interest rates move up 300 basis points on day two, and
• the borrower chooses to prepay on day two.[1]

In this example, since interest rates went up 300 basis points the yield-maintenance fee is zero. And since the loan has been prepaid, the IO is eliminated. Because the coupon strip never receives any principal payments, this means the coupon strip investor lost 100% of his investment on day two! The ironic part is that the holder of the par bond who receives principal is happy in this prepayment scenario, because although he does not get any prepayment fee either, he gets his principal back at par and can reinvest it at the higher market interest rates.

For the IO holder, a fixed percentage prepayment fee is a little less intuitive to understand, because it can be better or worse than a yield-maintenance fee depending upon a combination of factors, such as how high the fixed percentage prepayment fee is, at what point it can be exercised in the loan term, and which way Treasury rates move. Suffice it to say that a fixed fee generally affords better protection than a yield-maintenance fee in rising rate environments, but generally less protection in falling rate environments. This is because the IO holder receives the same fixed-percentage fee regardless of interest rate movements, versus a yield-maintenance fee that decreases to zero in rising rate environments.

Mythology

There is a myth that commercial borrowers do not prepay loans in a rising rate environment, because it is economically illogical to prepay an 8% loan in a 10% rate envi-

---

[1] The reason why a borrower might prepay their loan even when rates have increased 300 basis points is explained later.

ronment. Although this is an argument that is absolutely true for residential (homeowner) borrowers who generally only refinance for a lower rate or to buy a new home, it is a statement that is not true for commercial borrowers. This is because commercial borrowers sell or refinance their properties regardless of interest rate movements if they think they can realize some cash in order to finance their next deal.

The next deal earns commercial real estate owners development fees, ongoing management fees, and helps reduce their overhead costs per unit. For example, suppose a developer needs $2 million of equity to build a $10 million apartment project. This new project will generate an up-front development fee of at least 5 points or $500,000, and an annual management fee of 5% of gross income, which might be around $90,000 per year. In addition most of the overhead labor associated with the property will be covered by the project.

Now, the developer can raise the required $2 million from four potential sources. One source is the developer's bank account. This is rarely done. The second is equity dollars raised from third parties, but tapping this source is time-consuming and expensive. The third source is the developer's patient saving of excess cash flow from another property. For example, let's say another property the developer owns is realizing $600,000 of cash flow after debt service. In this case it would take 3.5 years for the developer to save $2 million. The fourth source, which is by far the most efficient and cheapest source, is from refinancing an existing property. For instance, let's say the property described just above has $200,000 of additional cash flow after debt service that is above the existing lender's pro-forma. This means the property has either appreciated or the borrower did not maximize his original financing. Either way, if the loan only has a yield-maintenance fee, and Treasury rates have increased enough, the developer can prepay the loan at par, refinance the property, and realize the necessary $2 million of loan dollars ($200,000/an 8% cap rate × an 80% loan to value limit), less transaction costs of perhaps $100,000. Since the loan on the existing property was prepaid at par, the IO was crushed.

This discussion highlights the fact that prepayments on commercial mortgages are not exclusively driven by interest rate movements.

Who Feeds First?

Another important factor in valuing an IO's prepayment option is how the prepayment fees are allocated to the various classes of certificates within the CMBS bond structure. In some CMBS structures, all of the prepayment fees first go to the IO holder until its original cash flows have been made whole on a present-value basis. Obviously, if the IO does not receive the first allocation of prepayment fees within the CMBS's waterfall, the IO may not be made whole, and its yield could suffer significantly.

Start The Modeling

As demonstrated above, there are many factors to consider when valuing an IO's prepayment (call) option. Exhibit 1 shows an analytic framework that puts all these factors into motion, and demonstrates how each of these factors affect the returns for two different IOs. These are actual IOs that are in the market, they are both from large conduit transactions with mixed collateral, and have similar average lives. They both have call protection on their underlying loans, but as Exhibit 1 demonstrates, the type of call protection differs dramatically.

Exhibit 1 shows the bond-equivalent yield I calculated for each IO under different Treasury curve shifts, and under different prepayment scenarios. Scenarios 1 and 2 are the most onerous scenarios. Scenario 1 assumes that 100% of the loans prepay at the end of their lockout periods, and pay their applicable prepayment fees. Scenario 2 assumes that 100% of the loans prepay in full at their earliest par call dates.

As the results in Exhibit I demonstrate, each IO differs radically in performance under different scenarios with different Treasury curve shifts. This is because the individual loans in the IO A pool have very short lockout periods, with yield maintenance for most of their terms, whereas the individual loans in the IO B pool are lockedout for most of their terms. Which scenario is right? There is no single right answer, but these matrices provide an analytic framework in which to evaluate the prepayment option cost for each IO.

I am not going to reveal what I calculated the prepayment (call) option cost to be for each IO, but suffice it to say it should be obvious that IO A has a much higher option cost because of its extremely volatile return characteristics. Investors must assign their own probability ratios for each scenario based upon their view of three items:

- Treasury curve shifts,
- the volatility of Treasury curve shifts, and
- the likelihood of borrowers prepaying under the different scenarios given the Treasury curve shifts (this is, by far, the most important assumption).

Exhibit 1: Prepayment (Call) Option Analysis

Treasury Curve Shift	Bond-Equivalent Yield Percentages							
	Scenario 1		Scenario 2		Scenario 3		Scenario 4	
	A	B	A	B	A	B	A	B
-300	51.8%	8.7%	0.1%	8.7%	30.7%	8.6%	5.7%	8.6%
-200	42.7%	8.7%	0.1%	8.6%	26.0%	8.6%	5.7%	8.6%
-100	34.6%	8.6%	0.1%	8.6%	21.3%	8.6%	5.7%	8.5%
0	26.0%	8.6%	0.1%	8.6%	16.5%	8.6%	5.7%	8.5%
+100	16.8%	8.3%	0.1%	8.3%	11.6%	8.4%	5.7%	8.5%
+200	6.7%	8.3%	0.1%	8.3%	6.5%	8.4%	5.7%	8.5%
+300	(1.9%)	8.3%	0.1%	8.3%	3.2%	8.4%	5.7%	8.5%
+400	(4.6%)	8.3%	0.1%	8.3%	2.3%	8.4%	5.7%	8.5%

1 = 100% of the loans prepay immediately after the lockout period ends.
2 = 100% of the loans prepay immediately at their first par call date.
3 = 50% of the loans prepay immediately after the lockout period ends, and 50% go to the full term.
4 = 50% of the loans prepay immediately at their first par call date, and 50% go to the full term.

DEFAULT (PUT) OPTION PRICING

When a commercial mortgage borrower defaults, the servicer has two alternatives: to foreclose and liquidate, or to restructure the loan. This section deals with the foreclosure and liquidation alternative, while the next section deals with the restructuring alternative.

A default that results in the foreclosure and liquidation of the property has the same effect on the IO as a prepayment without the prepayment fee. For instance, if 100% of the loans in a pool defaulted on day one, and all the loans were liquidated on day two, the IO would lose 100% of its investment. This is because liquidated loans do not receive any prepayment fees, and because the IO does not receive any principal upon liquidation. Conversely, the principal-based bonds would only lose the amount that was lost on the liquidation of the properties since they receive 100% of the principal.

How much of an IO's return is affected by defaults depends upon five factors:

• how many loans in the pool are in default,
• when the defaults occur,
• how long it takes to liquidate the properties,
• whether or not the servicer advances through liquidation, and
• how the IO certificate is structured.

The best way to understand how some of these factors affect an IO's returns is to compare the default option cost for two different IOs under a number of scenarios.

More Modeling

Exhibit 2 shows the default option cost I calculated for the two different IOs, assuming different default rates that occur at various points in time. The results for IO A in Exhibit 2 clearly illustrate the fact that the lower the default rate and the later a default occurs, the better the IO performs.

This means that the underwriter must determine how many borrowers will default and at what time. This requires an understanding of the loans in the pool, a knowledge of the historical default rates for that type of loan, and, most importantly, an opinion about how the loans will perform given their underwriting and financial margins.

IO Structure: Which Certificates are Stripped?

An IO can be structured by stripping the coupon from one, or from all, of the tranches in a CMBS issue. Knowing which tranches are stripped is very important, as the results in Exhibit 2 highlight.

For instance, under the 10% default scenario in Exhibit 2, IO A is significantly impacted while IO B is not impacted at all. This is because of the different structures of the two IOs. The IO A certificate is structured so that its cash flows are stripped off the entire CMBS issue, from the AAA down to the unrated tranches; thus even one default erodes its return. On the other hand, IO B is stripped off the notional balances of the certificates from the AA rated tranche down to the BB tranche, with a AAA tranche above the AA, and a B and non-rated class below that provide credit support to the BB. This means that up to 10% of the pool can default and IO B is not affected. This is because, upon liquidation, all the losses are absorbed first by the non-rated and B classes, and the recovered amounts upon liquidation pay down the AAA rated class first. Therefore, since IO B's cash flows are derived from the notional balances from the AA through BB tranches, its return is not affected in the 10% default scenario. Fascinating, IO B's structure is worth more than IO A's.

IO Structure: WAC Strip Versus Fixed Strip

For any IO, another important structural feature to consider is whether it is a WAC strip or a fixed strip. The importance of this structural feature is highlighted in Exhibit 2 under the 15% and 20% scenarios for IO B. The IO B's 15% scenario default option cost is higher than its 20% default option cost. How can a higher default rate be better than a lower default rate? Well, a higher default rate is never better, rather it is a matter of which loans in the pool default.

For example, assume a loan pool consists of the following:

Loan Pool

Assumptions	Principal Balance	Coupon
Loan #1	$50 million	12%
Loan #2	$50 million	8%
Total	$100 million	10%

Exhibit 2: Default (Put) Option Analysis

Default Starts in Month	One-Time Permanent Default Rates Default Option Cost for Each Scenario (Basis Points)							
	10%		15%		20%		25%	
	A	B	A	B	A	B	A	B
1	328	0	503	196	690	163	888	487
13	271	0	418	179	576	132	745	422
25	220	0	339	161	467	103	604	357
37	173	0	266	143	366	77	471	322
49	132	0	201	126	275	55	352	234
61	96	0	145	111	197	35	250	178

Notes: No prepayment fees are collected on defaulted loans. Foreclosure and liquidation take 12 months after default. Service advances through liquidation. No extensions. No restructures. Recovery rates upon liquidation are 100%.

Further assume there are two classes of certificates as follows:

Certificate Assumptions	Principal Balance	Coupon
Class 1	$100 million	9%
Class IO	$0	1%
Total	$100 million	10%

Also assume Loan #1 with the 12% coupon defaults. This means the new WAC would be 8%, not 10%. If the IO is structured as a weighted average coupon strip (WAC strip), the 9% Class 1 certificates would receive 8% on the $50 million, and the IO would receive nothing. On the other hand, if the IO certificate is structured as a fixed coupon strip (fixed strip), the IO would first be due 1% on the remaining $50 million, and the 9% coupon certificates would only receive 7% (8% − 1%). Likewise, an IO that has a loan pool with all the same coupons would have the same result as a fixed strip, because it would not matter which one defaulted since the coupon would always remain at 10%.

So, back to Exhibit 2. Since IO B is not a fixed strip but is a WAC strip, it is important to model the high coupon loans defaulting (the 15% scenarios) versus the average coupon loans (the 20% scenarios) in order to see how much the pool's coupon dispersion impacts its returns. Obviously this pool has a large coupon dispersion since 15% of the highest coupon loans defaulting hurts more than 20% of the average coupon loans defaulting.

IO Structure: How Much Is Stripped?

Another important structural feature to analyze is how much IO is stripped off of each class of certificate. The reason why this is important is best explained with an example. Assume the following pool and certificate assumptions:

Loan Pool Assumptions	Principal Balance	Weighted Average Coupon (WAC)
Total	$100mm	10%

Certificate Assumptions	Principal Balance	Class 1&2 Coupon	−	Pool WAC	=	Class IO Coupon
Class 1, AAA	$75mm	8.0%		10%		2.0%
Class 2, AA	$25mm	8.5%		10%		1.5%
Class IO	$0mm					
Total	$100mm	8.125%		10%		1.875%

In this example the AAA bond contributes 2% of coupon to the IO, and the AA contributes 1.5% of coupon to the IO, for a total weighted average IO coupon of 1.875% on the $100 million of certificates. Let us then assume $10 million of the loans in the pool default and are liquidated. Surprisingly, upon liquidation the higher the recovery rate, the lower the return to the IO. Perverse isn't it? This is because, upon liquidation, the recovered principal first pays down the senior classes of certificates, the AAAs, and it is the AAAs that are contributing the most to the IO. If the recovery rate is 100%, the AAA certificates are paid down $10 million, and the IO now receives 2% on only $65 million (versus the original $75 million), and 1.5% on the full $25 million. On the other hand, if the recovery rate is 0%, the IO continues to receive 2% on the full $75 million, and 1.5% on only $15 million (versus the original $25 million), because the AA certificates receive the first loss of $10 million. Therefore, in order to be conservative, the analyst should always run scenarios assuming a 100% recovery rate. Note that if all the certificates have the same coupons, and therefore the IO is receiving the same contribution from each class of certificates, the recovery rate does not matter.

CMBS IO RESTRUCTURE OPTION PRICING

The most overlooked option is the servicer's latitude in restructuring the underlying loans, but ironically it is the most important option the IO investor needs to analyze. If the CMBS structure allows the servicer to restructure a loan when the loan is either in default, or even worse, when a default is deemed imminent, it can mean disaster for the IO's performance. This is because upon default or imminent default, the typical workout entails encouraging the borrower to contribute capital to the property, and in return the lender will do one, or all, of the following to the loan:

- refinance the loan, if current rates are lower, and waive prepayment fees,
- lower the coupon rate to a level where the property's cash flow can cover debt service,
- write-off a portion of the loan, or
- extend the maturity date of the loan.

The IO's returns are significantly reduced if any of the first three restructure alternatives are implemented. Although the fourth alternative is actually good for the IO, usually the fourth is employed only in conjunction with one or all of the first three alternatives.

There are two ways the IO can be protected from the servicer's restructuring of the underlying loans. The best way is to have the IO structured as a fixed strip. As discussed earlier, a fixed strip IO receives its share of the coupon first, prior to any other class (maybe the AAA class is pari-passu). This means that if the servicer reduces the interest rate on a defaulted loan, the IO is indifferent because it continues to receive its fixed coupon strip of payments, and the lower rated classes of certificates absorb the reduced coupon payments. As a matter of fact, a fixed strip IO would perform much better than expected if every loan were extended and the interest rate reduced.

The second way an IO can be protected from the servicer's restructuring of the underlying loans is in the documentation of the CMBS issue. There are two slightly different ways the CMBS documentation can protect the IO. The first is if the servicer is restricted from agreeing to modify any material aspect of any mortgage loan, without the vote of 100% of the certificate holders. This means the only option open to the servicer is foreclosure, which is generally good for the IO since the servicer advances through liquidation, and because default to liquidation can take a long time, especially if the borrower declares bankruptcy. The second way the CMBS documentation can protect the IO is by allowing the servicer to restructure the loan at will upon default, but design the CMBS documentation so that if the loan is restructured the coupon amount paid to the IO is calculated as if the restructure had never occurred. This basically means that under restructure the IO is treated like a Fixed Strip, but retains its WAC Strip attributes both for voluntary prepayments and for defaults that result in liquidation.

SUMMARY

As this chapter indicates, the IO is the most volatile and least intuitive to understand of all the classes of securities within a CMBS structure. The only way to price an IO properly is to evaluate the prepayment, default, and restructure options embedded in every CMBS. The evaluation of these three options involves some serious scenario analysis, which is only as good as the assumptions that go into the scenarios.

An appropriate set of scenario assumptions requires that the investor thoroughly understand the following four items:

• the underlying collateral's call protection,
• know the collateral's historical default rates, and judge its future default rates,
• how the CMBS is structured, and
• how the IO certificate is structured.

Remember, when you buy an IO, you buy volatility — model it and get paid for it.

Chapter **9**

How CMBS Structuring Impacts the Performance of the Bond Classes

David P. Jacob
**Managing Director and
Director of Research & Securitization
Nomura Securities International, Inc.**

Lynn Tong
**Director
Nomura Securities International, Inc.**

INTRODUCTION

The structure of a CMBS deal can greatly affect the performance of each of the bond classes. For some deals the structuring process involves nothing more than taking a single loan or a pool of loans and cutting up the cash flow to fill the size of the rating classes as dictated by the rating agencies. Most often this results in a very conventional sequential deal. More sophisticated structuring analysis recognizes that the loan terms, the particular grouping of the loans, as well as the specific cash flow allocation scheme, can all have a substantial impact on the performance of the bond classes.

Many underwriters have no flexibility on loan terms since they do not originate the loans, some do not have much flexibility on the group of loans that go into the securitization as they typically bid on pools or packages from traditional lenders. For those underwriters who also originate the loans, the deal can be fine tuned by the choice of loan terms, the choice of which loans to pool together, as well as the cash

The authors would like to thank Bernard Lin, Edward Mikus, and Thomas Pogge for their helpful comments.

flow allocation scheme. As a result these deals can produce bonds that are more tailored to the needs of the passthrough fixed-income investor.

While the structuring of commercial and residential mortgage-backed securities is in many ways similar, there are some important differences. First, as we discuss in more detail later on, prepayment terms differ significantly. Commercial
mortgages generally require prepay penalties which must be allocated. Second, what
happens in a default is different. With commercial mortgages there are usually features which allow for extension and other modifications of the loans in the event of
balloon default. In addition, the servicer is required to advance scheduled principal
and interest in the event of a default. These cash flows need to be allocated. Third,
there is far less homogeneity in the cash flow of the loans in a commercial pool. This
can result in unusual payment patterns for some bond classes.

In this chapter, we examine select loan terms: how each affects a deal as a
whole and how differential performance of each loan under various scenarios influences
individual bonds. The focus of the chapter will be the slicing and dicing of cash flows,
through which prepay risk and default risk are allocated among the bond classes.

LOAN CASH FLOW: THE RAW MATERIAL

The raw material for structuring bond classes is the cash flow of the underlying mortgages. This includes principal (scheduled and unscheduled), interest, prepayment
penalties, and default penalties. The deal structure must allocate each of these cash
flows to a bond class, otherwise the cash will go to the residual class.

Principal

The amortization schedule of the underlying loans determines scheduled principal
payments. Loans can have terms ranging from bullet, where there is no amortization
at all, to full amortization over the term of the loan. Many intermediate combinations
are possible and have been implemented. There are very few loans with negative
amortization, since this increases the risk to the lender.[1] At the other extreme there are
instances where loans hyperamortize. This is a credit enhancement feature that is
sometimes added.[2] Some commercial mortgage loans have specified principal repayment schedules.

A recent innovation is a fully-amortizing loan with an anticipated repayment
date on which borrowers can repay the loans. If a borrower does not repay on that
date, excess cash from the related properties will be trapped to accelerate principal
repayment (*cash trap*) and to pay interest at a higher rate. Unlike the conventional
balloon loans in which a default is triggered if the balloon payment is not made on
maturity date, failure to repay the remaining loan balance on the anticipated repayment date is not an event of default so long as the monthly principal and interest pay-

---

[1] Some floating rate loans do allow some negative amortization.
[2] This situation might arise at a balloon default, where the borrower is required to use all excess net operating income (NOI) to repay the outstanding principal on his loan.

ments are received on scheduled payment dates. This gives borrowers more time to work on refinancing the loans without dragging the bonds through defaults. The higher loan rate and cash trap feature provide strong incentives for borrowers to speed up their refinancing process, thus reducing extension risk and weighted-average life variability on the bonds.

Interest

Interest payments can be fixed or floating. Generally, fixed- and floating-rate loans are not mixed into one pool. When they are, they are typically segregated to support floating and fixed tranches, respectively. In essence two deals are done at once. While residential deals, particularly agency deals, are backed by loans with coupon rates within a very narrow band, a commercial mortgage-backed deal can have a wide range of coupons. This is a result of two factors: mixed collateral (with a resulting diversity in quality, property type, loan terms, etc.) and different origination times at which interest rates were at different levels. When there is a wide range of coupons in the underlying loans, the weighted average coupon of the deal will vary over time as the various loans pay down. This will affect the bond classes differently.

Penalties

In addition to principal and interest, other sources of cash flow are prepayment penalties and default penalties. Prepayment penalties are further discussed in Chapter 4. Prepayment penalties arise when the borrower decides to voluntarily terminate his mortgage prior to the scheduled maturity date. The penalties serve as a deterrent to the borrower and compensation to the lender. In a multi-class deal, while the penalty still serves as a deterrent to the borrower, it may or may not compensate the investor. The allocation of these penalties is decided at the structuring level and varies greatly among deals. It can have an enormous impact on the value of the bond classes. We will discuss this later, and present an approach whereby one can ascertain whether or not the penalties are making CMBS investors whole in the event of a prepayment.

Default penalties are another source of cash flow. Typically these penalties are imposed in the event of a balloon default. (Whereas the likelihood of being able to collect any penalty from a default during the term of a loan is small, it is quite possible that, under balloon default, the property is generating sufficient income to pay the penalty. This penalty acts in a similar fashion to the cash trap, except that the lender receives the cash in the form of interest.) Like the prepayment penalty, where the default penalty goes in a multi-class deal is dictated by the structure. In many cases the default penalty does not go to the regular bond classes. Nevertheless, it still serves as a deterrent to the borrower against non-payment of the balloon.

LOAN CASH FLOW: HOW IT CAN AFFECT BOND CLASSES

The typical pooled commercial mortgage deal will contain mortgages with a variety of interest rates, maturities, and principal payment schedules. This dispersion is inevitable due to the different businesses and financing requirements of commercial mortgage borrowers. The lack of homogeneity in commercial mortgages can lead to some unusual characteristics in the resulting bond classes.

Principal Dispersion

A wide dispersion of balloon payment dates can lead to what is known as *duration drift*. This occurs when the duration of a bond does not decline linearly with the passage of time. While the duration of a pool of uniform fully-amortizing mortgages changes little over time, balloon date dispersion can lead to an extension of duration. For example, suppose the underlying collateral for a bond is two bullet loans with equal size and terms to maturity of 7 and 12 years. After 5 years the average life would be 4.5 years; however, after 7 years the average life becomes 5 years. This can cause the bond to underperform particularly in a positive yield curve environment. In a pro rata pay deal, where all bonds receive principal payments concurrently according to the ratio of their outstanding balances, the duration drift is similar for each bond. In a sequential-pay deal, where senior bonds must mature before subordinated bonds begin receiving principal payments, the largest bond is usually affected more than the other bonds as more balloons are generally required to pay it off. A good deal structure slices bonds to minimize the number of different balloon payment dates within each bond's principal payment window so as to reduce bond duration drift.

Another effect of balloon date dispersion is the possible extension of a senior class due to losses. For example, as shown in Exhibit 1, a $60 million senior bond and a $40 million subordinated bond are backed by two $50 million bullet loans. One loan matures in 5 years and the other matures in 10 years. In a pro rata deal, both bonds have a weighted-average life of 7.5 years if the loans do not prepay or default. In a sequential-pay deal, the weighted-average lives of the senior and subordinate bonds are 5.83 and 10 years, respectively. If the 5-year loan defaults in six months and only $10 million is recovered, the senior bond extends to 8.42 years. Because its original weighted-average life is shorter, the senior bond in the sequential deal is extended more by the loan losses. But it is better protected from losses than the senior bond in a pro rata pay deal in case the 10-year loan defaults after the 5-year loan matures.

Balloon date dispersion, coupled with sequential-pay structure, can result in a higher level of cash flow subordination and make deals less efficient. Though investors and borrowers may not notice this, they are both adversely affected by inefficiencies in any deal structure, for the additional costs are passed on to them. In a sequential-pay deal, principal payments received from loans must be passed through sequentially to bonds, beginning with the most highly rated. Of the loans with different balloon payment dates, the shorter ones tend to pay down the senior bonds and the longer ones tend to pay down the subordinate bonds. This creates inefficiency as the long-maturity subordinate bonds absorb more loan cash flows than the required level of deal subordination.

Exhibit 1: Effects of Loan Principal Dispersion on Bond Weighted-Average Lives

No Prepay No Default	Principal Payment Amount		Weighted AL of Bond
	Year 5	Year 10	
Loan 1	$50 mm		
Loan 2		$50 mm	
Pro Rata Pay Structure:			
Senior Bond	$30 mm	$30 mm	7.5 Years
Subordinated Bond	$20 mm	$20 mm	7.5 Years
Sequential Pay Structure:			
Senior Bond	$50 mm	$10 mm	5.8 Years
Subordinated Bond	$0 mm	$40 mm	10 Years
Loan 1 Defaults in 6 Months	Principal Payment Amount		Weighted AL of Bond
Recovers $10 million	Month 6	Year 10	
Loan 1	$10 mm		
Loan 2		$50 mm	
Pro Rata and Sequential-Pay Structure:			
Senior Bond	$10 mm	$50 mm	8.4 Years
Subordinated Bond	$0 mm	$0 mm	

For example, suppose a 7-year bullet loan with 40% subordination is combined with a 10-year bullet loan that has the same face amount with 10% subordination. This results in a deal with 25% subordination, in which the entire 7-year loan principal and 50% of the 10-year loan principal are used to pay the senior bond. The remaining 50% of the 10-year loan principal is used to pay the subordinate bond even though the 10-year loan requires only a 10% subordination. This situation is shown in Exhibit 2. The sequential-pay structure moves the subordination of the 7-year loan to the 10-year point. Assuming a 10% coupon for both loans and bonds, the cash flow allocated to the subordinate bond is over 27% of the total instead of the 25% required subordination. If the 10-year loan were otherwise identical to the 7-year loan and the deal's required subordination were 40%, the cash flow allocated to the subordinate bond would be over 43%.

Now, suppose we add a 20-year loan also with a 25% subordination into the deal. This loan lengthens the subordinate bond further to 20 years without reducing the deal's overall subordination level. 75% of the loan principal is used to pay the subordinate bond even though its own required subordination is only 25%. Over 33.5% of the deal's total cash flow is allocated to the subordinate bond. This addition, as shown in Exhibit 3, disproportionately increases cash flow allocated to the subordinate bond.

Exhibit 2: 10% Rate, Bullet Loan 7 Year, 40% Sub. and 10 Year, 10% Sub. Deal Sub. 25%, Cash to Sub. Bond: 27%

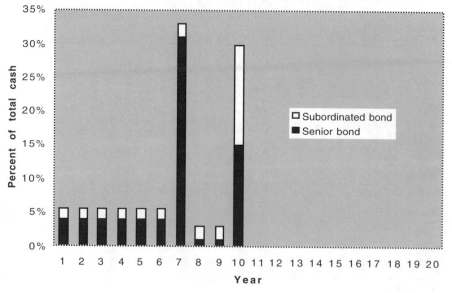

Exhibit 3: 10% Bullet, 7 Year., 40% Sub., 10 Year., 10% Sub. and 20 Year., 25% Sub. Deal Sub. 25% Cash to Sub. Bond 34%

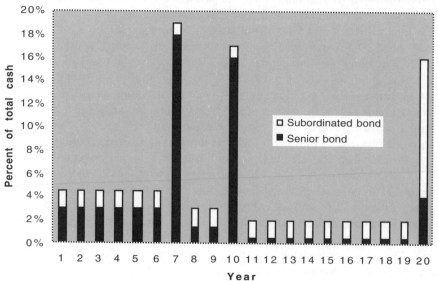

Clearly, loan term dispersion in a sequential-pay deal can lead to ineffi-ciency. For underwriters who securitize loans originated in-house, loan structuring is an integral part of deal structuring. Setting loan terms to meet individual borrower's financing needs and to improve efficiency in aggregate is one of the first steps towards creating good bonds. To better allocate loan cash flows to bonds, given an existing pool of loans with differing rates and terms, the balloon payment date or anticipated repayment date of a new loan should be far enough in the future to extend the senior bonds, but also near enough so as not to lengthen the subordinate bonds. This limits the reduction of, and possibly increases, loan cash flows allocated to the senior bonds relative to those allocated to the subordinate bonds. In the previous example, replac-ing the 20-year loan with a 10-year loan improves efficiency more than replacing it with a 7-year loan, everything else being equal.

Besides the benefit of increasing the senior bonds' cash flows relative to those of the subordinate bonds, extending the senior bonds in a positive yield curve environment reduces the necessary amounts of interest-only strips (IO). To reduce prepay risks to the senior bonds, interest points are stripped off of their coupon to keep their prices at reasonable levels. The stripped-off interest points, along with pre-pay risks, are allocated to the IOs. The IOs are thus more volatile and priced at wider spreads than their related senior bonds. When a senior bond is extended, it is priced at a higher yield. This by itself increases the financing cost of the senior bond, but the corresponding lower bond price allows an increase of the senior bond coupon and channels loan cash flows which would otherwise be passed through to the interest-only strips to the senior bond. Such cash flow transfer improves deal efficiency.

Coupon Dispersion

So far the discussion of the dispersion of balloon payment dates has assumed that the rate on the new loan is set reasonably close to the existing pool's weighted-average rate. In real CMBS deals, coupon dispersion is inevitable and is usually dealt with by creating interest-only (IO) classes from higher coupon loans and principal-only (PO) classes from lower coupon loans. Some deals pass through coupon dispersion directly to the bondholders in the form of weighted-average-coupon bonds (WAC bonds).

As mentioned above, interest-only classes can be created by stripping some interest points off of senior bonds. Similarly, they can also be created at the loan level by stripping interest points off of high coupon loans. Unlike IOs stripped from bonds, which are affected by the performance of the mortgage pool and the structure of the deal, IOs stripped from loans are primarily influenced by the perfor-mance of the loans from which they are created. These higher coupon loans are either originated under a different market environment at an earlier time or secured by riskier asset types. Loans from the first category present greater refinancing risk and those from the latter greater credit risk. While it may seem that such an IO is loaded with prepay risk and default risk, a well-structured IO is allocated prepay premiums to reduce the impact of loan prepayments and has the most senior claim among all bonds on available funds from all loans in case of a cash shortfall. Most deals do require that the servicer advances for cash shortfalls. With such advances, prepayment and default affect the IO stripped at the loan level the same way: the IO's notional balance is reduced and its weighted-average coupon is changed no matter how the loan exits the pool.

IOs stripped from bonds, on the other hand, are affected differently by loan prepayment and default. IOs stripped from senior bonds are better-protected from loan losses but are more exposed to loan prepayments and recoveries than IOs stripped from subordinated bonds. IOs from mezzanine bonds are better protected than IOs from both senior and subordinate bonds: the balance of its related bond remains intact while the senior bond balance is paid down and the subordinate bond balance is written down. Compared with IOs from bonds, IOs from loans have the advantage of being simple. Investors need only model the loans in a deal, but not the bond distribution priority, in order to analyze an IO stripped at the loan level. However, because they are always affected by any high coupon loan exiting the pool at any time, IOs stripped from loans provide limited flexibility for different investors to play out their views on the underlying loans and on the real estate market in general. IOs stripped from bonds can more easily be tailored to suit an investor's preferred risk / return profile. (For a detailed discussion of interest strips in CMBS, see Chapters 8 and 13.)

To increase the rate of a low coupon loan, a fixed portion of its principal is stripped into a PO. The loan's remaining principal combined with the entire interest results in a higher coupon. This process is conventionally called "ratio-stripping," as the ratio of PO to loan balance is fixed. To maintain the fixed ratio so that the higher coupon remains constant, the PO's balance must be reduced at the same rate as that of the underlying loan balance. Strips from different low coupon loans are combined to form a PO class. Depending on the deal structure and the specific loans from which it is stripped, the PO can be made senior. Whether it is senior or pari pasu to its underlying loans, the ratio-stripped PO is not affected by the dispersion of coupon rates as it receives no interest payment. It can benefit a great deal from prepayments, though it is unlikely that its underlying low coupon loans would prepay. Term default of these low coupon loans could benefit the PO if it is senior to the other bonds, as recoveries on such loans are likely to exceed the small fixed portions stripped into the PO.

WAC bonds present an interesting challenge to the conventional understanding of a fixed-income instrument. The dispersions in loan rates and maturities frequently leads to counterintuitive results in a WAC bond. During its lifetime a WAC bond can be transformed from a discount bond to a premium bond and vice versa without any change in the market level of interest rates. If the loans are prepayable, becoming a premium bond would tend to widen the bond spread, as it usually reduces the yield of a premium bond if it receives its principal payments earlier than expected. However, prepayment can be beneficial for a WAC bond if the loan exiting the pool has a below average coupon. The effect of increased bond coupon can more than offset the effect of faster premium amortization. If a high-coupon loan prepays, a premium WAC bond would be adversely affected by both the faster premium amortization and a lower coupon thereafter. And a discount WAC bond would not necessarily pick up yield as the reduction in future coupon income mitigates the benefits of faster discount accretion. Investors of WAC bonds must take care to suspend judgment based on their experiences with conventional fixed-income securities and investigate in detail the coupon variation over time under different prepay and default scenarios.

PREPAYMENT

We have discussed how dispersions in loan rates and terms affect CMBS deals, now we turn to the effects of loan prepayment. While homeowners prepay primarily to refinance their mortgages at cheaper rates, commercial borrowers often have other reasons to prepay, such as selling the properties or getting out of the business, etc. Prepayments in a rising-rate environment are not only possible, but likely, because such environments are often associated with a booming real estate market, which engenders many mergers, and also involves a reduction of yield maintenance premiums. (For a more detailed discussion of commercial loan prepayments, see Chapter 3.) Fortunately for CMBS investors, commercial mortgages usually have built-in prepay penalties that are so substantial that the allocation of prepay penalties is of greater importance than the allocation of prepay risks. Here we discuss the various forms of prepayment penalties common in commercial mortgages and how such penalties can be allocated to bondholders.

Penalty from Loans

Lock-out is a period during which borrowers are not allowed to prepay. It provides investors with the best call protection, but leaves borrowers with limited flexibility. If a loan were locked out for life, it could force the borrower to resort to technical default to prepay the loan. Usually, lock-out only covers the initial years of a mortgage. Thereafter prepayment is permitted with required prepay penalties discussed below. Some loans allow prepay without penalty after certain number of years.

   Yield maintenance premium is determined by how far (1) the sum of the amount prepaid and the present value of future cash flow after such a prepayment, falls short of, (2) the present value of future cash flow without such a prepayment. The cash flows are discounted at a spread over Treasury and the lender is conventionally known as "made-whole" when that spread is the same as the spread on the loan. In other words, the lender is rendered indifferent between receiving the originally expected cash flow and receiving cash flow altered by a prepayment along with a prepay premium. One way to determine if a premium is make-whole or not is to compare the total returns to maturity of the loan assuming no prepay and no default with total returns assuming prepayment and premium are received. The loan cash flows, including the yield maintenance premium, are assumed to be reinvested in loans with similar yields. The following example shows the comparison.

Exhibit 4: Total Return to Maturity as a Benchmark for "Make-Whole" Yield Maintenance Premium

	Lower Rate	Same Rate	Higher Rate
Treasury Yield	5%	6%	7%
Loan Rate @ T+300 bp	8%	9%	10%
No Prepay Total Return	8.70%	9%	9.30%
T+300 bp Discount Rate	8%	9%	10%
T+300 bp Yield Maintenance	$3.99	$0	$0
Total Return w/ Prepay Premium	8.70%	9%	9.58%
T+350 bp Discount Rate	8.5%	9.5%	10.5%
T+350 bp Yield Maintenance	$1.97	$0	$0
Total Return w/ Prepay Premium	8.56%	9%	9.58%
T+250 bp Discount Rate	7.5%	8.5%	9.5%
T+250 bp Yield Maintenance	$6.07	$1.97	$0
Total Return w/ Prepay Premium	8.85%	9.14%	9.58%
T-Flat bp Yield Maintenance	$17.32	$12.64	$8.20
Total Return w/ Prepay Premium	9.59%	9.86%	10.14%

Let's say the Treasury yield curve is flat at 6% and loan spread is at 3% over the curve. A 9% bullet loan with 10-year term can prepay in 5 years with yield maintenance premium. Market spreads for similar loans are assumed to remain unchanged at 300 basis points over Treasury and the loan is assumed to pay interest annually. Exhibit 4 shows yield maintenance premiums calculated at spreads of 300, 350, 250 and 0 basis points over Treasury and total returns associated with each premium under lower rate, same rate, and higher rate environments. Assuming no prepay and no default, total returns to maturity under the corresponding interest rate environments are 8.7%, 9.0% and 9.3%. In the higher rate environment, no yield maintenance premium needs to be paid by the borrower as prepayment benefits the lender. Prepayment of the 9% loan when prevailing loan rates are at 10% enables the lender to earn higher reinvestment income and increases the total return from 9.3% to 9.58%. Similarly, the lender can maintain the same total returns without any prepay premium if the loan is prepaid in the same rate environment. The T+250 yield maintenance premium more than makes the lender whole and raises the total return to 9.14% from 9.0%. This is also the case in the lower rate environment, where the T+250 premium raises the total return from 8.7% to 8.85%. The T+350 yield maintenance premium, on the other hand, leaves the lender short with a total return of 8.56%. And the T+300 makes the lender whole.

If, however, by the time of the prepayment the loan spread is tightened from 300 to 250 basis points over Treasury as the credit quality of the loan has improved and such an improvement was expected and priced into the original loan spread. Then, both the T+300 and T+350 yield maintenance premiums would fall short of making the lender whole. Only the T+250 yield maintenance premium can pass as a "make-whole" provision. Many commercial mortgages have yield maintenance premiums based on spreads tighter than the loan spreads at the time of origination in anticipation of improvements in the quality of underlying assets.

Treasury-flat yield maintenance premium is a stronger form of prepay deterrent. The premium is derived from discounting the future cash flows at corresponding Treasury rates instead of loan rates and is therefore higher. As shown by the total returns in Exhibit 4, where loan spreads are assumed to remain at 300 basis points, the lender gets a windfall if the borrower prepays in any of the interest rate environments. Any improvement in loan quality is unlikely to lead to sub-Treasury loan spreads and the lender will most likely be more than made whole upon prepayments.

Percentage prepay premium is another form of call protection on commercial mortgages. The premium is a percent of the prepaid loan balance and usually declines over time. A common type of percentage premium is the 5-4-3-2-1% each year for five years after loan lock-out ends. Percentage premium is perceived to be less effective than lock-out and yield maintenance. However, it may outperform yield maintenance premiums in a rising-rate environment, when the implicit reinvestment assumption of the yield maintenance calculation limits the amount a borrower must pay along with any prepayment. (See the right-most column of Exhibit 4.) Mixed in a deal, loans with different forms of call protection complement one another.

The most precise form of call protection is to permit prepayment only through *defeasance*. A portfolio of Treasury securities or Treasury equivalents which replicates future cash flow of the mortgage is purchased to defease future mortgage payments. The cost to borrowers who prepay is similar to the cost of Treasury-flat yield maintenance premium, while investors see no change in their bond payments as if loans were locked out for their entire term. With this form of call protection, investors reap further benefits: better credit on the assets remaining in the deal and no additional taxes since no prepayments and prepay premiums are distributed.

Penalty to Bonds

Allocating prepayment premiums from loans to bonds according to each bond's performance sensitivity to prepayment is a key part of creating good bonds. Here we discuss a few allocation methods currently in use in the market.

Lock-Outs on Bonds and Loans are Not the Same Many deals in the market pay prepay premiums only to bonds which receive principal prepayments and to IOs whose notional balances are reduced by such prepayments. However, bonds from a sequential-pay deal which are structurally locked-out at the time of a loan prepayment can still be affected by such a prepayment. Structural "lock-out" on bonds is different from a lock-out on loans. The following example illustrates the point.

Let's say a pool contains two bullet loans with equal balances and identical features except that one matures in year 7 and the other in year 10. The pool is cut into two sequential bonds with equal face amounts. If the loans do not prepay or default, the 7-year loan would pay off Bond 1 and the 10-year loan would pay off Bond 2 (see Exhibit 5a). If the 7-year loan prepaid in year 5, only Bond 1 would be shortened (see Exhibit 5b); however, if the 10-year loan prepaid in year 5, both bonds would be shortened from their original terms of 7 and 10 years to 5 and 7 years, respectively (see Exhibit 5c). Bond 2 is clearly affected by a loan prepayment that is passed through only to Bond 1, and Bond 2 should therefore be compensated for its foregone interest payments.

If loan rates are different and bond interest payments are based on the weighted-average of loan rates (WAC bond), prepayment of either loan would affect the bond's performance, as the remaining bond coupon would be different. If the 7-year loan has a higher coupon rate, then Bond 2 would receive a lower coupon after the 7-year loan prepays in year 5 (Exhibit 5b) even though Bond 2 does not shorten. Conversely, the prepayment of the 10-year loan in year 5 (Exhibit 5c) would raise Bond 2's coupon and possibly offset the adverse effects of its shortening.

Bond Yield Maintenance In general, allocating prepay premiums to bonds based on whether they receive the particular prepaid principal amounts leaves structurally "locked-out" bonds with insufficient compensation. Paying premiums to a WAC bond based on its weighted-average-life sensitivity to a specific prepayment is also undesirable. The impact of a prepayment on the entire bond cash flow must be taken into consideration. Better deals maintain bond yields through present value comparisons that are similar to yield maintenance premium calculation on loans. This method fairly compensates each bond without hinging its right to receive premiums on either receiving the current prepayment or having a shortened remaining weighted-average life. As with the underlying loans, the appropriate premium for each bond is determined by comparing the present values of its future cash flows with and without the prepayment. The cash flows are discounted at Treasury plus spreads which can be the same as the current bond spread, or tighter in anticipation of potential rating upgrades on the bond.

Unlike many large commercial mortgage loans, in which partial prepayment simply reduces the loan's future cash flows proportionately, a bond's risk/return profile can become very different after some underlying loans prepay. Therefore, the spreads over Treasury for computing the two present values can also be different from one another so as to price in the change of the bond's characteristics due to the specific prepayment. For example, if a loan prepayment shortens a bond significantly and the spread curve is positive, then the spread for computing the present value with the prepayment may be tightened accordingly. If, on the other hand, the shortened bond rolls down a positive yield curve so much that it becomes a super premium bond, then the spread for computing the present value with the prepayment may be widened to reflect the bond's increased exposure to future prepayments.

Exhibit 5: Effects of Loan Prepayment on Structurally "Locked-Out" Bonds

(a)

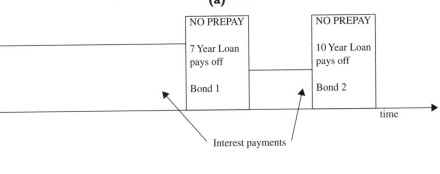

(b)

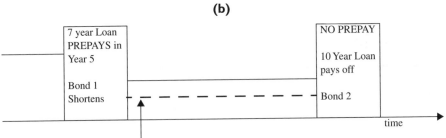

Bond 2 gets less interest in a WAC bond deal where the 7 year loan has a higher rate.

(c)

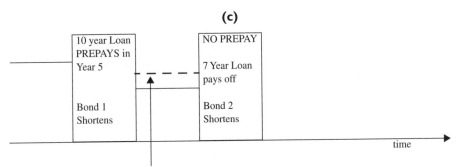

Bond 2 gets more interest in a WAC bond deal where the 7 year loan has a higher rate.

While it is fairly straightforward to implement the yield maintenance formula on the loan level, it can be computation intensive on the deal level with different loans prepaying at different periods. Because the effects of each prepayment on bonds can only be ascertained by passing cash flows from loans through the deal's distribution priority, the deal's debt rule must be generated for every period in which there is a projected prepayment to properly compute the incremental foregone cash flow and differential riskiness of each bond.

Exhibit 6: Schematic Graph Showing the Rising Average Bond Yield over Time Resulting from the Steep Credit Curve

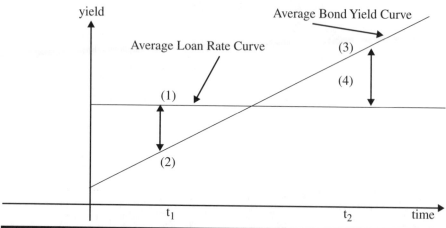

Make-Whole Premiums Do Not Pass-Through As described above, making bondholders whole is more complicated than making lenders whole, as loan prepayments not only reduce the affected bonds' future cash flows, but also change their risk profiles. Here we shall see that leaving such additional complications aside, make-whole provisions on loans still do not ensure make-whole on the bonds. This is because the average yield of affected bonds at the time of prepayment is unlikely to be the same as the coupon of the prepaid loan. The premium can be more or less than the necessary make-whole amounts on bonds. Exhibit 6 illustrates the point.

To simplify matters, let's assume a flat Treasury curve and unchanging spreads on loans and bonds. Assume also that all loans in the deal have the same rate, so the average loan rate is the same throughout the deal's life (the horizontal line in Exhibit 6). Because of the steep credit curve, the average yield of all the bonds increases over time as senior bonds are paid down and the deal's subordination level rises, assuming no defaults take place. If loans prepay at time t_1, the discount rates at which make-whole yield maintenance premiums are computed are different for the loans and the bonds: point (1) on the loan rate curve is the loan discount rate, and point (2) on the average bond yield curve is for the bonds. While the aggregate cash flow change must be the same for loans and bonds, the higher discount rate on the loans leads to insufficient premium available to make all of the bondholders whole. At time t_2, the opposite happens.

We have discussed briefly the various types of prepay penalties from commercial mortgage loans and compared the different allocation methods of such penalties to CMBS. To assess a bond's prepayment sensitivity, scenario analysis must be performed. As shown earlier, the performance of certain bonds is heavily influenced by specific loans and any average measurements would miss such linkages. The conventional measurements for prepayment, CPR and PSA, are more suitable for large pools of homogeneous residential mortgages than for commercial mortgage pools. One practical approach for CMBS investors is to identify the loans which influence the bond in question the most and then to develop plausible prepay scenarios to reveal the bond's performance sensitivity. Here is a look at an IO stripped from a senior bond. It is priced to yield 8.33% assuming no prepay and no default. Ignoring default for the time being, the worst case for the IO would be to have all prepayable loans prepay right after lock-out. The IO yield in that scenario turns out to be 9.05%, because the IO holders are more than made whole by prepay premiums. Without those premiums, the prepayment would have reduced the IO yield to 5.39%.

DEFAULT

Most CMBS deals rely solely on the cash flows from underlying loans and properties for credit enhancement. The deal's structure allocates credit risk deferentially among bonds. How a default affects a particular bond depends on various factors, such as the time of the default, the amount of the recovery, the characteristics of the defaulted loan in relation to those of the pool, the bond's position in the distribution priority and whether the servicer advances or not. The following example shows how the interaction of these factors can lead to surprising results.

Exhibit 7 shows the yield to maturity of an IO stripped off of mezzanine bonds under different default scenarios. The specific default and recovery rates are chosen for illustration only. The left-most column shows the months in which defaults take place and a 12-month foreclosure period, during which advances are made by the servicer, is assumed. First, let's look at the two columns under 10% default rate. The yields for the 70% recovery case are consistently higher than those in the 100% recovery case. This shows that the IO is primarily affected by recoveries from the defaulted loans as they prepay senior bonds and shorten mezzanine bonds. This also suggests that so long as default rate is low and losses do not reach the mezzanine bonds, *less recovery benefits the IO*. The declining yield as defaults occur later, common to both columns, is a result of the defaulting of specific loans, rather than a uniform percentage of each loan. In this case, the defaulted loans have below average coupons and the mezzanine IO happens to be a WAC IO. The effect of higher coupon after default more than offsets the effect of shorter life and the *earlier the default takes place the higher the IO's yield.*

The yields in the columns with 20% default rate tell a different story. While the yields in the case of 100% recovery are still higher for earlier defaults, the difference is much smaller, because the additional 10% of defaulted loans have higher coupon rates. In the case of the 70% recovery, yields rise as defaults take place later and they are consistently lower than yields in the 100% recovery case. This shows that loan losses have reached the mezzanine bonds and the IO is affected more by losses than recoveries.

Exhibit 7: Mezzanine IO Yield Profile with Loan Defaults

Foreclosure: Recovery:	12 months 70%		12 months 100%	
Default Month	10%	20%	10%	20%
1	9.825	7.218	9.297	8.400
13	9.729	7.533	9.200	8.380
25	9.639	7.821	9.109	8.363
37	9.552	8.079	9.022	8.347
49	9.469	8.307	8.938	8.332

As explained above, under certain circumstances some bonds can benefit from loan defaults. This can also happen when balloon defaults provide premium senior bonds and their corresponding IO strips with additional interest income, as the defaulted loans are extended. The payments during the extension period can be made by the borrower, advanced by the servicer, or paid out of the current interest of the subordinate bonds. Losses, if any, are allocated to the subordinate bonds. The senior bonds and IOs simply walk away with the extra cash.

The extension benefits, however, are tempered by the potential lower recovery if the servicer advances throughout the foreclosure period. Liquidation proceeds are applied first to the unpaid servicing fees and unreimbursed servicer advances before being applied to pay down bonds. Prolonged foreclosure with servicer advances could significantly reduce the available recovery for bonds. Better deals in the market today limit the amount advanced to the subordinate bonds. In our example, this means that the servicer will not advance so long as the current interest payments of the subordinate bonds can cover the shortfall caused by the defaulted loan.

The senior bonds would also be hurt if prevailing interest rates are higher at the time of balloon default, because the extra interest payments are below those on available alternative investments. The IOs, though, keep their windfall.

RESIDUAL

We have discussed how loan characteristics affect various bonds through pooling and cash flow allocation schemes. A few words about residuals are necessary, for deal structures affect their values and they in turn constrain the types of bonds created.

REMIC rules require that each deal must contain one residual interest to pay the taxes which approximate the difference between what would be owed on the loans and what is now owed on the bonds. Exhibit 6 can be used to illustrate the notion of "phantom income." The horizontal loan rate curve represents the REMIC asset (loans) income on which taxes would be paid by the lenders if there were not a REMIC deal. The average bond yield curve is the REMIC liability cost on which taxes are paid by the bondholders once a REMIC deal is done. Taxes due on the difference between these two curves, which difference is called "phantom income" because the residual holder does not receive it, must be paid by the residual holder to make the IRS whole. The total phantom income throughout the life of a deal is zero (turn the triangle with sides labeled (3) and (4) by 180 degrees), but the present value of taxes paid is positive as tax payments are made earlier and deductions are taken later. In a real deal these lines are not so straight. Structural variations and prepay/default assumptions complicate the valuation of a residual. In addition to the steep credit curve, greater dispersion of loan rates and terms, and further slicing of bond classes, could all change the shape of the average yield curves and increase residual tax liabilities. Evaluating a residual is therefore an integral part of structuring a CMBS deal and must be performed to limit any additional adverse tax consequences of a deal structure.

SUMMARY

In this chapter, we have discussed how bond performance can be affected by the structure of a deal, which includes its cash flow allocation scheme, and the particular grouping of loans.

Chapter **10**

Rating of Commercial Mortgage-Backed Securities

Joseph C. Franzetti
Senior Vice President
Duff & Phelps Credit Rating Co.

INTRODUCTION

The ratings of commercial mortgage-backed securities are opinions of credit worthiness. There are four major rating agencies currently involved in providing ratings for these types of securities. While there are a great many areas of similarity, there are unique aspects to each rating agency's approach. This chapter attempts to deal with the major rating issues, but is written from the view point of Duff & Phelps Credit Rating Company.

For over a decade rating agencies have been assigning ratings to commercial mortgage-backed securities. The structures are usually either bond type securities in which a mortgage and note on a cross-collateralized package of loans is pledged as collateral, or pass-through certificates in which the securities rated represent ownership in a trust that, in turn, owns certain mortgage loans.

This chapter was compiled from various reports produced by the Commercial Mortgage Backed Securities group at Duff & Phelps Credit Rating Co. Additional contributions were made by Patrick Sargent of Andrews & Kurth LLP.

The property types collateralized are normally retail, office, multifamily, industrial and other income-producing properties. The rating agency approach is to analyze the cash flow and value of the collateral as well as the mortgage and security structure. Issuers, their counsel, accountants and investment bankers present the collateral information, mortgage and security documents to be reviewed for the rating. Rating agencies rely on this information as well as other due diligence reports (i.e., appraisals, engineering and environmental reports) and legal opinions. Except as needed to disclose certain information in support of the analytical conclusions reached in the rating process, the information is usually kept confidential.

The rating process is comprised of four steps:

- preliminary assessment of the transaction based on a term sheet, financial statements and other relevant data,
- site visits, cash flow analysis and review of other outside due diligence information,
- review of deal structure, legal documents and legal, and
- Credit Rating Committee review and assignment of rating.

UNDERWRITING APPROACH

This section describes the rating approach to individual property analysis and underwriting. The main areas of analysis in the rating process are: (1) discussion of the market area and economy in which the property is located, including an examination of the competition, (2) analysis of the property's physical quality and location, and (3) analysis of the property's lease structure and financial attributes.

Market and Site Area

Location is the most important factor to the current and long-term viability of real estate. Site inspections are performed for the majority properties in the transaction, with the exception of large pool issues. In such cases, a statistical sampling determines the properties to be visited. The site inspection considers issues such as visibility and accessibility (ingress and egress), as well as convenience to major thoroughfares, transportation centers, employment sources, retail areas, hotel and hospital services, and educational and recreational facilities. Other factors that affect real estate marketability include compatibility with the surrounding neighborhood, recent and proposed development, and the strength of local real estate values.

The market area is defined on an individual basis and requires a broader analysis than the specific site review. The market area review includes an evaluation of competitive properties, supply and demand characteristics, and a review of nearby land use development for the defined market area. The market analysis also involves contacting local real estate professionals for current rental and sales information, vacancy levels, new construction and absorption.

For all property types, historical rental rates and occupancy levels, average lease terms and rent concessions are reviewed for the property as well as the market. The current demand, including historical and current absorption data, is reviewed. The corresponding supply, including projected additions along with the historical market occupancy, is also analyzed. The property's lease terms, including concessions, are compared with those currently prevalent in the market before real estate cash flow projections are developed. Information about property expenses is derived from the subject and competitive properties.

This information is compared with market averages found in industry reports such as those issued by the Building Owners and Managers Association (BOMA), the Institute of Real Estate Management (IREM), or the Urban Land Institute (ULI). Additional demographic data are collected from local and national sources. Where available, specific local or property type market surveys provide additional information on market characteristics. All information collected in the field is compared with information provided in the appraisal and/or other information submitted.

The market and site analysis is the most important component in analyzing a property. The demand for and marketability of the property are the primary determinants in analyzing its potential for continuous occupancy. While the site and market area review criteria apply to all property types, there are differences in the focus of review for various property types. The following paragraphs outline those unique property issues.

Office Properties

There is a wide range of office property types, with different qualitative considerations for each. Space in a central business district has significantly different site and market characteristics than a suburban office building. Similarly, the definition of "market area" for these property types would be substantially different.

Generally, office properties depend on the strength and stability of the market area as a desirable business location. The success of the location will depend on the area economy, which impacts the ability to attract stable tenants on a consistent basis. Construction in most markets peaked in about 1986 and declined rapidly to a halt thereafter. The supply moratorium has begun to have an impact. Vacancies have stabilized in most markets, though there remains a huge oversupply. However, recent demographic trends in unemployment suggest office users are requiring less space, which has slowed the absorption of the oversupply and may impact the future demand for space.

There recently has been a trend toward bifurcation in the office markets of most central business districts into those that are technologically capable of accommodating the modern business user and those that are not. The latter continue to suffer physical and functional obsolescence and may never return to competitiveness. Floor plate sizes and layout will affect marketability, as will access to transportation and similar business users. Replacement cost currently exceeds economic value, therefore, new construction is neither justified nor anticipated in the near term.

Office properties require significant cash infusion over time to provide for general capital expenditures and to provide for tenant improvements and related costs of re-leasing space. In fact, the owner's ability to access capital for these needs has proven to be an effective, competitive tool in attracting new tenants. The attendant volatility in office cash flow is directly accounted for in the underwriting process, by stabilizing the cash outflows and including them in our base-year cash flow estimate. Depending on the lease rollover pattern, this may result in the required build-up of some reserves over time, in anticipation of these costs.

Retail Properties

Retail properties include regional and super-regional malls, strip centers, power centers, free-standing stores, neighborhood shopping centers and specialty centers. Of primary concern to the success of retail properties is site visibility, access and area demographics. Most retail properties rely on automobile traffic for accessibility to the customer base. To draw tenants, the property must be well located with easy access to attract this customer base. For large shopping malls, a good location is identified by reference to the surrounding residential quality and density and traffic patterns. Small retail centers must be well positioned in comparison with other retail centers and also must have an adequate residential base.

Single-property retail financings are typically feasible only when the property dominates its location, has three or more good-quality anchors and when opportunities for new competition are limited by the absence of developable land. Particular attention is given to "dark anchor" risk, which pertains to the likelihood of an anchor closing down its operations while maintaining its lease obligations. This would have an obvious deleterious affect on the property, and is avoided by the inclusion of operating covenants or recapture provisions in the anchor lease with respect to conditions under which operations must be maintained.

The physical condition and layout of the property should be adequate for the modern retail user, with respect to its larger shop space requirements and parking needs. Sales and occupancy costs per square foot are the primary indicators of the property's performance. Trends over time are examined and comparisons with competitive properties and published sources such as the ULI publication "Dollars and Cents of Shopping Centers" are made. With respect to percentage rent, an analysis is conducted on historic sales numbers to ascertain their volatility. This is then used to determine a base-year sales number upon which to calculate an appropriate percentage rent estimate.

Industrial Properties

The qualitative review focuses on building clear heights, column spacing, bay depths, divisibility, truck-turning radius, and overall functionality and accessibility. Vital to industrial properties are local labor sources, proximity to supply sources and customers, major employers in the market area, and accessibility to rail lines and major roadways.

Quoted rents for industrial properties commonly include a significant portion of specialized amortized tenant improvement costs. When developing an underwriting cash flow it is important to calculate the "shell rent," or rent net of these costs, to perform similar comparisons. In general, flex space is considered less desirable collateral than light manufacturing or warehouse due to its significant office component, which renders this asset type susceptible to dramatic swings in rental rates.

Multifamily Properties

Multifamily properties are the most commodity-like of the income-producing property types and can experience supply changes in a relatively short period of time. An apartment market with historically low vacancies may experience substantial new construction, which could quickly create an oversupply. These new properties can be extremely competitive and may offer the latest in amenity packages that older properties cannot provide. Multifamily residents are typically on short-term leases and can easily "trade up" to new properties. Other factors, such as zoning changes and local economic trends may also significantly affect the stability of a market.

The barriers to entry for multifamily properties remain low, and this points toward increased competition in this market. The key factors in underwriting are the age and condition of the property, which will be partly affected by the adequacy of ongoing maintenance, and overall management quality.

The results of the qualitative market and site review are used to develop quantitative assumptions for market growth (supply and demand), expected turnover, rental rates and expense factors, and vacancy factors. The qualitative market and site analysis is used to evaluate the current and future marketability of the property. These calculations directly affect the assessment of a property's sale or refinancing risk.

Construction Quality

The construction quality of a property affects its current and future marketability as well as the ongoing cash flow stream. Factors such as age, functionality, efficiency of rentable space, energy systems and usage of space all contribute to required maintenance costs and capital expenditures. A property that requires significant amounts of operating expenditures or excessive repairs will have a decreased income stream, reducing cash flow and property value calculations. Properties requiring capital improvements or other nonrecurring capital expenditures are required to provide evidence of adequate reserve balances.

A property must appeal aesthetically and functionally to current and prospective tenants. A property's amenities, architectural design, parking, landscaping, utilities and security systems contribute to the attractiveness of the property for tenants and may affect potential marketability.

Management Quality

The management company is analyzed from the perspective of its historical performance and its financial strength.

In terms of the management track record, the following factors are considered: 1) the number of square feet of property under management of the same asset class as the collateral, 2) the qualifications and experience of the management team, including the leasing agents, 3) the ability to attract and retain high-quality tenants, 4) the ability to maintain a proper tenant mix and avoid excessive concentration of lease rollovers, 5) the ability to maximize the property's bottom line cash flow without sacrificing tenant credit quality or permitting deferred maintenance and 6) the adequacy of the accounting systems and capital expenditures budgeting.

A face-to-face meeting is conducted with the management team to ascertain their strengths or weaknesses in the categories listed above. With respect to financial stability, the industry is characterized by small, often thinly capitalized entities. Many management companies are the reincarnation of development companies that went bankrupt in the previous real estate recession. Consequently, a number of controls are required. For example, the management fee should represent adequate compensation for the services rendered. In the event that a replacement manager is sought, the fee should be high enough to attract competent interested parties. The subordination of this fee to the mortgage payment potentially accelerates the property's demise, due to lack of financial incentive for the property manager. On the other hand, this subordination puts creditors ahead of management.

Control over the cash flow from the tenants should be instituted. The most secure form is to set up a lock box account to which the tenants send all payments, thus circumventing the financial risk associated with management. The disadvantage of this is that it may hamstring the management from performing its usual functions. An alternative is to establish a "modified lock box," which is an account held by the trustee. The manager has access only in the amount exceeding the payment of principal and interest on the mortgage, property taxes, insurance and replenishment of any reserves that have been set up. This compromise method meets the dual objectives of maintaining cash control, and allows the manager the much-needed flexibility of access to the funds.

Insurance

Hazard Insurance should be provided by a creditworthy third party. Additionally, business interruption insurance will be required. This is to mitigate interruptions that could arise in cash flows to the bondholders, from events including a partial or full condemnation or casualty, or the necessity of structural work for any number of reasons. The same credit standards apply to this insurance provider as to casualty insurance, as described above.

Additional comprehensive public liability insurance should be provided, including blanket contractual and personal injury coverage.

If the property is located in an area identified by the U.S. Secretary of Housing and Urban Development as having special flood hazards and in which flood insurance has been made available under the National Flood Insurance Act of 1986, then coverage should be provided for this risk. Any other insurance, as may reasonably be required by the mortgagee to protect its interests, should be provided.

Leases/Tenants

Another important factor in determining the credit quality of commercial real estate is the quality and diversity of the leases and tenants. Diversity of leases refers primarily to variety in user and a variety of expiration dates. A mix of lease terms reduces the turnover risk at any one time during the term of the security. A diversity of tenants refers to the size and type of the business conducted by the tenants. Tenant diversity helps to protect the property from economic downturns or cycles in any specific industry. The credit quality of the tenants affects timely rent payments and lease renewals.

To make qualitative assessments regarding tenant profiles, rating agencies analyzes current leases and, where available, leases under negotiation. The rent roll submitted to rating agencies should include the following major provisions:

(1) number and identity of the tenants,
(2) amount, type (e.g., storage, penthouse) and location of space occupied by each tenant,
(3) rental rates (including percentage rent and escalation provisions),
(4) lease terms, including expirations,
(5) expense payment provisions, and
(6) renewal and/or cancellation options.

Where possible, lease abstracts should present this information in detail and disclose other lease requirements, such as free rent or early occupancy utility payments, security deposits, tenant improvements required, and brokerage commissions. In addition to the actual lease information, a payment history on a tenant-by-tenant basis is useful. All major tenants are analyzed on the basis of credit quality and payment reliability. This analysis often requires the submission of financial statements from key tenants and review of the full lease documents, including any operating agreements, main covenants, reciprocal easement agreements, etc.

A re-leasing vacancy period is assumed to occur in addition to appropriate leasing fees and concessions. The information analyzed during the lease and tenant review is used to develop the cash flow projections for the property. Quantifiable factors include rental rates and escalation provisions, free rent concessions, current and projected vacancy factors, operating expense allocations and tenant improvement requirements.

Renewal options are discussed with current management to determine realistic lease expirations. Leases with contractual rental increases or expense stops (caps) are considered favorable because they make cash flow projections more predictable.

QUANTITATIVE ANALYSIS

The maximum amount of mortgage debt for a given rating level will vary depending on a number of quantitative factors. These include the debt service coverage ratio, the loan-to-value ratio at commencement, the loan-to-value ratio at balloon date, fixed versus variable interest rate, and lease provisions including escalation clauses and rollover dates. There are also numerous security structure provisions that bear upon the debt amount including extension features.

Cash flow is a more reliable indicator of commercial property performance than value. The appraised value is nonetheless an important benchmark in the underwriting parameters. Current third-party appraisals should be provided on single-property financings. However, property value is subject to errors of estimation due to the unavailability of arm's length transaction data. Hence, there is the requirement of subjective determination of appropriate capitalization ("cap") rates. For this reason, rating agencies frequently will adjust the third-party approximation of the cap rate to reflect the uncertainty element in this key number and will recalculate the value on this basis. Likewise, the cash flow projection for the determination of value is internally reviewed and adjusted.

For all properties with medium- to long-term leases (generally retail, industrial and office), gross rental income used in the annual cash flows is calculated as the contract rental payments currently in place (as marked to market). Partial credit will be given to leases that are expiring in the coming year by assuming a probability of renewal. This probability assumption is also applied to the costs associated with rollover, namely tenant improvements, leasing commissions and downtime between leases. Leases that are at above-market rental rates will be adjusted down to market for this calculation. Industrial leases (flex space) will be adjusted to shell rents. Contractual increases are accounted for only when a specific dollar or percentage amount is stipulated if the amount does not exceed market rents or if the tenant is investment grade. Adjustments tied to the consumer price index or similar benchmark will not be given credit. The occurrence of a recent high inflation period, which will be imminently adjusted for under the terms of the lease, will be considered on a case-by-case basis. The overriding objective is to arrive at a representative stabilized estimate, not to reflect an above- or below-average inflationary environment.

A lease-by-lease analysis is performed for tenants representing greater than or equal to 20% of the total gross leasable area. Current rental income from all other tenants is calculated and projected over the holding period. In either case, annual lease rollover is estimated and tenant improvement, leasing and other costs are estimated based on a conservative renewal probability. In general, properties with occupancy levels above the market average are assumed to stabilize at market levels upon lease rollovers. Market rent and lease term, for the purpose of estimating revenue from new and renewal tenants, are based on recently signed leases in the building and/ or competitive properties (if available) or reliable local market statistics. The year-one operating statement or pro forma is used as the base year for all projections. Other income is based on historical collections and industry statistics.

All general operating expenses including property taxes, insurance, administrative, utilities, repairs and maintenance, and management fees are estimated. Estimates are taken from the property's historical operating results and/or industry standards for the market. When examining market data, expense-to-revenue ratios are compared to market averages. Properties with ratios higher than market are assumed to remain at the year-one level during the period of analysis. Properties with ratios below the market average are increased to the market average over the period of analysis. This is to reflect the loss of any operating efficiencies relative to the market due to the negative effect of the foreclosure process. Further increases may be warranted depending on the age of the property, level of occupancy and condition of the property and the market. Properties with below-average expense ratios are subject to escalation of operating expenses at a rate of not less than 5% per year.

The analysis examines the age, occupancy, size and type of the property in determining appropriate levels of reserves. Actual levels are taken from industry averages. Tax rates are assumed to remain constant. Unless otherwise indicated, a management fee ranging from 2%-5% of annual income is assumed.

It is assumed that stabilized properties remain at the lower of current or market occupancy levels. Absorption for properties that require lease-up to reach stabilization is based on the expected rate of the market absorption. The market's current overall occupancy is taken as the level for stabilized occupancy. In addition to this overall vacancy, lag vacancy is estimated based on lease rollover, the renewal probability, lease term and expected number of months of downtime between leases. A collection loss relating to the property type and tenant quality is also applied.

A stabilized occupancy number will be utilized by comparing the property's current occupancy with the market occupancy. This will be judged against historical tenant retention and the current lease structure.

Tenant improvements and leasing commissions are estimated and deducted from net operating income. Tenant improvement costs are projected based on the estimated renewal probability and degree of current build-out. Leasing commissions are based on the local commission structure and the renewal probability of leases.

Additional reserves are deducted for replacing or repairing capital items such as the roof, HVAC systems or parking lots. The amount varies depending on property condition, quality and type. Capital expenditures for upgrading or repositioning the property are only assumed to be incurred when the need is substantial. Such deferred maintenance must be taken into consideration and deducted from current cash. The amount deducted is based on engineering reports, appraisals or other sources. When such information is not available, estimates are made from industry cost estimating manuals.

CROSS-COLLATERALIZED STRUCTURES

The analysis of cross-collateralized and cross-defaulted loans includes elements of single-asset and pool analysis. The diversification of the pool is the primary determinant of the rating levels. However, most cross-collateralized pools have, to date, fallen short of the minimum size in terms of the number of loans to attain pool status. They frequently consist of fewer than 30 properties and commonly have concentration of a single asset type. This is due to the fact that these pools are primarily issued by medium- to large-sized developers that are seeking to refinance a portion of their overall portfolios, and that developers of this size have usually specialized in one or two property types. Their development expertise is usually limited to particular property types. This compares with non-crossed pools, the source of which is usually a portfolio lender, such as a life insurance company, conduit or other institutional lender, which are typically diverse across borrower, property types and geographic regions. For convenience, cross-collateralized and cross-defaulted pools are referred to here as simply "crossed." Non-cross-collateralized and non-cross-defaulted loans will be referred to as "non-crossed."

The critical distinction with crossed pools is the impact this has of significantly reducing the probability and severity of default, because each property's cash flow before debt service supports every other property in the pool. If, for example, there are 20 properties in the pool and there is currently a 2.0X debt service coverage (fixed rate), before a default becomes likely, cash flow would need to drop 50% or more *on a portfolio basis*. This contrasts with multiple-borrower pools whereby individual loans will default as cash flow deteriorates. There are therefore likely to be fewer defaults in a crossed structure, all other things being equal. In a non-crossed pool, individual loan defaults will result in losses if the liquidation price of the real estate falls short of the outstanding principal balance, including accrued interest and all related expenses allocated to each loan. However, in a crossed pool, the total liquidation proceeds from each and all of the properties are available to repay the outstanding principal.

Conversely, with a crossed pool, as individual properties deteriorate to the point where they would otherwise default if they were non-crossed, they are likely to be neglected by the owner/manager, thus exacerbating the diminution in real estate value. Certain early warning provisions may be included in the structure to mitigate this. Examples include debt coverage triggers to remove or substitute individual properties, or triggers to replace the management by vote of some predetermined percentage of the bondholders.

A properly structured cross-collateralized pool will require lower subordination levels. The rationale is that the pool benefits from diversification, and some of the losses that occur due to individual loan foreclosures are avoided. Also, no unrated subordinate piece will be required if the total LTV and DSCR are adequate on a pool basis to meet the minimum required for the rating. This contrasts with multiple-borrower, non-crossed pools, wherein even though the weighted-average LTV and DSCR may meet the target for the rating category, some subordination will be required. For this reason, it is far more common to see unrated subordinate tranches in non-crossed pools.

Single Assets

Single-asset financings are a subset of the cross-collateralized structures as described in the preceding section. The distinguishing characteristic is the concentration of risk.

When underwriting a single property, the risk of unanticipated events that could affect the property's cash flow is high. For example, despite extensive local market area analysis and discussions with the local zoning department, the risk of a new competitive property being constructed or retrofitted in close proximity to the collateral property is impossible to predict with certainty. Moreover, this one event could cause a default of the transaction. Any number of unanticipated events that adversely affect cash flow have the potential to trigger a default. This is in contrast to pooled transactions, in which the diversification of properties and leases mitigates this risk.

The underwriting parameters will reflect the individual property's specific characteristics. The heterogeneity of commercial real estate in terms of location, lease structure and physical characteristics results in a wide variance in the required LTVs and DSCRs for a given rating. It is not surprising that single properties with a large number of leases, each representing a small percentage of the overall cash flow, have formed the preponderance of single-asset financings. Regional malls most commonly fit this description.

DIVERSIFIED-BORROWER MORTGAGE POOLS

Mortgage pool securities are generally certificates that represent ownership interests in a trust. The trust owns a number of loans from individual borrowing entities that, generally, are not cross-collateralized. These loans are either a subset of a lender's loan portfolio or an aggregation from a conduit. In either case, the approach taken incorporates the following steps:

- evaluate the credit quality of the individual loans,
- determine the quality of the origination,
- assess the competence and financial capacity of the servicing function and
- review the aggregated pool statistics for mitigating circumstances or pool-wide exposures.

Loan Credit Quality

In evaluating the credit quality of each loan, rating agencies attempt to discern any unique strengths or weaknesses in the loan due to either specific property or loan features. These include among others: market conditions, location issues, physical construction, lease rollover and secondary financing. This analysis is achieved by:

- reviewing loan files or "long form" due diligence reports, including appraisals or market studies,
- analyzing financial statements and lease reviews,
- sensitivity analysis of cash flows,
- performing site inspections,
- reviewing tenant quality,

- adjusting cash flows to achieve a "marked-to-market" scenario,
- adjusting LTVs based on current cash flow and cap rates, and
- reviewing engineering and environmental reports.

Depending on the pool size, rating agencies will perform a detailed analysis and site visit on either the entire pool or a statistical sample. (For example, the sample is usually employed in loan pools in excess of 50 loans. The minimum sample is targeted to be 33% of the dollar amount of the pool with 50 properties being visited. The selection is based upon the pool diversity as well as potentially volatile asset types and geographic locations. In a pool of more than 50 loans, at least 75% of the loan pool due diligence information is reviewed in depth and 100% of the loan profile information.)

Quality of Origination

Rating agencies will review the circumstances of the loan originations to ascertain any potentially adverse selection situations. For a loan held in portfolio, the following questions will be asked, among others: Why is the loan being sold? What was the purpose for originating? What situations have changed in the organization? What competitive issues influenced the underwriting? What was the level of analytical rigor documenting the credit approval?

For loans from a conduit, rating agencies review the underwriting guidelines, decision-making process and incentives of the originators. The quality control and compliance issues must be reviewed to ensure that a consistent, thorough approach is taken by the conduit. Since these originations are designed particularly for third-party sales, rating agencies need to ascertain what risk-sharing proposals are in place to keep the conduit's focus on credit quality and compliance.

The representation and warranties a seller makes are critical to the rating process. While these may be provided in a variety of forms, overtime many have become commonplace. Aside from the actual representations and warranties made, rating agencies review how they are made. Did the seller go through a detailed analysis to make sure those "reps" are true? What procedures did they employ? This can be proven through third-party due diligence or other documentation. In cases where comfort cannot be achieved from the seller on the "reps," a highly rated entity would need to back up the seller's position.

Servicing Capabilities

The amount of flexibility the servicer/special servicer has in modifying defaulting loans can have a significant impact on the amount of loss mitigation for any particular pool. Modifications generally deal with the following:

- extending the maturity date,
- adjusting the amortization schedule,
- deferring interest payments,

• adjusting the interest rate,
• forgiving debt, and
• releasing or accepting collateral.

The most obvious situations are balloon loans that have good debt service coverage, but the borrower is unable to obtain a refinancing at maturity. Clearly, giving the borrower more time or restructuring to a fully amortizing loan would be appropriate. However, deciding on forgiving debt or deferring interest with the hope that the borrower can turn around a troubled property is a more difficult task.

The assessment of servicer flexibility must be governed by two issues. The first is the ability of the servicer to evaluate trouble situations and recommend courses of action that will result in maximizing net present value to certificateholders. The second is that their decision-making process and conclusion is fully documented and supplied to the trustee, not for affirmation, but to document the various alternatives entertained and that the optimal alternative was chosen.

Pool Analysis

Once the loan credit quality, origination quality and servicer quality have been assessed, an expected loss for the pool of loans is calculated. This loss is based on both the rating category and the factors discussed above. However, the higher the rating category the greater the loss tolerance that a pool of loans should be able to sustain. In other words, the pool should have a larger subordinate first loss piece or cash reserve in order to get a higher rating on the more senior certificates.

In sizing the loss expectation for any pool at a given rating category there are two primary factors:

• Probability of Loss: The probability that any particular loan will go into default, be foreclosed upon and liquidated.
• Loan Loss: The loss realized upon liquidation of that loan.

The conclusions reached in the analysis of the credit quality of the loan, the quality of its origination, the pool aggregation and the servicer, will be manifested in the determination of the probability and loan loss.

Probability of Loss

The elements that will have a material impact on whether a loan goes into default and is foreclosed upon and liquidated are:

• LTV/DSCR,
• property type,
• loan structure (i.e., balloon)
• fixed/floating interest rates,
• loan quality,

- seasoning of property and loan,
- management,
- ownership structure,
- barriers to entry/loan to replacement cost,
- cash flow volatility and
- recourse.

Loan Loss

The actual loss sustained by any mortgage loan upon liquidation will be affected by three major items:

- Obtaining the asset
    recourse
    state law
    foreclosure period
    ownership structure

- Time to sell
    location
    property type

- Costs to sell
    liquidation (cost to carry, legal fees, commissions, property protection expenses, improvement expenses, asset management fee)
    loan size

The loss expectation on any portfolio of loans is simply the summation of the products of each loan's probability of loss and anticipated principal loss.

There are then a number of macro issues (poolwide adjustments) that will impact the pool's performance, which are addressed through overall adjustments to the loss expectations. These are as follows:

- geographic diversification,
- overall environmental exposure,
- seismic exposure,
- servicer/special servicer flexibility capabilities,
- loan diversification,
- origination quality,
- information quality,
- cash control and
- reserves.

There are a number of items which, will have negative or positive impacts on the loss expected. These adjustments are outlined below.

Amortizing

Fully amortizing loans that obviate the need to refinance the property reduce the risks associated with a volatile credit market. However, fully amortizing transactions are generally of a longer term, which introduces the risks of changing neighborhoods, physical obsolescence and the need for capital improvements.

Seasoning

Seasoning represents the period of time that the borrower has been paying on the loan. A payment history, in and of itself, is neither positive nor negative. An unblemished payment history by a borrower is positive. What mitigates some of this positive, however, is that depending upon the year of origination, the property value and cash flow may have declined. Therefore, the quality of current information is critical when looking to assess the impact for seasoning.

Servicer/Special Servicer

The specific assessments of the servicer and special servicer will impact credit enhancement. If a servicer/special servicer used is deemed unacceptable, the transaction is probably not ratable. There is still a wide variety of quality differential even if the overall assessment is acceptable. Given this wide variety of quality and the ability to modify loans, credit enhancement can increase or decrease depending on the operational capability and financial capacity of the servicer and special servicer.

Origination Quality

Origination quality refers to the rigor of the individual underwriting. This includes the way that cash flows and value are assessed. Additionally, it deals with the strengths of legal documentation and covenant restrictions. While differentiation between excellent versus very good underwriting may not significantly change the quality of the collateral, poor underwriting can have a devastating impact, particularly when it comes to preservation and control of the asset. Similar to origination, determining information quality is a subjective analysis. We look for the information provided to be complete, recent, insightful and analytical.

Cash Control

Cash control is the ability of the lender to effectively get its hands on the property cash flow. This provides not only the ability to reduce the loss of collateral, but it is an effective tool for bringing a recalcitrant borrower into a more cooperative posture. This function ranges from sweeping accounts periodically to having tenants make payments directly to the servicer.

Reserves

Reserves are established at a loan level to make cash available to the property owners and lender for particular needs. These range from maintenance and capital items to tenant improvement and commissions. Additionally, reserves can be established for debt service in the event of significant tenant rollover. The reserves will reduce defaults due to short-term cash flow problems and act to preserve asset quality in the long term.

Floating Rates

Floating-rate loans that have caps will be tested assuming increasing rates over time. The specific analysis will be determined based upon the index used, the adjustment frequency and amortization adjustments. Typically, the stressed index rate used is its highest level over several business and economic cycles. The resulting adjusted debt service coverages will then be used in the tabular calculation of credit enhancement.

Asset Quality

The assessment of the differences among class A, B, C and D properties cannot be done in isolation. Superior/inferior asset quality differential should be measured within a particular submarket. The balance of existing stock of different asset classes versus the potential for new development potential needs to be measured. Generally, class A property is viewed more favorably because even in depressed economic situations, there is a trend to upgrade by tenants who remain in the market. Class A is also more accepted by institutional investors who would be purchasing or refinancing.

Barriers to Entry

Each market and submarket will be reviewed to determine the likelihood of new construction. This is done by property type. The determination of whether a market and property type have significant barriers to entry will not necessarily result in changes to credit enhancement since amortization and lease structure interrelate on this issue.

Cash Flow Volatility

Suffice it to say that properties with erratic cash flows due to tenant rollover or high expense ratios will require greater credit enhancement levels. The subjectivity in addressing this topic is due to a specific analysis of lease structure and whether current rents are below market rents. The level of reserves established will also positively contribute to mitigating cash flow volatility.

Loan Size

The particular dollar amount of a loan is not significant. However, the benchmark credit enhancement levels incorporate liquidation costs. Recognizing the fixed portion of the costs to foreclose and liquidate property, smaller loans may experience disproportionately higher losses. Therefore, for loans less than $3 million, the loss expectation will be increased because liquidation costs will be a higher percentage of the loan. Conversely, loans greater than $5-7 million should see some reduction as liquidation costs represent a smaller percentage of the loan.

Location

It is impossible on a poolwide basis to assess particular credit enhancement attributable to location. Generally, in-fill locations are more desirable given a supporting population base and a lack of available land. Differentiation between suburban and urban is only significant given the property type and the local market demographics and submarket supply/demand.

Concentration

Generally, state concentration of should be avoided. However, certain markets are more resilient than others. Concentration in any market is a risk. Diversifying into markets that are considered substandard will not positively impact credit enhancement. Individual loan or borrower concentrations in excess of 5% of the pool are analyzed on a loan-by-loan basis. Issues of importance are borrower structure (single-purpose entity) and property quality. Generally, the more concentrated (more than 5% in any category) the greater the credit enhancement needed. Depending on loan quality, the adjustment can be significant.

Small Pools

Generally, a small pool is defined as fewer than 50 loans or where an individual loan(s) exceeds 5% of the pool. The analysis in these cases becomes much more loan-by-loan. As a result, individual borrowers that are not structured as special-purpose entities with nonconsolidation opinions become a much greater risk, due to any individual loan having disproportional impact on the entire pool. Individual property leases and tenant performance will also be reviewed more specifically, given that tenant bankruptcy and rollover create more pronounced risks.

Small pools also create a greater risk of timely payment of principal. Balloon risk is measured against the maturity in the certificate. With few loans, which potentially mature within the same time period, these small pool transactions need to have certificate maturities significantly beyond the mortgage maturities to allow for liquidation of assets. The credit enhancements needed for small pool transactions are usually analyzed using more of a direct sizing approach.

STRUCTURAL AND LEGAL CONSIDERATIONS

In commercial MBS programs, the primary structural goal is to isolate the assets or collateral that will generate the cash flow to investors. Outside credit risks or exposure should be removed to the greatest extent possible.

Typically, assets are transferred to a bankruptcy-remote special-purpose vehicle (SPV or Issuer) that is limited to only business relating to the assets to be acquired (an SPV may be a corporation, partnership or trust). Consequently, the SPV should not be able to incur additional debt or obligations that might enable a creditor to bring action against it that could interfere with payments to the investors.

The SPV should also be structured to reduce the possibility that a bankruptcy court, in a proceeding involving the parent or other affiliate, would order substantive consolidation of the assets of the SPV with those of its parent or affiliate. Assuming the SPV is bankruptcy remote, the transfer to the SPV should further be structured to be a true sale so that the assets will not be deemed a part of the transferor's estate (in the event of the transferor's bankruptcy) pursuant to Section 541 of the United States Bankruptcy Code (the Bankruptcy Code).

The focus of this section will be on debt obligations using commercial mortgages as collateral, although many of the points will apply to certain aspects of passthrough transactions as well.

Issuer/SPV Criteria

A nonconsolidation opinion of counsel will generally be required stating that, in the event of a bankruptcy proceeding involving the parent, the assets of the SPV will not be substantively consolidated with those of the parent. The issuer/SPV (or, in the case of passthrough securitizations, the seller or depositor) should satisfy certain criteria:

- The corporate charter, partnership agreement or trust document, as the case may be, should limit the business and operations of the issuer to activities related to acquisition and holding of the specific assets, issuance of the securities and other activities necessary and appropriate to carry out the foregoing.

- The issuer should be restricted from incurring additional debt unless (1) the debt would not result in a reduction of the current rating, (2) the debt is fully subordinate to the rated debt (provided rating agencies approve LTV and coverage limits) or (3) the debt is rated at the same or higher level as the existing rated debt and would not impair the current rating.

- So long as the securities are outstanding, the issuer should not be able to (1) change the limitations set forth in the charter or other governing instrument, (2) dissolve or liquidate prior to payment in full of the securities or (3) merge with any entity, or transfer or pledge any of its property or assets, except under certain limited conditions. (See "Transfer Restrictions.")

- The SPV and, where applicable, parent or other affiliate, should provide the following "separateness" undertakings:

    1) SPV should be adequately capitalized.
    2) SPV should maintain its books and records separate from its parent and affiliates. It should prepare separate tax returns, or if part of a consolidated group, it should be shown as a separate member.

3) The SPV should utilize its own letterhead and telephone and should maintain an office distinct from its parent.

4) All transactions with the parent or any affiliate should be on an arm's-length basis and pursuant to enforceable agreements.

5) SPV should be held out to the public by SPV and its parent as a separate and distinct entity. There should be no commingling of assets or funds with any other entity.

6) At least one director of the SPV should be an outside director not affiliated with the parent or any of its affiliates.

7) Regular board meetings should be held to approve SPV activities; transactions with affiliates must be approved by the outside director(s).

8) The transfer of assets to the SPV should be adequately disclosed to transferor's creditors.

9) The parent and identifiable creditors should agree not to voluntarily place the SPV into bankruptcy proceedings. The SPV should be restricted from filing a voluntary bankruptcy or other insolvency proceeding unless it is approved by all directors, including the outside director.

10) The SPV should not guarantee or pay debts or other obligations of the parent or any other entity; the parent will not guarantee obligations of the SPV other that indemnification of certain limited obligations to underwriters.

11) Any common employees or overhead shared with affiliates should be appropriately allocated and charged.

In mortgage conduit programs, the SPV criteria and substantive consolidation concerns arise at two levels: 1) at the seller/depositor level where the mortgage assets are being pooled and 2) at the borrower level where each mortgage is originated. A pool of loans from a single owner or small group of owners merits close attention to the SPV criteria and delivering of a nonconsolidation opinion. As the pool increases in size and diversity, the severity of the impact of substantive consolidation with respect to a single borrower on the pool as a whole diminishes.

True Sale versus Pledge

A transaction should be structured to ensure that the SPV has complete and absolute ownership of the assets used to secure the securities issued. Accordingly, the transfer of the assets from the parent/affiliate to the SPV should be treated as a true sale or, if made as a capital contribution, as an absolute conveyance. In the case of a pass-through transaction, the seller/depositor must convey all right, title and interest in the assets to the trustee for the benefit of the certificateholders. An opinion of counsel to the issuer generally will be required to the effect that the assets will not be deemed property of the transferor under Section 541 of the Bankruptcy Code. The courts often look to the intent of the parties and the true nature of the transaction. Factors considered by the court in determining whether or not the transferor retains any equity ownership in the assets transferred to the SPV include:

- The amount of recourse to the transferor; any amount in excess of historical losses may cause the transaction to be viewed as a secured pledge.
- A determination of which party bears the risks and enjoys the benefits of ownership of the assets.
- The relation between the fair value of the assets and the price paid.
- Whether or not the seller retains any rights in the assets (e.g., right of substitution, redemption or repurchase).
- Whether or not collections from the transferred assets are segregated from any other assets that may be held by or retained by the transferor. If the transferor act as servicer, detailed servicing agreements should be included and segregated accounts used.
- How the parties treat the transaction for tax, accounting and regulatory purposes.
- The intent of the parties, particularly as indicated by the language of the documents.

Fraudulent Conveyance/Transfer

In some instances, it will be necessary to ensure that the transaction will not be deemed a fraudulent conveyance or fraudulent transfer under applicable state law or Section 548 of the Bankruptcy Code. Section 548, which is similar in many respects to the various state fraudulent conveyance or fraudulent transfer codes, provides that the trustees may avoid any transfer if the debtor: (1) made the transfer with actual intent to hinder, delay or defraud any creditor or (2) received less than a reasonably equivalent value in exchange for such transfer and either (a) was insolvent at the date of the transfer or became insolvent as a result of the transfer, (b) was engaged in business for which its remaining capital was unreasonably small or (c) intended to incur debts beyond its ability to pay. A legal opinion may be required, which may rely on extrinsic evidence of solvency and value, such as MAI appraisals and independent fair value certificates.

Other Legal Opinions

Opinions of counsel to the issuer generally must be rendered to the rating agencies regarding the following matters:

Legality/Enforceability All documents relating to the transaction must be legal, valid, binding and enforceable in accordance with their terms. They should have been duly authorized, executed and delivered by the issuer (and the parent or other transferor, with respect to the transfer of assets to the issuer). They should not conflict with or violate the issuer's organizational documents, bylaws or any agreements or orders by which the issuer is bound, or any applicable laws or regulations. Such documents include the following:

Trust Indenture

Sale/Transfer Agreement
    Pooling and Servicing Agreement
Mortgages/Leases
    Other Security or Collateral Agreements

Security Interest/Perfection In the case of a debt transaction using an indenture, an opinion that the trustee will have a first perfected security interest in all assets comprising the trust estate that are pledged or transferred to the trustee for the benefit of the investors is required.

Issuance of Securities In the case of a debt transaction, an opinion that the notes or bonds are validly issued and entitled to the benefits provided for in the indenture is required. In pass-through transactions, an opinion that the certificates are legally issued and created pursuant to the terms of the pooling and servicing agreement or trust agreement and are entitled to the rights and benefits set forth should be provided.

Credit Enhancement Similar opinions also are required from appropriate counsel with respect to any credit enhancement documents, such as letters of credit, interest swap and cap agreements, insurance policies, surety agreements, master leases or guarantees.

Trust Indenture/Trustee

Minimum requirements necessary in the indenture are:

- Eligible investment criteria for investment of trust funds will be established. All investments should be 'AAA' rated instruments or U.S. government securities (i.e., cash equivalents).
- All funds held in a corporate trust account must be segregated from other accounts. Funds held in trust should be adequately collateralized pursuant to Office of the Comptroller of the Currency regulations.The indenture should require immediate investment of funds into eligible investments.
- Cash flow of funds within the indenture will be reviewed and determinations made as to:
    Priority of distributions: principal, interest, fees, expenses and subordinate classes.
    Release of funds from the indenture.
    Receipt of investment income, and whether such income will first replenish a reserve account or similar accounts.

Indemnification of Trustee/Limits on Liability Standard provisions generally are acceptable; however, a "gross negligence" standard is not. The trustee will not be relieved from liability for, or indemnified against, its own action or inaction that constitutes negligence.

Provision of Reports Trustee must take notice of defaults with respect to failure of issuer to provide timely reports, statements and certificates required by the transaction documents. Also, trustee should affirmatively check compliance with minimum ratings of insurance company, servicer or other entities on a regular basis.

Requirements of Trustee A minimum long-term debt rating of 'A' is required if trustee is obligated to make advances directly or as back-up to servicer, otherwise a rating of 'BBB' is required. Back-up servicing or advancing function may be required. Minimum capital surplus of $50 million is required.

Bondholder Vote In many instances a majority or super-majority is acceptable for major decisions. However, a 100% vote is required to reduce interest rate, change the term/maturity or reduce the principal and change voting percentages. Other items may require full bondholder approval.

Redemption Provisions Whether or not there will be any requirements for or limitations on early, optional or mandatory redemptions will be determined.

Defeasance of Securities Requires deposit of collateral with appropriate maturities and a ratings equivalent to or better than the securities being defeased (as described in "Eligible Investments" under Trust Indenture/Trustee).

Pooling and Servicing Agreement/Master Servicer

In the case of pass-through securities where a pooling and servicing agreement is utilized, many of the considerations under "Trustee Indenture/Trustee" above will apply, together with an evaluation of the master servicer and the following points:

- Representations and warranties as to mortgage loans/assets conveyed to trustee will be confirmed. Seller/depositor should have a cure or repurchase obligation as to any material breach.
- Trustee/custodian should review mortgage file(s) to determine completeness within 30 to 120 days after closing.
- If the master servicer will have any advancing functions (e.g., principal and interest payments, taxes and insurance), they should be through foreclosure and liquidation.
- Detailed servicing and accounting records must be maintained; 30-, 60- and 90-day delinquency and default status reports and certifications should be provided quarterly.
- Collections should be remitted to the trustee on at least a monthly basis. A segregated account must be utilized.
- Master servicer may not resign or be removed until a qualified substitute servicer has been appointed.
- Property inspections should be performed on a regular basis (e.g., once per year and after 60 days delinquency).

- Special servicers may also be required to handle defaulted and troubled loans. Limits on servicer's authority to modify and reform loans should be established.
- Amount and source of compensation will be considered along with the priority in distribution of trust funds.
- Servicer should monitor borrowers' compliance with minimum insurance carrier rating policy coverage requirements.
- In general, the same criteria regarding financial statements will apply as in "Trust Indenture/Trustee" above, except that property operating statements, audited for each property, should be provided in a pool of fewer than 20 loans. If all properties are owned by the same borrower, then the statements should be provided for each property, but audited only as to the pool.

Forms of Credit Enhancement

Various types of credit enhancement are involved in rated transactions, including letters of credit, senior/subordinate structures, master leases, surety bonds, insurance policies, reserve funds and over collateralization. Consideration will be given to the legal and other criteria required for each of these types of credit enhancements.

CREDIT LEASE-BACKED TRANSACTIONS

There are a variety of structure types that fall under the general description of credit lease. At one end of the spectrum is the triple net, bondable (sometimes referred to as "hell or high water") lease. This lease type is created specifically as a financing instrument, and is intended to be bond equivalent. Subject to certain structuring requirements, the financing backed by this lease will most commonly receive a credit rating equal to the long-term secured credit rating of the lessee/obligor. At the other end of the spectrum are leases with credit tenants that contain risks or obligations unrelated to the lessee. Examples of these are leases that provide for certain landlord obligations with corresponding rent offsets, and cancellation provisions upon the occurrence of certain events.

The transaction may be structured as a sale/leaseback between the corporation and a wholly owned subsidiary created by the corporation solely for the purpose of financing. Alternatively, the lease may be an obligation between the corporation and a third-party entity, usually a partnership associate of the real estate development company. In either case, that entity must meet the minimum bankruptcy remoteness requirements. If the minimum provisions are met, these transactions can be structured with a minimum 1.00X DSCR. These issues are discussed in this policy.

Collateral

The security is collateralized by the mortgage or deed of trust, assignment of rents, and the lease and lease guarantees, if any. Technically, while a lease guarantee is often provided, it is not necessary from a credit rating standpoint. Guarantees will be needed from rated parent entities where an unrated subsidiary is the tenant. Corporate guarantees provide no additional protection over and above the legal obligation of that same entity under the terms of the lease.

The following is an outline of the minimum requirements to qualify for bondable lease treatment and hence a credit rating that "flows through" to the senior rating of the company.

Triple Net, Bondable Leases: Major Provisions

- All operating expenses, such as real estate taxes, utilities, insurance, and repair and maintenance costs, and any other financial obligations, must be the responsibility of the tenant. The landlord's obligations should be limited to providing the leased improvements.
- The lease must be noncancelable under any circumstances, including a property casualty or condemnation event. It must also be nonassignable.
- Any purchase option granted to the lessee must be at a price greater than or equal to the then outstanding principal balance of the debt, plus any accrued interest and prepayment penalty.
- Further indebtedness is not permitted. Exceptions to this include nonforeclosable debt to the extent that this does not impair the bankruptcy remoteness of the entity and certain liens such as mechanics liens and easements.
- An estoppel certificate will be require from the tenant confirming the lease terms. This becomes particularly important with newly constructed properties.
- All rental payments are to be directed to a separate account held in the trustee's name for the benefit of the security holders. The borrower must not have access to this account.
- An environmental indemnification should be provided by the lessee.

Certain due diligence reports may be required such as structural and engineering reports, MAI appraisals, Phase 1 environmental reports, and when necessary, Phase 2 studies.

Cancellation Provisions

There are certain risks commonly found in credit leases, the most significant of which relate to casualty and condemnation clauses. A lessee's obligations under a true triple net bondable lease will be unaffected by either casualty or condemnation. However, there are many leases that fall short of this standard, but which can nonetheless receive similar treatment to a bondable lease with inclusion of a number of provisions.

A common lease provision is to allow, at the tenant's option, the lease cancellation upon either the occurrence of a casualty (such as fire or other hazard) that either 1) causes a specified dollar amount (commonly $100,000) of damage during the last two years of the lease or, 2) during the last five years, the damage exceeds a certain percentage (often 50%) of the then replacement cost of the improvements. A casualty of below the specified percentage or dollar amount, or a casualty occurring prior to the allowable cancellation period, results in no lease cancellation and will not affect the timeliness of payments to the bondholders.

There are several ways to mitigate these risks. One method would be to structure the bonds to fully amortize by the time the casualty cancellation window begins. For example, if there is a 25-year lease with the lease provisions described above, the bonds could be amortized over 20 years, thus creating a structure that is equivalent to bondable because the bonds would be retired prior to the beginning of the cancellation options.

Alternatively, bonds can be amortized over 25 years if there is servicer advancing or some other mechanism in place to ensure payment of the outstanding principal balance should the tenant elect to cancel. The bonds could be structured so that insurance proceeds would over collateralize the outstanding principal balance by at least two times. For example, if a casualty were to occur in year 21 of a 25-year lease, the tenant elected to cancel its lease and the minimum expected insurance proceeds at the lease cancellation trigger were $500,000, the bonds should be amortized to $250,000.

The amount of over collateralization and the number of offsets or cancellation provisions that will be permitted will be a function of the rating level desired. Liquidity will be needed to cover any timing delays with respect to receipt of insurance proceeds. This can be either in the form of an upfront reserve, or an escrow funded from cash flow over time, or a commitment by the trustee to advance funds during this period in the amount deemed recoverable. In either event, escape clauses of this nature will necessitate a detailed replacement cost estimate from an engineering firm to assist in determining the degree of over collateralization required.

The government can impose certain requirements with respect to building codes, such as those imposed with the passage of the Americans With Disabilities Act, sprinklers and facade repair, which may result in required modifications to the improvements. It is a risk if these potential changes are not specified as obligations of the tenant in the lease. This risk increases with the age of the property and the length of the lease term. Reserves will be required for these potential costs, which will be calculated on a per-property basis if there is no cross-collateralization.

Condemnation or eminent domain risk will be extensively analyzed to determine the probability of a partial or total taking of the land, parking area or the building to the extent that such a taking could effect the lease. This is accomplished through interviews with local zoning and Department of Transportation authorities, visually inspecting the property and studying any available adjacent land. Aerial photographs are frequently provided in the underwriting package when condemnation risk is an issue. If a reasonable likelihood of a condemnation is deemed to be present as determined by the due diligence process, the lease will not be treated as bondable. Rent abatement as a result of these provisions should be prohibited and specifically stated as such within the lease.

Portfolios of diverse credit leases can be pooled with tranches rated and sized according to the relative size of the lease stream. Alternatively, diverse leases can be pooled with rated tranches created that do not directly match the size of the individual credits. In the latter case, the sizing of the various rated tranches would be DSCR and LTV driven.

SERVICER

The servicer's capabilities and knowledge are critical to the performance of a pool. The following section describes the analysis of the servicer.

The general areas of analysis include the servicing history; financial condition; quality of originations; breadth and depth of experience in categories such as loan size, property type, geographic regions and problem loan issues; administrative capabilities; and systems and personnel of the servicer. This policy lists the information required to be provided to rating agencies. In some cases, the servicer under review is also the originator of the loans. In these situations, the term "servicer" also refers to originator and all areas of origination and servicing are evaluated by rating agencies in their review.

The ability of the servicer to facilitate timely payment of interest and principal, especially in the event of collateral shortfalls, is factored into the structured finance rating. The servicer assessment should not be misconstrued as a securities rating. The servicer assessment indicates that specific conditions have or have not been met to allow the servicer to participate in a structured finance transaction.

Historical Experience

It is important that the servicer be able to demonstrate that it has gained the broad depth of experience needed to adequately service a commercial real estate structured finance transaction. The evaluation includes an analysis of the servicer's historical performance in order to assess previous performance and to determine whether there are any developing trends that may effect future performance. The historical growth of the portfolio, both on a total and annual basis, and the resulting impact on performance is reviewed to determine the company's flexibility and potential capacity.

The length of time that a servicer has been in operation provides an indication of the company's experience through various business and market cycles. Companies with a minimal history must be carefully evaluated to determine the viability of the operation. Taken into consideration are such situations in which the servicer is a subsidiary of a larger company or when senior management consists of a group of professionals with substantial combined experience. While the current business organization may have limited operating experience, points such as the prior experience of a seasoned senior management team and the support of a strong parent entity are factored into the assessment process.

Performance of the servicer's own portfolio or portfolios serviced on a contract basis is analyzed with an emphasis on delinquencies, gross and net loss experience, foreclosures and recoveries as a percent of the outstanding principal balance serviced. It is important to factor in changes such as growth or decline in portfolio balances that may skew the statistics in a misleading way. Static pool data are preferred. Growth or declines in portfolios will be reviewed when determining trends in statistics.

Consistency in performance indicates that a portfolio is performing well during times of various economic stress. Anomalies caused by individual loans or borrowers will be reviewed when analyzing the statistics. The current mortgage loan portfolio of the servicer will be analyzed along various parameters. The servicer will be required to have maintained a servicing portfolio size of at least $100 million in commercial mortgage loans over the past 12 months. The required level of expertise by loan size, property type and geographic region must be commensurate with the pool(s) to be serviced. While limited levels of experience will be considered for specific pools with corresponding loan characteristics, a lack of broad expertise will be reflected in the assigned assessment

The historical performance of the portfolio is analyzed by reviewing delinquency and default reports. The adequacy of tracking procedures is determined. The procedure for handling delinquencies is reviewed to assess timeliness of response, level of consistency regarding follow-up on open items, evidence of uniform adherence to procedures and overall effectiveness of the system. Levels of delinquency and amounts recovered will be reviewed for consistency and trends.

The servicer's policy for the loan workout process is analyzed. Levels of authority and procedures for decision making are reviewed. Unlike single-family mortgage loans, commercial loans involve more options when loans become delinquent, including the ability to extend maturities, forgive interest or provide equity infusions. The servicer must exhibit flexibility as well as the ability to recognize and evaluate the available alternatives within the context of the parameters of the pooling and servicing agreement. The servicer must clearly demonstrate a track record of negotiating successful outcomes to delinquent loan situations and the ability to maximize loan recoveries.

Operations

The quality of a servicer's personnel is measured in terms of experience, knowledge and commitment. The support of senior management is evaluated during the review process. Interaction with management, supervisors, collectors, credit analysts and other operational personnel provides a basis for our qualitative assessment.

The familiarity of management with the portfolio assets is vital to the proper planning for systems, policies, procedures and the hiring of competent staff. Management's prior experience is important in order to anticipate potential problems and to create plans to address those difficulties. In addition to its experience, management must demonstrate its competence and its commitment to the business. The size of the servicing staff relative to the number of accounts and level of complexity of the accounts serviced is an indication of the effectiveness of the operations.

Management should be focused on the business of servicing commercial mortgage loans. To the extent that the servicer is engaged in servicing of other lines of business, these will be reviewed as to their performance. In addition, the management and future business plan of the other lines of business are reviewed to insure that the other businesses will not detract from the overall business plan of the servicer to be rated.

Originations

If the servicer services loans originated by the organization, the stability of a servicing portfolio is directly linked to the quality of the origination process. Stringent approval standards generally result in a high-quality portfolio with lower-than-average delinquencies and losses. In the event that the servicer originates its own loans or accounts, rating agencies analyze the originations process to determine its impact on servicing operations.

Because uniform standards for underwriting commercial real estate loans have not been well established, they may vary greatly among originators. Important considerations include lending guidelines for DSCRs and LTVs, the experience of credit analysts and underwriters, credit approval processes, levels of approval authority, documentation requirements and degree of information verification.

Personnel granting credit should be either in a supervisory position or under the careful supervision of experienced management. Rating agencies evaluate the training required for credit-granting positions and the established levels of credit approval. For example, loans with above-average loan balances should be approved only by personnel with considerable experience. Many originators require additional executive or loan committee signatures for the approval of above-average dollar amounts. Management should provide established guidelines for the approval process and signature requirements. A lack of control over lending authority has a negative impact on the review results.

Loans must be well documented so that a credit approval or denial may be adequately supported. Any exceptions to policies encompassing originations, credit approval and servicing should be clearly documented.

The servicer's history is compared with information on the credit approval standards. If management at one time utilized more or less stringent standards, the review analyzes delinquencies and defaults for corresponding changes in portfolio performance.

The ability of an entity that has, to date, serviced only its own originations to service a third-party portfolio must be demonstrated.

Documentation

Originators should demonstrate that all loans are documented using standard documentation. A sample of files will be reviewed for completeness. Diligent tracking of documentation indicates that the servicer can monitor the approval process and has timely information about its operations. Storage of documentation must be safe from theft, fire and other disasters. Provisions must be made for duplication of lost loan files and documentation. Documentation includes legal documents (i.e., notes, mortgages or leases), credit bureau reports, appraisals, title policy, insurance policy, audited financial statements, engineering reports, environmental studies and other information as applicable or required by law.

Audit Policy

The results of internal and external audits will be reviewed. All audit results should be received regularly by management. Irregularities and management's actions are discussed during the assessment. Regulatory audits are also reviewed.

Servicing Capabilities

Servicing capabilities encompass written procedures, cash management, real estate tax collection, late payment collection, property insurance maintenance, loan classification policies, computer systems and reporting capabilities. The servicer must have well-documented servicing and collection procedures. The rationale for various procedures will be discussed with management.

Procedures A review of the servicer's written procedures and policies indicates whether they are comprehensive and well organized. Policies should be reviewed by management and updated regularly to reflect any changes in the legal, regulatory and/or economic environment. Documented procedures provide a guide for management as well as staff personnel to perform the servicing in a consistent and acceptable manner. They should clearly and adequately address the servicing and collection process in a concise manner that employees can easily understand. They should be consistent with the current volume of business as well as expected future growth. The policies should address areas such as general servicing, the collection process, insurance and tax payment maintenance, title search and maintenance and legal issues. Custodial issues of where documents are stored and the level of accessibility for actions such as a collateral withdrawal should be addressed.

Cash Management The cash management operations must be closely supervised by management to ensure the security of cash receipts. Safety procedures for on-site cash collection should encompass the authority to handle funds by a limited number of persons, the secure storage of funds while on-site, and the prompt deposit of funds to appropriate accounts. Ideally, a lock box system is employed for the collection of principal, interest and escrow receipts.

Customer Services Customer service personnel provide an important link between the servicer and its clients. The department must be adequately staffed and equipped to promptly respond to requests for account information and assistance. Any authority that customer service personnel have to forgive late fees or to exercise similar discretionary control must be disclosed so that its impact on security and cash flow may be assessed. Also, rating agencies discuss with management the philosophy of the department, which includes its approach to customer complaints, response time, and resolution of problems.

Collection Capability As delinquencies on obligations progress into defaults, the ability of the servicer's collection department is tested. Collection procedures should be sufficiently rigorous to produce an acceptable recovery rate on losses. Rating agencies discuss with management the training and level of experience of collection personnel, the supervision of collection efforts and the monitoring of collections.

The policies should provide for timely follow-up on all delinquent loans and for contact with a borrower as soon as a loan is past due. Any agreement to pay should be pursued and, if obtained, should be monitored for compliance. Continuous contact should be made as a loan moves through the delinquency cycle and becomes more severely past due.

Computer System and Reporting Capability The servicing process should be automated to provide up-to-date data on the loans, standard investor reports and ad hoc reports as requested. Computer systems must have the capacity to adequately track all loans currently serviced. Computer systems should have the capability to be expanded, or capital resources must be available to support any expected growth.

A servicer must frequently back up the computer system used for servicing. An acceptable disaster recovery plan must be established and documented to expedite a fast recovery of data in the event of a temporary or permanent loss of data.

The servicer must be capable of producing periodic reports (at least monthly) that accurately reflect the performance of the loans. The reports should be usable at all levels of the organization. The servicer must be able to produce reports that are consistent with monthly reporting requirements. These reports should include the operating performance and occupancy levels, if available, collection of payments, cash reserve balances, letter of credit balances, delinquencies, recoveries and losses. The reports should highlight delinquency and default categories. Consistent definitions for each of these terms should be in place. Responsibility for the review of delinquency/default reports should be established. Quality control procedures should be in place and constant monitoring of adherence to follow-up procedures should be implemented

Human Resources

The effectiveness of a servicing business depends on the quality of management and operations personnel. The quality of a servicer's personnel is measured primarily in terms of experience, knowledge and commitment, particularly with reference to the type of real estate being serviced. During a servicer review, the quality of personnel is evaluated by review of profiles and interviews with select employees. Interaction with management, supervisors, credit analysts and other operational employees form the basis for the rating agencies' evaluation of the quality of servicing personnel.

Although experience may be measured in terms of length of time working in the servicing area, the breadth of knowledge and competence gained during that time is more difficult to measure. Management's familiarity with the commercial real estate property types serviced is vital to the proper planning of systems, policies, procedures, and especially, hiring of competent staff.

Management's prior experience is important in order to anticipate potential problems related to its business and to create plans to address those difficulties. Management's knowledge of servicing and the property types that it services is evaluated by examining its stated goals, plans and procedures for coordinating the servicing operations.

In addition to experience, management must demonstrate its competence and commitment to the business. This includes not only possessing effective management skills, but also a track record of achievement in meeting stated goals. Management's commitment to servicing is reflected in its readiness to modify or add to existing capabilities. Management's commitment is also reflected in the existence and completeness of internal auditing procedures for monitoring ongoing operations. Rating agencies give special consideration to a high turnover frequency among top management. Such turnover may indicate dissatisfaction with corporate policies and goals and may result in inconsistent management supervision in the future.

The size of the servicing staff relative to the number of loans serviced is an indication of the effectiveness of operations. The servicer's ratio of staff to loans, compared with other industry servicers, should indicate whether there are any inefficiencies or potential staffing pressures. A discussion with management includes an overview of training procedures and staff development programs. Training should prepare staff to administer uniform policies and procedures. Employee turnover rates and trends provide insight into employment desirability, motivation and advancement opportunities.

Additionally, management is asked about any past litigation or pending legal action involving the company or any principals of the company. A legal search may be performed by rating agencies in order to obtain legal information about the parties.

Financial Condition

The financial condition of servicers varies substantially and plays an important role in the ability of the servicer to continue to perform its contractual obligations over the extended period of time involved in a structured financing. Overall financial condition will be reviewed to determine long- and short-term financial stability.

Some servicers have support from a strong parent, while others may be start-up operations with limited working capital. Although a new servicing operation may be managed by professionals with extensive experience, limited capital resources may restrict its ability to properly staff and equip operations in order to expand or to remain competitive. During the review, management should address future expansion and staffing needs that will require additional capital and the proposed sources of that capital.

A financial analysis of all lines of business will be performed if the company is a multiline business in which commercial real estate servicing is a part of the overall company business plan. The chief financial officer should discuss the financial condition of the corporation and the corporate business objectives.

Analysis of the servicer's financial statements indicates its ability to make servicer advances, if required, and demonstrates its immediate viability. A servicer must exhibit the ability to remain in existence for the life of a transaction. If there is a possibility that the servicer may not continue operations or may become unable to fulfill its obligations under securitization documents, provisions must be included to provide for a substitute or back-up servicer. If the servicer is not yet earning a profit, then the financial statements should disclose the source of working capital. If the servicer is supported by a strong parent, management should be prepared to discuss the reliability of capital infusions, advances and other types of financial support as well as the potential for a severance of the relationship and covenants involving intercompany borrowing and dividends of income. A business plan should outline a start-up servicer's projection of growth and profitability.

The financial viability, as well as the servicing capability, of a new servicing operation is very unpredictable. Such servicers may be required to submit periodic financial statements to rating agencies in order that any deterioration may be detected immediately.

Long-term viability is, in part, reliant upon diversification of income sources. Rating agencies view the servicer's viability as at risk if a significant portion of the servicer's income is earned from a single client.

INFORMATION GUIDELINES

The following eight exhibits provide guidelines as to what information should be provided. These items are particular to Duff & Phelps Credit Rating Co. However, there are numerous similarities with other rating agency formats. The timely and accurate provision of this information helps to facilitate the rating process.

Each transaction is unique, therefore, some of these exhibits may not apply to all transactions. Additionally, there may be other information needs that present themselves during the rating process.

Exhibit 1: Submission Package

The following information and documents are to be submitted as part of the rating. This information will vary depending upon whether the transaction involves a large pool, small pool, single property, new loan or existing loan.

(1) A term sheet from the underwriter explaining the financing structure of the transaction. This explanation should include the bond structure, identification of the principal parties in the transaction, identification of the underlying credit enhancement and description of the mortgage loan structure.

(2) Information concerning the servicer.

(3) A market analysis.

(4) Information concerning the property management and leasing company will include the track record and depth of experience in managing and leasing the property in the market area. A history of the property management and leasing company should be included along with an organizational structure, financial reporting and record keeping for projects managed. A history of the on-site management and management turnover at the projects should be supplied. Information on property maintenance and prior and anticipated capital expenditures for replacements and improvements is required.

(5) An engineering report is required showing the adequacy of the utilities of the property at full capacity, the structural condition, foundation, framing, roof and floor strength, and condition of all services such as the heating, ventilating, air conditioning, fire and safety systems. The engineering report also should discuss compliance with all zoning and building codes and other appropriate governmental requirements (including environmental and waste disposal) and an overall evaluation of the construction quality, design and appearance. There should be an evaluation of rehabilitation work or capital improvements planned, expected or needed.

(6) The property's historical operating results for the past five years with an audited report for at least the most recent year and pro forma 10-year cash flow projections. Market support for all assumptions underlying the projections concerning lease turnover, rental rates and expense increases should be included.

Exhibit I (Concluded)

(7) Copies of all executed commercial leases or lease abstracts. The location of each tenant in the property should be supplied. The lease abstract should show the tenant's name, space occupied, location of space, rental rate, lease term and types of expense payments and options (extension, expansion, renewal termination and the rights and options of tenants, and right of first refusal). Other information that should be provided to the rating agency includes rental concessions provided in the leases, side letters, broker's commission requirements, tenant improvement payments, percentage rents, and security deposits.

(8) Insurance policies.

(9) Representations and warranties from the servicer and issuer as described in Exhibit 8.

(10) Environmental reports

Upon receipt of all of the above information, the rating agency will perform a property site inspection and analysis of the proposed transaction. The rating agency relies on the accuracy and completeness of the information supplied and assumes no responsibility for verification.

Exhibit 2: Portfolio Submission Package

In order to process mortgage pool transactions, the following data items should be submitted to the rating agency in spreadsheet form.

- Property Address
- Property Type
- Gross Square Footage
- Net Rentable Square Footage
- Number of Units
- Property Age
- Owner/Borrower
- Property Manger
- Lien Status
- Property Valuation
- Date of Property Valuation
- Source of Property Valuation
- Three years historical operating information including at a minimum:
    Total Revenues (net of vacancies, credit losses, etc.)
    Occupancy %
    Total Expenses (excluding capital expenditures)

Exhibit 2 (Concluded)

- Capital Expenditures
- Date/Period of NOI Compilation
- Source of NOI Compilation
- Next ten years of scheduled lease rollover (commercial properties only, expressed as % of GLA)
- Original Loan Amount
- Loan Origination Date
- Payment History
- First Payment Date
- Payments Frequency
- Current Loan Amount
- Loan Maturity Date
- Remaining Term to Maturity
- Original Amortization Period
- Remaining Amortization Period
- Loan Balance at Maturity
- Loan Interest Rate
- Loan Interest Rate Index
- Loan Interest Rate Margin
- Loan Modification Details, if applicable
- Any additional loan information required to accurately calculate expected loan payment schedule, such as rate caps, floors or reset information
- Current and original DSCR and LTV

Exhibit 3: Market Studies – Scope of Work

Conceptually, market studies prepared for the rating agency should resemble an abbreviated MAI appraisal both in format and content. The studies must be prepared by a third-party appraiser or consultant who is not personally or professionally associated with the borrower.

Although "boiler plate" introductions and definitions can be eliminated, as well as the Cost Approach, most elements found in the Income and Sales Comparison Approaches should be presented and analyzed. It is important that all sections include not only charts summarizing data, but a narrative analyzing how the data relate to and affect the subject. Adjustments should be made to all comparables and rates and each analysis should be conclusive within a narrow range. As mentioned, the Cost Approach can be eliminated; however, a land analysis should be included if there is a substantial amount of excess land or if the consultant/appraiser determines the subject's value is approaching land value.

Exhibit 3 (Continued)

The following is an outline of items that must be included in submitted market studies. Although this format is flexible, it represents the minimum scope acceptable to the rating agency.

Cover Letter General cover letter identifying the property and briefly summarizing the scope of work completed for the client.

Executive Summary Summary of property data, value/rate range conclusions and any special assumptions.

Introduction Brief section that includes:

- Identification of Property
- Subject Photos
- Scope of the Report: more detailed explanation of the agreed upon procedures and scope of work completed
- Date of Inspection: include the dates of inspection and by whom
- Assumptions & Limiting Conditions

Area/Regional Analysis Expanded, conclusive section that includes the following items. The focus should be on identifying historical and future trends that would affect the subject property and the possible short and long-term economic conditions for the area

- Area map
- Delineation of the metro or regional area under analysis
- Population statistics and demographics
- Employment: Total employment, employment by industry, and unemployment rate
- Largest Employers
- Military Bases
- Transportation Linkages
- Recent and proposed developments that would impact the area
- Conclusion

Neighborhood Analysis Brief section describing the immediate area surrounding the property. The focus should be on historical and future trends as well as any recent or proposed developments impacting the area. The section should include:

- Neighborhood Map
- Delineation of neighborhood boundaries

Exhibit 3 (Continued)

- Description of land uses in neighborhood and estimate of how much land is developed
- Historical trends in property values and household income
- Access and transportation linkages
- Recent and proposed developments
- External Obsolescence - note if there are any external, economic conditions negatively impacting the value or marketability of the property
- Conclusion

Property Description A brief, but complete, narrative describing the subject property which includes:

- Age, size, construction, layout, building characteristics, amenities, parking, functional utility, deferred maintenance, recent/proposed capital improvements, fire safety and security.
- Size, shape, access, ingress/egress, functional utility, flood hazard and surrounding
- land uses.
- Zoning classification, parking ratio requirements, floor area ratio requirements, if subject is legal and conforming use.
- Current assessment, date of the property's next assessment, current taxes, historical tax rate trends and any personal or gross receipt taxes incurred by the property.

Market Area Analysis Extensive market analysis of the property type as well as the trade area for retail properties. Once again, the focus should be on historical and future trends impacting the property and its competitiveness relative to comparable properties. This section should include:

- Definition of Market and/or Trade Area
- Supply – current and historical
- Vacancy figures - current and historical
- Absorption data
- Demand – description of demand generators for the area
- Competitive Properties - description of competition and how the subject relates
- Trade Area statistics: household income, general demographics, sales figures
- Conclusion

Exhibit 3 (Continued)

Market Data Presentation and Analysis

Expanded and detailed section containing most items found in the Income Capitalization and Sales Comparison Approaches. This section is viewed as the most important section of the report and should be well supported with narrative discussions and conclusive within a reasonable range.

1) Income and Expense Data

Subject's Historical & Budgeted Operating Statements

Income Comparables: detailed presentation of competitive properties

Income Comparable Analysis & Market Rent Estimate: Analysis of the comparable properties, how they relate to the subject and conclude to a market rent range for the subject not to exceed 15%. If space within the subject varies (i.e., anchor vs. mall space or upper-level vs. lower-level office space), separate market rate ranges should be estimated.

Expense Analysis & Expense Comparables: Discuss significant increases or decreases in expenses exhibited by the subject in recent years and how it relates to the subject's current budget. If the property is not stabilized or is undergoing a major transformation, it may be necessary to include expense comparables to justify subject's projected expenses.

Tenant Improvements: Text discussing both the subject's current allowance for tenant alterations, what is being offered in the market and a range estimate within 15% of an appropriate allowance.

Leasing Commissions: Text discussing both the subject's current commissions structure, what is being offered in the market and a range estimate within 15% of appropriate commissions for the subject.

Reserves: Estimate of an appropriate annual reserve to allow for replacement of short-lived components of the property.

2) Comparable Sales Analysis

Improved Sales: Detailed presentation of comparable sales, which includes both physical and income characteristics of the property. Any unusual sale or financing conditions of the transaction should be disclosed.

Improved Sales Analysis: Analysis of the comparable properties, how they relate to the subject and conclude to a market value range for the subject not to exceed 15%.

Exhibit 3 (Concluded)

3) Investment Parameters and Indices Capitalization Rates
Presentation and discussion of both published and/or conducted surveys as well as the capitalization rates indicated by the comparable sales. Narrative should also conclude to a range estimate not to exceed 50 basis points for both first-year (going-in) and terminal (reversion) capitalization rates.
Discount Rates: presentation and discussion of both published and/or conducted surveys as well as the discount rates indicated by the comparable sales. Narrative should also conclude to a range estimate not to exceed 50 basis points.

Exhibit 4: Property Condition Survey Policy

I. Subject Research Review

The consultant should address public information regarding past, current and possible future engineering problems, which would include the following:

• compliance with building codes,
• compliance with zoning,
• current utilities in place,
• architectural drafts and documentation,
• systems reviews such as HVAC and elevators,
• safety issues such as ADA and fire codes, and
• flood plain status and/or earthquake stability where applicable.

II. On-Site Review

A physical inspection should be conducted not only to confirm findings from the research review, but also to gain an insight into the overall condition of the subject property. The physical inspection should include the following:

• Conducted by on-site maintenance personnel.
• Review of maintenance request and maintenance completion records.
• Full physical inspection of structure as well as systems.

III. Report

The final review should include a summary of pertinent items including deferred maintenance and items in need of immediate attention. Identified maintenance items should include estimates of both repair and replacement costs, as well as estimated remaining life of major building components, such as roof, if repaired and if replaced.

Exhibit 5: Environmental Policy

One of the areas that can adversely affect the cash flow is the cost of maintaining the property to the strict environmental standards set forth by the EPA and other state and local authorities. Foreclosure and liquidation analysis is also a part of the rating process, and case history suggests that the foreclosing entity can be held as partially responsible, since the legal standard is "Strict and Joint and Several Liability."

With these aspects in mind, we have assembled a minimum criteria for environmental reviews that, if followed, should help us to identify not only past and current problems, but should help to identify areas that, when addressed, prevent future problems as well.

I. Subject Historic Review

The consultant should review public information regarding past, current and future environmental problems including the following:

- Chain of title and land use records from 1940 to the present.
- Aerial photographs, fire insurance maps and environmental permits.
- City inspection reports and fire department response records.
- Rent roll and interview of on-site personnel and/or tenants.
- Historical and current use of surrounding area.
- DNR Wetlands designations.

II. Regulatory Review

The consultant should review databases in an effort to identify sites that have an impact on the subject property. The following federal and state lists are among the most comprehensive.

- Federal: NPL, CERCLIS, RCRA, FINDS, ERNS.
- State: SPL, LUST, UST, SWLF

A radius of one mile from the perimeter of the subject property should be used when identifying problem sites in general. A radius of one-half mile from the perimeter of the subject property should be used when identifying USTs and LUSTs.

III. Geological Review

Resources such as topographical maps, that help to determine both surface and subsurface migrations should be reviewed to assess the flow of potentially harmful materials.

Exhibit 5 (Continued)

IV. Physical Site Inspection

A physical inspection of the site should be made not only to confirm findings from the various reviews, but to determine the existence of any other environmental concerns. The inspection should take an all-encompassing approach to include:

- Surrounding area review of listed sites to assess their impact on the subject property.
- Description of the subject land and improvements including likely surface migration.
- Notation and explanation of abnormalities such as distressed vegetation, odors, stains, spills, wells, etc.
- Identification of above/underground storage tanks with opinion of physical condition.
- Description of utilities such as water supply and sewage, and inspection of transformers with conclusive determination of the existence of PCBs.
- Use and storage of hazardous materials.
- Asbestos, Radon and Lead: All suspect sources of these materials should be identified, sampled, and tested for level of contamination. Properties suspected to contain high levels of these materials should have separate tests conducted to reveal the true volume of materials.

V. Property Summary Report

The report provided by the consultant should include the following:

- Detailed account of procedures and reviews.
- Listing of requested unobtained information with explanation (i.e., source not available in subject city.)
- Full documentation of items utilized in the review process including a plotting of the environmental concerns in the surrounding area.
- Topographical map indicating direction of surface and subsurface flows.
- Conclusive statement of areas of concern with recommendations and cost estimates for further action.
- The report should be reviewed and signed by a person of authority, as well as by the consultant who should hold proper licensure in the subject's state.

VI. Response to Items

The questions that arise from Phase I reviews should be addressed prior to our review. An overall summary of reports should be presented to the rating agency along with the individual property reports. This summary should include results from the Phase I reports, results of any further testing that was recommended in the initial report and a plan of action for any unresolved items.

Exhibit 5 (Concluded)

VII. Proper Responses

- Confirmation that source of contaminant was properly addressed.
- Testing wells along property line adjacent to any "dirty neighbor."
- Test and confirm everything.
- All problems listed with proper authority.
- Estimates on remediation costs.

Exhibit 6: Lease Abstracts

Required Lease Abstract Data

- Project
- Lessor
- Lessee
- Parent Company, if any
- Guarantor
- Date of Lease
- Commencement Date
- Expiration Date
- Location
- Use of Premises
- Square Feet (Gross, Net, etc.)
- Operating and Name Covenant
- Expense Stop Formula
- Base Rate
- Rent Escalations
- Base Year
- Percentage Rent and Breakpoint Schedule
- Rent Concessions
- Security and Other Deposits
- Operating and Maintenance Expenses, Common Area
- Charges and Taxes
- Brokerage Commissions
- Lessee Improvement Costs
- Late Payments and Penalties
- Cancellation or Termination Rights
- Any Defined Liquidated Damages for Early Termination
- Rights to Reduce or Expand Leased Area
- Rights to Assign or Sublease
- Unfunded Lessor Obligations
- Renewal Options

Exhibit 6: (Continued)

- Lessor's Recapture Provisions
- Options to Purchase
- Rights of First Refusal Options
- Unusual Lease Provisions
- Non-Compete Clauses
- Required Store Hours (Retail)
- Tenant Estoppel Provision

Required Operating Agreement Abstract Data
- Project
- Parties
- Date of Operating Agreement
- Commencement Date
- Expiration Date
- Location
- Use of Premises
- Square Feet
- Operating and Maintenance Expenses, Common Area
- Charges and Taxes
- Cancellation or Termination Rights
- Any Defined Liquidated Damages for Early Termination
- Rights to Reduce or Expand
- Renewal Options
- Recapture Provisions
- Non-Compete Clauses
- Required Store Hours (Retail)

Exhibit 7: Suggested Guidelines for Acceptable Agreed-Upon Procedures

For the rating of single-borrower transactions, the rating agency needs to attain a high level of confidence in the propriety of the portfolio's operating statements. This level of confidence can be achieved one of three ways. The preferred method is to receive an audit opinion on each individual property's operating statement. Another alternative is to obtain an audit opinion on the roll-up operating statement of the portfolio as a whole. With an audit opinion on the portfolio as a whole, an audit of the individual properties is not necessary. The last and least preferred alternative is to perform certain agreed-upon procedures on each individual property in order to obtain "audit level certainty" on the operating statements for the portfolio as a whole.

Exhibit 7 (Continued)

The objective of the agreed-upon procedures is to provide assurance that the portfolio's operating statements are free of material misstatement. There are five objectives that must be met when designing the procedures.

- **Existence** Do the assets and revenues exist?
- **Completeness** Do the statements reflect all of the transactions of the entity and are they accounted for in the proper period?
- **Rights & Obligations** Do the assets and revenues belong to the entity, without restriction, unless otherwise noted?
- **Valuation** Are the values of the assets and revenues properly reflected?
- **Presentation & Disclosure** Are financial data properly described, classified and disclosed?

What follows is an outline of the minimum procedures that would be required to be performed in order for the rating agency to accept the use of agreed-upon procedures as an alternative to the preferred audited portfolio operating statement.

General

Meet with ownership/management to achieve an overall understanding of the properties within the portfolio, their operations and accounting procedures.

Obtain and read third-party reports such as appraisals, engineering and environmental reports to gain added insight into the properties.

Obtain and read the unaudited historical operating statements of the properties for the previous three years and any year-to-date information, including information regarding recurring capital expenditures from these periods.

Obtain current year operating budgets and net operating forecasts (including recurring replacements) for the annualized current year. Compare historical operating statements to the forecasts and discuss any variances greater than 5% on income items and variances greater than 3% on expense items with management. Comment on the reasonableness of these assumptions based on discussions with management, market research, historical results and professional judgment.

Obtain management-prepared monthly budget-to-actual report and determine if any actual line item amounts differ from what was budgeted by more than 10%. Inquire of management as to why this variance occurred. Comment on reasonableness of these assumptions based on discussions with management, market research, historical results and professional judgment.

Make inquires regarding pending litigation and other issues that may effect the cash flow of the properties. If litigation is pending or if legal expenses for a particular law firm exceed $25,000 for the year, obtain a letter from counsel describing the litigation and the expected resolution.

Exhibit 7 (Continued)

If hotel properties are included, review franchise and management agreements, including rights of termination, reporting requirements and overall terms.

If retail properties are included, review anchor tenant's leases for recapture rights, co-tenancy clauses and cancellation rights.

Market

Conduct interviews with property management personnel as to each property's operating performance, market and competitive trends, its physical condition and need for capital improvements.

Visit the properties and observe the site to obtain an understanding of the general market conditions; randomly compare rent rolls to actual physical occupancy of space.

Drive the surrounding neighborhood and competitive market area to determine competition, location attributes, access to commercial services, employment centers and other amenities.

Interview property management of three selected competitive properties for each subject property in the portfolio as to rents, vacancies and market conditions for their respective property.

Obtain and analyze economic and demographic information for the market in which each property is located. Market data should be comprised of population, number of households, household income, inflation, employment trends and projections and other pertinent information.

Obtain market reports that identify historical and projected occupancy, rental rates, absorption, percentage rent, expense passthroughs (if applicable) and concessions.

In those instances in which the information is available, identify proposed additions to supply in terms of size, timing and target market.

Revenues

Obtain historical operating statements, current rent rolls, total occupancy costs and historical percentage changes in rents. Consider trends in the data, discuss any variances greater than 5% on any income line-item with management. Comment on reasonableness of these variances based on discussions with management, market research, historical results and professional judgment.

If disclosed, obtain the prior year's partnership tax return and trace the individual property's rental revenue per the operating statement to the tax return.

Calculate the average monthly rental revenue per occupied unit from the previous three years. Analyze the average annual occupancy rate and average monthly revenue per occupied unit, looking for any unusual amounts in comparison to historical, neighborhood and property-type data.

Exhibit 7 (Continued)

Obtain rental growth/inflation rates, releasing and capital improvement assumptions for the next two years for each property, utilizing historical occupancy levels, historical releasing experience, required future capital improvements, local and regional market projections.

Judiciously select three current leases from each property and assess whether the information presented on the rent roll for each selected lease is confirmed by what is stated in the lease. Trace the rent for these tenants from the rent rolls to appropriate cash receipts journals and validated bank deposits, noting any exceptions.

For each property, trace one month's cash receipts per the cash receipts journal to the appropriate property general ledger, noting any exceptions.

Review the latest available aging of tenants accounts receivable for indications of collectability problems.

If retail properties are included, compare actual percentage rent collected to what should be collected based on the tenant's actual sales and the lease terms.

If retail properties are included, randomly verify that the pass-through income collected is confirmed by what is provided under the terms of the lease.

Expenses

Obtain historical operating statements, total occupancy costs and historical percentage changes in expenses. Review prior year's property administration, marketing and leasing, and service contract expenses for each property as classified in the unaudited, historical operating statements. For any type of expense that represents more than 5% of revenues, select one month of expenses from the general ledger and agree the expenses recorded to invoices from vendors. Note any exceptions. In addition, recompute the management fee in accordance with the terms described in the management agreement.

Obtain an understanding of management's policy regarding capitalization of expenditures. Review each property's detailed general ledger for the prior three years for repairs and maintenance expense. From the cash disbursements ledger, select payments to vendors for maintenance services greater than $2,500 and agree those to vendor invoices to determine whether the item is properly categorized.

Review each property's prior three year's personnel costs as classified in the unaudited, historical operating statements. Select two pay periods from the previous three years and agree the recorded payroll expense from the general ledger to the payroll register.

Compare historical and projected expenses to national industry standards and local expense levels indicated in market reports and/or interviews.

Agree the total amount of the prior three year's property taxes recorded for each property to the paid property tax bills. Conduct interviews with the tax appraisal district and the local utility companies that service the properties. Determine historical tax/utility rate increase/decreases and where available, obtain projections for the next two years.

Exhibit 7 (Concluded)

Interview management to understand the terms of the historical and projected "blanket" hazard insurance coverage. Compare this information with interviews with insurance agents and other retail property managers. Obtain schedules of insurance in force for each property. Agree the total amount of insurance expense for the prior three years for the properties to the appropriate schedules of insurance, noting any exceptions. In addition, obtain a schedule detailing the allocation of the prior three year's insurance expense to the individual properties.

Inquire of management as to the methodology employed in allocating expenses performed at the partnership level for the individual properties.

Review each property's past three years of utility expenses as classified in the unaudited, historical operating statements. For any type of utility expense (electricity, water and sewer, gas and oil) greater than 5% of revenues, agree one month's recorded expense to the appropriate month's paid bills.

Exhibit 8: Representations and Warranties

The following comprise certain basic representations and warranties to be delivered in connection with commercial mortgage securitizations. This list is not all-inclusive and may be modified or expanded depending on the specific terms and structure of a given transaction. This list is intended only as a general guideline for the scope and substance of typical provisions.

1. Mortgage Loan Schedule
The information with respect to each mortgage loan is true and correct in all material respects at the date or dates the information is given.

2. Ownership of Mortgage Loans
Immediately prior to the transfer and assignment of the mortgage loans to the purchaser, the seller is the sole owner of each mortgage loan and transfers the lease free and clear of all liens. Additionally, each mortgage loan should be a whole loan and not a participation interest in a mortgage loan.

3. Ratios
The debt-service-coverage ratio and loan-to-value ratio with respect to each mortgage loan are not to be less than *XXXX* and *XXXX*, respectively, as of the cut-off date.

4. Payment Record
No mortgage loan is delinquent beyond any applicable grace period nor more than 30 days delinquent at any time subsequent to origination, without giving effect to any applicable grace period.

Exhibit 8 (Continued)

5. First-Lien Mortgage

Each mortgage is a legal first lien on the mortgage property, subject only to (a) the lien of the current real property taxes, ground rents, water charges and sewer rents, and assessments not yet due and payable, (b) exceptions and exclusions specifically referred to in lender's title insurance commitment or policy (including rights of way and easements), none of which materially interferes with the current use of the mortgaged property or the security intended to be provided by the mortgage, and (c) other matters to which like properties are commonly subject, none of which materially interferes with the current use of the mortgaged property or the security intended to be provided by such mortgage (collectively, "permitted encumbrances"). A UCC financing statement has been filed and/or recorded in all places necessary to perfect a valid security interest in the personal property, if any, granted under such mortgage; any security agreement, chattel mortgage or equivalent document related to and delivered in connection with the mortgage loan establishes and creates a valid and enforceable first lien and first priority security interest on the property described, provided that enforceability may be limited by bankruptcy or other laws affecting creditor's rights or by the application of the rules of equity.

6. Assignment of Leases and Rents

The mortgage file contains an assignment of leases or an assignment of rents (assignment of leases) either as a separate instrument or incorporated into the related mortgage, which creates, in favor of the holder, a valid, perfected and enforceable lien of the same priority as the related mortgage, in the property and rights described; provided that the enforceability of such lien is subject to applicable bankruptcy, insolvency, reorganization, moratorium, and other laws affecting the enforcement of creditors' rights generally, and by the application of the rules of equity. The seller has the full right to assign to the purchaser such assignment of leases and the lien created thereby as described in the immediately preceding sentence. No person other than the mortgagor owns any interest in any payments due under the related leases.

7. Valid Assignment

Each assignment of mortgage and related assignment of leases has been duly authorized, executed and delivered by the seller in recordable form, in order to validly convey the seller's interest to purchaser.

Exhibit 8 (Continued)

8. Waivers and Modifications

None of the terms of any lease, mortgage note, mortgage or assignment related to a mortgage loan have been impaired, waived, altered or modified in any way, except by written instruments, all of which are included in the related mortgage file (and, to the extent necessary, all such waivers, alterations and modifications have been filed and/or recorded or submitted for record in all places necessary to perfect, maintain and continue the validity and priority of the lien of the mortgage). The related lessee, mortgagor or guarantor, if any, has not been released, in whole or in part, from its obligations related to the mortgage note, other than pursuant to releases previously approved in writing by the seller or any affiliate, copies of which are included in the related mortgage file.

9. No Offset or Defense

There is no right of rescission, offset, abatement, diminution, defense or counterclaim to any mortgage loan (including the defense of usury). The operation of any terms of the mortgage note or the mortgage, or the exercise of any rights under the agreement, will not render the mortgage note or the mortgage unenforceable, in whole or in part, or subject to any right of rescission, offset, abatement, diminution, defense or counterclaim (including the defense of usury or the violation of any applicable disclosure or consumer credit laws). No right of rescission, offset abatement, diminution, defense or counterclaim has been asserted with respect thereto.

10. Mortgage Status

Neither the seller nor any prior holder of any mortgage loan has satisfied, canceled, rescinded or subordinated the mortgage in whole or in part, released the mortgaged property in whole or in part from the lien of the mortgage, or executed any instrument that would effect any such satisfaction, cancellation, rescission, subordination or release. The terms of the mortgage do not provide for a release of any portion of the mortgaged property from the lien of the mortgage.

11. Condemnation

To the best of the seller's knowledge, there is no proceeding pending for the total or partial condemnation of any mortgaged property.

12. Legal Compliance-Origination

All requirements of relevant federal, state and local law, rules and regulations have been satisfied or complied with in all material respects as they relate to the origination, funding servicing and the terms of the mortgage loans, including, without limitation, usury, truth in lending, real estate settlement procedures, consumer credit protection, equal credit opportunity or disclosure.

Exhibit 8 (Continued)

13. Title Insurance

The lien of each mortgage is insured by an ALTA lender's title insurance policy (or a binding commitment) or its equivalent, as adopted in the applicable jurisdiction. The policy insures the seller, its successor and assigns, as to the first priority lien of the mortgage in the original principal amount after all advances of principal, subject only to permitted encumbrances, none of which, individually or in the aggregate should interfere with the current use of the mortgaged property or materially detract from the benefit of the first priority lien of the mortgage. The seller or its successors or assigns are the sole named insured of the policy, and the policy is assignable to the purchaser without the consent of or any notification to the insurer. No claims have been made under such policy and no prior holder of the related mortgage has done anything, by act or omission, and the seller has no knowledge of any matter that would impair or diminish the coverage of such policy. The insurer issuing such policy is qualified to do business in the jurisdiction in which the mortgaged property is located, and the policy contains no exclusion for or affirmatively insures (a) access to a public road, (b) that there are no encroachments of any part of the buildings thereon over easements (except for any mortgaged property located in jurisdictions where such affirmative insurance is not available) and (c) that the area shown on the survey is the same as the property legally described in the mortgage.

14. No Holdbacks

The proceeds of each mortgage loan have been fully disbursed, or, in cases of partial disbursement, there is no requirement for future advances. To the best of the seller's knowledge, all requirements imposed by the originator to completion of any on-site or off-site improvements and to disbursements of any escrow funds have been complied with. Construction of the improvements on the mortgaged property are complete.

15. Mortgage Provisions

The mortgage note, mortgage and assignment of leases for each mortgage loan contain customary and enforceable provisions for commercial mortgage loans secured by properties such as the mortgaged properties, so as to render the rights and remedies of the holder adequate for the realization against the mortgaged property of the benefits of the security, including realization by judicial, or if applicable, non-judicial foreclosure subject to the effect of bankruptcy and similar laws affecting the rights of creditor and the application of principles of equity.

Exhibit 8 (Continued)

16. No Mortgage Default

There is no default, breach, violation or event of acceleration under the mortgage note, mortgage or assignment of leases, and no event that, with the passage of time or the giving of notice, or both, would constitute a default or event of acceleration, nor has the seller waived any such default. No foreclosure action or other form of enforcement has been threatened or commenced with respect to any mortgage.

17. Other Collateral

Each mortgage note does not, and has not since the date of origination of the related mortgage loan, secured by any collateral except the lien of the related mortgage, as assignment of the related leases, and any related security agreement. The mortgaged property does not secure any other mortgage loan not represented by the related mortgage note. No mortgage loan is cross-defaulted with any other mortgage loan nor is any mortgage loan secured by the mortgaged property that secures another mortgage loan.

18. Trustee Under Deed of Trust

In the case of any mortgage that is a deed of trust, a trustee, duly qualified under applicable law to serve as such, is properly designated and serves in accordance with applicable laws. No fees or expenses are payable to the trustee under the deed of trust, except in connection with a trustee's sale after default by the mortgagor or in connection with the release or the mortgaged property or related security for the mortgage loan following the payment of the mortgage loan in full.

19. Leases

The seller has delivered the purchaser a complete schedule of all leases with respect to each mortgaged property as of a date not more than 30 days prior to the closing date set forth in the attached schedule (XXX). Based on mortgagor representations, tenant estoppel certificates and other documents obtained by the seller, (i) the information contained therein is true and correct in all material respects, (ii) such leases are in full force and effect, and (iii) no default by the mortgagor or the lessees has occurred under such leases, nor, to the best of the seller's knowledge, is there any existing condition which, but for the passage of time or the giving of notice, or both, would result in a default under the terms of such lease. (Applicable to commercial loans with anchor tenants; multifamily properties may refer to attached rent roll.)

Exhibit 8 (Continued)

20. Lease Termination

No lease may be amended, terminated or canceled, and the lessee may not be released from its obligations, except under are certain limited events relating to material damage to, or destruction of, the mortgaged property, or condemnation of less than the entire mortgaged property, which, in any case, the lessee in good faith determines will render its continued occupancy and use of the remainder of the mortgaged property economically unsound, or condemnation of all the mortgaged property. (Applicable to retail/office loans.)

21. Condition of Mortgaged Property

Each mortgaged property is in good repair and condition, free of any material damage.

22. Local Law Compliance

Each mortgaged property is in compliance with all applicable laws, zoning ordinances, rules, covenants and restrictions affecting the construction, occupancy, use and operation of such mortgaged property. All inspections, licenses and certificates required, including certificates of occupancy, whether by law, ordinance, regulation or insurance standards to be made or issued with regard to the mortgaged property, have been obtained and are in full force and effect.

23. Environmental Compliance

In each mortgage, the mortgagor represents and warrants that it has not and will not use, cause or permit to exist on the related mortgaged property any hazardous materials in any manner that violates federal, state or local laws, ordinances, regulations, orders, directives or policies governing the use, storage, treatment, transportation, manufacture, refinement, handling, production or disposal of hazardous materials. The mortgagor agrees to indemnify, defend and hold the purchaser and its successors and/or assigns harmless from and against any and all losses, liabilities, damages, injuries, penalties, fines, expenses, and claims of any kind whatsoever (including attorney's fees and costs) paid, incurred, or suffered by, or asserted against, any such party resulting from a breach of any representation, warranty or covenant given by the mortgagor under the mortgage. A Phase I environmental report has been conducted by an independent licensed (if required), reputable environmental engineer in connection with each mortgage loan, which did not indicate any non-compliance or existence of hazardous materials. To the best of the seller's knowledge, the mortgaged property is in material compliance with all applicable federal, state and local laws pertaining to environmental hazards, and no notice of violation of such laws have been issued by any governmental agency or authority.

Exhibit 8 (Continued)

24. Opinion re Mortgage Enforceability

Each mortgage file contains an opinion letter(s) from counsel to the mortgagor which opines that, among other things, (A) the mortgage note, the mortgage, the assignment of leases, the UCC-1 or UCC-3 financing statement and all other documents and instruments evidencing, guaranteeing, insuring or otherwise securing the mortgage loan are genuine, and that each is the legal, valid and binding obligation of the maker, enforceable in accordance with its terms, except as the enforcement may be limited by bankruptcy, insolvency, reorganization, receivership, moratorium or other laws relating to or affecting the rights of creditors and by general principles of equity (regardless of whether such enforcement is considered in a proceeding in equity or at law) (B) all parties (other than the originator) to the mortgage note, the mortgage, the assignment of lessee, the UCC-1 and UCC-3 financing statement and each other document and instrument evidencing, guaranteeing, insuring or otherwise securing the mortgage loan have legal capacity to enter into the mortgage loan and to execute and deliver the mortgage note, the mortgage, the assignment of leases and other documents and instruments, (C) all necessary approvals, consents and authorizations required to be obtained by any party (other than the originator) have been obtained, and (D) the mortgage note, the mortgage, the assignment of leases and other documents and instruments have been duly authorized, executed and delivered by the parties (other than the originator).

25. Insurance

Each mortgaged property and all improvements are covered by insurance policies providing coverage against loss or damage sustained by (i) fire and extended perils included within the classification "All Risk of Physical Loss" in an amount sufficient to prevent the mortgagor from being deemed a co-insurer, and to provide coverage on a full replacement cost basis; and the policies contain a standard mortgagee clause naming mortgagee and its successors as additional insureds; (ii) business interruptions or rental loss insurance, in an amount at least equal to 12 months of operations of the mortgaged property; (iii) flood insurance (if any portion of the mortgaged property is located in an area identified by the Federal Emergency Management Agency as having special hazards); (iv) comprehensive general liability insurance in amounts as are generally required by commercial mortgage lenders, and in any event not less than $2 million per occurrence; (v) workers' compensation insurance; and (vi) other insurance as applicable to specific circumstances and criteria. The insurer in each case is qualified to write insurance in the relevant jurisdiction and has a claims paying ability rating from the rating agency of lot less than 'A'. The insurance policies contain clauses providing they are not terminable and may not be reduced without 30 days prior written notice to the mortgagee, and all premiums due and payable through the closing date have been made. No notice of termination or cancellation with respect to any such policies has been received by the seller.

Exhibit 8 (Continued)

26. Loan Underwriting

Each mortgage loan complies with all of the terms, conditions and requirements of the seller's underwriting standards in effect at the time of origination of such mortgage loan.

27. Status of Mortgage Documents

The mortgage note, related mortgage, any guaranty, assignment of leases and/or rents, security agreement, and chattel mortgage, each instrument delivered and all other documents evidencing, securing, guaranteeing, insuring or otherwise relating to the mortgage loan are genuine and the legal, valid and binding obligation of its maker, enforceable in accordance with its terms, except as such enforcement may be limited by bankruptcy, insolvency, moratorium or other laws affecting the enforcement of creditors' rights, or by the application of the rules of equity.

28. Inspections

The seller has inspected or caused to be inspected each related mortgaged property within the last 12 months.

29. Taxes and Assessments

There are no delinquent or unpaid taxes or assessments (including assessments payable in future installments), or other outstanding charges affecting any mortgaged property which are or may become a lien of equal or coordinate or higher priority than the lien of the mortgage.

30. Liens

There are no mechanics' or similar liens or claims that have been filed for work, labor or material. There are no claims outstanding that under applicable law could give rise to such lien, affecting the related mortgaged property which are or may be a lien prior to, or equal or coordinate with, the lien of the related mortgage.

31. Mortgagor Bankruptcy

To the best of the seller's knowledge, no mortgagor is a debtor in any state or federal bankruptcy or insolvency proceeding.

32. Fee Simple Interest

Each mortgaged property consists of an estate in fee simple in real property and improvements owned by the mortgagor. The buildings and improvements on the mortgaged property are owned by the mortgagor and used and occupied for commercial purposes in accordance with applicable law.

Exhibit 8 (Continued)

33. Loan Terms

No mortgage loan has a shared appreciation feature, other contingent interest feature or negative amortization.

34. Transfers and Subordinate Debt

The mortgage contains a "due on sale" clause that provides for the acceleration of the payment of the unpaid principal balance of the mortgage loan if, without the prior written consent of the holder, the property subject to the mortgage, or any interest therein, is directly or indirectly transferred or sold. The mortgage prohibits any further pledge or lien on the mortgaged property, whether equal or subordinate to the lien of the mortgage, without the prior written consent of the holder. (Any exceptions must be approved by the rating agency.)

35. Financial Statements

Each mortgage requires the mortgagor to provide the holder with quarterly and annual operating statements, rent rolls and related information. Annual financial statements must be audited by an independent certified public accountant upon the request of holder.

36. Escrow Deposits

All escrow deposits and payments relating to each mortgage loan are in the possession or under the control of the seller, and all amounts required to be deposited by the applicable mortgagor under the related mortgage loan documents have been deposited, and there are no deficiencies regarding them. All such escrows and deposits have been conveyed by seller to purchaser and identified as such with appropriate detail.

37. Selection Process

The seller has taken no action in selecting the mortgage loans for sale, assignment and transfer to the purchaser which, to the seller's knowledge, would result in delinquencies and losses on mortgage loans being materially in excess of delinquencies and losses on the seller's actual portfolio of commercial mortgage loans.

38. Borrower Concentration

As of the closing date, not more than 5% of the aggregate outstanding principal amount of the mortgage loans have the same mortgagor or, to the seller's best knowledge, are to mortgagors which are affiliates of each other. (Exceptions should be noted. Indicate whether non-consolidation opinions have been provided.)

Exhibit 8 (Continued)

39. Single-Purpose Entity

Each mortgagor is either a corporation or a limited partnership whose organizational documents provide that it is, and at least so long as the mortgage loan is outstanding will continue to be, a single-purpose entity. (For this purpose, "single-purpose entity" shall mean a person, other than an individual, which is formed or organized solely for the purpose of owning and operating a single property, does not engage in any business unrelated to such property and its financing, does not have any assets other than those related to its interest in the property or its financing, or any indebtedness other than as permitted by the related mortgage or the other mortgage loan documents, has its own books and records and accounts separate and apart from any other person, and holds itself out as being a legal entity, separate and apart from any other person.) If the foregoing entry is a limited partnership, (i) one general partner must be a single-purpose entity, and (ii) the partnership agreement must provide that the dissolution and winding up or insolvency filing of such limited partnership requires the unanimous consent of all general partners.

40. Servicing

No other person has been granted or conveyed the right to service the mortgage loans to receive any consideration in connection therewith.

In the event representation (32) regarding fee simple interest cannot be made, the substance of the following representations regarding ground leases should incorporated and approved by the rating agency.

41. Ground Leases

With respect to any mortgage loan secured by a mortgage constituting a valid first lien on an unencumbered interest of the mortgagor as lessee under a ground lease of the related mortgaged property, but not by the related fee interest in such mortgaged property, the seller represents and warrants that:

(i)The ground lease or a memorandum regarding it has been duly recorded. The ground lease permits the interest of the lessee to be encumbered by the related mortgage and does not restrict the use of the related mortgaged property by such lessee, its successors or assigns in a manner that would adversely affect the security provided by the related mortgage. There has been no material change in the terms of such ground lease since its recordation, except by written instruments, all of which are included in the related mortgage file.

Exhibit 8 (Continued)

(ii)The lessor under such ground lease has agreed in writing and included in the related mortgage file that the ground lease may not be amended, modified, canceled or terminated without the prior written consent of the mortgagee and that any such action without such consent is not binding on the mortgagee, its successors or assigns.

(iii)The ground lease has an original term (or an original term plus one or more optional renewal terms, which, under all circumstances, may be exercised, and will be enforceable, by the mortgagee) that extends not less than 10 years beyond the stated maturity of the related mortgage loan.

(iv)The ground lease is not subject to any liens or encumbrances superior to, or of equal priority with, the mortgage. The ground lease is, and provides that it shall remain, prior to any mortgage or other lien upon the related fee interest.

(v)The ground lease does not permit any increase in the amount of rent payable by the lessee thereunder during the term of the mortgage loan. (Exceptions must be provided to the rating agency).

(vi)The ground lease is assignable to the mortgagee under the lease hold estate and its assigns without the consent of the lessor thereunder.

(vii)As of the date of execution and delivery, the ground lease is in full force and effect and no default has occurred, nor is there any existing condition which, but for the passage of time or giving of notice, would result in a default under the terms of the ground lease.

(viii)The ground lease or ancillary agreement between the lessor and the lessee requires the lessor to give notice of any default by the lessee to the mortgagee. The ground lease or ancillary agreement further provides that no notice given is effective against the mortgagee unless a copy has been given to the mortgagee in a manner described in the ground lease or ancillary agreement.

Exhibit 8 (Concluded)

(ix)A mortgagee is permitted a reasonable opportunity (including, where necessary, sufficient time to gain possession of the interest of the lessee under the ground lease through legal proceedings, or to take other action so long as the mortgagee is proceeding diligently) to cure any default under the ground lease which is curable after the receipt of notice of any default before the lessor may terminate the ground lease. All rights of the mortgagee under the ground lease and the related mortgage (insofar as it relates to the ground lease) may be exercised by or on behalf of the mortgagee.

(x)The ground lease does not impose any restrictions on subletting that would be viewed as commercially unreasonable by an institutional investor. The lessor is not permitted to disturb the possession, interest or quiet enjoyment of any subtenant of the lessee in the relevant portion of the mortgaged property subject to the ground lease for any reason, or in any manner, which would adversely affect the security provided by the related mortgage;

(xi)Under the terms of the ground lease and the related mortgage, any related insurance proceeds or condemnation award (other than in respect of a total or substantially total loss or taking) will be applied either to the repair or restoration of all or part of the related mortgaged property, with the mortgagee or a trustee appointed by it having the right to hold and disburse such proceeds as repair or restoration progresses, or to the payment of the outstanding principal balance of the mortgage loan, together with any accrued interest.

(xii)Under the terms of the ground lease and the related mortgage, any related insurance proceeds, or condemnation award in respect of a total or substantially total loss or taking of the related mortgaged property will be applied first to the payment of the outstanding principal balance of the mortgage loan, together with any accrued interest (except in cases where a different allocation would not be viewed as commercially unreasonable by any institutional investor, taking into account the relative duration of the ground lease and the related mortgage and the ratio of the market value of the related mortgage property to the outstanding principal balance of such mortgage loan). Until the principal balance and accrued interest rate are paid in full, neither the lessee nor the lessor under the ground lease will have the option to terminate or modify the ground lease without the prior written consent of the mortgagee as a result of any casualty or partial condemnation, except to provide for an abatement of the rent.

Chapter **11**

Defaults on Commercial Mortgages

J. Zachary Monsma
Structured Finance Analyst
Fitch Investors Service, L.P.

Janet G. Price
Structured Finance Analyst
Fitch Investors Service, L.P.

INTRODUCTION

A major impediment to commercial mortgage research has been the desire of lending institutions to keep proprietary loan-level "information confidential. With the advent of CMBS, however, there has been a flow of loan-level information through the public and 144A markets. This chapter summarizes the results of a Fitch default/payoff study focusing on the effects of specific loan characteristics on the average annual default and payoff rates for certain loans during the four-year analysis period. Characteristics studied include debt service coverage ratio (DSCR), property type, loan size, interest rate type (fixed/floating), loan type (balloon/ fully amortizing), and geographic location. The appendix to this chapter explains the research methodology employed.

DATA BASE

To analyze the effects of specific loan characteristics on the performance of commercial mortgages, Fitch created a data base that tracks loan-level information from qualifying multiborrower CMBS transactions it has rated.

Special thanks is given to Sandeep Garg for his contribution in preparing this chapter.

Exhibit 1: Transactions

	Seasoning (Years)	Number of Loans	Securitization Balance ($ Millions)
RTC 1991-M6	3.3	391	651.5
RTC 1991-M7	3.3	595	240.4
RTC 1992-M3	3.0	1,345	523.5
RTC 1992-C4	2.8	2,745	932.6
RTC 1992-C5	2.8	3,623	884.3
RTC 1992-CHF	2.5	1,763	1,460.3
SASCO 1993-C1	2.1	679	520.7
RTC 1993-C3	1.3	979	444.1
The New England	1.3	193	881.9
Average/Total	2.9	12,313	6,539.3

Each CMBS deal included in this study was originated prior to 1994 and had more than 100 loans. As indicated in Exhibit 1, applying this criterion yielded nine transactions containing 12,313 loans that totaled $6.5 billion and had an average seasoning of 2.9 years as of May 1995. These nine pools include multifamily or mixed commercial collateral; transactions with features such as specialized property types or credit lease-backed loans, which could skew results, were not included in the study.

Fitch input the loan-level data from underwriter-provided information at the origination of the transaction. In certain cases, loan characteristics were manipulated so that each loan had consistent treatment. For example, in the calculation of DSCR, only loans with 12 months of historical net operating income (NOI) were included, and debt service payments were adjusted to reflect market interest rates. DSCR for floating rates was calculated based on a 10.5% interest rate, which approximates the maximum rate experienced on most floating-rate loans between 1991 and May 1995. In addition, not all loans have complete information for all loan characteristics. For instance, only 2,229 loans have DSCR, due to the unavailability of information or operating statements that did not meet Fitch's requirements.

Today, Fitch's data base is predominantly composed of thrift-originated loans that were securitized by the Resolution Trust Corp. (RTC). These loans dominate the data base because RTC pools were among the first to enter the market in 1991 and, therefore, have the most history for analysis. The RTC pools also have a relatively large number of loans compared with more recent CMBS pools.

Notwithstanding the heavy concentration of RTC collateral, Fitch believes that many of the insights from this study are applicable to commercial mortgages in general. Of course, the results of the analysis, particularly the rates of default and payoff, are reflective of this portfolio and the economic climate to which it was exposed. A breakdown of Fitch's data base by various loan characteristics is depicted in Exhibit 2.

Exhibit 2: Data Base Distribution

Region

	Count
West	4,272
Midwest	2,884
Northeast	2,189
Southwest	1,632
Southeast	1,336

Property Type

	Count	Percent
Multifamily	4,404	36
Other	2,480	20
Office	1,976	16
Industrial	1,575	13
Retail	1,526	12
Lodging	238	2

DSCR

Number of Loans:	2,229
Number Missing:	10,084
Mean (x)	1.72
1st Quartile (x)	1.01
Median (x)	1.29
3rd Quartile (x)	1.85

Loan Type

	Count	Percent
Fully Amortizing	6,016	54
Balloon Loans	5,074	46

Balance

Number of Loans:	12,313
Number Missing:	0
Mean ($)	542,700
1st Quartile ($)	49,220
Median ($)	127,000
3rd Quartile ($)	372,500

Rate Type

	Count	Percent
Fixed Rate	5,315	57
Floating Rate	6,990	43

ANALYSIS

The assessment of commercial mortgage performance relies on the examination of two risks: the probability of default/payoff and the severity of loss. This study focuses solely on the default/payoff component of this assessment. Fitch's data base also tracks mortgage loss statistics; however, since losses are typically realized 12 to 24 months (and often longer) after the date of default, it is still premature to gather sufficient data for meaningful analysis. In addition, preliminary results show that loss characteristics are highly dependent on deal structure and the qualifications and incentives of the servicers and special servicers involved.

For this study, a default was defined as a loan that was 60+ days past due on a scheduled debt service payment or a matured balloon payment. Typically, either of these events triggers a transfer of the loan to the special servicer. To avoid double counting, a loan is considered a defaulted loan even if it becomes current at a later date. This means that no loan can default more than once. A payoff was defined as a full payment of principal and interest by the scheduled date of maturity. Defaults and payoffs have been updated in the data base through May 1995.

Fitch believes it is important to examine the likelihood of payoffs in conjunction with the likelihood of default, because, when analyzing the credit of a pool of mortgages, the event of a payoff eliminates the loan's future ability to default. As a simple example, take an initial pool of 10 mortgages that has experienced one default and one payoff. In this case, there are now only eight loans that have the possibility of future default. If this same pool had only one default and no payoffs, however, there would be nine loans that have a future possibility of default. Thus, the second scenario is more uncertain and "risky."

Fitch used regression analysis on its data base to predict the default and payoff rates for each loan characteristic studied. Overall, the regression analyses proved to be highly accurate in estimating default rates. Although the regression analyses of payoffs yielded less conclusive results, they were still considered reliable by statistical methods of assessment (see the appendix).

The analysis was adjusted to take into account the period of time that various loans had been outstanding, i.e. the amount of time they had to default or pay off. For the purposes of comparison, default and payoff results are stated as average annual rates. In addition, the rates of default and payoff are based on loan count, not loan balance. The effect of loan balance was examined by means of a separate analysis discussed later.

One concern regarding the makeup of the data base is that the average loan size is $525,000, which is smaller than most commercial mortgage loans. To address this, Fitch analyzed a subset of its data base that excluded all loans less than $500,000. This analysis gave Fitch comfort regarding the validity of its results because it did not produce results substantially different from those based on the total data base in terms of the overall conclusions or the ranking of property types, states, and other characteristics studied.

The default and payoff results presented in the following sections are representative of the economic climate over the four years studied and should not be compared with default rates used in Fitch's rating model, which is based on a Fitch commercial mortgage default study dated June 8, 1992. Results from that study are based on a more severe economic environment that was determined to be an 'A' level stress. This study does not attempt to predict the rate of default or payoff over the life of a loan, and neither study attempts to predict the timing of defaults or payoffs.

Default/Payoff Analysis by DSCR

The average annual default and payoff rates for the 2,229 loans for which DSCRs were available are indicated in Exhibit 3. Not surprisingly, as the DSCR drops, the default rate increases and the payoff rate decreases.

Exhibit 3: Default/Payoff by DSCR

Loan DSCR (x)	Average Annual Default (%)	Average Annual Payoff (%)
2.80	1.7	10.4
2.40	2.3	10.0
2.00	3.1	9.6
1.75	3.7	9.4
1.60	4.1	9.3
1.45	4.5	9.2
1.30	5.0	9.0
1.20	5.3	8.9
1.10	5.7	8.8
1.00	6.1	8.7
0.85	6.7	8.7
0.65	7.5	8.6
0.45	8.4	8.4
0.25	9.5	8.2

The DSCR had a dramatic effect on loan default rates. In fact, the default probability ranged from 1.7% to 9.5%, among the widest ranges for any loan characteristic analyzed, indicating this to be one of the factors that could most significantly affect loan performance. These findings support Fitch's use of DSCR as the primary analytical tool in rating mortgage portfolios. Some notable points are discussed below:

- The higher the margin between the property income and its debt service, the better the chance that the property can continue to pay its debt service, refinance its balloon payment, or take advantage of a low interest rate environment to refinance. In addition, low DSCRs, particularly those below 1.0x, indicate loans that likely have outstanding debt in excess of current market value, which constrains the borrower's ability to sell a property.
- Interestingly, there is no "cliff" at 1.0x DSCR representing the event of default, only a steeper slope representing a higher likelihood of default. In other words, DSCR below 1.0x does not automatically trigger the event of default. This is due to the fact that NOI is reflective of a particular year and is not always representative of the collateral's long-term ability to pay debt service. Furthermore, borrowers can dip into reserves, defer management fees, or "come out of pocket" to meet debt service if DSCR falls below 1.0x. Even with a fixed debt service payment, DSCR can be variable due to fluctuations in cash flow caused by retenanting or short-term economic shocks.

Exhibit 4: Default/Payoff by Property Type

Default Experience

Property Type	Avg. Annual Default (%)
Warehouse	2.0
Multifamily	3.5
Industrial	3.8
Office	4.3
Retail	4.5
Lodging	5.1

Significance Matrix*
(x indicates statistically significant differences)

	WH	MF	IN	OF	RT	LO
WH	—	x	x	x	x	x
MF	x	—	o	x	x	x
IN	x	o	—	o	x	o
OF	x	x	o	—	o	o
RT	x	x	x	o	—	o
LO	x	x	o	o	o	—

Payoff Experience

Property Type	Avg. Annual Payoff (%)
Warehouse	14.3
Office	13.6
Industrial	11.9
Lodging	11.7
Retail	11.0
Multifamily	10.8

Significance Matrix*
(x indicates statistically significant differences)

	WH	OF	IN	LO	RT	MF
WH	—	o	x	x	o	x
OF	o	—	o	x	x	x
IN	x	o	—	o	x	x
LO	x	x	o	—	o	o
RT	o	x	x	o	—	o
MF	x	x	x	o	o	—

* The relative default and payoff rates between various property types are statistically significant (see the appendix) to the extent depicted in the above significance matrixes. The matrixes can be read in accordance with the following example: the multifamily default rate of 3.5% is not significantly different from that of industrial at 3.8% (indicated by an "o"), but it is significantly different from that of retail at 4.5% (indicated by an "x").

- The fact that the average annual default rate was 1.7% at the high DSCR of 2.8x indicates the inherent riskiness of commercial real estate as an asset class, especially given the relatively low volatility in the real estate economic environment from 1991 to May 1995, the period of our analysis. For example, the ability of a property to meet debt service can depend on whether a single large tenant renews its lease.
- Payoff rates shown may not continue, because our analysis period encompasses a time in which liquidity returned to the market after a long dry spell, supplemented by a period of low interest rates.
- Of note, the default rates should not be compared to Fitch's model, which uses lifetime default rates based on an 'A' economic stress.[1]

Default/Payoff Analysis by Property Type

The average annual default and payoff rates are indicated in Exhibit 4. The property-type information was available for nearly every loan in the data base.

[1] See Fitch Research on "Commercial Mortgage Stress Test," dated June 8, 1992.

In general, Fitch believes that diversity of property types within a single portfolio is a strength, once the particular property-type risks are addressed. Fitch's analysis distinguishes between property types by applying appropriate underwriting criteria to cash flows and applying market interest rates and amortization terms when calculating DSCR for deal sizing. In addition, for certain property types, such as lodging, default probabilities are increased. Fitch's observations on the property-type results are presented below:

- Our analysis showed that office and lodging properties were more likely to default than multifamily and warehouse properties. In general, office and lodging properties demonstrate more volatile financial performance due in part to high capital costs upon lease rollover for office properties and high operating leverage on hotels. Multifamily properties, on the other hand, generally show more stable cash flows and, thus, are expected to have lower defaults. These findings support Fitch's current underwriting, which addresses these risks by applying conservative assumptions to office cash flows and increasing the default probability for hotels.
- Warehouse properties defaulted less than industrial properties as a whole. The industrial property type includes manufacturing and "flex space" properties, which generally require more capital, or are more user-specific, and thus are more susceptible to tenant rollover risk. Somewhat surprising, however, was the magnitude of warehouse's strong performance. Fitch will continue to study this property type to better understand its strong performance in the sample tested.
- Contrary to expectations, retail properties were among those most likely to default. A probable explanation for this result is the preponderance of low-quality, and often unanchored, strip centers that make up the bulk of the retail product in RTC portfolios. Fitch believes that well located, anchored retail properties, especially regional shopping centers, would perform better than the retail sample in its data base. This result reinforces Fitch's negative view toward unanchored or low-quality retail properties, which is reflected by the use of a higher market interest rate in calculating debt service coverage for these properties.

Default/Payoff Analysis by State

Fitch's analysis was limited to states with at least 250 loans. The average annual default and payoff rates for these states are indicated in Exhibit 5. Also shown is the "other" category, which combines the remaining states.

Fitch addresses geographic diversity in its analysis by increasing the default probability in the state or region with the highest concentration, with the view that some regions will boom while others bust over the life of a transaction. Assessing a higher probability of default for the highest geographic concentration accounts for the risk that the region will suffer from poor economic performance. For regions that are projected to have declining economic performance due to identifiable factors, additional subordination may be required. Generally, the concentrations are assessed at the state level, with consideration given to diversity within a state. In addition, regional concentrations are assessed if they are significant. Fitch's observations on the state analysis are presented below:

- The default analysis shows geographic clustering by region. For example, the states of the Pacific Northwest were clearly the best performers, while those of the Northeast were among the worst. These ends of the spectrum are in line with the performance of these regional commercial real estate markets during our analysis period of 1991–1995.
- The Pacific Northwest was not a region that was significantly overbuilt during the 1980s, and it has seen strong demographic trends in the early 1990s, which probably contributed to the low default rates and above-average payoff rates for Oregon and Washington.
- The Northeast is a very mature, industry-based region that has seen out-migration and a deterioration of some urban centers. New York and New Jersey had both high default rates and low payoff rates.

Exhibit 5: Default/Payoff by State

Default Experience		Payoff Experience	
State	Average Annual Default (%)	State	Average Annual Payoff (%)
Oregon	1.4	Indiana	17.0
Washington	1.4	Illinois	16.6
Florida	2.8	Oregon	16.0
Indiana	2.9	New Mexico	15.6
Pennsylvania	3.0	Pennsylvania	15.0
Illinois	3.1	Colorado	14.3
Colorado	3.4	Other*	13.7
Texas	3.5	Ohio	13.5
Ohio	3.7	Washington	12.8
Minnesota	3.9	Kansas	12.4
New Mexico	4.0	Louisiana	11.9
Other*	4.3	New York	11.6
Arizona	4.3	Florida	11.7
Kansas	4.3	Texas	12.5
New Jersey	4.6	Arizona	10.6
California	4.7	New Jersey	9.7
Louisiana	5.8	California	8.8
New York	6.2	Minnesota	8.4

* All remaining states in the data base.

Exhibit 6: Default/Payoff by Loan Size

Loan Size ($000)	Average Annual Default (%)	Average Annual Payoff (%)
375	4.7	9.3
625	5.5	8.1
875	6.0	7.4
1,250	6.6	6.7
2,750	8.0	5.6
4,000	9.2	4.8
7,500	10.8	3.9

- Despite bad press about the California economy, the default rate, though high, was still less than that of New York and Louisiana. However, California loans were among the least likely to pay off, which suggests that there were few lending institutions willing to refinance these properties. Included in the California default/ payoff rates are the effects from any earthquakes that occurred during the period of analysis. Fitch assesses a higher probability of default for loans in California to reflect the earthquake risk.
- Florida was among those states least likely to default. It is well documented that Florida, and the Southeast in general, has benefited from the strongest demographic growth in the country. Unfortunately, the sample has only a small number of loans in other Southeastern states, so further analysis is not available for this region.

Default/Payoff Analysis by Loan Size

Two contradictory schools of thought exist on loan performance in relation to loan size. Some believe that larger loans result in more intensive due diligence or are made to more "professional" property operators and, therefore, are less likely to default. Others believe that borrowers of smaller loans have more of an incentive to "beg, borrow, and steal" to meet their debt service obligations because their livelihood is often more directly tied to the performance of the underlying property.

As shown in Exhibit 6, loan size affects the probability of default and payoff, with small-balance loans outperforming large-balance loans. Currently, Fitch's analysis does not distinguish between larger and smaller loans. Though the results are compelling, Fitch believes it is premature to bring loan size into its analysis as explained below; however, the relationship between loan size and default/payoff rates needs to be monitored on an ongoing basis:

- The results are likely skewed, since some of the loans from RTC pools had significant amortization at the date of securitization (most RTC loans were originated by thrifts during the 1980s, but not securitized until the early 1990s under the RTC). Greater amortization typically results in a lower loan-to-value ratio (LTV) and, therefore, makes the loan less likely to default. This amortization effect may also explain why smaller loans paid off at a higher rate. Loans with low LTVs are less of a risk to lenders and are much easier to refinance. Data indicating the loan size at loan origination, rather than at securitization, would have made Fitch's loan size analysis more meaningful; however, this information was not available or not reliable for most RTC loans. Future studies will better analyze the effect of loan size as more non-RTC multiborrower deals are added to Fitch's data base.

• The losses associated with a default are not reflected in this analysis. Because there are certain fixed costs associated with foreclosing or otherwise resolving defaulted loans, losses for smaller loans can be very high as a percentage of loan balance. Fitch will continue to monitor this result as more defaulted loans are resolved.

Default/Payoff Analysis by Interest Rate Type

The average annual default and payoff rates are indicated in Exhibit 7. Both results were found to be statistically significant (see the appendix).

Loans with floating interest rates were more likely to default and less likely to pay off than those with fixed interest rates. Fitch addresses the risk of floating-rate loans in its ratings analysis by calculating debt service coverage using a stressed rate (typically 13%–14%) or the interest rate cap, whichever is lower.

• The results support the conventional wisdom that floating-rate loans are more likely to default over time due to the volatility of interest rates. Often, even modest increases in rates after a period of low rates creates a stressed environment because borrowers have received financing based on a certain level of debt service payments, and property cash flow may not rise with interest rates. In fact, the interest rates during the analysis period were relatively low, with the highest rates occurring in late 1991 and early 1995. Since the loans were performing when securitized in 1991 or later, the only period of substantial increases in rates would have occurred in early 1995.

• The high percentage of payoffs among fixed-rate loans was likely the result of a period of low interest rates, especially in 1993, causing many fixed loans to refinance. Floating-rate loans automatically benefit from low rates and do not provide the same motivation to refinance. This payoff rate may not continue, because loans that did not refinance during the low interest rate period were likely unable to do so, which would indicate adverse selection.

Exhibit 7: Default/Payoff by Interest Type

Interest Rate Type	Average Annual Default (%)	Average Annual Payoff (%)
Fixed	3.1	14.7
Floating	4.7	8.4

Exhibit 8: Default/Payoff by Loan Type

Loan Type	Average Annual Default (%)	Average Annual Payoff (%)
Fully Amortizing	2.4	12.8
Balloon	5.9	10.9

Default/Payoff Analysis by Loan Type

The average annual default and payoff rates are indicated in Exhibit 8. Both results were found to be statistically significant (see the appendix).

Loans with ballooning principal balances defaulted more and paid off less than loans with fully amortizing principal balances. Fitch assesses balloon risk in its credit rating analysis by stressing debt service at a market refinance interest rate and giving subordination credit for fully amortizing loans. The following point, however, should be kept in mind when using the statistics in Exhibit 8. The balloon date is a critical juncture for a loan, since it will either pay off or default. Thus, the results above are dependent on the maturity schedule of the loan portfolio in the study. Future results will be more meaningful, because the transactions will have matured and lifetime rates for balloons and fully amortizing loans can be compared.

GOALS AND APPLICATIONS

The goal of this study is not only to report and comment on past performance, but also to identify performance characteristics that can be used to improve current and future analysis. The actual default and payoff rates presented should be used with caution, because they are representative of the collateral pool analyzed and the analysis period from 1991 to mid-1995. However, the results do provide valuable insights into commercial mortgage default risks, such as: the critical role DSCR plays in defaults and payoffs versus other loan characteristics; the ranking of property types; the clustering of delinquency and payoffs by regions; differences in the performance of fixed-rate loans versus floating-rate loans; and the fact that payoffs are not explained to the same degree by the variables that predict defaults. The results also have a more direct application in the analysis of conduit-originated loans because of the similarities between conduits and thrift product.

For instance, thrifts tended to originate smaller loans on class B to class B– quality properties to less sophisticated borrowers. This lending niche developed because thrifts were unable to match the larger commercial banks' and insurance companies' lower cost of funds and, therefore, were required to lend for higher yields. Today, conduits have similar pressures, and Fitch believes that in many ways they are originating loans with characteristics similar to those of 1980s thrift product, although at today's underwriting standards and with securitization, involving ratings, as an ultimate goal.

APPENDIX — RESEARCH METHODOLOGY

Fitch used a regression analysis on its data base to estimate the default/payoff rates for each loan characteristic in this report. Specifically, a logistic regression (rather than ordinary regression) analysis was used due to the existence of both discrete and continuous independent variables in our data base. Property type is an example of a discrete categorical variable. Loan size is an example of continuous data.

The validity of Fitch's regression results was assessed for each loan characteristic using the deviance statistic, the P-value, and by comparing the actual results from the data base with the calculated results from the regression using the Hosmer-Lemeshow goodness-of-fit test. Calculated default rates were determined to be highly accurate, while payoffs, although less accurate, were still considered reliable predictors. In other words, the defaults could be explained to a high degree based on the loan characteristics analyzed, whereas payoffs seemed to be influenced by other variables not included in the data base.

A separate regression analysis was performed on each loan characteristic in this report. Each regression analysis was based on three variables: the individual loan characteristic, the seasoning (the amount of time between securitization and the date the data base was updated), and the dependent variable of default or payoff. It is important to include the effect of seasoning, because not all loans have been exposed to the market for the same period of time. For example, the earliest transactions in the data base had only multifamily loans, and, therefore, the average seasoning for multifamily loans is 3.1 years, while industrial properties were included only in later transactions and have an average seasoning of 2.7 years. The rates of default and payoff presented in this report account for these differences.

Isolating each loan characteristic in a separate regression analysis is equivalent to assuming that the other loan characteristics are uniformly distributed throughout the data set. This approach does not result in default and payoff rates that are independent of other characteristics in the data base. For example, the fact that lodging properties have larger average loan balances than multifamily properties was not accounted for when comparing their relative default percentages. It is not inappropriate to examine one loan characteristic at a time without stripping out the effects of other loan characteristics, because certain loan characteristics are often "bundled together" as a result of market forces. In other words, the fact that lodging properties have a larger average loan balance than multifamily properties is typical, since lodging properties as a whole have larger average balances than multifamily properties.

Fitch also performed a regression analysis that incorporated all of the loan variables in the same analysis so that the independent effect of individual variables on loan performance could be assessed. Fitch used the results from this alternate analysis in conjunction with the analyses presented in this report to confirm that both sets of results are generally consistent in terms of their conclusions. For example, even after stripping out the effect from each of the characteristics analyzed, floating-rate loans defaulted more often than fixed-rate loan.

For categorical loan characteristics (property type, state, loan type, and interest rate type), Fitch determined whether relative default/payoff rates were statistically significant using a least significant difference test to a 95% confidence level. This analysis was performed to compare the calculated annual default and payoff percentages and answer questions such as: "Is the 4.3% default rate for office loans significantly different from the 3.5% default rate for multifamily loans?" Since these rates are, in fact, statistically different, it can be said with 95% certainty that office loans default more often than multifamily loans. Had they not been statistically significant, Fitch would not have differentiated between the default probabilities of these two property types.

Chapter **12**

Assessing Credit Risk of CMBS

Patrick Corcoran, Ph.D.
Vice President
Nomura International Securities, Inc.

Duen-Li Kao
Director of Investment Research
General Motors Investment Management Corp.

INTRODUCTION

Commercial mortgage-backed securities (CMBS) are bonds that are collateralized by commercial mortgage loans. In turn, these commercial mortgage loans are collateralized by underlying real estate property.[1]

In 1993, many first time investors in CMBS were persuaded by yields that seemed hugely attractive relative to any reasonable calculation of losses. As more and more investors became persuaded that commercial real estate prices had bottomed, spreads narrowed steadily. Today's narrower spreads call for a vehicle for more carefully assessing CMBS fundamentals. At the same time, with real estate prices having, in our view, bottomed in most markets, the analysis must proceed in the context of a fundamentally improved real estate outlook. This chapter attempts to fill this need. Eventually, as the emerging market in CMBS develops, assessing the credit experience of these new bonds directly will be possible. At this point in time, however, such a track record is unavailable. Hence, our approach is to assess the track record available in the default experience of the underlying commercial mortgages. From this record we then infer the likely credit outlook for CMBS.

---

[1] Much has been written recently concerning problems of residential mortgage-backed securities and related derivative securities in handling prepayment risk. Residential mortgages of course can be prepaid fully at any time. In contrast, commercial mortgages generally have very strong protection against early prepayment. This protection takes the form of absolute prohibitions against prepayment (called lockout) as well as prepayment penalties (so-called yield maintenance provisions). The key point is that the recent problems relating to residential mortgage backed securities have nothing to do with CMBS.

Our chapter proceeds as follows. The first section lays out our empirical model. Our model links the delinquency experience of life insurance company loans to the changing prices in the real estate asset markets. To move from a delinquency model to a credit loss model, we need to examine the various credit events in commercial mortgages and the consequent losses. This is the subject of the second section. The third section of the chapter shows how the credit model can be used to project losses for CMBS. The final section attempts to synthesize the outlook for the real estate markets and the implications for CMBS credit risk.

THE EMPIRICAL DEFAULT MODEL

It was an early insight of the options literature that a lender/investor in a risky bond could be viewed as owning a Treasury bond plus a short position in a put option to the borrower. In the case of a commercial mortgage, the lender had, in effect, sold the borrower a put option on the underlying property. The borrower could put or sell the underlying real estate property to the lender at a strike price equal to the unpaid loan balance. Interest income over and above the Treasury coupon rate represented the option premium received by the lender for the sale of the underlying put option.

In the absence of transaction costs or other considerations involved, borrowers would always default on their loans if the property value were to fall below the value of the outstanding loan balance. This is especially the case for commercial mortgages which are generally non-recourse.[2] The lender has recourse only to the borrower's real estate collateral and not to his other assets. However, in a series of important articles, Kerry Vandell has argued that commercial mortgage borrowers do not exercise the default option "ruthlessly," as described above.[3] Instead, loan defaults are less than ruthless just as they are for residential mortgages. Vandell's findings heighten the importance of having an empirical default model which captures the actual response of borrowers and lenders to changing real estate markets.

In this options framework, mortgage losses and defaults are negatively related to changing real estate prices. This relationship is shown in Exhibit 1. Falling real estate prices, such as occurred from 1988-1992, raise loan-to-value (LTV) ratios and, hence, expected losses (position B). Rising real estate prices reduce LTV ratios and eventually drive losses to minimum levels (position C). Beyond this point, further increases in real estate prices (position D) do not materially reduce losses.

---

[2] By comparison, in corporate bonds, the options paradigm has proved much more difficult to apply because the underlying "equity" concept is not as well defined. The non-recourse nature of commercial mortgages greatly simplifies the issue in this case.
[3] Kerry D. Vandell, "Predicting Commercial Mortgage Foreclosure Experience," *Journal of American Real Estate and Urban Economics Association* 20 (1992), pp. 55–88, and "Handing Over The Keys: A Perspective on Mortgage Default Research, "*Journal of American Real Estate and Urban Economics Association* 21 (1993), pp. 211–246.

Exhibit I: Commercial Mortgage Losses, Real Estate Values, and LTVs

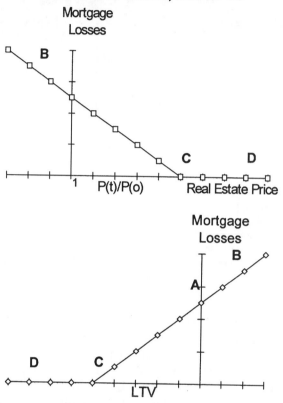

The Relationships

In our empirical model, we link American Council on Life Insurance (ACLI) data on loan delinquencies with the NCREIF Index (formerly called the Russell-NCREIF index) of property returns and property prices. These data reveal the aggregate linkage between loan performance and real estate prices both by region and major property type beginning in 1988.

The loan performance data are available for the nine major census regions. We combined several of these census regions to produce a six-region division that roughly follows the one proposed by Wurtzebach, Hartzell, and Shulman.[4]

---

[4] Wurtzebach, Charles, David Hartzell, and David Shulman, "Refining the Analysis of Regional Diversification for Income Producing Real Estate," *The Journal of Real Estate Research* (Winter 1987), pp. 89–95. Their approach focuses on larger regions that are economically homogenous. The six regions are as follows: (a) North East (the Mid Atlantic census region); (b) Old South (adds together the South Atlantic and East South Central census regions); (c) Mid West (the East North Central census region); (d) Mineral Extraction (adds together West South Central and Mountain census regions); (e) Farm Belt (the West North Central census region); and (f) Pacific (the Pacific census region).

Exhibit 2: Delinquency Model

Sector	Regional Price	Sector Price	Constant	Steady State	R^2 (Percent)	Standard Error (%)	Estimation Period
Apartment	-12.61	-17.68	33.51	3.22	31.5	2.11	1991: Q1
	(4.3)	(2.4)	(5.2)				1993: Q2
Industrial	-26.58	2.74	25.83	1.99	63.7	1.77	
	(12.8)	(1.7)	(16.2)				1988: Q1
Office	-25.88	-4.24	33.33	3.21	63.4	2.19	to
	(10.1)	(2.5)	(17.3)				1993: Q2
Retail	-12.78	-9.04	24.47	2.65	66.4	1.36	
	(7.7)	(6.4)	(17.7)				

Notes:

a. The regional variable corresponds to the eight regional "divisions" in the NCREIF Index. These divisional price indices capture price movements for a combination of property types within the region.

b. The sector indices measure changes in property prices at the national level but specific to the property sector. Thus, the apartment equation focuses on the national apartment index in the NCREIF database. Since the apartment index has only been available since 1991, the estimation period for the equation is shorter than for the other equations.

c. Regression coefficients are numbers in the top row. T-statistics are in second row in parentheses.

d. Since both the regional price variable and the sector price variable measure today's real estate relative to loan origination, their normalized value corresponding to unchanging prices is unity. Thus, if real estate prices do not change, the "steady state" delinquency rate is the sum of the three regression coefficients.

For each major sector, we estimated separate statistical relationships to explain loan delinquencies. For example, industrial loan delinquencies in the six regions are negatively related to changes in the price of industrial real estate properties. To capture the price changes for industrial properties we use a national index for industrial property prices and a regional index for commercial property prices. The regional index represents properties of different sectors combined together. We followed the same approach in the other sectors (see Exhibit 2).

As shown there, the coefficients on the real estate price variables reveal a powerful negative relationship between the frequency of delinquent loans and real estate prices. The especially important role of the regional price variable in all the sector equations testifies to the important role of regional diversification. In the past 20 years the various sub-regions within the U.S. economy have experienced ongoing rolling recessions with relatively low correlations among these regions. This implies that CMBS investors can achieve a substantial gain from a portfolio that has strong regional diversification.

Looking at delinquency rates for the first quarters of 1990 and 1992 (Exhibit 3) provides a visual sense of the diversity among regions. In the earlier period (top panel), the Mineral Extraction region exhibits the highest loan delinquency rates within each property sector. Two years later (bottom panel), the Mineral Extraction delinquency rates were at the low end for each property type (except apartments).

Exhibit 3: Regional and Sector Delinquency Rates
Panel A: First Quarter 1990

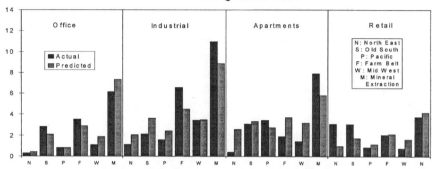

Panel B: First Quarter 1992

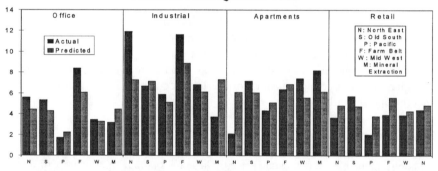

The sensitivity of loan delinquencies to changing real estate prices can be illustrated graphically (Exhibit 4, left hand panel). The lines represent the combined impact of both regional and sectorial prices on delinquency rates for large life insurance company loan pools. On the left panel, the intercepts of the lines on the vertical axis represent the "steady state" delinquency rates also shown in Exhibit 2. These delinquency rates correspond to unchanged real estate prices and an initial LTV ratio of 72%.[5] Notice that for these large life insurance company loan pools, an increase in real estate collateral prices of between 8% and 12% is sufficient to reduce projected delinquency rates to zero.

With respect to LTV ratios, an important characteristic of life company portfolios in the 1988-1993 period was relatively large dispersion of LTV ratios. This large dispersion arose because of wide variation in underwriting standards in

---

[5] The average reported LTV for life company new loans is about 72%. As discussed above, abnormally high dispersion of LTVs means loss estimates reported in this chapter are on the high side. Two subsequent papers utilize our model to deal more explicitly with this issue and thus present more balanced estimates. See Patrick J. Corcoran, "Debt and Equity in the New Real Estate Markets," *Real Estate Finance* (Fall 1995), reprinted in *Fixed Income Solutions*, Thomas S.Y. Ho (ed.) (Burr Ridge, IL: Irwin Publishing Co. 1996), and Duen-Li Kao, "Default Risk Based Pricing in a Two-asset Setting," *Fixed Income Solutions*, 1996.

1988-1989, near the top of the real estate cycle. Moreover, subsequent to 1989 when delinquencies rose sharply, life company lender "involuntarily" refinanced many poorly performing loans at high LTVs.

Over the period 1988-1993, reporting life insurers originated new loans at an average LTV ratio of 72%. This average life portfolio's LTV is the benchmark from which the impact of changing real estate prices must be computed.

The right hand panel of Exhibit 4 translates the changing real estate prices into changing LTV ratios. As shown, our results implies that a reduction in LTV ratios from 72% to the mid-60s is sufficient in each sector to reduce expected delinquency rates to zero.

The differences and similarities among the different sectors are also interesting. The retail sector loans have the lowest sensitivity to changing real estate prices as shown by the flat slope in the retail line. The industrial sector loans also have a moderate flattish slope and, in addition, have the lowest position of any of the delinquency lines in the graph. Finally, the office and apartment sector show the highest sensitivity (steepest slope) to changing real estate prices. In fact the position of the office and apartment relationships on the line is virtually identical. This does not mean that office and apartment loans had identical delinquency records in the eighties. Rather the office sector was more overbuilt and experienced much larger price declines, pushing office delinquencies much further up the curve than the apartment loan sector.

Other Factors
A number of other factors have an important bearing on the relationship between loan delinquencies and real estate prices. These factors may operate very differently in the future than they did in the 1988-1993 period when the model was estimated. Let us consider a number of these factors:

Exhibit 4: Sector Delinquency Rates, Real Estate Values, and LTVs

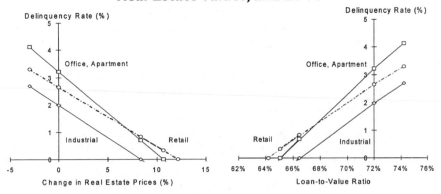

Exhibit 5: Break-Even Changes in Real Estate Prices
10-Year Mortgage

Amortization (Years)	Mortgage Coupon Rate (%)				
	6	7	8	9	10
15	-7.96	-7.59	-7.25	-6.91	-6.59
20	-4.29	-3.96	-3.65	-3.36	-3.09
25	-2.66	-2.38	-2.11	-1.88	-1.66
30	-1.77	-1.52	-1.30	-1.11	-0.95

LTV Ratio Dispersion A rise in the dispersion of the LTV distribution means that more loans are at the high end of the distribution. With the same average LTV, more loans will end up delinquent than in a narrower distribution. In the 1988-1993 period, falling real estate prices contributed greatly to high dispersion for LTVs. However, for portfolios of new loans invested in 1994 and flat real estate prices going forward, the LTVs in these portfolios have much lower dispersion.

The Maturity of the Loan Portfolio The maturity of the life insurer portfolio in the years 1988-1993 was approximately 3½ years. This reflected the fact that new loan origination's typically had a maturity of about 7 years. With a seasoned loan portfolio this translated into existing loans having average maturity of about 3½ years. Moreover, between 1988 and 1993 the maturity of this seasoned portfolio was virtually unchanged. So our data reveal nothing about the impact of changing maturity and loan seasoning on delinquencies.

Our data set does not allow us explicitly to examine the role of amortization — the return of principal on a gradual basis over the life of the loan. Even with unchanging real estate prices, amortization causes a gradual improvement in LTV ratios over time. Hence, delinquencies should also be improving over time. In terms of Exhibit 1, the loan pool "rolls down" the delinquency curve. As shown in Exhibit 5, a 10-year mortgage with an 8% coupon rate can sustain declines in real estate prices over its life-time ranging from 1.30% per year for a 30-year amortization schedule to 7.25% for a 15-year write-off period and still maintain its original LTV ratio.

In projecting the performance of new loans, it will be important to account for the impact of amortization on the LTV ratio. The vast majority of life company loans are amortizing loans that typically have a 25 year amortization rate. Studies by Mark Snyderman confirm that commercial mortgages experience positive seasoning.[6,7] Snyderman documented the amount of seasoning that is very close to expectations with a 25-year amortization.

[6] Mark P. Snyderman, "Commercial Mortgages: Default Occurrence and Estimated Yield Impact," *Journal of Portfolio Management* (Fall 1991), pp. 82–87, and "An Update on Commercial Mortgage Default Costs Using Insurance Regulatory Data," *Real Estate Finance Journal* (Summer 1994).
[7] Positive seasoning means improved creditworthiness of loans as they season or get older. Amortization is the most obvious reason for positive seasoning because it reduces the loan's LTV even with unchanged real estate prices. A second issue is whether mortgage loans with unchanging LTV may change in creditworthiness over time. Our model simulations in this chapter assume not, but this is an area for further research. In the corporate bond area, for example, researchers have found negative seasoning for investment grade bonds and positive seasoning for junk bonds [see Duen-Li Kao, "Illiquid Securities: Issues of Pricing and Performance Measurement," *Financial Analysts Journal* (March/April 1993), pp28–35, 77.]

258 Assessing Credit Risk of CMBS

MOVING FROM DELINQUENCY AND FORECLOSURES TO A CREDIT LOSS MODEL

When a borrower misses timely payment of interest or principal on a commercial mortgage, the loan is technically in default or delinquent. In the ACLI statistics delinquent those loans are those that are behind in scheduled payments 90 days or more. Once delinquent, a loan can emerge from delinquency in one of two ways. First, the lender may foreclose on the property to settle the debt. Because the borrower has the option to sell the property himself prior to foreclosure, loans settled in the foreclosure process have higher losses. Snyderman's study found a loss severity of 36% for foreclosed loans originated between 1972 and 1986, tracked up to 1991.[8] This means that loss of interest and principal amounted to 36% of the outstanding loan balance.

On the other hand, delinquent loans can also emerge as so-called restructured loans in which the borrower and lender mutually agree to alter the original terms of the loan. The lender might agree to reduce the coupon or to forgive past failures to meet scheduled interest. (With non-recourse loans lenders have had a strong incentive to restructure loans.) With restructured loans, the borrower might agree to repay missed interest and principal payments either immediately or over the remaining life of the loan.

Unfortunately we know almost nothing about an important loophole in the rescheduled loans — their loss severity. Of loans that became delinquent in the 1970's and 1980's, approximately half emerged as restructured loans (see Snyderman [1994]). The other half emerges as foreclosures. Snyderman's study *assumes* that the loss severity for restructures is 18% compared to 36% for foreclosures but provides no evidence to support this assumption.[9]

Using Snyderman's assumption, the *average* delinquent loan will experience a loss severity equal to

$$\left(\frac{1}{2}\right) \times 18\% + \left(\frac{1}{2}\right) \times 26\% = 27\%$$

Notice that this is far below the average loss severity on corporate bond defaults, which is generally estimated to be around 60%.[10]

---

[8] Snyderman, "An Update on Commercial Mortgage Default Costs Using Insurance Regulatory Data," *op. cit.*

[9] Our own view is that an 18% loss severity is probably too high for normal real estate markets. An examination of ACLI historical statistics suggests that borrower waiting times in delinquency were much longer in the 1970's and early 1980's than the very difficult 1988-1993 period. We feel that lenders dealt with delinquent loans very aggressively in 1988-1993 because expected losses were large. (They also had encouragement from the NAIC capital guidelines to do so.) In more normal or favorable real estate markets, prospective losses may have been *negligible* making patient restructuring the optimal strategy for lenders. Without further empirical study of the matter, however, a strong case cannot be made for Synderman's assumption or for any other.

[10] See Edward I. Altman, "Defaults and Returns in High-Yield Bonds: Analysis Through 1993," Merrill Lynch & CO., 1994, and Moody's Investors Service, *Corporate Bond Defaults and Default Rates: 1970–1993*, Special report, 1994.

To move from loss severity to the computation of losses, we use the standard formula:

Loss = (Loss Severity) × (Delinquency)

Suppose our model is projecting a delinquency rate of 1% per year if real estate prices remain at today's levels. In other words, a total of 1% of loans would normally emerge each year either as restructures or foreclosures. Applying the above formula means that the annual loss is (0.27) × (1%) or 27 basis points of loss per year.

When this loss severity is used in conjunction with our steady state delinquency rates, the losses seem quite high. For example, the retail sector delinquency rate is 2.65% per year.

This means that a pool of retail loans with initial LTV of 72% under the condition of flat real estate prices experience losses of (0.27) × (2.65%) or 71 basis points per year. The question naturally arises: if the prices of the real estate collateral properties are not falling (on average), where do the losses and delinquencies come from? The answer lies in the LTV ratios of loans originated during our model estimation period (1988-1993). The unusually high LTV *dispersion* during the period resulted in a relatively large number of high LTV loans with high losses. Because much of this high historical LTV dispersion is irrelevant for projecting loan losses for new loans made today, our model projections tend to be overly pessimistic.

Risk-Neutral Credit Spread

We can use the notion of the risk-neutral credit spread to calculate the impact of the losses computed above on the price of a commercial mortgage whole loan or security. The risk-neutral concept has been discussed by several researchers.[11] Its applications to pricing commercial mortgages and private placements were also reviewed elsewhere.[12] The idea is that a risk-neutral investor should use the Treasury curve to value the cash flow of a risky bond net of expected credit losses. In other words, the discounted value of the nominal cash flow using the risky bond discount rate is equivalent to discounting the net of loss cash flow using the Treasury curve. Mathematically, the simplified relationship can be stated as:

$$\frac{\text{Promised cash flow}}{\text{Discount rate with credit risk spread}} = \frac{(\text{Promised cash flow} \times \text{Credit loss adjustment})}{\text{Treasury discount rate}}$$

whereby *credit loss adjustment* is a function of delinquency rate, relative probability of foreclosure and restructuring, and their respective loss severities.

---

[11] See Jerome S. Fons, "The Default Premium and Corporate Bond Experience," *Journal of Finance* (March 1987), pp. 81–97; Thomas Y. S. Ho, *Strategic Fixed Income Investment* (Homewood, IL: Dow Jones-Irwin, 1990); and Duen-Li Kao, "Valuation: Fair Trading," *Balance Sheet* (Winter 1992/1993), pp. 15–19.

[12] See Duen-Li Kao, "Valuation: Fair Trading," and "Illiquid Securities: Issues of Pricing and Performance Measurement," *op. cit.*

This concept is useful for figuring the decline in a bond's price or elevation in its up-front yield that is sufficient to just offset anticipated credit losses. Continuing the previous example of calculating loss, suppose that a commercial mortgage carries a 8.5% coupon with a 10-year term and 20-year amortization schedule while comparable Treasury rate is 7.5% semi-annual compounded (s.a.). With the assumptions of delinquency rate of 1% and a credit loss of 27 basis points per year, the "fair or intrinsic" value of credit losses for this mortgage would be $17 per $1,000 face value.[13] Note that this analysis focuses only on the losses associated with credit risk. It ignores the values related to the security's illiquid nature (i.e., the value of illiquidity option) and the yield maintenance provisions (i.e., the value of prepayment option).[14]

The credit loss model can also be used to derive the spread required to compensate the possible credit loss. That is, given an assumed delinquency rate and related credit losses, one can calculate the required coupon rate on a mortgage. Using the example above (1% delinquency, a 10-year mortgage with a 20-year amortization and a 7.5% Treasury rate), additional yield spread of 27 basis points (s.a.) would be required to compensate future credit losses for this mortgage traded at par[15]. If delinquency rate increases to 2% per year, the required credit-loss yield spread would be 53 basis points for a marginal increase of 26 basis points. Note that future periodic cash flows are adjusted by cumulative delinquency rates, which results in a non-linear relationship between price and delinquency rate under the credit loss model. As shown in Exhibit 6, the marginal increase in required credit loss yield spread actually declines as delinquency rate increases.

Another application of this credit loss model is deriving implied delinquency rate (i.e., delinquency rate implied by the market quoted mortgage yield).[16] Suppose that a 10-year par-mortgage demands 9.0% coupon amortized over 20 years with similar term Treasury rate of 7.5% (167 b.p. spread, semi-annual compounded) with 50 basis points of this yield spread related to liquidity and prepayment options. With the same assumptions of foreclosure propensity and credit losses as above, we can derive the implied delinquency rate of 4.80% per year. If the future delinquency rate is anticipated to be lower than the implied rate, the mortgage would appear to be cheap.

Assessing Losses for CMBS

The key point in analyzing losses for CMBS is that they are derived from the underlying whole loans. All cash flows net of underwriting and servicing fees flow through to the bond holders. In a simple passthrough structure, for example, the credit experience of the bonds would simply mirror that of the whole loans.

---

[13] The calculation assumes the bond is held to maturity.

[14] For the discussion of implications of these two options, see Patrick J. Corcoran and Duen-Li Kao, "Implications of Asset Illiquidity,." in Edward I. Altman and Irwin T. Vanderhoof (eds.) *The Financial Dynamics of the Insurance Industry* (Burr Ridge, IL: Irwin, 1993), pp. 197–211.

[15] Since the assumed 20 year amortization rate reduces the LTV in this example, real estate prices must be assumed to decline sufficiently to keep the LTV at a level consistent with 1% delinquency rate. This is also the case in the example in the subsequent paragraph.

[16] A similar analytical framework was used to evaluate high-yield bonds in Peter Niculescu, "Breakeven Default Rates," Goldman Sachs Fixed Income Research, November 1990.

Exhibit 6: Relationship Between Delinquency Rate and Required Credit Loss Spread

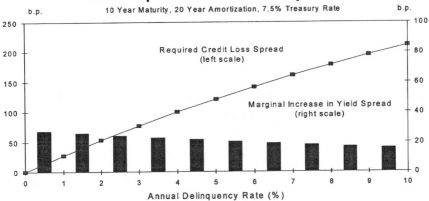

Exhibit 7: Simple Subordinated Junior/Senior Bond Structure

Whole Loans	CMBS
Commercial Mortgage Loan Pool ($72 Million) LTV = 72%	Senior Bonds ($54 Million) (Effective LTV = 54%)
	Subordinated Bonds ($18 Million)

More commonly, however, credit enhancement is provided to senior bonds through subordination of the claims of junior bondholders. For example, suppose we have a $100 million diversified pool of retail properties with average LTV of 72%. Suppose further that the junior bondholders assume the first 25% of credit loss liability. The situation then looks as shown in Exhibit 7.

From the perspective of the senior bondholders, the 25% subordination of the junior bondholders is equivalent to obtaining additional equity in the underlying real estate properties. This means that the senior bond has a credit outlook equivalent to loans on the underlying properties with 54% LTV.

The junior bonds have loss exposure for the entire $72 million pool of loans. Their position is comparable to the capital or surplus of a bank or insurance company lender. The senior bondholders' position is comparable to that of bank deposits (without deposit insurance) or insurance company policyholders.

Assuming real estate prices have bottomed in most markets, we need to determine the appropriate assumption for an *increase* in real estate prices over the life of the loans. Because the above examples we examine involve negligible risk of credit loss for the senior bondholders, we shall focus our credit analysis on the subordinate bonds.

Before turning to that analysis, we briefly review the real estate outlook to support our assertion that prices have bottomed and will be at least rising modestly in the next several years. In this setting, it is worth noting briefly that the primary issue for senior bondholders in today's real estate environment is not credit risk at all but rather uncertainty in the timing of cash flows. An analysis of this issue is beyond the scope of this chapter.

THE CMBS OUTLOOK AND
THE REAL ESTATE OUTLOOK

Our approach to assessing the CMBS credit outlook is derived directly from the real estate market. The period 1986-1993 commercial real estate markets experienced the largest declines since the Great Depression. Beginning in 1993-1994, it has become clear even to casual market observers that real estate prices have bottomed in most markets. Moreover, prices have bottomed at levels that are far below replacement costs. The substantial discounts of real estate asset values to replacement cost essentially preclude new supply in these markets because returns to new development activity are negative.

With real estate prices flat to modestly rising over the next several years, the stage is set for CMBS to perform very strongly. The argument is not that real estate prices will surge dramatically. It is merely that prices have bottomed and will rise modestly.

In this setting, three factors bear positively for CMBS investments: (1) From the perspective of economic theory, a "bottom" for real estate prices is defined in inflation-adjusted terms. Thus, even if prices do not rise subsequently in real terms, nominal real estate prices would keep pace with the general level of inflation. As noted below, a modest rise in real estate prices has a very significant impact on CMBS. (2) The advantage of modestly rising real estate prices for CMBS is that LTVs and associated delinquencies will be trending downward even for a non-amortizing loan. In the case of amortizing loans, however, amortization achieves the same effect even with unchanged real estate prices. (3) From a longer run perspective, real estate prices are expected to rise faster than inflation. With prices so far below replacement cost in so many markets, the resulting absence of new supply will put upward pressure on asset prices. With general inflation expected to run 2% to 3% over the next several years, and allowing for a modest 1% appreciation over and above inflation, a conservative expectation is that real estate prices will rise 3.5% per year.

As noted above, our model projections are likely pessimistic for new loan portfolios because of the high LTV dispersion in the model's estimation period. To explicitly offset part of this bias, a user can make a simple technical adjustment to the model by accounting for a small amount of inflation. In this case, in the example above, a 3.5% inflation rate would actually correspond to a somewhat smaller "true" rate of real estate price appreciation.

Exhibit 8: The Impact of Amortization

Security Information	
Maturity: 10 Years	Coupon Rate: 10.0%
Average Life: 6.97 Years	Treasury Rate: 7.5%
Subordination: 25%	Collateral: 100% Retail
	Rating: Triple-B

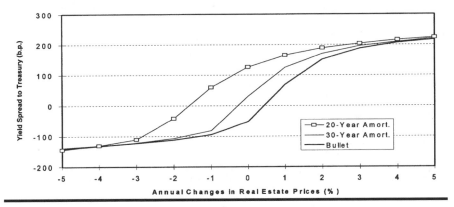

Annual Changes in Real Estate Prices (%)

Credit Analysis for Subordinate CMBS

Let us return to our example in Exhibit 7. Against a pool of properties worth $100 million, we have commercial mortgage whole loans of $72 million. Our subordinate bondholders have the $18 million first loss exposure.

Suppose further that the subordinate bonds have a coupon of 10%, a maturity of 10 years, and a triple-B (BBB/Baa) rating and that (for simplicity) the Treasury yield curve is flat at 7.5%. Exhibit 8 looks at risk neutral credit spreads for three different bonds with different rates of amortization.

First and foremost notice that the net spread in our expected range of increases in real estate prices (at least 3.5% per year) is at or above 200 basis points per year. By comparison, in today's market triple-B corporate bonds exhibit a yield spread about 100 basis points above the 10-year Treasury. Using Altman's 1993 default tables suggests a credit charge of about 37 basis points per year for a net corporate spread of 63 basis points.[17]

Secondly, the powerful impacts of amortization are evident in adverse scenarios. For example, if real estate prices do not change at all over the life of the bonds, the net spread for the bullet (zero-amortization) is minus 50 basis points. Why is this the case? With no change in real estate prices and no help from amortization, the delinquency rate for the retail loan pool remains at its steady state level of 2.65% per year. This results in losses of approximately 2.65% × 0.27 or 71 basis points per year

---

[17] The calculation assumes a 30% recovery price on defaulted, cash-pay subordinated bonds and a 10-year cumulative default rate of 4.8%. Similar to the case of analyzing "B" class CMBS, the seasoning (negative) effect of triple-B bonds on annual default rates is also considered.

to the loan pool which are absorbed entirely by the subordinate bondholders. Thus, the debit to the net spread is roughly four times (corresponding to subordination of 25%) 71 basis points which exceeds the nominal 250 basis point spread to Treasuries and makes the net spread for the bullet slightly negative.

At zero real estate inflation, the net spread with 30 year amortization is +30 basis points. The spread with 20 year amortization is +120 basis points. Viewed a bit differently, to reduce the net spread with 20 year amortization to -50 basis points, which is the bullet's net spread at zero inflation, the rate of real estate inflation must be reduced about 2% (from zero to − 2%). In other words, in this example 20 year amortization is worth 2% of real estate price inflation.

Thirdly, our net spread calculations for the subordinate bond are sensitive to our assumptions about loss severity. Suppose, for example, we used a foreclosure loss severity of 25% (versus 36% in base case) and a restructure loss severity of 10% (versus 18% in base case).[18] The justification would be the favorable point we currently occupy in the real estate cycle with prices having bottomed and no new supply in sight. With zero inflation in real estate prices and no amortization, losses for the whole loans are roughly 47 basis points per year (versus 71 basis points for the base case). The net spread for the subordinate bullet bond in Exhibit 8 is 100 basis points higher at zero inflation. Notice that the assumed differences in the whole loan loss rate are amplified by a factor of four because the subordination is 25%. If subordination were only 10%, the amplification factor would be ten times.

Exhibit 9 provides additional detail for the subordinate bond assuming 20 year amortization for the whole loan pool. The top panel shows that the break-even point to Treasuries occurs when cumulative losses are between 3.5% to 4%. Higher cumulative losses go with lower real estate inflation rates. The bottom panel shows that the subordinate bonds with 20 year amortization are quite robust with respect to assumed real estate price inflation, especially in our expected (3.5%) range.

Exhibit 10 examines the sensitivity of the junior bond to the amount of subordination. Recall our base case has 25% subordination. Exhibit 10 contrasts this bond with an alternative bond assumed to bear the same coupon (10%) and lower subordination (10%). The increase in cumulative losses causes the net spread of the junior bond with 10% subordination to decline more rapidly since the same losses are spread over a narrower base.

In practice, the junior bond with 10% subordination would not carry the same coupon as the subordinate bond with 25% subordination. Exhibit 11 carries the analysis a step further. It shows, at a variety of real estate inflation rates, the coupon required on the junior bond with 10% subordination to equate its net spread to that of the junior bond with 25% subordination. For example, in our expected range of at least 3.5% real estate inflation, a coupon about 300 basis points above the 7.5% Treasury rate would equate the net spreads.

---

[18] This assumption is equivalent to the case discussed in Patrick J. Corcoran, "Assessing the Risks for New Real Estate Loans," *Real Estate Review* (Spring 1994), pp. 10–14, and Patrick J. Corcoran, Dale Fathe-Aazam, and Alberto Perez-Pietri, "The Role of Commercial Mortgages in Fixed Income Investing," *Pension Real Estate Association Quarterly* (January 1994), pp. 26–30.

Exhibit 9: Sensitivity of "B" Class Yield Spreads

Security Information	
Maturity: 10 Years	Coupon Rate: 10.0%
Average Life: 6.97 Years	Treasury Rate: 7.5%
Amortization: 20 Years	Collateral: 100% Retail
Subordination: 25%	Rating: Triple-B

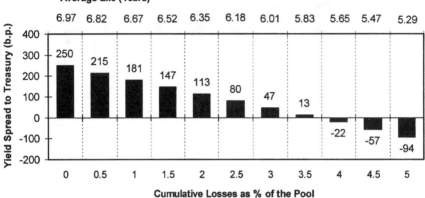

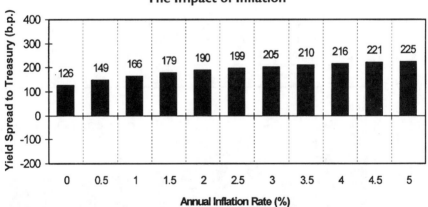

Exhibit 10: The Impact of Subordination Percentage

Security Information	
Maturity: 10 Years	Coupon Rate: 10.0%
Average Life: 6.97 Years	Treasury Rate: 7.5%
Amortization: 20 Years	Collateral: 100% Retail
	Rating: Triple-B

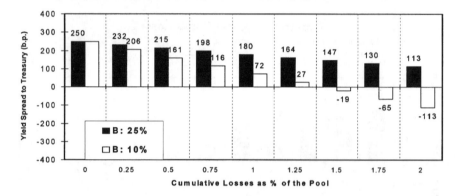

Exhibit 11: Expected Inflation Rates
and Required Coupon Spreads

Security Information	
Maturity: 10 Years	
Average Life: 6.97 Years	Treasury Rate: 7.5%
Amortization: 20 Years	Collateral: 100% Retail
Subordination: 10%	

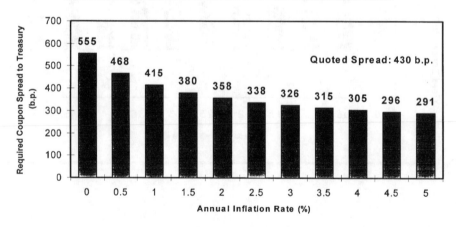

Exhibit 12: Comparison of CMBS and Corporates

	BBB		BB	
	CMBS	Corporate	CMBS	Corporate
Nominal Spread	250	100	430	250
Exp. Credit Loss (1, 2)	-40	-37	-113	-123
Net Credit Spread	210	63	317	127
Recovery	73%	30%	73%	30%
Cumulative Default	2.2%	4.8%	2.3%	15.7%

Note:
(1) Loss calculation considers seasoning effect of default.
(2) Real estate price change: 3.5% per year.
(3) Default statistics for CMBS are pool-level.

Suppose the 10% subordinated bonds were rated Double-B (BB/Ba) and traded at a spread of 430 basis points in the market. Since the market spread of this bond exceeds the required coupon spread of 315 basis points (at 3.5% inflation), the 10% subordinated bond looks attractive relative to the junior bond with 25% subordination.[19]

The 10% subordinated bond also looks attractive relative to a comparable corporate bond. The expected net credit loss spread for this CMBS is approximately 325 basis points at a 3.5% inflation rate.[20] By comparison, at the time of this analysis, double-B corporate bonds demanded a yield spread about 250 basis points above the 10-year Treasury. Again, using Altman's 1993 default tables suggests a credit charge of about 123 basis points per year for a net double-B corporate spread of 127 basis points[21]. The double-B CMBS appears to offer excellent value versus the comparable corporate bond even after adjusting for credit losses. Exhibit 12 summarizes the comparison of CMBS and corporate bonds for double-B and triple-B credit quality.

CONCLUSION

This chapter examines the credit outlook for commercial mortgage-backed securities (CMBS) using a framework which integrates real estate and bond analysis. The use of the risk-neutral credit spread concept allows the user to weigh the losses in any real estate scenario against the up-front yield promised in the bond market. Account is taken of the relative probability of foreclosure and restructure, and the respective loss

---

[19] No allowance is taken here for the fact that the bond with lower subordination is a riskier bond since the net spread concept is risk neutral.
[20] The market quoted spread for this 10% subordinated, Double-B rated CMBS is 430 basis points. The coupon rate is 115 basis points higher than what is required under a 3.5% inflation scenario (430 basis points minus 315 basis points). This 115 basis points plus the break-even spread of 210 basis points mentioned above result in a net credit loss spread of 325 basis points.
[21] The assumptions underlying the calculation are the same as those of Triple-B case (see footnote 9) except for the 10-year cumulative default rate of 15.7%.

severities. We modeled commercial mortgage delinquencies using data from 1988-1993, a period representing the worst commercial real estate markets since the Depression. Combining the results of our model with conservative estimates of loss severities, we established a prudent framework for assessing CMBS credit risk.

Chapter *13*

A Framework for Risk and Relative Value Analysis of CMBS: Theory

David P. Jacob
Managing Director
Director of Research & Securitization
Nomura Securities International, Inc.

Galia Gichon
Associate
Nomura Securities International, Inc.

Dan Lee*

Lynn Tong
Director
Nomura Securities International, Inc.

INTRODUCTION

In this chapter, we discuss basic issues that should be analyzed when tackling a CMBS deal. These issues relate to the underlying real estate, the mortgages, and the

---

* At the time this chapter was written, Dan Lee was a Vice President at Nomura Securities International.

bond classes of a CMBS deal. Specifically, we discuss five issues that we deem particularly important that potential investors in CMBS should be aware of. First we look at the various types of call protection of commercial mortgages (yield maintenance and lock-out provisions) and their impact on the cash flow of the bonds in a CMBS deal. Bond investors are sometimes under the impression that yield maintenance and lock-out offer the same benefit. We dispute this notion and offer an explanation. Second, we discuss the many adjustments that should be made to the net operating income for the different property types of commercial mortgages. The third issue we discuss is the influence balloon loans have on CMBS bonds. Potential investors should be aware of basis risk. This is the fourth issue we discuss. Finally, we look at interest strips in commercial mortgages.

YIELD MAINTENANCE VERSUS LOCK-OUT

Commercial mortgages have the distinct advantage of greater cash flow certainty than residential mortgages due to their significant call protection provisions. Commercial mortgages are either locked-out from prepayment, or the borrower is required to pay a substantial penalty if prepayment is permitted (or some combination of these two features). Many of these penalties are designed to make the investor/lender whole. A make-whole penalty should make the investor indifferent to the prepayment. This can be calculated as the difference between (1) the present value of the future cash flows at the time of prepayment assuming no prepayment had occurred (i.e. before taking the prepayment into account) and (2) the sum of the amount prepaid plus the present value of the future cash flows after taking the prepayment into account.

When a loan is completely locked-out, its cash flows remain intact. The borrower cannot refinance. As a result, the cash flow from tranches that typically get carved out of the whole loan can not change due to borrower refinancing. On the other hand, when the prepayment protection comes in the form of a penalty, the cash flow stream is affected. The allocation algorithm of the structure dictates how much of the penalty each class receives. As we show below, *under certain circumstances, even if the penalty is sufficient to make a holder of the whole loan indifferent, there may not be sufficient funds to make all the bond classes whole.* In these cases, the investor would have done better by investing in deals backed by locked-out whole loans.

For example, consider a $100 million 10-year bullet loan with a 9% coupon priced at par that is tranched into 2 classes. Suppose further that, the first class is $90 million face value with an 8% coupon priced at par, and the second class is a $10 subordinated class that pays 18% and is also priced at par. If the borrower prepays at the end of year three, when rates have dropped by 100 bp the make whole penalty on the whole loan would be $5.21 million. The issue is how much should each tranche receive. In many deals the yield maintenance penalty is allocated on a pro rata basis, i.e. on the basis of percentage prepaid. If we were to allocate this penalty based on the percentage prepaid, the senior class would receive $4.69 million, and the junior class would receive $0.52 million. However, based on the make whole principal the senior class ought to receive $4.85 million, and the junior class should receive $0.392 million.

Not only are these numbers different than those computed based on a pro rata formula, there is a $30,000 deficiency. If the loan had been locked out, this problem would not arise.

As a second example, suppose that the same $100 million 10-year bullet loan is tranched into a $90 million senior class with an 8% coupon, a $10 million junior class with an 11% coupon, and a coupon strip of 0.7% on a notional balance of $100 million.[1] In this case if the loan prepays at the end of three years when rates are 100 bp lower, the senior tranche is still due $4.85 million, and the junior class should get $0.487 million. The sum of these is more than the amount that comes in from the loan. Moreover, if all of the penalty were paid to these two classes there would be nothing left to pay the coupon strip. In practice, in situations like this, two things are done to make the coupon strip more attractive. First, the strip is usually priced with a higher yield than the regular bond classes. Second, some of the yield maintenance penalty is usually diverted to the strip class. Once again this problem would not arise, had the underlying loan been locked out.

Why does this problem arise? The answer lies in the yields at which the tranches are priced relative to the whole loan. When the yields on some of the tranches are above the whole loan yield, there may not be sufficient money to make them whole. Since the dollar duration weighted average yield of all tranches over the life of the deal is not mathematically equivalent to the internal rate of return of the loan one can not expect to get the same number by computing the make whole yield maintenance penalty for the underlying loan, and the sum of the penalties computed for each tranche. Thus, while a make whole yield maintenance penalty serves as economic compensation for the whole loan, it does not necessarily make all of the bondholders whole. On the other hand, tranches backed by loans which are locked out, continue to receive payment as planned and thus, do not have the same degree of reinvestment risk.

PITFALLS IN CALCULATING NOI

The two most-used statistics for quickly assessing the risk of commercial real estate loans are the loan-to-value ratio (LTV) and the debt service coverage ratio (DSCR). In this section we discuss some of the variations that are used in calculating net operating income (NOI), the primary component of DSCR. Lenders, rating agencies, and underwriters, compute this all-important number in different ways, some more conservatively than others. In order to compare deals, investors need to understand these differences and if possible make appropriate adjustments. From a credit standpoint, it is the amount and consistency of future NOI that is relevant.

---

[1] Investors should be made aware of the allocation of prepayment premium. Prepayment allocations range from fixed percentages to only allotting premiums to a tranche being paid down at the time.

The question is how to make this estimate. At the time of this writing, where the real estate market is in the process of recovering from the worst period, rating agencies and lenders prefer to use historical NOI to project the future. They believe that it is conservative to use NOI from a period in which real estate was languishing. Presumably, at the point in the real estate cycle when things are beginning to turn down, recent historical NOI may not be conservative.

Some of the blame for the bad performance of loans during the 1991 to 1992 period was attributed to the use of projected cash flows, where estimates of ever increasing NOI made the loans look like a sure thing. Nevertheless, in some cases the use of projected cash flow is correct. Projected cash flow can be used for retail and office properties when there are signed leases in place, even if the tenants have not yet moved in.

No matter how the initial NOI estimates are derived, the most important analysis should focus on the proper adjustments to NOI. The adjustments vary by property type. *NOI on retail properties should be adjusted for lease expirations since there are usually some leases that expire before the maturity of the loan.* Properly underwritten loans will have their NOI adjusted downward to account for tenant roll over and leasing commissions. In addition, the current leases should be compared to market rents. If the rents are above average, they should be adjusted downward.

We have seen some deals where DSCRs are quoted using NOIs without such adjustments. This can lead to a significant overstatement of DSCR and lead the investor to believe that the loans are of better quality. In Exhibit 1, we look at an actual deal to assess the difference in DSCR with and without these adjustments. With the adjustments, the DSCR drops from 1.40x to 1.28x. An investor should query their dealers about these adjustments even though the rating agencies have made the adjustments. At a minimum, an investor should use the rating agency DSCR, and not the dealer quoted DSCR. If there is more than one rating agency on a CMBS deal, investors should compare DSCRs and corresponding adjustments.

Exhibit 1: DSCR for an Actual Deal With and Without Adjustments

Property	DSCR with Tenant Rollovers and Leasing Commission Adjustment	DSCR without Tenant Rollovers and Leasing Commission Adjustment	Percent Change
Retail Property #1	1.29	1.45	12.66
Retail Property #2	1.32	1.32	0.00
Retail Property #3	1.24	1.40	12.68
Retail Property #4	1.28	1.42	10.31
Total Weighted Average	1.28	1.40	8.98

Adjustment for Management Fees

Fees are either fixed or based on a percentage of revenues. Management fees for hotel properties may be based on percentages of room and non-room revenues, whereas retail centers may base management fees on base rent and a percent of sales. While some lenders and underwriters may use lower estimates for management fees, the rating agencies typically have their own estimates, which vary by property type. For example, fees for hotels are generally assumed to be 5% for hotels, and 6% for nursing homes. Some dealers try to play down the relevance of management fees since they are often subordinate to debt service. This is incorrect, because if management is not paid the property will deteriorate.

Adjustments for Capital Expenditures and Repairs

These adjustments vary by property type. For multifamily properties, an assumption of $250/unit per year is common. Congregate care facilities usually calculate the reserve on a per bed basis. Maintenance and repairs need to be funded out of cash flow. Therefore, reserves need to be set aside for these. In addition, reserves are usually required for some portion of capital expenditures as well.

Although reserves for capital expenditures (capex) and repairs and maintenance may be part of the original loan agreement, the required amount of reserves varies greatly and sometimes may not be sufficient. Indeed, in a recent study, the International Society of Hospitality Consultants (ISHC) noted that the often used standard of 3% of gross revenues for hotels, way understates realty. On average the ISHC found that limited service hotels have reported repair and maintenance expenses equal to 5.21% of gross revenues. Moreover, the study indicates predictable spikes in CapEx. The first major expenditure is for room renovations which are generally required around year 6. Then at around year 15, replacement of major items, such as boilers, HVAC, plumbing, etc. occurs. These items are not related to revenue, and should be projected separately. In addition to making initial adjustments for these items, investors need to analyze on an on-going basis how closely reality is tracking the original assumptions.

BALLOON EXTENSION AND CMBS

Many commercial mortgage loans collateralizing commercial mortgage-backed securities are balloon loans that require a substantial principal payment (balloon payment) on the final payment date. Such balloon loans are perceived to be more risky than fully amortizing loans because the repayment of the final balloon amount depends on the borrower's ability to either sell the mortgaged property backing the loan or refinance the loan.

Several factors influence the borrower's ability to accomplish either of these goals. These factors include the absolute and relative level of available mortgage rates at the time of sale or refinancing, the market or appraised value of the mortgaged property, the financial condition of the borrower, the borrower's equity in the mortgaged property, the operating history of the property, the prevailing tax laws and general economic conditions, and the availability of credit for the type of mortgaged property.

The failure of the borrower to make the balloon payment constitutes an event of default. The loan then becomes due upon demand, and may undergo several modifications. While the loan is being worked out, the loan inevitably experiences an extension. During the period of extension, the interest rate charged on the mortgage loan may increase to a higher rate (default rate). The default rate can be a fixed rate, a floating rate, or a rate equal to the greater of the two, but always limited by the applicable laws. Concurrently, any excess cash flow from operations may be used to pay down the loan balance.[2] The exact definition of excess cash flow differs from loan to loan but is typically equal to the net operating income from the mortgaged property with or without regard to depreciation and appreciation less monthly payment of interest at the default rate and principal deemed due, actual capital expenditure, tenant improvement expenditures, leasing commission expenditures, and payments into any reserves required under the mortgage loan documents.

When a balloon loan is combined with other balloon loans and fully amortizing loans to securitize a CMBS deal, a balloon extension impacts the CMBS tranches differently with respect to the timing and the amount of total principal and interest received depending on what the servicer does, whether the tranches are being paid down or not at the time of the extension, whether the coupons on the tranche are weighted-averaged or not, whether the tranches are premiums or discounts, whether the tranches are coupon strips or not, and whether the tranches are senior or junior classes.

Upon a balloon payment default, the servicer of the deal has an opportunity to modify, waiver, or amend the terms of the mortgage loan in accordance with the servicing standards set forth in the pooling and servicing agreement, if such action is likely to produce a greater recovery on a present value basis than liquidating the mortgage loan outright. Material changes to the loan terms will result in the principal and interest cash flow stream that is different from the original cash flow stream. This change will cause the tranches to be paid down differently. The servicer is also obligated to advance any monthly payments of principal and interest deemed due but not paid by the borrower but to the extent that the servicer deems recoverable from the future borrower payments and property liquidation proceeds. If the servicer does not advance, the tranches will get paid down at a slower pace by the amount of principal deemed neither paid nor advanced. If the servicer advances, the tranches may extend anyway since the servicer does not advance the entire balloon payment amount but rather the monthly payment of principal and interest calculated as if the loan continues to amortize.

The tranche that would have originally been paid down from the balloon payment will most likely have a longer average life (assuming an eventual full principal

---

[2] This method is also known as the "cash trap" method and was originally used with non-performing CMBS deals.

repayment) as a result of the balloon extension. The tranche will not extend only if there exists another loan with equal or larger principal paydown for that month that would have gone to a subsequent tranche had the extension not occurred. The tranches which follow the tranche that would have been paid down by the balloon payment may or may not extend. In general, since there is a greater chance that the collateral as a pool will get back on track to paying down the principal as originally planned as time progresses, the later the original tranche paydown, the less likely the tranche will extend.

The total amount of interest received will depend on the coupon of the tranche. If the coupon on the tranche is a weighted-average rate, then the coupon may stay higher or lower than originally expected depending on whether the extended balloon loan has a coupon rate that is higher or lower than the weighted-average rate, respectively.

If a tranche is a premium, then the average life extension is somewhat mitigated by the collection of a higher coupon for a longer period. This mitigation is especially true of an interest-only strip whose notional balance would have been retired by the balloon payment. The extension allows such an interest-only strip to collect additional interest payments that the tranche holders did not expect to receive for as long as it takes to pay down the notional balance. Thus an investor concerned with the balloon extension should invest in the interest-only strip to gain from such an event. These results are generally true whether the default interest, the additional interest collected from the loan now paying a higher default rate, is passed on to the CMBS tranches or not.

The credit priority of the tranches also plays a role in how much cash flow is received. In some deals, the servicer does not make full interest and principal advances for the benefit of the most junior tranche. As a consequence, the most junior tranche may experience a delay in the receipt of its interest and principal. Also, if the extended balloon loan is eventually liquidated, and a loss of principal occurs, then the losses realized will likely result in the principal write down of the junior tranches. This write down may never be recovered by the tranches. Incidentally, it is possible that that the average lives of the remaining tranches with higher credit rating may extend as well after liquidation depending on the composition of the remaining mortgage loans in the collateral pool. It is also possible that this increase in the average life of a tranche sometimes can provide for the collection of a much higher total interest payment amount for the tranche while maintaining identical maturity dates as before.

BASIS RISK IN CMBS

In several floating rate CMBS deals, the adjustable-rate mortgages collateralizing the deal are based on one index such as COFI (Cost of Funds Index) while the floating rate bonds issued are based on another index such as LIBOR. Because of the index mismatch, if in a given accrual period the index of the bond rises faster than the index of the collateral, then the coupon rate on the bonds may exceed the net mortgage rate of the collateral. As a result, there may not be enough interest payment flowing in from the collateral loans to pay the full coupon interest to the bondholders in that accrual period. Basis risk refers to this potential risk of bondholders not collecting a full monthly interest payment because of the coupon mismatch between the collateral and the bonds.

Dissimilar indices are not the only cause of basis risk. Basis risk can also occur if the coupon reset dates, reset frequency, periodic reset caps, life caps and life floors do not coincide for both the collateral and the bonds. If the definitions of indices, such as LIBOR, stated in the collateral loan documents and the deal prospectus supplement are different, then basis risk can also exist. In many deals, the senior class can mitigate losses caused by an exposure to basis risk through the use of a reserve fund or the right to access cash flows initially allotted to a more junior class. Almost always, however, such support is capped so that the basis risk is never completely eliminated.

Deals that have bonds exposed to basis risks include Daiwa Mortgage Acceptance Corp. 1993-1 (Daiwa 93-1) and many CMBS issued by the RTC. In Daiwa 93-1, the collateral contains loans based on COFI and different U.S. Treasury yield indices while the most senior bond issued is based on LIBOR. RTC deals have included collateral loans with numerous different indices and bonds with either COFI or LIBOR as indices. In FDIC REMIC Trust 1994-C1, the collateral contains loans tied to Prime Rate, COFI, 1-year CMT, 2-year CMT, 3-year CMT, 5-year CMT, and other indices while the bonds issued have coupons tied to LIBOR.

In order to counter basis risk, investors should seek deals in which the indices, the reset dates, the periodic reset frequencies, the periodic reset caps, life caps and life floors are identical for both the collateral and the bonds, so that basis risk cannot arise.

INTEREST STRIPS IN COMMERCIAL MORTGAGES

In this section we discuss some of the issues related to interest strips in commercial mortgages. This should be of interest to all CMBS investors, even those who do not directly invest in strips, since any premium bond implicitly contains a strip. Moreover, as we discuss below, some bond classes may be receiving a portion of their coupon from strips off of other classes.

In an environment with a credit curve with a positive slope, it is common to strip a portion of the interest due to the senior classes in order to keep the prices of these classes reasonably close to par. These interest strips, while sometimes referred to as IOs, do not have the same risks as those in the residential mortgage market. The primary risk to interest strip holders is the reduction of the notional principal caused by prepayments.

Prepayments can arise either due to refinancing or foreclosure following a default. In the residential market, there are no barriers to refinancing, thus, when interest rates fall, homeowners prepay their mortgages, thereby reducing the notional principal amount on which the interest strip payments are based. Default rates are relatively low in the residential market. In contrast, refinancing risk is much less of a factor in the commercial market than for residential mortgages because of the strong call protection features such as lockouts and yield maintenance penalties. The focus of prepayment analysis in commercial mortgages, therefore, tends to be related to default risk.

Commercial interest strips generally have the same ratings as their related senior classes. While losses due to defaults are unlikely to reduce the principal amount due to the senior classes in a CMBS transaction, they have the same effect as prepayments. For a regular bond class this translates into a change in the average life, usually (but not always) making it shorter. For bonds priced at a premium this reduces the return. However, there could be an offsetting factor if the yield curve is positively sloped. In this case the shortening of the average life could cause the price to rise as the bond "rolls down" the curve.[3] For an interest only class, the erosion of notional principal is always a negative, since future cash flows are curtailed. As a result, these classes are priced at significantly wider spreads than their related bond classes. For example, in NASC-94-MD1 the A3x class was priced 200 basis points wider than the class from which it was stripped.

Whether or not the investor is adequately compensated by this additional spread, is a function of the structure, probability of default, loss severity, and probability of prepayment.[4] For example, in a multiborrower deal, depending upon one's view about loss severity versus default rates, the interest class stripped off of a single A class may be a better value than the one stripped off of a AAA class. Unless there are huge losses (sufficient to wipe out the credit support for the A class), the single A's corresponding principal remains intact, whereas the AAA's principal is reduced. This is because recoveries are used to paydown the AAA principal balance first, thus eroding the value of the corresponding interest strip. On the other hand losses are allocated from below, so that if losses are extremely high the A class could be wiped out first; however, the losses would have to wipe out all the classes and equity underneath the A class.

The analysis is different for a deal backed by a single loan. In this case, following foreclosure, both classes will cease receiving interest. The only advantage the AAA strip has is that if there is a shortfall in the recoveries it has priority to receive the interest that is due from prior periods. In Chapter 17, a framework is introduced which can be used to value the interest strip taking into account the possibility of default.

The characteristics of commercial strips vary greatly by deal. Some interest strips pay fixed rates on their notional principal balances, such as the four strip classes in NASC-94-MD1. Others pay a weighted average rate which will vary over time based on the paydown experience of the underlying loans. These interest strips are called WAC (weighted average coupon) strips. The effective yield will vary based on the default and prepayment experience. Interest strips can be created from either

---

[3] The price goes up as the cash flows get priced at lower rates at the short end of the yield curve.
[4] In the case of prepayment penalties, the allocation scheme can vary, which can dramatically alter the performance of the strip class.

fixed rate or floating rate classes. In situations when the floating rate class is capped, and the cap on the tranche is set to be the same as that of the underlying loans, there may be insufficient funds to pay the interest only class (This will occur when the underlying loans reach the cap). In these situations it is said that the strips pay interest subject to an available funds cap. The Heller deal brought by First Boston (Manufactured Housing Community Series 1994-MHC1), contains such an interest strip. The interest strip in KRT Mortgage Securities Trust 92-1, on the other hand, is not subject to available funds. This is because the underlying loans are uncapped.[5]

Two features of commercial mortgage-backed securities are of particular importance to the interest strip investor. Both of the features are the responsibility of the servicer. The first is *servicer advances*, the second is the *extension feature for balloon loans*.[6] When a borrower fails to make a payment, the servicer is usually required by the pooling and servicing agreement to advance the payment as long as it deems the amounts advanced to be recoverable. Servicers do not advance a balloon payment, but are required to advance interest and scheduled principal payments through foreclosure. Thus, when a default occurs, the bondholders continue to receive their cash flows until the property is sold. This feature is very beneficial for an interest strip holder since the cash flows are front loaded compared to other bond classes. Since all the interest strip investor gets is interest, the longer the certificate stays outstanding the better off he is.

The extension feature which comes into play at the balloon date can be even more valuable. In most deals the servicer has the right to grant an extension to a borrower who is able to continue regular payments in order to enable the borrower to seek refinancing. Under these circumstances the interest strip receives cash flow beyond the original expected maturity date. This can greatly enhance the yield for the interest strip holder. Regular bond class investors may be ambivalent about the benefits of extension particularly if interest rates had risen. These investors should consider purchasing interest strips as a hedge against extension risk.

In situations where there is limited call protection, investors may use strips to stabilize performance of discount bonds. When prepayments speed up, yields on the strips decline, but yields on the discount bonds increase as their weighted average lives shorten. If prepayments are slow, the yield on discount bond classes declines, but the yield on the interest strips increases as coupon is received for a longer period of time. In NASC-94-MDII and NASC-94-C3, "mix bonds" with these characteristics were created. In these cases instead of offering stripped interest classes, the interest cash flows were added to the coupon of lower rated classes which otherwise would have been priced at a discount. The prepayment sensitivity of such mix bonds is much lower than those of each of its components.

Such mix bonds are generally superior to synthetics, created by buying a senior interest strip and a subordinate bond separately. This is true for a number of

---

[5] Note although the underlying loans were also uncapped, the borrower was required to purchase caps in order to be able to pay interest in a high interest rate environment.

[6] For more detailed information on the role and functions of the servicer, see Chapter 5.

reasons. First, the mix bonds are cheaper than synthetics, because all the cash flows are priced at the subordinate bonds' spreads which are much wider than those of the stand-alone senior interest strips. Second, unlike synthetics created from strips and discount bonds from different deals, mix bonds are backed by the same collateral, so there is no mismatch in timing and amount of prepayment. Lastly, there is less paperwork in buying one class.

There are two ways mixed bonds can be created. One is to get the payment priority of the strip (that is now part of the subordinated class) to be equal to that of the interest of the senior class from which it was stripped. We call this the "senior strip structure." The other way is for the strip cash flows to have the same payment priority as the interest of the subordinated class with which it has been combined. We refer to this as the "junior strip structure." The impact of the priority is felt upon default if the servicer does not advance. If the servicer does advance the impact of the priority is felt when recoveries are received following foreclosure. When a recovery is made, available cash flow is allocated based on priority. The order of priority is starting with the most senior class outstanding, current interest, interest owed from past periods, and principal. If there are sufficient funds, payments are then made to the next most senior class in the same way, and so on down through the junior classes. When the mix bond is a senior strip structure, the mix bond will receive current interest and interest owed pari pasu with the bond from which it was stripped. In the junior strip structure, the mix bond has to wait until all classes above it get paid. So in a case where there are insufficient funds to pay interest to subordinated classes, it is possible that a mix bond from a senior strip structure would receive the interest due to its strip component. Thus, it would appear that from the mix bondholder's perspective the senior strip structure is better.

One situation in which the mix bond holder from a junior strip structure receives more cash flow is when the servicer does not advance during the foreclosure period, net recovery is available for distribution after foreclosure, the deal remains outstanding after recovery, and the total realized losses allocated to the bonds do not exceed the original principal balance of the mix bond.

Here is how it would work. The interest shortfall incurred during the foreclosure period is paid out of the net recovery. In a senior strip structure, as the strip component of the mix bond is *pari pasu* with interest on the senior classes, more of the net recovery is used to pay interest before the senior classes receive principal payments. In a junior strip structure, the portion of net recovery which would otherwise be paid to the interest strip component of the mix bond is used to retire the senior classes. The senior classes in a junior strip structure are therefore entitled to less future interest payments than their counterparts in a senior strip structure, because their ownership interest in the remaining mortgage pool is reduced by the additional principal repayment equal to the interest amount NOT paid to the strip component of the mix bond.

The write-off upon recovery on the mix bond in a junior structure is thus less by that same interest amount than the corresponding write-off in a senior structure. If total realized losses do not exceed its principal, the mix bond's unpaid interest shortfall will be paid by the time it is scheduled to receive principal repayments after all senior classes have matured. At maturity, the mix bond in a junior strip structure will take a greater principal write-off than the mix bond in the senior strip structure. This delay in the principal write-off on the mix bond in a junior strip structure entitles such a mix bond to greater interest payments than its counterpart in a senior strip structure is entitled to.

The following example illustrates the above. Consider a mortgage pool of $100 million which consists of two loans of $50 million each with a 12% coupon rate. For the sake of simplicity, neither loan is assumed to amortize over its term. One loan matures in four years and the other matures in nine years. The pool is divided into two classes, an $80 million senior class with a 11.5% coupon rate, and a $20 million junior class (mix bond) earning a 12% coupon on its own principal balance (discount subordinate component) and 0.5% on the senior class's balance (interest strip component). (See Exhibit 1.) Monthly interest from the pool is $1,000,000 with $500,000 from each loan. Monthly interest to the senior class is $766,667 and monthly interest to the junior class is $233,333 of which $200,000 is attributable to the discount subordinate and $33,333 to the interest strip. During the 47 months before the 4-year loan matures, total interest payments of $36,033,333 and $10,966, 667 are made to the senior and junior classes, respectively. (See Exhibit 3.)

Let's say the 4-year loan defaults upon maturity and the foreclosure period lasts 18 months during which the servicer does not advance payments. (See Exhibit 4.) At the end of the 18-month period, only 1% of the loan balance is lost. Thus in month 66, available cash for distribution is $50,000,000 consisting of $49,500,000 net recovery from the defaulted 4-year loan and $500,000 of interest from the 9-year loan. A $9,000,000 (0.12 / 12 × $50,000,000 × 18) interest shortfall is accumulated during the 18-month period.

Exhibit 2: Summary of Collateral and Securities

		Face ($)	Coupon (%)	Balloon	
Collateral	Loan 1	50,000,000	12.00	48	
	Loan 2	50,000,000	12.00	108	Yield
Securities	Senior	80,000,000	11.50	103	11.027
	Mix Bond	20,000,000	14.00	90	16.106
	– Discount Subordinate	20,000,000	12.00		
	– Interest Strip	20,000,000	12.00		

Exhibit 3: Interest Payable To Each Class

		Monthly ($)	47 Months Total Interest Paid ($)
Senior	11.5% × 80mm =	766,667	36,033,333
Mix Bond		233,333	10,966,667
– Discount Subordinate	12.0% × 20mm =	200,000	9,400,000
– Interest Strip	0.5% × 80mm =	33,333	1,566,667

Exhibit 4: Available Cash Allocation During Foreclosure and Recovery

Loan 1 defaults on balloon date and gets 99.00% 18 months later. During the 18-month foreclosure, only interest on Loan 2 is available: $500,000 per month.

	Senior Interest Strip (A and Interest Strip are pro rata)			Junior Interest Strip		
	Interest Paid ($)	Shortfall ($)	Total Shortfall ($)	Interest Paid ($)	Shortfall ($)	Total Shortfall ($)
Senior	479,167	287,500	5,175,000	500,000	266,667	4,800,000
Mix Bond	20,833	212,500	3,825,000	0	233,333	4,200,000
– Discount Subordinate	0	200,000	3,600,000	0	200,000	3,600,000
– Interest Strip	20,833	12,500	225,000	0	33,333	600,000

Upon recovery in month 65, 49,500,000 net proceeds and 500,000 interest are available.

	Senior Interest Strip (A and Interest Strip are pro rata)			Junior Interest Strip		
	Interest Paid ($)	Principal Paid ($)	Interest Shortfall ($)	Interest Paid ($)	Principal Paid ($)	Interest Shortfall ($)
Senior	5,941,667	43,800,000	0	5,566,667	44,433,333	0
Mix Bond	258,333	0	3,800,000	0	0	4,433,333
– Discount Subordinate	0	0	3,800,000	0	0	3,800,000
– Interest Strip	258,333	0	0	0	0	633,333

If there is no further default, then total interest paid:

	Senior Interest Strip (A and Interest Strip are pro rata)			Junior Interest Strip		
	Remaining Balance($)	Interest / Month($)	Total to Maturity ($)	Remaining Balance($)	Interest / Month($)	Total to Maturity ($)
Senior	36,200,000	346,917	14,570,500	35,566,667	340,847	14,315,583
Mix Bond	13,800,000	153,083	6,429,500	14,433,333	159,153	6,684,417
– Discount Subordinate	13,800,000	138,000	5,795,000	14,433,333	144,333	6,062,000
– Interest Strip	36,200,000	15,083	633,500	35,566,667	14,819	622,417

Exhibit 4 (Continued)

$50,000,000 repayment is paid:

	Senior Interest Strip (A and Interest Strip are pro rata)		Junior Interest Strip	
	Interest	Principal	Interest	Principal
Senior	0	36,200,000	0	35,566,667
Mix Bond	3,800,000	10,000,000	4,433,333	10,000,000

Total P & Ivpaid:

	Interest	Principal	Yield (%)	Interest	Principal	Yield Difference(%)	Basis Points
Senior	65,170,500	80,000,000	11.0628	64,915,583	80,000,000	11.0659	0
Mix Bond	21,829,500	10,000,000	10.4239	22,084,417	10,000,000	10.4189	0

If Loan 2 defaults on balloon date & gets 99.00% 18 months later, 49,500,00 recovery is paid as interest of 19 months and principal

	Senior Interest Strip (A and Interest Strip are pro rata)		Junior Interest Strip	
	Interest	Principal	Interest	Principal
Senior	6,591,417	36,200,000	6,476,097	35,566,667
Mix Bond	6,708,583	0	7,457,236	0

Total P & Ivpaid:

	Interest	Principal	Yield (%)	Interest	Principal	Yield Difference(%)	Basis Points
Senior	71,415,000	80,000,000	11.0497	71,050,833	80,000,000	11.0659	0
Mix Bond	24,585,000	0	5.9278	24,949,167	10,000,000	10.4189	11

In a senior strip structure, the senior class and the interest strip of the mix bond share the $500,000 interest from the 9-year loan during the 18-month fore-closure period and receive monthly interest payments of $479,167 ($766,667/ $800,000 × $500,000) and $20,833 ($33,333/$800,000 × $500,000), respectively. This leaves a total interest shortfall of $5,175,000 (18 × ($766,667 – $479,167)) on the senior class and $3,825,000 (18 × ($33,333 – $20,833) + 18 × $200,000) on the mix bond of which $225,000 is shortfall on the interest strip component. Interest due each class in month 66 is that month's interest plus the total interest shortfall, which is $5,941,667 for the senior class, $258,333 for the strip compo-nent and $3,800,000 for the discount subordinate. The $50,000,000 available cash is used to pay first the interest on the senior class and the interest strip compo-nent; the remaining $43,800,000 is then applied to reduce the principal balance of the senior class to $36,200,000 from $80,000,000. The subordinate discount receives no payment and writes down its balance to $13,800,000 from $20,000,000. This changes the pool ownership between the senior and junior classes from 80/20 to 72.4/27.6 and entitles the senior class to monthly interest of $346,917 going forward and the mix bond to $153,083. By the end of the ninth year, when the second loan matures, the $50,000,000 principal will be used to pay off the senior class ($36,200,000), then to pay the mix bond's interest shortfall on account of the discount subordinate ($3,800,000), and then to pay the mix bond's principal ($10,000,000 of the $13,800,000 outstanding). The senior and the junior classes will have received total interest payments of $65,170,500 and $21,829,500, respectively, and the junior class (mix bond) will have written off $10,000,000 of its principal balance: $6,200,000 upon recovery of the 4-year loan and $3,800,000 at maturity.

In a junior strip structure, on the other hand, the senior class takes all of the $500,000 interest paid on the 9-year loan during the 4-year loan's 18-month foreclosure period. This leaves a total interest shortfall of $4,800,000 (18 × ($766,66 –$500,000)) on the senior class and $4,200,000 (18 × $233,333) on the mix bond. Of the $50,000,000 available cash in month 66, $5,566,667 is paid as interest, and the remainder as principal, to the senior class so as to reduce its out-standing balance to $35,566,667. The junior class has a total interest shortfall of $4,433,333 and writes down its balance to $14,433,333. This changes the pool ownership from 80/20 to 71.13/28.87 and entitles the senior class to monthly interest of $340,847 going forward and the mix bond to $159,153. The $50,000,000 principal of the 9-year loan will be used upon maturity to pay off the senior class and the interest shortfall on the junior class, leaving $10,000,000 for the junior class's principal. The senior and the junior classes will have received total interest payments of $64,915,583 and $22,084,417, respectively. The junior class (mix bond) will have written off $10,000,000 of its principal balance: $5,566,667 upon recovery of the 4-year loan and $4,433,333 at maturity.

SUMMARY

When analyzing a CMBS deal, all facets of the deal, from the real estate, to the loan terms, to the bond structure, should be considered equally. Each part of the deal has its own nuances and should be researched accordingly. Once an investor is more familiar with the different types of product, he can analyze a deal properly. It is important to note that no two CMBS deals are the same. If the bond structure seems similar, then the real estate collateral is different or the loan terms vary. However, an investor can be prepared as long as he knows what to look for and the right questions to ask.

Chapter 14

A Framework for Risk and Relative Value Analysis of CMBS: Practice

David P. Jacob
**Managing Director and
Director of Research & Securitization
Nomura Securities International, Inc.**

Galia Gichon
Associate
Nomura Securities International, Inc.

INTRODUCTION

The best opportunities for investors lie in differentiating between deals and bond classes. Bonds of the same rating and stated average lives will produce very different performance results. Relative value analysis of any bond class in CMBS must consider the spread relative to the combination of the following factors: (1) the quality and valuation of the real estate; (2) the underwriting and structural aspects of the loan; and, (3) the cash flow characteristics of the bond structure. Without analyzing these three components, the investor could wind up with a return that is inferior to the offered spread.

In the third quarter of 1995, there was a flurry of conduit deals that were brought to the market. In total $1.7 billion of small loan deals were priced. Exhibit 1 lists the deals along with some basic information.[1] In this chapter, we review and

---

[1] Prudential Securities Funding Corp. also came out with a conduit deal on 7/28/95 for $105.6 million. However, this deal was privately placed and a prospectus was not available. For the purposes of this analysis, we did not include this deal.

compare these deals starting with the underlying real estate, followed by an analysis of the loans, and conclude with the structures. This analysis should serve as a basis for comparison with other deals.

REAL ESTATE COMPARISON

Exhibit 2 gives a breakdown of the seven deals by property type. Four of the seven deals had a large retail component. The other property type that was heavily represented was multifamily. These two sectors of the real estate market may have already experienced much of the increase in value in this recovery cycle at the time of this analysis, and thus the upside in value on these properties is now less than in some of the other sectors such as office, hotel, congregate care and industrial.

LOAN ANALYSIS

Loan analysis should be divided into two parts. First, one needs to look at the quality of the pool. Second, an analysis of the structural features of the loans should be done. As can be seen in Exhibit 3, the collateral quality varied substantially. The weighted average debt service coverage ratings (DSCRs) ranged from 1.33x to 1.60x and the weighted average loan-to-value (LTV) ratios ranged from 61% to 71%

Exhibit I: Deals Summary

Deal	Underwriter	Balance	Date	Servicer	Special Servicer
ASC 95-D1	Nomura Securities	$210.88	8/7/95	Midland Loan Services, L.P.	Midland Loan Services, L.P.*
ASW 95-C1	Donaldson, Lufkin & Jenrette	$293.04	7/25/95	Boatman's National Mortgage, Inc.	Lennar Partners, Inc.
FNMA 95-M2	NationsBanc	$216.14	6/21/95	EQ Services, Inc.	EQ Services, Inc.
JPM 95-C1	JP Morgan	$172.17	7/28/95	Banc One	AMRESCO 61% Banc One 39%
MCF 95-MC1	Citibank/ Smith Barney	$228.78	8/2/95	Citibank N.A.	J.E. Robert Company, Inc.
ML 95-C1	Merrill Lynch/ ING Securities	$216.01	7/17/95	Fleet real Estate Capital, Inc.	Appointed by junior class
MSC 95-GAL1	Morgan Stanley	$257.88	7/20/95	General American Life Insurance Co.	Banc One

* The special servicer may be replaced by the subordinate class of certificates as long as the new servicer is approved by each Rating Agency.

Exhibit 2: Property Type Breakdown (% of Deal)

Deal	MF	Hotel	Office	Retail	Industrial	Sr. Housing	Self Storage	Other
ASC 95-D1	41	25	0	11	0	9	1	13
ASW 95-C1	49	1	6	42	1	0	0	0
FNMA 95-M2	100	0	0	0	0	0	0	0
JPM 95-C1	21	11	1	52	15	0	0	0
MCF 95-MC1	67	5	2	15	3	8	0	1
ML 95-C1	19	9	19	46	7	0	0	0
MSC 95-GAL1	7	0	17	58	16	0	0	1

Exhibit 3: Collateral Description

Deal	% Sub	DSCR	LTV (%)	DSCR Range	LTV Range	# of Loans	% Balloon	Average Loan Size	Largest Loan	Rating Agency
ASC 95-D1	29	1.53x	64	1.25x–3.44x	30%–84%	62	81	$3.46	$11.21	Fitch, S&P
ASW 95-C1	28	1.33x	68	1.19x–2.05x	42%–71%	78	100	$3.76	$17.92	D&P, Moody's
FNMA 95-M2	10	1.33x	71	1.15x–1.74x	50%–89%	71	96	#3.17	$9.76	NA
JPM 95-C1	33	1.52x	64	0.59x–2.60x	45%–74%	79	68	$4.78	$13.48	S&P
MCF 95-MC1	30	1.60x	66	0.97x–6.51x	27%–85%	79	68	$2.90	$12.29	Fitch, S&P
ML 95-C1	37	1.46x	80	1.04x–2.36x	38%–117%	54	99	$4.00	$13.65	Fitch
MSC 95-GAL1	29	1.58x	61	1.15x–3.02x	29%–82%	97	95	$2.66	$22.09	Fitch, S&P

The weighted average statistics, however, can be deceiving. For example, in two of the deals, there were loans with DSCRs below 1.00x and one deal had loans with LTVs above 100%. The lower quality of these pools seems to have been recognized by the rating agencies in the form of higher subordination. Since loans in conduit deals are generally not cross-collateralized, one would certainly expect defaults in these pools. Thus investors in the lower classes of these deals should demand extra compensation. Moreover, while the AAA bond class would not experience losses due to the substantial subordination, nevertheless, there is likely to be great average life uncertainty associated with such pools. This occurs because the recoveries from foreclosures are paid to the most senior class first. As a result, it is impossible to predict when the AAA bond holder will receive his principal. Thus, even investors in the AAA class from a low quality pool need extra spread to compensate for the average life uncertainty.

While cross-collateralized and cross-defaulting is not usually found in conduit deals, it is available in other CMBS formats such as MegaDeal pools. An investor will be willing to pay up for cross-collateralization since it greatly reduces the volatility of net operating income (NOI) and as a result reduces the probability of default. In a recent study, it was shown that "default risk resulting from a 2 asset cross-default clause, can be reduced by over 50% of non-recourse default risk when asset values are uncorrelated."[2]

Many studies of loan defaults indicate that year of origination and source of origination are the two best predictors of loan default experience. Three of the seven deals had sizeable percentages of their loans originated prior to 1991. The real estate market bottomed in 1993. At the time of this analysis, we expect multifamily and retail loans originated in 1993 and 1994 (and hotel loans originated in 1994 and 1995) to be the best performing loans in this real estate cycle.

Another point to consider is that four out of the seven deals had loans that were materially modified. According to a recent research report "previously modified loans that ultimately are foreclosed upon have significantly lower loss recoveries." The authors found the average recovery for these loans to be 58% of the loan balance compared to 78% for non-modified loans.[3]

Two other factors should be considered in the loan quality analysis. First, with respect to the deals with large retail concentration, only ASC 95-D1 had its NOI adjusted for Tenant Rollover and Leasing Commissions. Thus, the sustainable coverage ratios could very well be less than stated. Investors should always request coverage ratios based on these adjustments to NOI.[4]

The other issue is the value calculation in the LTV. In our view, at the time of this analysis, both multifamily and retail have much less upside than they used to since they bottomed earlier and have been bid up substantially. This makes their LTV numbers less conservative than in the past.

---

[2] Paul Child, Steven Ott, and Timothy Riddiough, "The Value of Recourse and Cross-Default Clauses in Commercial Mortgage Contracting," *Journal of Banking and Finance*, 1994.

[3] Brian Ciochetti and Timothy Riddiough, "Loss Severity and Its Impact on Commercial Mortgage Performance," unpublished manuscript, December 1994.

[4] For a further discussion, see Chapter 13.

Exhibit 4: Call Protection Schedule
(Weighted Averages in Months)

Deal	Lockout Period	Yield Main Formula Period	Yield Main Percent of Principal Period	Free Period	Maturity	Lockout as Percentage of Maturity
ASC 95-D1	121	14	6	22	163	74
ASW 95-C1	46	31	4	20	101	46
FNMA 95-M2	25	46	26	18	115	22
JPM 95-C1	40	27	28	9	104	38
MCF 95-MC1	23	39	39	74	175	13
ML 95-C1	28	23	32	11	94	30
MSC 95-GAL1	42	54	23	3	122	34

After the analyzing the pool quality and underwriting standards, the investor should turn next to call protection, balloon risk, and default provisions. Even though bond performance is very dependent on call protection, many investors do not adequately analyze this component. They often forget that the rating agencies are not evaluating this risk. Exhibit 4 shows the call protection on each of the deals. Call protection must be done, first at the loan level, and then at the bond level. Call protection comes in the form of: lockout, yield maintenance, percentage penalties or any combination of the three.

Lockout is the most straightforward method to analyze and provides the best protection. Yield maintenance, if properly designed can fully compensate the whole loan investor. Yield maintenance is calculated by computing the difference in the present value of the cash flows had the prepayment not occurred minus the present value of the remaining cash flows after taking into account the prepayment plus the prepaid amount. In addition, the yield maintenance formula can also incorporate compensation for potential spread tightening by discounting at some spread to treasuries that is narrower then the initial spread. This provides additional penalty and gives the investor a windfall. Percentage penalties pay the investor a premium by applying a percentage (usually declining with time) to the amount prepaid.

Both yield maintenance and percentage penalties represent financial disincentives to the borrower prepaying. They operate differently and need to be evaluated as such. On the one hand, percentage penalties are not related to the market and therefore overcompensate when rates stay the same or move up, but can be woefully insufficient when rates drop. Thus, they do not operate to provide a disincentive in the environment when most borrowers would like to prepay. On the other hand, real estate owners prepay even in a rising rate environment. This typically occurs when property values rise along with rising income. Indeed a study of the NCREIF database indicates annual turnover of 4%-5%. As a result investors should look to see if the underlying loans are assumable. To the extent that they are not assumable, lockout provides greater protection then yield maintenance because it assures the investor that he will not receive voluntary prepayments.

In a rising rate environment, the percentage penalty still provides some compensation, whereas the yield maintenance penalty only provides compensation for a rise in rates equivalent to its spread maintenance component. While most investors feel that they do not need a great deal of compensation for prepayment in this environment, this is incorrect if they purchased the loan at a premium. Moreover, an investor in a strip class in a CMBS deal needs compensation regardless if rates move up or down.

DEFAULT ANALYSIS

Default analysis should include what happens in a default. In a default, the servicer is required to advance scheduled principal and interest through foreclosure. Balloon payments do not have to be advanced. In six out of the seven deals the servicer advances are paid to all classes. In ASC 95-D1, advances are not paid to the most junior outstanding class. We view this feature as added protection for the senior classes for two reasons. First, the servicer often owns the most junior class. Thus, a conflict of interest could exist. The servicer might have an incentive to delay the foreclosure process. Second, to the extent a junior class receives advances, it hurts the senior classes in the event of insufficient recovery in foreclosure.

The servicer often has the right to modify terms of the loans in a default. Modifications can include lowering the coupon, changing the maturity, etc. This can be detrimental to the bondholder, particularly if his coupon is based on a weighted average of the outstanding loans. Only two of the seven deals did not allow coupon modifications.

Balloon loans add an extra layer of risk since the borrower may have difficulty refinancing the loan. In the case of a balloon default, the servicer usually has the right to extend the loan. This extension is viewed negatively from the senior bond holder's perspective, because this event usually coincides with a credit deterioration, and might coincide with a rise in interest rates. In some cases the servicer is limited as to the amount of extension. In other cases, disincentives are put in place to discourage the borrower from waiting for better financing. Two such disincentives are default rate penalties and the trapping of excess net operating income.

Exhibit 5 summarizes default features, for these deals.

STRUCTURAL ANALYSIS

Following the analysis of the loans, the investor should examine the impact of the structure on his bond class. The senior subordinated structure almost always requires that principal from loans be used to pay down the most senior outstanding class. While this is good from a credit standpoint, it may hurt certain bond classes. Strips always get hurt by early payments. Even though penalties can offset this, there may not be enough penalty coming from the loans. The specific structure dictates how each class is paid. Investors need to examine the bond performance in rising and falling rate environments to see if, indeed, the penalty allocation makes the bond whole to a no prepayment case. Yield tables alone cannot give this information.

The only fair way to pay penalty is if it is based on a make-whole present value calculation. Two of the conduit deals (ASW 95-C1 and MSC 95-GAL1) only allocated penalty to bond classes that were receiving principal when the prepayment occurs. This is obviously not make-whole. If a bond class shortens due to a prepayment, it may still suffer, particularly if this occurs in a falling interest rate environment. Three deals (JPMC 95-C1, MCF 95-C1 and ML 95-MC1) allocated penalty only to the interest strip classes. This results in the other classes, particularly the AAA class not being made whole in an environment where interest rates drop and there is a prepayment.

RELATIVE VALUE

Exhibit 6 shows the spreads where these deals were originally priced as available in the press. What is remarkable is how close these spreads are to each other. What should be obvious at this point is that these deals should *not* trade at the same levels. For example, why should the AAA from ASC 95-D1 trade at a similar spread to the AAA from JPMC 95-C1? The ASC-D1 deal has 74% weighted average lockout compared to JPMC 95-C1's 38%. The JPMC 95-C1 deal also requires 4% more subordination. On a collateral basis, the JPMC 95-C1 deal has loans with DSCR less than 1.00x. However, the most important point is that if the JPMC 95-C1 deal has any voluntary prepayments, all prepayment penalty is allocated to the interest only classes. Therefore, in the event of a prepayment the AAA bond holder is short changed.

Exhibit 5: Default Analysis

Deal	Coupon rate Increase Upon Default	Trap Excess NOI	Balloon Extension	How Long Balloon Extended?	Modifications Allowed	Advance to Junior Class
ASC 95-D1	Yes	Yes	Yes	Indefinite	No	No
ASW 95-C1	No	No	Yes	36 months	No	Yes
FNMA 95-M2	No	No	Yes	36 months	Spec Serv may	Yes
JPM 95-C1	No	No	Yes	36 months	Spec Serv may	Yes
MCF 95-MC1	No	Yes	Yes	60 months	Yes	Yes
ML 95-C1	No	No	Yes	36 months	Spec Serv may	Yes
MSC 95-GAL1	No	No	Yes	12 months	Spec Serv may	Yes

Exhibit 6: Comparative Spreads

Deal	AAA	AA	A	BBB
ASC 95-D1	+85/7.5 yr.	+120/14 yr.	+145/15 yr.	+200/17 yr.
ASW 95-C1	+80/5 yr. +90/7 yr.	+115/9.4 yr.	+130/10 yr.	+190/10 yr.
FNMA 95-M2	+50/6 mo LIBOR +67/3.1 yr. +80/6.7 yr. +115/10 yr.			
JPM 95-C1	+82/5.9 yr. +90/9.4 yr.	+113/10 yr.	+140/10 yr.	+190/10 yr.
MCF 95-MC1	+90/3.5 yr. +90/7.5 yr.	+115/10 yr.	+143/12.6 yr.	+190/15.5 yr.
ML 95-C1	+90/5.2 yr.	+110/7 yr.	+140/7.8 yr.	+190/9.3 yr.
MSC 95-GAL1	+80/3 yr. +95/9 yr.	+110/10 yr.	+135/10 yr.	+190/10 yr.

Exhibit 7: Distribution of AAA Spreads

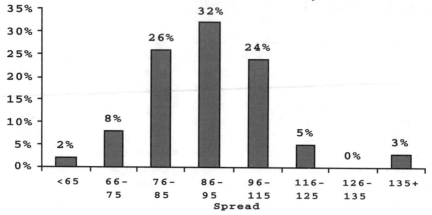

Source: Nomura Securities International, Inc.

Relative Value Model for CMBS

The rating agencies do a significant amount of work when analyzing a set of collateral before assigning ratings to a CMBS deal that is created from that collateral. The rating is meant to capture the risk of default and loss. While not all investors agree precisely with the rating agencies' conclusions, by and large, the market agrees with their general assessments and therefore prices AAA bonds with tighter spreads than AA bonds, etc. Nevertheless, as shown in Exhibits 7, 8, and 9, even within rating categories there remains a large dispersion of spreads. Thus, the rating alone does not explain the spread at which CMBS trade.

In this section we present the results of our model, which evaluates numerous factors that explain this variation. We analyzed new issue spreads on CMBS deals for the years 1994, 1995 and the first quarter of 1996. We fit the data to an equation and tested the statistical significance of the model. We found that different variables were important in explaining spreads for different rating categories. Here we show the results for AAA rated bonds down to BBB. Later in this section we use the model to rank several recent CMBS deals.

In approaching this study we considered two types of variables. First, we wanted to include in the regression those variables which investors considered important, but which were unrelated to credit events and therefore not considered in the rating assignment. The variables of this type that we considered were average life, prepayment protection, price level, and liquidity.

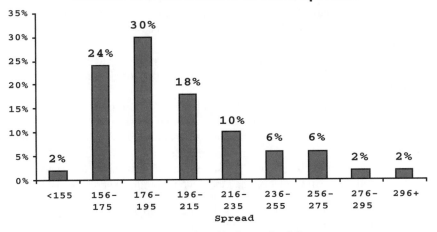

Exhibit 8: Distribution of AA Spreads

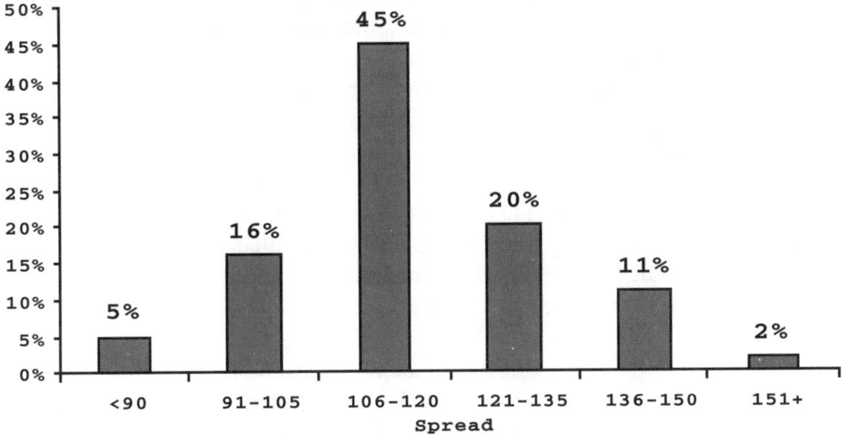

Source: Nomura Securities International, Inc.

Exhibit 9: Distribution of BBB Spreads

Source: Nomura Securities International, Inc.

To measure prepayment protection we considered two variables, the number of years of lockout as a percent of number of years to maturity as of the date of securitization, and the number of years of prepayment penalty as a percent of number of years to maturity as of the date of securitization. For the case of the AAA bonds, only the lockout variable showed up as a factor in the regression. We included a variable to measure the price level of the bonds, because investors tend to trade bonds priced above par at wider spreads. To measure liquidity we used the size of the issue.

The second type of variable we included was related to the quality and type of the collateral. While presumably this should be already incorporated into the rating and therefore the spread, the quality can affect the performance of the bonds beyond what is captured by the rating. In our view, AAA bonds from lower quality collateral should trade wider than AAA bonds that are backed by higher quality collateral. This is because the bonds from the lower quality pool will experience greater cash flow variability, even though the likelihood of losses is similar to that for the bonds backed by the higher quality collateral. Another reason that spreads on the AAA bonds from lower quality collateral can trade wider is that they may be shunned by some investors who feel uncomfortable with the increased likelihood of defaults occurring on the underlying loans. Moreover, the lower the quality of the collateral the greater the disagreement among rating agencies and investors about the appropriate subordination. This includes if there were any loans in the underlying collateral with an LTV greater than 100% or a DSCR less than 1.00x. In addition, we tested property type because many investors have clear preferences. For example, many favor multi-family properties over hotels.

To measure the quality of the collateral we used the percent subordination below the AAA level. We also considered the year of origination by pre- and post-1992. The idea here is that loans that were originated prior to 1992 were likely to be more risky, either because they had been modified, lacked good property data, etc. We considered diversification by property type in our tests. Tranches that had split ratings were also taken into consideration.

One last variable that was included was an indicator variable for whether the deal was priced in 1994 or 1995 or 1996. This was necessary because we know that on average spreads tightened.

For the AAA sector, using eight variables we were able to explain 69% of the variation in the spreads. The F statistic and the t statistics for all the coefficients were found to be significant.

So much for the statistics. Now for the interpretation. Suppose a AAA tranche, which represents 65% of a deal, has a 5-year average life, is locked out for 2.5 years out of 10 years, is $100 million in size, its underlying loans were originated after 1992, there are no loans with an LTV greater than 100% or a DSCR less than 1.00x, has a coupon of 6.20%, 5-year Treasuries are at 5.40%, and was issued October 30, 1995. Based on this information the model would predict a spread of +83 bp.

- The *average life* coefficient can be interpreted as follows: for every 1 year longer in average life, the market requires *3.99 bp more* in spread for AAA bonds.

- The *percentage of total maturity that is locked out* coefficient can be interpreted as follows: AAA bonds that have 10% greater lockout as a percent of maturity, trade *18.25 bp tighter.*
- The *percent subordinated* coefficient can be interpreted as follows: AAA bonds from deals that have 10% greater required subordination trade *6.66 bp wider.*
- The deals whose loans were *originated before 1992* coefficient can be interpreted as follows: for AAA bonds from deals whose loans were originated before 1992, trade *6.61 bp wider.*
- The *ratio of coupon to Treasury* coefficient can be interpreted as follows: for AAA bonds, if the ratio of the bond's coupon to Treasury rates is larger by 0.1 the spread is *greater by 4.96 bp.*
- The *LTV greater than 100%* coefficient can be interpreted as follows: for AAA bonds from deals whose loans had an *LTV greater than 100%*, the spread is *wider by 8.83 bp.*
- The *DSCR less than 1.00x* coefficient can be interpreted as follows: for AAA bonds from deals whose loans had a *DSCR less than 1.00x*, the spread is *wider by 5.92 bp.*
- The *time issued* coefficient can be interpreted as follows: for every *100 days since March 30, 1994*, AAA bonds traded *tighter by 2.52 bp.*

At this point a number of observations can be made. The signs of the coefficients were all in the expected directions. This means the model and the variables make a great deal of sense. The market clearly cares about lockout from prepayments and pays more for it than for prepayment penalties. (Whether or not this is the correct price to pay for prepayment protection is analyzed in Chapter 17 on the theoretical valuation of CMBS using option pricing theory.) It is interesting to note that the percent subordination is an explanatory variable despite the fact that the rating takes this into account. We infer from this that the market as a whole prefers AAA bonds backed by loans of high quality.

What is interesting to note also is the variables that did not add anything to the model. Property type, diversification, and number of borrowers were analyzed, but none of these were helpful in explaining the variation in the spread.

For the AA sector, the first thing to note is that the coefficient of determination (R-squared) is 68%. What is very interesting, is to note the fact that certain variables are not as important or not important at all for explaining the variation in the AA bonds even though they were very significant in explaining the variation in spreads in the AAA bonds. For instance, the prepayment protection is a lot less significant. This should be expected since the first bond in the sequential structure is the AAA and it provides some prepayment protection for the AA class.

In our view, while this is somewhat true, the shortening of the AAA class due to prepayments still can have significant impact on the AA classes. For the same reason it appears that the fact that a AA bond might be priced above par, is not considered as important by the market. (Also fewer AA bonds are high premiums.) Note that average life falls out of the model.

In the model for AA bonds we added a new variable to reflect the fact that bonds at the AA level often have split ratings. Naturally one would expect such bonds to trade at wider levels. According to the model, split rated AA bonds trade on average +17 bp wider than non-split rated bonds.

The last sector we look at is the BBB sector. In the BBB sector the R-squared is only 55% and the F value while statistically significant is substantially lower than for the AAA and AA sectors. Nevertheless, some useful observations can be made. First, the variables representing call protection completely dropped out of the model. At the BBB level, investors are more concerned with the quality of the collateral, the size of the tranche, and the average life. Even the property type as indicated by the coefficient which measures the response to the percent of hotels in the deal becomes relevant.

Besides being useful as an explanatory tool the model can be used to assess relative value when comparing deals. By plugging the parameter values for the deal that is being analyzed into the model, one can compute the expected spread. By comparing this number with the actual spread one can determine whether or not the market spread is relatively high or low. In Exhibit 10 we show the model spreads and the actual spreads for five bonds priced in the first quarter of 1996.

The richest of the five deals presented in Exhibit 10 was the MSC 1 96-BKU1/ A. It had the least call protection and other than being backed by multifamily collateral we see no reason why it should trade at +75 bp. The cheapest of the five deals was the SBMS VII 1996-C1/ A-2. This deal was well diversified and had good prepayment protection, yet traded at +95 bp.

A regression based model is not a fundamental valuation like an OAS approach, but rather a reflection of the market's pricing. This model does, however, provide a relative valuation and gives the investor a framework for accounting for the important variables.

Exhibit 10: CMBS Deals Done in First Quarter 1996: AAA Tranches

Deal/Tranche	Date	Model Spread	Actual Spread	Relative Value
CBM 1996-1/ A-2	1/24/96	95	90	rich
JPM 1996-C2/ A	1/24/96	84	90	cheap
MSC 1 96-BKU1/ A	1/31/96	85	75	rich
SASCO 1996-CFL/ A-2B	2/9/96	111	105	rich
SBMS VII 1996-C1/ A-2	2/27/96	85	95	cheap

Chapter **15**

Investing in Subordinate CMBS Bonds

Jojy Mathew
Manager of Product Marketing
SS&C

Elazar Katz
Chief Information Officer
Commercial Assets, Inc.

INTRODUCTION

Commercial mortgage backed securities (CMBS) are bonds backed by commercial mortgages. Typically, the bonds are structured into a senior/subordinate structure whereby one group of bonds called the subordinate, or junior classes, provides credit enhancement to another group of bonds called the senior classes. The junior classes protect the senior classes by agreeing to write down their balance to cover losses incurred on the mortgages.

The junior classes are purchased at a deep discount. Priced correctly, they have the potential to be extremely profitable, but like other risky instruments, they must be analyzed intelligently. The process of analyzing, comparing, purchasing, and monitoring subordinate CMBS bonds is the topic of this chapter. From the perspective of the subordinate class buyer, we will discuss conducting due diligence on the properties, analyzing mortgage loan features, and reviewing noteworthy features of CMBS structures.

Investing in subordinate tranches can be a lucrative field for the sophisticated investor as witnessed by the increasing number of players entering this arena. Strong real estate expertise is a prerequisite for entering the field. In addition, a thorough understanding of structured finance must also be developed. The bond structure controls the allocation of loss to specific bond classes. Understanding the risk to a subor-

297

dinate class requires simultaneous analysis of the real estate and the bond structure. The combined risk profile of a subordinate class can be described as follows:

Real Estate Risk: It is the income generated by real estate properties which enable the borrower to meet debt service obligations. Real estate risk covers the reduction in the property's income generating capacity.

Mortgage Default Risk: Mortgage default risk is the risk of the borrower defaulting on mortgage obligations. In addition to the real estate risk, default risk takes into account the borrower's incentive to make payments, and loan features which allow support from performing properties to non-performing ones.

Bond Write-down Risk: This is the risk of having the loss allocated to the bond you own. This risk takes into account the loss-allocation rules as defined by the CMBS structure.

Understanding the various risks associated with subordinate CMBS bonds is key to effective pricing and, ultimately, successful management of a subordinate CMBS portfolio.

ANALYZING SUBORDINATE CMBS BONDS

Analysis of a subordinate bond follows the risk components outlined above. Due diligence of the properties underlying the collateral is usually the first step in the process. Next, loan-related factors are evaluated. Finally, CMBS structural factors must be reviewed in detail.

Due Diligence of the Underlying Properties

Since the underlying properties are the sources of possible loss, a buyer of credit-support bonds must conduct due diligence similar to what an equity investor in the real estate would do. The investor should first familiarize himself with the underwriting criteria. Next, the individual loan files should be requested. Information has to be gathered describing loan terms, balances, rates, payment history, delinquency, and default history. Loan files should be scrutinized for existence of environmental and engineering reports, the existence of any negative comments on management of the property, and finally, audited income statements should be compiled.

Income statements should be reviewed with a critical eye. Line-items should be reviewed for appropriateness. One time payments (such as insurance reimbursements) should be removed. Expenses should be reviewed for reasonableness and inclusiveness. Careful validation of the income statements is critical because they will be used not only to determine the debt service coverage ratio (DSCR) but also to estimate the property's value.

Estimating property value is an important component of the real estate analysis. There are a number of methods to estimate a property's value. Among them are cost of replacement and price of comparable properties. One method which is more meaningful for income-producing properties is based on the property's ability to generate income. In this method the property's value is estimated by dividing annual net operating income by a *capitalization rate* (*cap rate*). The cap rate reflects the annual return to the investor assuming that the property maintains its value and is perpetually held. The cap rate reflects the investor's subjective belief regarding the required return from the property.

    Maintenance reserves should also be carefully evaluated for adequacy. Sufficient reserves need to be set up to insure that near term repairs do not drop income below an acceptable level. There is no substitute for a visual check of the property or a thorough engineering report to gauge whether the reserves set aside are adequate. Maintenance surveys should list major predicted repairs and estimated reserves for each repair.

    Environmental hazards can be an expensive liability. An engineering survey must be done not only for the property itself, but for neighboring properties as well.

    Processes should be established and systems should be implemented to track and predict the real estate performance. There are many advantages to implementing this framework using a database management system (DBMS). The DBMS provides a common platform for collecting data from various sources. In the initial evaluation stages of a subordinate bond, the investor is often provided spreadsheet files by the underwriter containing property level data. This data should be incorporated into the DBMS. Missing fields of information can be augmented from the loan files. Evaluation routines need to be created to generate the various cash flow components of the real estate. A detailed description of the system parameters needed for real estate modeling can be found in the systems section of this chapter.

Mortgage Default Risk: Reviewing the Loans

The next step in evaluating the subordinate class involves analyzing each loan in detail. Important measures of a loan's default risk is debt service coverage ratio (DSCR), and LTV (loan-to-value). The DSCR is the ratio between available income and the required debt service. The LTV is the ratio between the loan balance and the value of the property. While the DSCR is an indicator of the property's ability to support the debt service, the LTV is a predictor of the borrower's incentive to do so.

    One feature which reduces the risk of default is the existence of *cross default/cross-collateralization clauses*. When multiple properties are owned by the same borrower, cross-collateralization allows the use of cash flows from performing properties to cover debt service on non-performing ones. Cross default allows foreclosing of any properties in the cross-default group to cover defaulted loans.

    Prepayment locks and yield maintenance clauses may not be directly involved in the default equation but they, too, have an impact on the risk of default. Generally, prepayments have a positive impact on default risk. Loans which are prepaid drop out of the CMBS structure and do not require any more credit support. While it can be argued that borrowers who prepay may not be the troubled ones, all properties are susceptible to adverse economic or demographic changes. Both prepayment locks and yield maintenance clauses may have a negative impact since they prevent or discourage early prepayment.

In analyzing the loans' risk of default, we focus on two time spans: (1) ongoing debt service and (2) refinance at balloon date. The analysis of ongoing debt service and refinance at the balloon date is similar, except that for analyzing the refinance risk, assumptions must be made regarding conditions at the balloon date. High on that list will be assumptions regarding prevailing interest rates at the refinance date. Interest rate levels determine the required debt service and impact the DSCR. To forecast net income at the balloon date we must make some subjective assumptions regarding future vacancy rates, future rent rates, future utilities and tax rates, and neighboring construction and saturation rates which may influence an investor's determination of cap rates. Based on these assumptions, an income stream is generated for the refinance date. Based on the forecasted income stream, the property's value can be estimated using the assumed cap rate. In determining the property's future value, due consideration must be given to the impact of aging. Using the forecasted value, the LTV at the time can be computed. Based on the income stream and the required debt service, the DSCR can be computed.

Analyzing The CMBS Structure

Once the analysis of the properties and the loans have been completed, probability of default can be estimated. By adding assumptions regarding the costs of resolving the delinquencies, we can arrive at an expected magnitude of loss for each loan. The probability of loss should be computed separately for ongoing debt service and for the balloon date. Once the cash flows and losses are estimated, the CMBS bond structure rules should be applied to direct cash flows and losses to the appropriate classes. To do so requires modeling software that can express the CMBS rules and generate the expected cash flow for each CMBS class.

Several programs exist on the market today which are capable of modeling bond structures. These tools allow the analyst to translate the rules appearing in the CMBS prospectus or private placement memorandum, into statements in a modeling language. Once the model is created, the analyst can feed default and loss assumptions for each of the loans. The model then generates cash flows and losses, and allocates them to the appropriate bond classes. From the cash flows, the model computes various financial benchmarks (yield, duration, average life, etc.).

Choosing a modeling system is a matter of personal preference. Consideration should be given to the software's flexibility to cope with current and envisioned rules, user friendliness, and the existence of a library of modeled structures. This library is useful for analyzing deals offered on the secondary market and for comparing the behavior of a new investment against similar historical ones. Once the model is created or downloaded from the library, the bonds should be tested under a variety of scenarios across a broad range of economic scenarios.

Some features of bond structures are especially relevant to the buyer of subordinate classes. There are several structuring topics that are especially noteworthy,

Multiple junior classes appear in many CMBS transactions. Losses are almost always allocated to the subordinate classes in reverse order, with the class of the highest numerical order being written down first. *Reserve funds* can be found in the deal structures of many CMBS transactions. The priority of cash flow allocations to a reserve account often impacts timing of cash flows received by subordinate bonds.

There are pools specifically directed to tranche groups. The collateral loans backing this type of structure are grouped into pools. All adjustable-rate mortgages might be grouped into one pool, while fixed-rate mortgages are grouped into another. The cash flows from each loan group is directed to a separate group of bonds. From a modeling standpoint, having to contend with multiple collateral streams adds another level of complexity. Single property transactions have appeared in recent years. Since these deals provide less diversification of real estate, subordinate investors must perform careful due diligence.

Some additional bond types which are often found in CMBS structures are mezzanine bonds, interest only bonds, and principal only bonds. Mezzanine classes are positioned between the junior classes and the senior classes in their order of exposure to losses. Interest only (IO) or principal only (PO) classes help balance the interest cash flow received from the mortgages and the interest cash flow required to service the bonds. If the rate on the mortgages exceeds the rate required for the bonds, the extra spread can be funneled to an IO class. Conversely, if the rate on the mortgages is insufficient to cover the rate of the bonds, a PO class can be created. By foregoing interest payments altogether, the PO class increases the cash available for interest payments to the other classes.

DATA RESOURCES

Data can be gathered from various sources. Some services specialize in collecting market data on occupancy rates, rent levels, expenses, and so forth. Additional data such as new developments, saturation levels, and demographic trends can be collected from local contacts. Local contacts can also be invaluable for providing insight into neighborhoods, and determining benchmark, vacancy rates, rent rates, and expenses. Data collected in the context of researching specific issues can be recycled and made available as benchmark information for other properties. It cannot be emphasized enough that the key to re-use of the data is smart classification and labeling categories. It is in this area that maximum advantage can be gained from a cooperation between the real estate and computer systems professionals.

While some investors develop short cuts for doing due diligence on properties, this is not always a recommended practice and may vary in applicability from one property type to another. While multifamily properties may be more comparable, retail or office properties may rely on specific anchor tenants or be affected by specific lease contracts.

SYSTEMS RESOURCES

Establishing systems to manage CMBS subordinate tranche investments requires an integrated system. The two critical components include a real estate modeling component and a CMBS bond structure modeling component.

The system should allow modeling of real estate, loans, and bond structure in one consistent framework. Loan cash flows and losses must be passed on to the bond structure to evaluate the various risks associated with investing in CMBS subordinate tranches.

Real Estate Modeling

The primary objective of the real estate component is to generate forecasted net operating income (NOI) for the real estate underlying the CMBS transaction. The parameters controlling income generation need to be described in a meaningful and consistent manner. For some property types (i.e., multifamily), an analyst may rely on historical or market-specific benchmarks for vacancy rates and rent rates. Other property types may require more property-specific data such as a description of leasable areas, major tenants, and lease covenants.

It is to be expected in analyzing the properties that not all the required property data may be available. In those cases where an alternative source of data is needed, a database of market and property statistics can be extremely useful. A good platform to build such a repository of data is a DBMS. The database needs to be designed in such a way as to allow an analyst to store historical and current market data, and retrieve it in a meaningful way. It is in this area that the real estate professional and the systems analyst need to work together. Consideration must be given to the underlying logic which allows substitution of alternative data when specific property data are missing. Some issues to be addressed are:

- What constitutes a similar market?
- Which properties belong in a comparable group?
- Which industry averages should be computed and how should they be applied?
- What constitutes a sufficient sample?
- What should be the fall-back strategy if sufficient data are not available for the most comparable region or property type, etc.?

In addition to planning the substitution logic, thought must be given to how data will be collected and entered into the database. Topics to consider when designing the database and related software are:

- Sources of data regarding specific markets
- Meaningful categories for tagging and labeling data so that the system can find comparables

- Standards and translation rules to allow data from different sources to be brought into a common format
- Information gained thorough ongoing monitoring of existing properties to help analyze new acquisitions.

In designing the database, an analyst must keep in mind how the data will be used to evaluate expected cash flows from the properties. Once the database is designed, an analyst needs to implement software which will access the database as needed and generate the required cash flows.

To accommodate varied borrower needs, many different types of commercial mortgages have been developed. New types of loans are added every day. Notable mortgage types include amortizing fixed, graduated payment, tiered payment, adjustable rate, interest only/balloon, and partially amortizing/balloon. Software must be developed or acquired to generate the debt service requirement of each of these loan types.

Having generated both the expected property NOI and debt service requirement, a comparison can be made of the two cash flows to evaluate default potential risk. The analysis should point out magnitude of shortfalls and estimated timing.

Multiple scenarios and "what-if" analysis would be required to assess the sensitivity of forecasts. In generating the various scenarios, an analyst would be simultaneously using data from property records, market statistics, and "what-if" assumptions introduced by the analyst. It is extremely important to manage and document the sources of data that are input into each scenario.

Finally, it is critical to understand that whenever assumptions are made, whether based on personal experience or system automation, these assumptions should be displayed on reports and screens as much as possible. Computer-generated reports are treated with reverence, many times unjustifiably so. The best single measure to prevent GIGO (garbage in/garbage out) is to present all assumptions to the final decision maker. Most of the reports available are deficient in this area. This is probably the most neglected area in most systems today. Where report titles exist, they should be meaningful ("Cash Flow 1" is just not good enough).

If you are building your own system, a good way to report your assumptions is to keep a table of assumptions and titles which should appear on each desired report. Logic can be built to show different assumptions based on property type or region (e.g., if property type = retail, show major tenant list and lease highlights, if property type = multi-family, show region benchmarks).

Bond Structure Modeling

The CMBS bond structure modeling process can be thought of as a three-tier process. The first tier involves creating a model that will generate collateral cash flows. The second tier, often called the "waterfall," is the process of taking the collateral cash flows and aggregating them into buckets of cash flows. These cash flow accounts are set up to stage cash flow allocations to the senior classes apart from the subordinate classes. The final tier involves defining the tranches and directing cash flows from the waterfall to the tranches, based on a set of payment rules.

The bond structure needs to receive cash flows from the real estate model. Prepayment and default information created in the debt service versus NOI analysis must be passed on the bond structure system for a truly integrated dynamic analysis. It is often not enough to pass to the bond structure summary level cash flows. Bond structures may have rules that handle scheduled payments, prepayments, and recoveries differently.

The waterfall is a staging process that creates funds to be distributed to tranches based on a set of predefined rules. In a typical CMBS structure, various layers of the deal have priority over others in terms of how cash flows are allocated from the available collateral cash flows. For example, in a simple senior-subordinate structure, the senior interest has the highest priority. Next in line is the senior principal followed by interest payments to the subordinate class, subordinate principal, and rights to any excess allocated to the residual. The system needs to distinguish between senior and subordinate tranches, and allocate the incoming cash flows within the tiered structure. The system should be able to define various interest, principal, reserves and letter of credit accounts, and designate each fund's level of priority in the waterfall. Flexible waterfall functionality is important in modeling cross collateralized deals, and distributing yield maintenance payments.

Loss allocation and distribution is a vital part of modeling a CMBS deal structure. Loss allocation logic allows the user to channel losses of principal due to defaults, delinquencies, and foreclosures from the collateral to the bond structure. Loss allocation parameters determine when the balance of a subordinate tranche is written down due to principal losses from the collateral. Loss logic is also necessary in determining flow of funds from recoveries.

As discussed above, the primary purpose of the waterfall is to create accounts of cash flows from the collateral based on the pooling rules of a bond structure. The system's built-in capabilities and formula logic should provide flexibility in modeling the waterfall. The modern CMBS deal utilizes fund structures extensively and should be considered in choosing a system.

In choosing a modeling system for bond structures, consideration should be given to existing structure types and foreseeable structural innovations. Some of the current tranche principal types include: collateral PO strips, PACs, TACs, accretion directed bonds (ADs), Z-bonds, and sequential (SEQ) support bonds.

While some classes have a fixed interest rate, others have a floating interest rate which follows a specified index. Modeling the interest payments to a floating rate class requires forecasting the behavior of the underlying index and computing the class interest rate. Future index values can either be retrieved from assumption tables, computed using formulas, or generated by interest rate models. Additional functionality should be provided for incorporating floors, caps, and margins to compute the class interest rate.

Finally, in modeling the bond structure, the system must allow implementation of allocation rules for principal, interest, and losses. Systems available in the market today use tables, language scripts, formulas, or a combination of the three to express these rules.

To allow evaluation and comparison of projected bond cash flows, the system should be able to calculate all common financial benchmarks (i.e., price, yield, duration, convexity, OAS). In analyzing subordinate classes, real estate default and loss adjusted price-yield tables are commonly used.

Basic reports include tranche cash flow reports, price/yield and yield/price tables, and percent outstanding tables. Custom reporting capabilities are also a plus in generating management reports and presentations. Graphics functionality should also be considered when evaluating a system.

The ability to export cash flows to other applications, such as spreadsheets, offers extended flexibility for analytics and reporting. Interfaces to other systems within your organization should also be evaluated, including trading systems, asset/liability management systems, and accounting systems.

Analyzing CMBS subordinate classes is a tedious process based on a large volume of data and involving many assumptions. A good system will organize available information, automate the evaluation process, and produce meaningful reports. The system's modeling capabilities should be robust enough to contend with all current and foreseeable structures. Finally, the system should allow easy transition from acquisition to monitoring mode, with minimal effort.

CONCLUSION

Investing in subordinate CMBS classes is a multi-disciplinary endeavor, bringing together real estate, finance, and systems professionals. While this need to integrate knowledge from different fields may be a barrier to some, it is also a source of opportunity for the sophisticated investor. A good management team and an organization conducive to open communication are keys to success.

Chapter **16**

High Yield Commercial Mortgage-Backed Securities

David P. Jacob
Managing Director and
Director of Research & Securitization
Nomura Securities International, Inc.

Galia Gichon
Associate
Nomura Securities International, Inc.

INTRODUCTION

In this chapter we will discuss investing in high-yield commercial mortgage-backed securities (CMBS). In the first section, we first look at the value of investing in long maturity CMBS. In the second section, we focus on subordinated classes of CMBS as an alternative to direct real estate investment either on a levered or unlevered basis.

SUBORDINATED CLASSES OF CMBS AS ALTERNATIVES TO REAL ESTATE EQUITY

Subordinated classes from commercial mortgage-backed securities offer alternatives to direct real estate investment either on a levered or unlevered basis. To support this view, we begin by demonstrating that at cap rates prevailing as of this writing, unless an investor is expecting very significant and sustainable increases in net operating income, the expected returns from BB, B, and unrated CMBS are substantially higher than those from direct real estate investment over a wide range of scenarios. Following the presentation of expected returns, the issue of control is discussed and we conclude that unless the investor is also managing the property he should never be in the first loss equity position. Institutional money managers whose job it is to produce returns for their investors, should leave the first loss equity position in the hands of the expert property manager.

Real estate is an important asset class for investors. It is imperfectly correlated with stocks and bonds and as such plays an important role in portfolio diversification. In the past an investor who desired to place money in this asset class, had two choices, direct real estate investment (levered or unlevered), or commercial mortgages. The real estate equity investment had potential upside and downside risk, but also had significant real estate management requirements. The commercial mortgage had less upside and downside, and hopefully less real estate management requirements. Today's investor is not limited to these options. Instead an investor is presented with a smorgasbord of investment possibilities to gain exposure to the real estate asset class. The astute real estate investor needs to be able to determine at any point in time, which opportunity provides the most favorable risk-reward trade-offs.

Expected Performance Profiles

Consider a property with an NOI of $9 million per year. An investor can either buy the real estate outright or purchase the property and finance a portion. Suppose that the investor can finance 65% at 8.79% (Treasuries plus 269 basis points). Alternatively, the investor could purchase the lower rated classes of a CMBS deal that could be created from the debt that is used to finance the property. Exhibit 1, describes how the CMBS structure is created from the loan. The loan is tranched through a credit subordination mechanism which requires available funds to be applied to the most senior bond classes first. While the B and BB rated bonds are junior to the AAA, AA, A, and BBB rated bonds, they still have the 35% equity cushion below them. Thus, in order for these bonds to experience losses in foreclosure, the property would have to decline by 35%. In today's market the B rated bond would have a yield of Treasuries plus 650 basis points, and the BB rated bond would have a yield of Treasuries plus 450 basis points.

In Exhibits 2, 3, and 4 we compare the expected 5-year total returns on the levered and unlevered equity investments for annual changes in net operating income ranging from –5% per year to +5% per year to the returns on the B and BB rated bonds, assuming the property could be purchased at a 8.5%, 9.5%, or a 10.5% cap rate. Exhibit 5 lists the assumptions used in the total rate of return analysis, and Exhibit 6 lists the numerical returns.

Exhibit 1: Investment Options and CMBS Spreads

Various Options of Investment

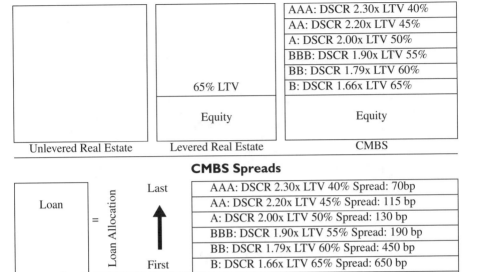

Unlevered Real Estate	Levered Real Estate	CMBS

65% LTV / Equity (Levered Real Estate)

CMBS:
AAA: DSCR 2.30x LTV 40%	
AA: DSCR 2.20x LTV 45%	
A: DSCR 2.00x LTV 50%	
BBB: DSCR 1.90x LTV 55%	
BB: DSCR 1.79x LTV 60%	
B: DSCR 1.66x LTV 65%	
Equity	

CMBS Spreads

Loan = Loan Allocation (Last → First)

AAA: DSCR 2.30x LTV 40% Spread: 70bp
AA: DSCR 2.20x LTV 45% Spread: 115 bp
A: DSCR 2.00x LTV 50% Spread: 130 bp
BBB: DSCR 1.90x LTV 55% Spread: 190 bp
BB: DSCR 1.79x LTV 60% Spread: 450 bp
B: DSCR 1.66x LTV 65% Spread: 650 bp
Equity

Exhibit 2: Levered Equity versus High Yield CMBS
8.5% Cap

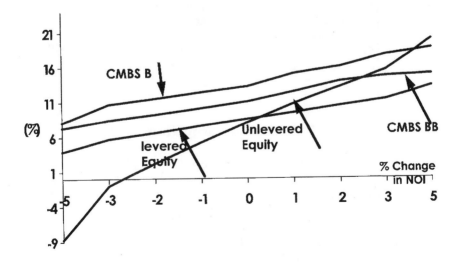

Exhibit 3: Levered Equity versus High Yield CMBS 9.5% Cap

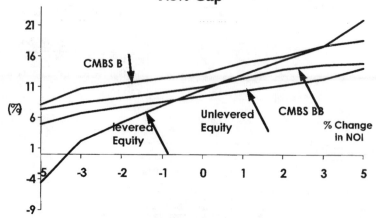

Exhibit 4: Levered Equity versus High Yield CMBS 10.5% Cap

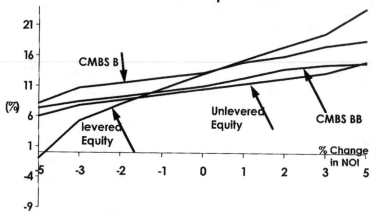

Exhibit 5: Assumptions

- NOI: $9million/year
- Percent annual change in NOI: -5% to +5%
- Percent annual change in NOI assumed each year for 5 years
- Initial loan-to-value: 65%
- Mortgage: 20 year maturity and 8.79% couon (T + 2.69%)
- Cap rates: 8.5%, 9.5%, and 10.5%
- CMBS spreads — BB: +450, B: +650
- Equity holder defaults when NOI < debt service
- All equity cash reinvested at initial cap rates, all bond cash reinvested at bond's initial yield

Exhibit 6: Returns

8.5% Cap Rate

% Change in NOI	-10	-5	-3	-2	-1	0	1	2	3	5	10
CMBS BB	-7.26	7.26	8.37	9.18	10.06	11.01	12.36	13.85	14.59	14.86	15.49
CMBS B	-2.95	8.09	10.71	11.53	12.44	13.23	14.99	15.99	17.73	18.57	19.19
Levered	-32.93	-8.72	-1.02	2.25	5.25	8.04	10.65	13.13	15.48	19.91	29.77
Unlevered	-0.65	3.89	5.73	6.65	7.57	8.50	9.43	10.36	11.29	13.17	17.88

9.5% Cap Rate

% Change in NOI	-10	-5	-3	-2	-1	0	1	2	3	5	10
CMBS BB	-7.26	7.26	8.37	9.18	10.06	11.01	12.36	13.85	14.59	14.86	15.49
CMBS B	-2.95	8.09	10.71	11.53	12.44	13.23	14.99	15.99	17.73	18.57	19.19
Levered	-24.30	4.60	2.23	5.21	7.98	10.59	13.05	15.40	17.64	21.88	31.44
Unlevered	0.43	4.93	6.75	7.66	8.58	9.50	10.42	11.35	12.27	14.13	18.82

10.5% Cap Rate

% Change in NOI	-10	-5	-3	-2	-1	0	1	2	3	5	10
CMBS BB	-7.26	7.26	8.37	9.18	10.06	11.01	12.36	13.85	14.59	14.86	15.49
CMBS B	-2.95	8.09	10.71	11.53	12.44	13.23	14.99	15.99	17.73	18.57	19.19
Levered	-17.36	-0.95	5.22	7.98	10.56	13.01	15.34	17.58	19.72	23.80	33.09
Unlevered	1.51	5.97	7.77	8.68	9.59	10.50	11.42	12.33	13.25	15.10	19.76

As can be seen in Exhibit 2, for this range of annual changes in NOI the B rated bond almost uniformly outperforms the other investment alternatives. For no change in NOI, the levered equity purchased at a 8.5% cap rate shows the worst performance. Obviously, the investor entering into this transaction expects NOI to increase. As NOI increases, the investor's total return is enhanced both through the income component and the higher value at the end of the 5-year holding period. Many real estate investors mistakenly believe that they give away this upside when they purchase bonds. This is absolutely incorrect. As NOI increases, the coverage ratios on the bond classes improves, which in turn decreases the likelihood of default. This would tend to cause the spread on the bonds to tighten which leads to a higher ending price at the end of the 5-year holding period. While the increase in return is not as dramatic as in the case of the levered equity position, the B and BB rated classes are so cheap relative to the equity that it requires at least a 5% annual increase in NOI for each of the next five years for the levered equity position to outperform the CMBS bonds.[1]

On the down side, the levered equity gets hammered as NOI drops. The levered equity holder bears the weight of the decline in the value of the real estate and drop in NOI. On the other hand, the bonds while trading down due to spread widening

---

[1] The return profile for the B and BB rated bonds can be made to be more aggressive by levering these positions. This is shown later in the chapter.

in recognition of the increased likelihood of default, continue to receive their full coupon unless NOI drops sufficiently to induce a default.[2]

The B rated bond dominates the BB for this range of changes in NOI, as NOI continues to decrease and the equity holder defaults, the BB bond can do better since losses will be allocated to the B bond first. However, if the loss is so large that both classes get wiped out, it is possible for the total return to still be better on the B since it earned the higher coupon.

Exhibits 3 and 4, show the same comparison where the real estate can be purchased at a 9.5% and 10.5% cap rate, respectively. Obviously, at a 10. 5% cap rate the return profile for the levered equity is much improved. Unfortunately for the investor, real estate prices have already increased in many markets. This is because the market has already priced in an increasing NOI. As a result, today's real estate investor needs a greater increase in NOI to beat B rated CMBS.

An important point for an investor considering this strategy is that in order to benefit from improving NOI, he should seek the longest maturity B and BB rated bonds. This is because if NOI increases and spreads tighten the impact will be greater the longer the duration of the bond. In fact, it is somewhat inappropriate to compare the performance of short maturity CMBS to equity real estate, since equity itself has a long duration. In Exhibit 7, we compare the performance of the BB and B bonds from the prior examples assuming that they are either 10-year or 20-year bonds. For example, if NOI were to increase by 3% annually the 20-year B rated bond would provide almost 230 basis points annual extra return over the 10-year bond. We discussed this part earlier in the chapter.

Unrated Bond Classes

Thus far we have considered only the BB and B rated bonds. Often there is another class of bonds that is junior to these classes, but senior to the equity. These classes offer still higher potential returns. For example, in a deal issued in the last quarter of 1995, the unrated class was offered at par with a 22% coupon. An investor who manages to assemble a portfolio of these bonds could withstand a number of defaults and still do very well.

Control Issues

One of the major reasons cited by real estate investors for preferring real estate equity is the issue of control. They feel that they are better able to influence the performance of the real estate when they are in an ownership position. While there is some validity

---

[2] The difference between a single borrower and multiple borrower/pool deal. In the multiple/borrower pool deal, the B and BB rated bonds could get entirely wiped out before the pool of equity gets entirely wiped out. Therefore, if one is concerned about the down side, we recommend that the real estate buyer create a portfolio of B and BB rated bonds from many multi-borrower pool deals or single borrower deals, where the real estate analysis can be done and monitored. By creating a portfolio of these bonds the real estate investor is able to gain the benefits of diversification, which are not attainable by purchasing one or two single B classes from a CMBS backed by a large diversified pool

to this argument when comparing first loss debt securities to whole loans in the event of default, in our view, this issue is way overblown when comparing first loss debt to first loss equity. First, as we just discussed, investors in real estate should only be in the first loss equity position if they are managing the property. If they are not managing the property, then they have already given up a certain amount of control, and their interests are not properly aligned with those of the property manager.

Exhibit 7: Comparison of BB and B Bonds Assuming 10- or 20-Year Maturities

Moving Up the Credit Curve

	Time to Next Level (months)	NOI Growth		
		1%	2%	3%
BB	43	43	22	10
BBB	95	95	69	43
A	117	114	104	78
AA	134	119	117	95
AAA	155	155	155	114

Leveraging the B and the BB Bonds

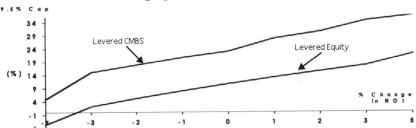

Difference Between 20-Year Maturity and 10-Year Maturity Total Returns

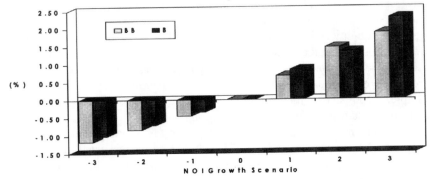

How does the investor in the first loss debt compare to the investor in the first loss equity as a property begins to deteriorate and NOI is dropping? If the equity investor is the manager, he obviously is in control until foreclosure subject to the restrictions placed upon him by the covenants in the mortgage agreement. He can cut expenses, reposition the property, or do whatever it takes to get the property back on track. At this point the investor in the B rated bond can do little. (Of course, he is still clipping his coupon.) As NOI continues to drop and coverage ratios reach a certain level, the servicer is usually empowered to replace the property manager. If a default actually occurs, the equity holder completely loses control, whereas the first loss debt investor's interests are served by the special servicer whose function it is to maximize the total proceeds in the foreclosure process.

VALUE IN LONGER MATURITIES

Investors in high yield CMBS pay-up for short maturity bonds. For example, BB CMBS with a 5-year average life might trade at 375 basis points over the 5-year Treasury, whereas a 15-year average life BB class will trade at about +450 basis points to the 10-year Treasury. In this chapter we argue that for comparable investment horizons, there is more value in the longer average life bond classes. We analyze some of the reasons that are offered by investors for preferring the shorter classes, and come to the conclusion that many of these explanations are illogical, and as a result, investors may be missing a tremendous opportunity.

Longer Duration Benefits More from a Spread Tightening

CMBS trade at wide spreads to Treasuries for a number of reasons. Obviously a good portion of the spread is to compensate the investor for credit risk. In addition, today's investor is being paid for liquidity risk, and for being first in a relatively new emerging market. Investors are also demanding excess spread because of the perceived (and actual) relative lack of ongoing property level information. This type of excess spread is typical in new markets. As markets mature and become better understood, and more ongoing information is made available through various services, this liquidity and information premium will disappear causing the portion of spread attributable to these factors to narrow. This is a trend which is independent of credit risk. The investor in a longer average life/duration bond gains more from a spread tightening than the investor in a shorter average life/duration bond. For example, a 100 basis point tightening adds 5% to the return of a 5 year duration bond, compared to 10% for a 10 year duration bond.

If the investor in high yield CMBS proves to be correct in his analysis, and the credit quality (coverage ratios, LTV, and demand for real estate) improves, the spread will tighten. The longer duration bond will, once again, benefit more. While it is true that a spread widening will hurt the longer duration bond more, the whole point of the credit analysis is to identify credit risks that the market has mispriced.[3] Finally, most investors believe that we are still in the early stages of the real estate recovery. Therefore, in general, one would place a higher probability on spread tightening than on spread widening for the sector as a whole.

Structural Considerations

Longer maturity high yield CMBS are typically backed by fully amortizing loans which are less risky than loans with balloon payments. The senior-subordinated structure prohibits the payment of principal to junior classes prior to senior classes. Thus, lower rated CMBS that are structured from longer term fully amortizing loans tend to have long average lives. In order to create short life lower rated classes, the underlying loans will usually have balloon payments. The risk of a borrower not being able to roll over a balloon loan is significant. The first loss tranches backed by these loan leverages this risk, whereas, first loss tranches carved from fully amortizing loans, do not face this risk. Thus, in a scenario where real estate values decline or interest rates rise the borrower may be unable to roll over his loan, and be forced to default potentially causing a loss to the first loss tranche.

Even if the borrower is permitted an extension, the B piece holder may suffer since these tranches are often priced at a discount. This is also an important consideration for deals backed by non-performing collateral since if the foreclosure process takes longer than expected, the average life of the B piece holder will extend and if the bond was purchased at a discount the investors yield will be lower than anticipated. When the underlying loan is fully amortizing this risk does not arise.

Another benefit to investors in long maturity lower rated CMBS backed by fully amortizing loans, is that they have the amortization working in their favor. Another way of saying this is that CMBS have built-in deleveraging which leads to upgrades in their rating. This is in sharp contrast to corporate bonds where improving financials usually lead to an increase in debt. Moreover, in CMBS even if the property is not appreciating in value, at least the numerator in the loan-to-value ratio is declining with time. In other words as time passes and the underlying loans amortize, the loan-to-value declines. Therefore, over time the tranche moves up the credit curve.

Amortizing the Up Front Cost of Analysis

Investors who purchase lower rated classes of CMBS typically spend a great deal of time analyzing in detail the income generating properties which are collateralizing the underlying loans. Analysis of the individual properties' financial condition and prospects is intensive. Whereas the senior bond buyers will rely on the rating agencies for most of this sort of analysis, first and second loss buyers are more sensitive to defaults which result in losses, and by the same token benefit more if their analysis correctly indicates that the possibility of default is remote. Essentially this buyer is doing simi-

---

[3] Assuming that interest rates and credit risk for CMBS are not correlated, non-callable CMBS are positively convex, and therefore, the gain from a spread tightening would exceed the loss from a similar size spread widening.

lar analysis to that performed by the equity investor. However, it takes as much due diligence to analyze a piece of real estate backing a 5-year loan as one backing a 15-year loan. Shouldn't the investor look to amortize this cost over a longer period?

Forward Credit Spreads Are Unrealistically High

One of the implications of wider spreads for longer maturity bonds is that there is an expectation in the market of wider spreads in the future. For example, suppose the spread for a 5-year BB is at +300, and the spread for a 10-year BB is at +350, and the Treasury curve is flat at 7%. Then the implied 5-year BB spread, 5 years from now is +400 basis points. Another way to look at this, is that to break even over the 10-year holding period, an investor in the 5-year assumes that he will be able to roll over his position at a spread which is 100 basis points wider than today. This seems to be an extreme scenario to be used as a base case for analysis.

Theoretical Basis

On a theoretical level, we know that a bond with credit risk can be thought of as a riskless bond plus a short position in a put option on the value of the underlying asset. While it is true that the value of the option increases with term to maturity, it increases at a rapidly decreasing rate, particularly for amortizing securities. Thus, large differentials in spread for longer maturities are not justified, and therefore represent an opportunity for investors.

Incorrect Arguments for Investing in Shorter Maturities

There are a number of arguments that investors use to support their view about shorter maturities. One argument that is often put forth for preferring shorter maturities is the possibility that if the credit quality improves, the bond may be called away. If this were to happen, shorter maturities would not under perform as much as longer bonds. While this is an appropriate argument for high yield corporate bonds, it is less of an argument for commercial mortgages since most commercial mortgages have significant call protection either through complete lockout and/or through yield/spread maintenance provisions. Thus, if interest rates were to drop and/or borrower quality were to improve and the loan is locked out, an investor would benefit more from the longer maturity B-tranche. Also, for example, if a commercial mortgage with spread maintenance down to Treasuries flat were called, the investor in a long maturity ought to be very happy, since he effectively can reinvest his proceeds in Treasuries and earn his original yield.[4]

Another often cited reason for shying away from longer maturities, is that the probability of default is greater for longer maturities. This is not really a fair comparison. The comparison has to be done for similar investment horizons. For example, there is no reason to believe that a 15-year loan is any more likely to

---

[4] Of course, this presumes that the penalties are allocated on an economic basis to each of the bond classes in the deal.

default in the first five years of its life, than a 5-year loan. Or equivalently, if one has a 15-year horizon, rolling over 5-year bonds will likely expose the investor to the same risk of default as that of the 15-year bond. Moreover, as we noted earlier, the short lower rated classes are often backed by balloon loans, and these have a greater risk of default at the 5 year horizon, than a tranche which is backed by a fully amortizing loan.

CONCLUSION

In summary, we believe that investors should strongly consider longer maturity BB and B classes, particularly when they are backed by fully amortizing loans. And if they are concerned about the interest rate risk associated with the longer duration, they can always reduce their duration with other instruments or even consider a combination of fixed rate and floating rate CMBS to achieve their duration targets.

Chapter 17

An Options Approach to Commercial Mortgages and CMBS Valuation and Risk Analysis

David P. Jacob
Managing Director and
Director of Research & Securitization
Nomura International Securities, Inc.

Ted C.H. Hong
Director
Nomura International Securities, Inc.

Laurence H. Lee
Senior Research Analyst
Nomura International Securities, Inc.

INTRODUCTION

Investment in commercial mortgages and commercial mortgage-backed securities (CMBS) is receiving increasing attention from mainstream fixed-income investors. Yet, much of the quantitative technology that has been developed for analyzing relative value in such areas as residential mortgage-backed securities (MBS) and corporate bonds has not been applied to commercial mortgages. Investors in agency mortgage-backed securities and callable corporate bonds, for example, have used

319

option pricing to determine fair value for securities whose cash flows are uncertain due to the possibility of an early call. Commercial mortgages typically have greater call protection than residential MBS and corporate bonds, although they still have some callability. Most commercial mortgages have lock-out periods followed by a period during which a penalty is applied to premature principal payments, followed in turn by a free period. The technology applied to other fixed-income instruments to value these features could be used for assessing risk and relative value in commercial mortgages and CMBS.

In addition to the risk of early principal payment, commercial mortgages, like corporate bonds, are subject to the risk of losses in a foreclosure following a default. Pricing methodology described in academic journals has been applied to this risk for corporate bonds, but for a variety of reasons it has not proven to be practical.[1] The analysis and valuation of this risk for commercial mortgages using similar quantitative analysis, while discussed in the academic world, has not been applied in the market for commercial mortgages.[2]

The need for improved tools has increased with the introduction of securitization, where the most popular method of credit enhancement is the senior-subordinated structure. Whole loans are aggregated and their cash flows are then allocated to create securities with credit ratings from AAA down to B and unrated. As a result, the risk of loss due to default is leveraged up in the junior classes and leveraged down in the senior classes. The analogy in the residential MBS area is the creation of planned amortization class (PAC) bonds and support tranches where the PAC bond has leveraged down prepayment risk and the support bond has leveraged up prepayment risk. Moreover, the senior subordinated structure requires that recoveries from foreclosures first be used to pay senior bondholders. From the perspective of these bondholders a prepayment event has occurred, even though the unscheduled cash flow came about due to a credit event. Nevertheless, it must be considered in the valuation and risk of these AAA rated securities.

When an investor looks at a CMBS deal it would be useful to know whether or not the AAA class at 90 basis points over Treasuries is a better value than the B class at a +600 basis point spread. How should one compare the risk of a bullet loan with one that amortizes? How does the risk of default affect the value of a security trading at a premium? What is the fair value of an interest-only strip when

---

[1] The complexity of the capital structure of a corporation and the possibility of a leveraged buyout make the application of the option approach less practical for corporate bonds. For more details on the option approach to pricing default risk in high yield bonds, see Richard Bookstabber and David P. Jacob, "Controlling Interest Rate Risk," Chapter 8 in *The Composite Hedge: Controlling the Credit Risk of High-Yield Bonds* (New York: John Wiley & Sons, 1986).

[2] There has been some work published in this area. See Chapter 12 and Patrick J. Corcoran "Commercial Mortgages: Measuring Risk and Return,"*Journal of Portfolio Management* (Fall 1989);Sheridan Titman and Walter Torous, "Valuing Commercial Mortgages: An Empirical Investigation of the Contingent Claims Approach to Pricing Risky Debt," *Journal of Finance* (June 1989); and, Paul D. Childs, Steven H. Ott, and Timothy J. Riddiough, "The Pricing of Multi-Class Commercial Mortgage-Backed Securities," Working Paper (December 1994).

the loans underlying the deal have percentage penalties versus yield maintenance, versus lockout. This chapter describes a two-factor contingent-claims theoretic framework and applies option pricing methodology to commercial mortgages to answer these questions.

In the next section we outline the elements of valuation and the basic analytic approach to pricing commercial mortgages. Following this, we apply the approach to commercial whole loans and show the effects of each factor on the value of the mortgage. Next, a multi-class senior-subordinated deal is evaluated. We then use the model to look at the relative risk of different securities. Finally, we draw some conclusions, discuss practical issues relating to the model, and propose some future applications. In the appendix we show some of the mathematics behind the model.

THE ELEMENTS OF VALUATION

The value of all real estate securities is contingent upon the value of the underlying real estate asset since they each have a claim on this asset. For example, the equity holder has a residual claim on the income stream after the debt holder is paid. If the income from the real estate asset is insufficient to meet the debt obligation and a default results, the debt holder has a claim on the real estate. Usually, the equity holder defaults only when the value of the real estate is less than the value of the loan and in when income is insufficient to pay debt service. The debt holder, in this case, will receive the smaller of the debt payment or the value of the real estate and the equity holder receives nothing.

The analytic approach we use is to view the owner (lender/investor) of a commercial mortgage as having a long position in a credit risk-free, non-callable mortgage, a short call option, and a short put option. The commercial mortgage investor/lender (debt holder) has written an option to the borrower (equity holder) to call (prepay) the debt, and an option to put (default) the real estate to the debt holder. That is,

Commercial mortgage = (Default-free and non-callable mortgage)
– (Call option) – (Put option)
PREPAYMENT   DEFAULT

As compensation for writing these options the debt holder receives a spread over the yield on Treasury bonds usually in the form of a higher coupon. Therefore, in order to value the commercial mortgage, one can value the risk-free cash flows and the associated call (prepayment) and put (default) options. To properly value the options, the default and prepayment options need to be analyzed *simultaneously* since as we will show they are interrelated.

To value the options we need to define what circumstances would cause the property owner to exercise his options.

Prepayment option — triggering conditions: Prepayment is triggered for two reasons:

    a. economic benefit from refinancing which occurs if
       1. the general level of interest rates drop.
    or
       2. the property value increases, thus allowing the borrower to refinance
          at a tighter spread to Treasuries.
    or
    b. Owner wants to sell property and the mortgage is not assumable.

For condition *a* to be viable net operating income (NOI) must be sufficiently greater than the scheduled payments required under the new rate, since otherwise the borrower would not qualify for the loan. If the borrower does qualify, he will refinance so long as the present value of the future promised payments minus the value of the options (fair market value of the debt including its embedded options) is greater than the face value of the remaining debt plus refinancing costs such as prepayment penalties. Thus, as interest rates drop (for newly originated fixed-rate mortgages) and as the quality of the property improves the likelihood of refinancing increases since under these circumstances the market value of the debt increases.

In addition, property owners sometimes want to realize the return on their properties particularly as the tax benefits of ownership decline through time. If the mortgage is assumable or a substitution of collateral is permitted, the owner could sell the property with the loan remaining intact. Otherwise the owner would have to prepay the mortgage. Another situation that could occur that would lead to prepayment even in a rising rate environment is if the property appreciates in value, and the owner desires to re-leverage the property. If the mortgage note prohibits additional financing (this almost always the case for CMBS), then the borrower must first repay his loan.

Empirical evidence on commercial mortgage prepayments by Abraham and Theobald reported in Chapter 3 suggests that when it is economic for commercial property owners to prepay, they do so at an even faster rate then owners of residential properties. Moreover, turnover rates in property ownership indicate that even if refinancing is uneconomic property owners sell their properties to realize profits. For example, Abraham and Theobald found that the cumulative prepayment rate for low coupon mortgages that were outstanding for 10 years was 82.4%.[3]

Default option triggering option conditions: For the property owner to exercise his default option there are two necessary conditions.

    i) Net operating income is less than the current period's scheduled mortgage
       payment[4]
    and

---

[3] This is one reason why interest strips from CMBS deals that have lockout provisions as opposed to simply yield maintenance are far less risky and should trade
at tighter spreads.

[4] Net cash flow might be more appropriate, but here we use NOI for simplicity.

ii) The market value of the property is less than the market value of the debt.[5]

For a non-callable mortgage, default will never be necessary for a rational borrower if the NOI is enough to cover debt payment. Default starts to occur when the NOI is insufficient to meet the debt service. When that happens and the property value is also less than the value of the debt, the default option would be exercised. Both conditions are necessary because if the property value is greater than the value of the debt, but the NOI is insufficient to pay the debt service, the property owner would attempt to sell the property and payoff the debt rather than go through foreclosure.

Default as a method of prepayment — triggering conditions: Sometimes the property owner may try to use a default as a method of prepaying so as to avoid the prepayment penalty and/or lock-out feature.[6] In this case, the triggering conditions for default are more complicated. The conditions would be triggered to default as follows:

i) The NOI has to be greater than the payments that would be required at the time if the loan were to be refinanced.

and

ii) the present value of the future promised payments minus the value of the options (fair market value of the debt including its embedded options) is greater than the face value of the remaining debt plus foreclosure expenses.

If these two conditions hold the borrower can default, go through foreclosure, pay off the face value of the debt with the proceeds, and then refinance. This situation can arise when interest rates drop and property value and NOI increase, but the loan is either locked-out or there is a stiff prepayment penalty. In this case if the foreclosure expenses are not too onerous, the borrower has an incentive to default. It is unclear, however, how the courts would treat this situation. It is possible that the bankruptcy judge would force the borrower to compensate the lender.

The Combined Default and Prepayment

Since the call and put options are embedded in the mortgage debt, the call option and the put option cannot actually be separated. The incentive to prepay as we have discussed is linked not just to the general level of interest rates, but to the ever changing level of operating income of the property and the resulting available refinancing spread. Thus, the value of the prepayment option is related to factors that affect the value of the default option. Similarly the incentive to default is related to the level of interest rates which in turn affects the value of the prepayment option. Moreover, borrowers who either prepay or default terminate the contract of the mortgage. This results in the termination of both options. Our triggering conditions, thus, do not work independently, but need to be evaluated simultaneously.

[5] The market value of the debt is the present value of the future promised payments plus the current payment that is due minus the value of the options.
[6] Experts in bankruptcy law feel that in a true default, prepayment penalties could be construed by the judge as usury and therefore disallowed.

Exhibit 1: Prepayment Option of a Commercial Mortgage

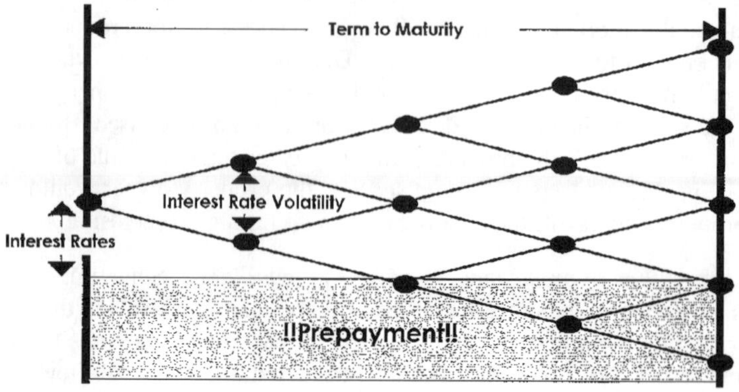

Source: Nomura Securities International, Inc.

To visualize the triggering process for the prepayment option, look at Exhibit 1. The horizontal axis measures time. The vertical axis tracks interest rates which in turn determines the present value of the promised payments. As time passes, interest rates can move up or down. As interest rates drop, the market value of the debt increases above the face value making it economically worthwhile for the borrower to refinance.

A lock-out or penalty reduces the value of the call option since it lessens the likelihood of the option being exercised. In general, the longer the term to maturity and the more volatile the interest rate, the more valuable the prepayment option since the likelihood of exercise increases.

In order to visualize the triggering process for a loan default, we make use of the metaphor of a drunk person walking along the edge of a cliff trying to go from point A to point B. The closer he is to the edge when he begins his walk, the more erratic his walk, and the longer the distance from point A to point B, the more likely he will fall off the cliff before reaching point B. Similarly, in the case of an income generating property, the more volatile the NOI, the greater the initial loan-to-value (LTV), the lower the debt service coverage ratio (DSCR), and the longer the maturity of the debt, the higher probability of default prior to maturity. In Exhibit 2 the horizontal axis measures time to maturity. The vertical axis measures the level of NOI and LTV. As time passes NOI and LTV can move up or down. If NOI/LTV moves down/up sufficiently, the property owner will default and hand the keys of the property to the lender.

Determinants of Option Values

Now that we have defined the conditions that lead to the exercise of the options, we need to identify the determinants of the options' values. The value of the embedded options depends upon many factors. The direct determinants are

1. Current balance of mortgage
2. Term to maturity of mortgage
3. Mortgage payments including interest and principal, and the amortization schedule

Exhibit 2: Default Option of a Commercial Mortgage

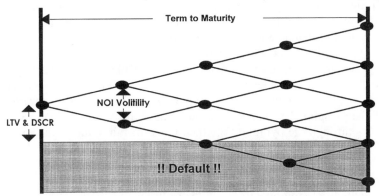

4. Prepayment terms and penalties
5. Net operating income from the collateral property
6. Volatility of net operating income
7. Terms of default and foreclosure costs
8. Interest rates
9. Volatility of interest rates
10. Correlation between interest rates and net operating income

The first four items specify the information necessary to calculate the promised cash flows of the underlying mortgage. This information in conjunction with current and the potential future interest rates are necessary for calculating the value of the prepayment option. Items 5, 6, and 7 which relate to the property are essential for valuing the default option. The last three items are critical for valuing all assets, including the mortgage, the real estate, and the options.

The Valuation Process

The process of interest rates and net operating income determine the entire valuation procedure of the commercial mortgage and its embedded options. In our framework, we assume that interest rates and NOI are the two underlying building blocks. The property value which is the present value of all future NOI's can be calculated from interest rates and NOI. To solve for the option values, a two-dimensional binomial tree or pyramid is constructed (by combining Exhibit 1 and Exhibit 2) based on the assumptions of the process and volatility governing future NOI and interest rates.[7]

---

[7] When a multi-class commercial mortgage-backed security is evaluated, the path-independent condition for the remaining balances of the bond classes does not necessarily hold. Fortunately, so long as the underlying loans satisfy the path-independent condition, Monte Carlo simulations which randomly select a finite number of paths from a virtually infinite number of paths can be utilized to calculate the option values. Since a huge path selection process is involved, variance reduction techniques turn out to be very important to improve the sampling method.

For every path of interest rates there is a whole set of possible paths of NOI. The tree will specify the future cash flows of the mortgage under the full range of interest rates and NOI scenarios. Once the pyramid is created, the value of the property can be calculated at each node of the pyramid.[8] Similarly other relevant variables such as LTV and DSCR can be calculated as well. At each node, the action taken by the borrower (prepayment, default, or scheduled payment) determines the cash flow that the debt holder receives. The option values and the fair value of the mortgage can then be calculated by discounting the cash flows backward in time through the pyramid. The values are equal to the expected discounted value of the cash flows through the pyramid. The theoretical or fair value of the commercial mortgage can be obtained by combining these terms.

Option-Adjusted Spread Since the market value or market price of a financial security may differ from its fair value, the fixed-income market has developed the concept of *option-adjusted spread* (OAS).

OAS is a spread relative to the Treasury curve, quoted in basis points, which is used for measuring the relative value of securities with a series of uncertain cash flows. The OAS can be obtained by calibrating the theoretical present value to the current market price. The theoretical present value takes all possible cash flow streams discounted by the corresponding discount rates and weighted by assumed probabilities. The OAS, thus, is a constant spread added to the risk-free interest rate and is used as the discount rate for the corresponding cash flows. The procedure involves solving for the spread which equates the price obtained via discounting the cash flows to the market price.

The larger or more positive the OAS, the cheaper the security is relative to its theoretical value. The OAS can be thought of as the risk premium which the investor would earn if he repurchased or hedged, at fair value, the options that he has implicitly shorted by owning the security. The concept of OAS was originally introduced to analyze relative value in residential mortgage-backed securities and callable corporate bonds, where the borrower's prepayment option substantially negatively impacts the value of these securities. If the OAS is positive/negative, then the investor is receiving more/less than he should have for shorting the embedded options.

Parameter Estimation and Practical Considerations Like all option models, a number of parameters need to be estimated and assumptions need to be made regarding the process governing the random variables. In our case, we need to have an estimate for the volatility of NOI for the property, the volatility of interest rates, and the correlation between these. If the loan or a security is backed by a number of properties, then we also need the correlation matrix of NOI of all the properties.

---

[8] In our model we specify a term which indicates the growth rate, if any, in the NOI. We define the property value to be equal to NOI/(R − R × G) where R equals prevailing interest rates, NOI is net operating income, and R × G is the growth rate in NOI. R − R × G equals the traditional cap rate.

Regarding interest rates there is a voluminous body of literature which addresses the interest rate process necessary to properly price fixed-income income options and to satisfy the arbitrage-free condition for the term structure of interest rates.[9] In this chapter, we use the Black, Derman, and Toy model and its binomial tree to calibrate the interest rate lattice to the initial yield curve.

To empirically estimate the NOI volatility, we first used the Russell/NCREIF Property Index (RNPI) despite all of its drawbacks.[10] The RNPI index is the most widely quoted index for real estate property performance. It provides data such as net operating income and appraisal value of commercial buildings by region and by property type on quarterly basis. We also used the RNPI series to estimate the correlation between interest rates and net operating income. The 6% volatility of NOI that was estimated from the large and diversified pool of properties that underlie the RNPI series greatly understates the true NOI volatility of individual properties. Based on our own data we expect the volatility of NOI to range between 9% and 15%. There are differences by property type. As we would expect multi-family properties have lower NOI volatilities and hotels tend to have higher volatilities. In practice one needs to estimate the volatility for the property in question.[11]

One way to calibrate the NOI volatility assumption is to see what pattern and level of defaults is produced using the parameter assumptions. In Exhibit 3 we show the actual average cumulative default rates for investment grade and speculative grade corporate bonds as a function of time as computed by Moody's Investors Service for the years 1970- 1994. One can see that for the high quality debt the marginal default rate starts out low and increases over time. On the other hand, the marginal default rate for the speculative grade debt declines over time. The reason for this is that lower quality debt that survives the early years has a decreasing probability of defaulting. Whereas, high quality debt has an increasing (or at least non-decreasing) chance of defaulting as time passes.

---

[9] Ho and Lee used a binomial tree to create an arbitrage-free interest rate model. See Thomas S.Y. Ho and S.B. Lee, "Term Structure Movements and Pricing of Interest Rate Contingent Claims," *Journal of Finance* (December 1986). Black, Derman, and Toy also constructed a binomial tree model and, furthermore, allowed various volatilities for the entire term structure. See Fischer Black, Emanuel Derman, and William Toy, "A One-Factor Model of Interest Rates and its Application to Treasury Bond Options," *Financial Analysts Journal* (January-February 1990). Hull and White created a trinomial tree and provided a closed form solution for arbitrage-free model in continuous time. See John Hull and Alan White, "One-Factor Interest-Rate Models and the Valuation of Interest-Rate Derivative Securities," *Journal of Financial and Quantitative Analysis*, (June 1993). Both Jamshidian and Chan assumed a variety of interest rate process to calibrate to the term structure. See Farshid Jamshidian, "Forward Induction and Construction of Yield Curve Diffusion Models," *Merrill Lynch Research* (March 1991); and, Y.K. Chan, "Term Structure as a Second Order Dynamical System, and Pricing of Derivative Securities," *Bear Stearns Research*, 1992.

[10] The Russell/NCREIF property index is an appraisal-based index of property returns and values. This index represents data collected from the Voting Members of the National Council of Real Estate Investment Fiduciaries. Many researchers feel that the appraisal process causes the data to significantly understate the price volatility. The volatility of the income component, on the other hand, might be representative for a large pool of assets.

[11] Specific features such as cross-collateralization, which would lower NOI volatility need to be modeled.

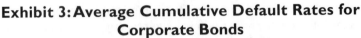

Exhibit 3: Average Cumulative Default Rates for Corporate Bonds

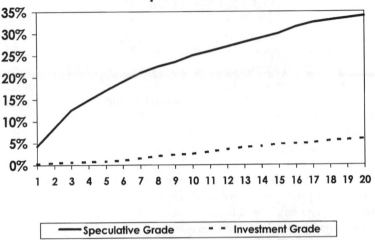

Speculative Grade   - - Investment Grade

Source: Moody's Investors Service.

In Exhibit 4 we show the marginal default rates for high quality (low LTV) and low quality (high LTV) loans that are implied by our model using an assumption of 15% volatility of NOI. In Exhibit 5 we show the implied cumulative default rates. The pattern is very consistent with the Moody's data and demonstrates the ability of the model to differentiate the default pattern associated with different quality loans. Moreover, the level of defaults, while higher than what Moody's found for corporate bonds, in our view represents a conservative level of defaults.[12]

Aside from parameter estimation, there are some practical considerations when implementing the model that differ from the theory. The theory assumes the following conditions: (1) liquidity, (2) symmetry of market information, (3) optimal exercise, and (4) refinancing ability.

Liquidity refers to how easy it is to buy or sell real estate and commercial mortgages in the secondary market. The theoretical model assumes that transactions costs are low and that the markets are very liquid. Symmetry of market information refers to whether borrowers and investors have the same information. Optimal exercise refers to how efficiently the borrower exercises his options if arbitrage opportunities emerge. Refinancing ability refers to the fact that financing is based solely on the property consideration irrespective of the borrower. Even though many of these conditions do not hold in practice, the model provides value by incorporating in a single framework the primary factors driving the value of the mortgage. As a result it becomes useful as a relative value tool and for comparing risk.

---

[12] The cumulative default level after 10 years implied the by the model for a 70% LTV loan with an initial DSCR of 1.5X using a 15% NOI volatility is about 26%. Moreover, the implied loss severity is about 19%, both of these statistics exceed the levels found with the historical data. We feel that our standard of 15% NOI volatility is conservative.

Exhibit 4: Implied Marginal Default Rates for Commercial Mortgages

50% LTV

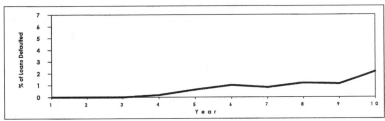

90% LTV

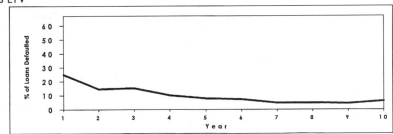

Source: Nomura Securities International, Inc.

Exhibit 5: Implied Cumulative Default Rates for Commercial Mortgages

50% LTV

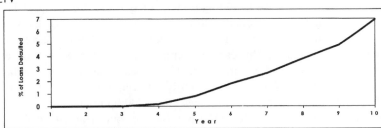

90% LTV

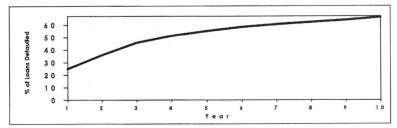

Source: Nomura Securities International, Inc.

330 An Options Approach to Commercial Mortgages and CMBS Valuation and Risk Analysis

COMPARATIVE ANALYSIS

In this section we use OAS as the measure to analyze the factors that affect the value of a commercial mortgage. In the next section, we apply the framework to a multi-class CMBS structure. In order to use the model to analyze the factors affecting the value of a commercial mortgage, we could either keep the spread constant (OAS), and see how the price varies as we change each of the factors. Or, we could keep the price constant and see how the factors affect the OAS as we change each of the factors. We adopt the latter approach since, in general, the market sets the price.

Since the OAS is considered compensation for shorting options, the OAS decreases for a fixed mortgage price as the default or prepayment risks increase. The degree of risk exposure depends upon the characteristics of the mortgage debt, the performance of underlying collateral as well as the economic factors such as interest rates. We analyze default risk with respect to four factors — DSCR, LTV, volatility of NOI, and mortgage maturity date. These factors are the usual measures of risk quoted in real estate markets for analyzing default risk.

In this section we use as an example, a commercial mortgage with a 10 year maturity, 9% coupon, initial DSCR of 1.50x, initial LTV of 70%, initial risk-free interest rate of 7%, and volatility of 11% and 15% for interest rates, and NOI, respectively.[13] Thus, the initial spread of the loan is +200bp. A correlation of 0.2 between interest rates and NOI is used. We assume that the loan follows a 30 year amortization schedule and pays a balloon payment at the end of year 10. *Initially, we assume that the mortgage is noncallable.*

Debt Service Coverage Ratio (DSCR)

The debt service coverage ratio (DSCR) is defined as the annual NOI divided by annual cost of debt service including principal payments. Normally, as DSCR gets larger, the probability of default and a resulting loss decreases. Thus, as DSCR increases the value of the default option decreases. As a result for a fixed-income price the OAS increases. This can be seen in Exhibit 6 for a wide range of DSCR. Moreover, as DSCR gets very large, further increases do not result in a higher OAS.[14] For lower initial values of DSCR, the OAS is lower, indicating that the investor is really getting on average something less than +200 bp implied by his coupon. For example, at a DSCR of 2.50x the OAS is 170bp, or equivalently the default option is worth +30bp.

As one would expect the model shows that the OAS line for a bullet loan always lies below the line for the amortizing loan, since the amortizing loan has a built-in risk reduction mechanism. Even though both loans start with the same LTV, the LTV of the amortizing loan decreases through time, thus reducing its risk. The model computes the value of the amortization to be worth 30-40bp.

---

[13] To reduce the number of calculations we assumed a semi-annual pay mortgage.

[14] Since we kept initial LTV constant at 70%, the OAS does not increase much above 180 bp. Thus, the probability of default does not go to zero. In reality LTV would likely to lower and the OAS would go to +200bp.

Exhibit 6: OAS versus DSCR: Default Option

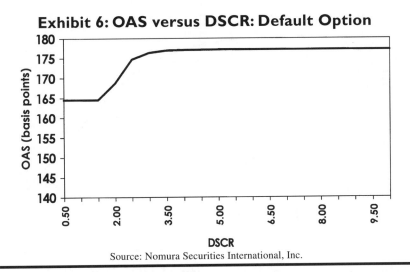

Source: Nomura Securities International, Inc.

Loan-To-Value Ratio (LTV)

The loan-to-value ratio (LTV) is defined as the ratio of loan amount to the value of the collateral property. This ratio is frequently used as a measure of leverage to assess the level of protection from default. A lower LTV loan is considered more credit worthy due to its better default protection. In terms of OAS, the OAS should increase as the initial LTV drops since the probability of a default and a loss decreases. This can be seen in Exhibit 7. When the LTV is sufficiently low, the loan is so default-protected that the OAS will start to level off. Lower initial LTVs do not lead to further increases in OAS. At this point the probability of default is near zero and the OAS equals the nominal spread of +200bp.

The impact on OAS due to change of LTV is more significant for bullet loans than amortizing loans.[15] This is because, as we stated earlier, the amortizing loan has a built-in LTV decreasing mechanism to automatically reduce default risk over time.

Volatility of Net Operating Income

The more volatile a property's income stream, the greater the probability of default. From the model's perspective volatility of NOI affects value because with greater volatility there will be more paths under which income will be insufficient to pay the debt service and under which the value of the property declines below the value of the debt (see Exhibit 2). Thus, given a mortgage price, the corresponding OAS decreases as the volatility increases. Exhibit 8 clearly indicates this result: the greater the volatility of NOI, the lower the OAS. It should be clear from the graph that at a 70% initial LTV, the volatility of NOI has a profound influence on the value of the loan.[16]

---

[15] A bullet loan pays no principal until the maturity and then the entire principal amount is fully paid. The amortizing loan pays principal according to its amortization schedule until the maturity and then the remaining principal amount is fully paid.

[16] Note that for sufficiently high LTV, as NOI volatility increases to a certain level, the OAS levels off.

Exhibit 7: OAS versus LTV: Default Option

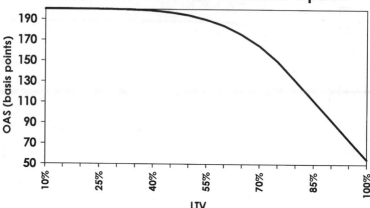

Source: Nomura Securities International, Inc.

Exhibit 8: OAS versus Volatility of NOI: Default Option

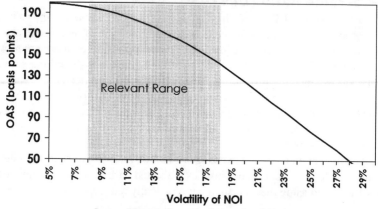

Source: Nomura Securities International, Inc.

This parameter enables investors to estimate the required excess spread for different property types. For example, mortgages on hotels or other property types with relatively high operating margins should offer higher spreads than mortgages on property types such as multi-family which tends to have a more stable income stream, assuming the same initial LTV and NOI. In practice, loans and CMBS backed by hotel or office properties tend to have lower initial LTVs (in the case of CMBS greater subordination which translates into a lower effective LTV) and therefore the difference is not reflected in the spread.

Term to Maturity

As previously shown in Exhibit 2, the longer the term to maturity, the higher default risk is. This is because there is more time for things to go bad. The cumulative probability of default increases as the term to maturity lengthens. As a result, the OAS should decrease as the term to maturity lengthens. Our model shows that OAS decreases as term to maturity increases, particularly for the higher quality loan (see Exhibit 9). On the other hand, when the loan starts out as a lower quality loan, increasing the maturity of the debt can actually lead to increasing OAS indicating increasing value. At first this seems strange, since the probability of default should increase with time. There are two reasons for the odd result. First, even though the cumulative probability of default increases, with a longer term to maturity the time to default is pushed further into the future. [17] Second, when a loan is really at risk of default, additional time gives the property owner some chance of getting the property back on track. An analogy can be made to a sporting event. Suppose a team is down by seven runs. It would far prefer it to be the first inning instead of the ninth, whereas the team that is ahead by seven runs would prefer that it be the bottom of the ninth inning.

Another interesting phenomenon is that even for the higher quality loan, after a certain point the OAS stops declining and even rises a bit until it levels off. This happens because even though the probability of default increases, on a present value basis, this added risk of default does not add much to the expected loss. The result is interesting in that it shows that longer term to maturity does not necessarily mean greater risk.

Valuing the Prepayment Option

Thus far we have assumed that the commercial mortgage was completely non-callable. In reality, while most commercial mortgages are more call-protected than residential mortgages, many have free periods. For example, the borrower in a 10-year balloon mortgage may be locked-out from prepayment for five years, and then is permitted to prepay. In addition, many commercial mortgages do not have lock-out provisions, but instead prepayment penalties which come in a variety of forms. The investor in the mortgage needs an ability to place a value on the lock-out and/or penalties in order to properly compare investment alternatives.

In order to analyze the effects of callability we continue with our example where we assumed a commercial mortgage with a 10-year maturity, 9% coupon, initial DSCR of 1.50x, initial LTV of 70%, initial risk-free interest rate of 7%, interest rate volatility of 11%, and NOI volatility of 15%. We assume that the loan follows a 30-year amortization schedule and has a balloon payment at the end of year 10. In addition, we assume that the loan is fully callable after 5 years without penalty at par.

Naturally, if the loan is also callable, the investment is less attractive. As a result, the OAS is lower as can be seen in Exhibits 9, 10, and 11. For our prototype loan with 70% LTV and 1.5x DSCR, the investor is really only getting +145 bp instead of the stated spread of +200 bp. It is interesting to note that the difference gets larger for lower quality loans. This is because the option to call in lower quality debt is even more valuable.

---

[17] This is similar to the results found in Robert Merton, "On the Pricing of Corporate Debt: The Risk Structure of Interest Rates," *Journal of Finance* (May 1974).

Exhibit 9: OAS versus Term to Maturity: Default Option

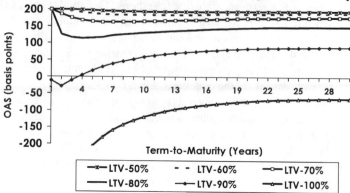

Exhibit 10: OAS versus DSCR: Refinance and Default Options

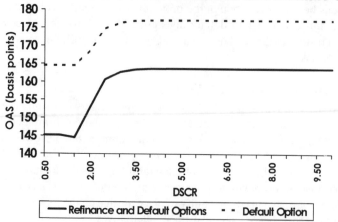

Exhibit 11: OAS versus LTV: Refinance and Default Options

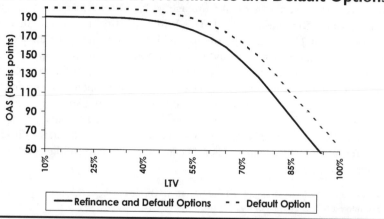

Exhibit 12: OAS versus Volatility of NOI: Refinance and Default Options

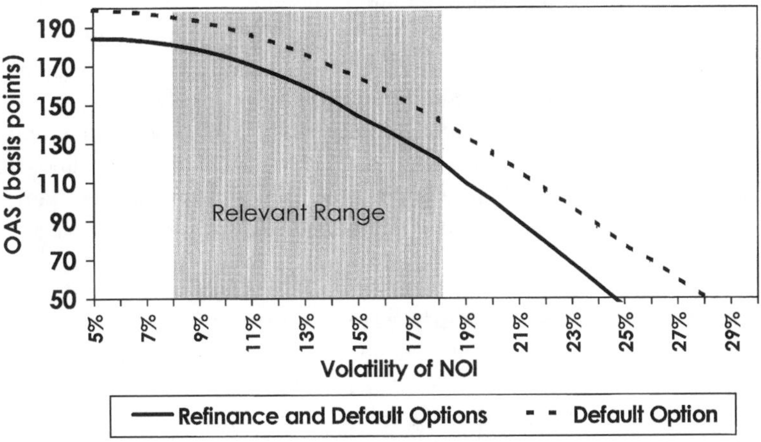

Exhibit 12 shows the OAS versus volatility of NOI. Once again, if the loan is callable, the OAS is lower.

In addition to the issues of callability there are factors which, while not discussed here, have an impact on value and show up in the OAS. These include the particular penalty structure; what happens in a default, extension, and modification provision in a balloon default; the price of the loan (assumed in all of the above analysis to be priced at par[18]); the shape of the yield curve; etc. All of these can be analyzed by the model.

VALUING MULTI-CLASS COMMERCIAL MORTGAGE-BACKED SECURITIES[19]

Thus far, we have applied the model to the valuation of a commercial mortgage. In this section we use the model to analyze multi-class commercial mortgage-backed securities. Securitization is the process of converting financial assets that produce cash flows into securities that trade in the financial markets. The cash flows from the loans are used to pay the certificate holders. Often many loans are pooled together in the securitization. A single class of bondholders can be created or there can be numerous classes. In addition to creating liquidity, the securitization process can be used to alter credit quality through various means of credit enhancements. These credit enhancements can

---

[18] If the investor purchased the loan at a deep discount, a default could be a favorable event if the proceeds from the foreclosure are sufficient. Similarly, a loan purchased at a premium will suffer if there is a default even if the foreclosure process only recovers the par amount

[19] Note that there will be some differences in the valuation results since in this section we use Monte Carlo simulation rather than obtaining an exact solution from the binomial tree.

take the form of guarantees, over collateralization, or senior-subordination. Today, senior-subordination is used almost exclusively. By creating a credit and payment prioritization, credit risk is reallocated among the bond classes. Typically, all principal payments that are made by the borrower(s) are used to pay off the most senior outstanding bond class, whereas losses are allocated to the most junior outstanding class. This process effectively decreases the LTV of the most senior bond class.

Because the losses are mostly absorbed by the junior classes, the senior class has more credit protection than its underlying collateral. By utilizing subordination, one can create securities which have higher credit ratings than the underlying collateral. The rating agencies set the effective LTV and DSCR requirements in each deal in order to achieve the desired bond ratings.

A Simple Sequential CMBS Structure

The question which investors would like to be answered is: Which has better value — the AAA bond at +85bp or the BBB bond at +190 bp? Our model can be used to help answer this type of question. We use the following example to demonstrate the application of the model.

We start with the same type of loan as in the prior section, i.e. a 9% coupon, 10-year balloon loan with a 30-year amortization schedule, Treasury rates at 7%, NOI volatility of 15%, interest rate volatility of 11%, and a correlation of 20% between interest rates and NOI. For analytic purposes we assume that instead of a single $100 million loan, we have a pool of ten $10 million loans with LTVs ranging from 54% to 90% (weighted average 70%) and DSCRs ranging from 1.94x to 1.11x (weighted average 1.5x).

Exhibit 13 depicts a typical CMBS deal.[20] In the deal, the C class is structured as the most junior tranche which provides credit support to the A and B classes while the B classes provides support to the A classes. Since the collateral is priced at par and has a coupon of 9.00%, the senior tranches whose yields are below that of the collateral will have prices above par, and the junior classes will have prices that are at a discount.

As was the case with the unstructured commercial mortgage, when the NOI volatility is low, the OAS is almost equal to the stated yield spread.[21] At higher levels of NOI volatility, the OAS declines. As expected, the largest declines take place in the most junior classes since they are the first to absorb losses caused by defaults. Interestingly, the OAS also declines for the most senior class. This is because the recoveries from defaults are used to pay the most senior classes first. Since, in this example, the senior classes are priced at a premium, the premature receipt of principal at par leads to a degradation in the bond's yield. (In Exhibits 14 and 15 we show the results for a case when the senior bonds are priced at a discount. In that situation the OAS of the senior bonds initially increases as the NOI volatility increases.)

---

[20] In this example, the spreads are reasonably representative of the market as of the fourth quarter of 1995. However, the sizing of the tranches is a bit too conservative. In particular, the unrated class is too large. As a result this deal would not have been done since the arbitrage is negative.

[21] As before this is true for a flat Treasury yield curve. If the Treasury curve were positively sloped the OAS would still be below the stated yield spread due to the dispersion of the cash flows.

Exhibit 13: An Example of a Sequential Structure of CMBS: Default Option (10 Loans)

Class	Size ($MM)	Aver Life	Rating	Price	Yield Spread	OAS 6% Volatility	OAS 10% Volatility	OAS 16% Volatility	OAS 30% Volatility
A-1	65	9.33	AAA	107.08	90 bp	89	82	71	63
A-2	5	10.00	AA	105.39	120 bp	120	120	120	120
A-3	5	10.00	A	103.32	150 bp	150	150	150	150
B-1	5	10.00	BBB	100.00	200 bp	200	200	200	197
B-2	5	10.00	BB	88.05	400 bp	400	400	400	332
B-3	5	10.00	B	77.96	600 bp	600	600	590	245
C	10	10.00	N/R	38.63	2000 bp	1963	1868	1610	563
Loan	100	9.56	N/A	100.00	200 bp	195	186	163	72

Note: Each tranche is priced at spread over its benchmark Treasury.

Exhibit 14: OAS versus Volatility of NOI for Senior Tranches: Discount Bonds Default Option

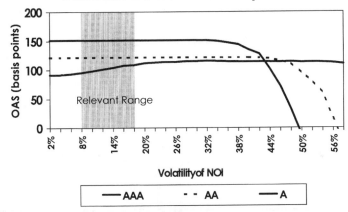

Exhibit 15: OAS versus Volatility of NOI for Senior Tranches: Discount Bonds Refinance and Default Options

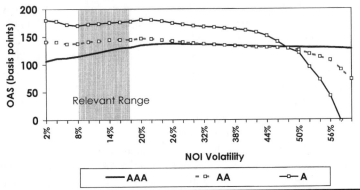

Exhibit 16:An Example of a Sequential Structure of CMBS: Refinance and Default Options (10 Loans)

Class	Size ($MM)	Average Life	Rating	Price	Yield Spread	OAS 6% Volatility	OAS 10% Volatility	OAS 16% Volatility	OAS 30% Volatility
A-1	65	9.33	AAA	107.08	90 bp	34	30	22	15
A-2	5	10.00	AA	105.39	120 bp	77	76	77	86
A-3	5	10.00	A	103.32	150 bp	117	119	122	128
B-1	5	10.00	BBB	100.00	200 bp	180	182	186	192
B-2	5	10.00	BB	88.05	400 bp	421	419	418	393
B-3	5	10.00	B	77.96	600 bp	655	649	632	373
C	10	10.00	N/R	38.63	2000 bp	2170	1977	1645	262
Loan	100	9.56	N/A	100.00	200 bp	177	167	140	32

Note: Each tranche is priced at spread over its benchmark Treasury.

Exhibit 17: OAS versus Volatility of NOI for Senior Tranches: Premium Bonds with Default Option

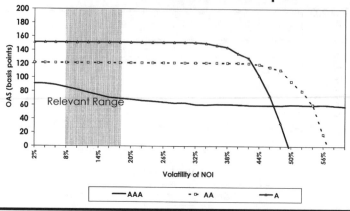

There are several other points worth noting. First, the most protected classes are the AA, A, and BBB. Their OAS changes the least as a function of NOI volatility since they are not the first to absorb losses or recoveries. Second, the BBB CMBS at NOI volatilities above 9% appears to be a better value than the underlying loan if the two are offered at the same stated spread. Finally, the lowest rated classes appear to be the cheapest unless NOI volatilities substantially above observed levels are assumed.

In Exhibit 16, we allow the loans to be callable after 5 years without penalty. This substantially hurts the value of the most senior classes, particularly because they are priced at a premium. This is why a complete prepayment lockout on these classes is so important and valuable. The subordinate classes can actually benefit as shown by the improvement in their OAS because they are priced at a discount.

Exhibits 17 and 18 show that only at substantially higher levels of NOI volatility does the A rated bond have a lower OAS than the AA and AAA rated bonds. The conclusion is that the market is paying up too much for the higher rated classes.

Exhibit 18: OAS versus Volatility of NOI for Senior Tranches: Premium Bonds with Refinance and Default Options

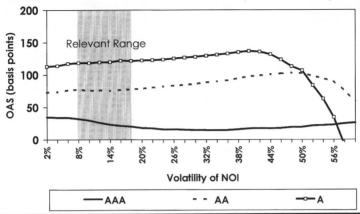

Subordinate Bonds

The subordinate bond classes (B-pieces) in a CMBS deal are usually priced at a discount. Our analysis shows that the OAS of the B-pieces remains wide compared to the senior tranches even when a volatility as high as 18% is assumed for the NOI. This indicates the market view on the B-pieces is very conservative.

Interest-Only Strips

As we noted earlier, since senior bonds are priced with lower yields than the collateral, they would have prices substantially above par if they had the same coupon. Since many investors do not want to purchase premium bonds, interest is stripped off and interest-only (IO) classes are created.[22] Interest is usually stripped in order to price the senior class close to par or at low premium in the CMBS deal. It is in the interest of the issuer to create the strip class if the proceeds from the strip class and the par bond is greater than the proceeds from a premium bond. Since the price of an IO strip is more sensitive than its principal bond with the same credit rating, it is traded at a much wider spread. Exhibit 21 takes the deal that we have considered and strips three IOs from three A-classes in order to create discount bonds. Notice how the OAS on the AAA class increases as NOI volatility increases, as shown in Exhibits 14 and 15. This is because the bond is priced at a discount and any early payments from recoveries in a default are paid at par.

IO strip classes have special characteristics, which make the use of an OAS model in their valuation extremely useful. Since interest is paid only when the notional principal is outstanding, when the notional principal upon which the IOs payments are based is reduced, the amount of interest paid to the IO holder declines. There are two ways in which the erosion of notional principal can occur. The reduc-

---

[22] This can be done either at the loan level or the bond class level.

tion in principal takes place due to either losses or due to principal payments. In the case of a loss, the senior-subordinated structure requires that the loss be allocated to the most junior outstanding class. Thus, IOs which are stripped from the AAA bond are relatively insulated from erosion of principal due to the allocation of losses. On the other hand, erosion of principal also occurs due to principal payments. The senior-subordinated structure requires that the most senior outstanding class receive principal payments. Thus, even a minor amount of prepayments leads to the erosion of principal associated with the IO stripped from the AAA bond. Principal payments can be either voluntary or involuntary. Voluntary prepayments are related to refinancing or the selling of the property. The IO holder, thus, derives considerable protection from prepayment protection features.[23]

Involuntary principal payment is a slightly more subtle concept. It arises from recoveries from foreclosure proceedings. These recoveries also must go to the most senior outstanding class. Thus, high defaults with a high rate of recovery also can erode the principal of the IO stripped from the most senior bond. The senior IO holder is in the odd position in the case of a default of hoping for zero recovery.

As can be seen in Exhibit 21 the IO stripped from the AAA bond is more sensitive to the volatility of NOI. At a high levels of volatility the OAS can become negative. While we do not show it here, adding the call feature would also negatively impact the IO class.

Investors should be willing to pay up substantially for IO's that are backed by •well call protected loans. Note that while we assumed immediate foreclosure, the foreclosure process on average takes about a year. This would substantially improve the value of the IO classes.

Exhibit 19: OAS versus Volatility of NOI for Subordinate Tranches: Default Options

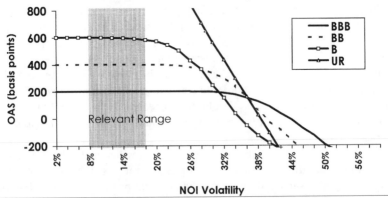

---

[23] Lockout, however, provides better protection than yield maintenance for two reasons. First, while yield maintenance serves as a disincentive, in the event of prepayment the IO holder may not be allocated his fair share. More importantly, as we mentioned earlier property owners may want to prepay even when interest rates rise. In this in instance there is no yield maintenance to distribute.

Exhibit 20: OAS versus Volatility of NOI for Subordinate Tranches: Refinance and Default Options

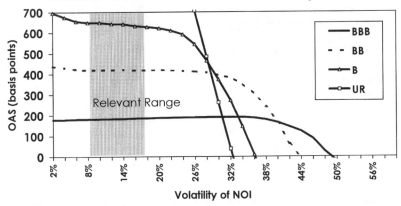

Exhibit 21: An Example of a Sequential Structure of CMBS: Default Option

Class	Size ($MM)	Aver Life	Rating	Price	Yield Spread	OAS 6% Volatility	OAS 10% Volatility	OAS 16% Volatility	OAS 30% Volatility
A-1	65	9.33	AAA	94.21	90 bp	93	98	108	115
A-2	5	10.00	AA	91.92	120 bp	121	121	121	121
A-3	5	10.00	A	90.03	150 bp	151	151	151	151
B-1	5	10.00	BBB	100.00	200 bp	201	201	201	197
B-2	5	10.00	BB	88.05	400 bp	401	401	401	332
B-3	5	10.00	B	77.96	600 bp	601	600	590	245
C	10	10.00	N/R	38.63	2000 bp	1963	1868	1610	563
AAA IO	65*	5.11	AAA	12.71	220 bps	174	37	-185	-339
AA IO	5*	5.25	AA	12.36	320 bps	321	321	321	321
A IO	5*	5.25	A	12.20	350 bps	351	351	351	351
Loan	100	9.56	N/A	100.00	200 bp	195	186	163	72

* Notional amount
Note: Each tranche is priced at spread over its benchmark Treasury.

Exhibits 21 and 22 confirm our view that interest strips from bonds that are neither the first nor the last in the sequential structure are the least risky. This is because (1) they are protected from erosion of principal due to losses, (2) there are bond classes below them, and (3) they are protected from principal payments by bond classes that are in front of them. Interestingly, the market does not price them that way. The AAA strip is typically priced at a tighter spread than the AA strip, which in turn is priced at a tighter spread than the A strip. For example, in Exhibit 22, the OAS of the IO stripped from the most senior class declines rapidly as the volatility of NOI and the ensuing default rate rises. The IO strips from the AA and A rated bond classes are actually less risky in a more volatile market. This suggests that less senior IO strips should be traded at a tighter spread.

Exhibit 22: OAS versus Volatility of NOI for Interest-Only Strips: Default Option

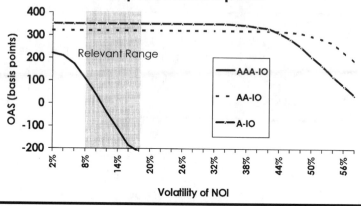

DISPERSION OF LOAN QUALITY

Investors need to give serious consideration to the diversity of the loans backing the bond classes in a CMBS deal. In the prior CMBS examples, we assumed there were ten loans with a range of LTVs and DSCRs. While the average LTV was 70% and the average DSCR was 1.5x, the dispersion in quality generally has a negative impact on the bond classes. In Exhibits 23 and 24 we compare the OAS versus NOI volatility for the AAA bond and the unrated class assuming a ten loan portfolio and a single loan portfolio. In general, one can see that the dispersion lowers the OAS. For the unrated class this is obvious. As the most junior class, it suffers the downside of the lower quality loans without an equal benefit from the higher quality loans. The AAA bond on the other hand gets hurt if it is priced at a premium, since the lower quality loans will increase the likelihood of defaults leading to recoveries which get paid to the AAA class. At higher levels of NOI volatility, the AAA benefits from the dispersion because the lower quality loans default, and the remaining pool consists of much higher quality loans.

RELATIVE RISK OF CMBS BOND CLASSES

Up to this point we have used OAS model mostly as a tool for pricing and assessing relative value. The model, because it is based on the evaluation of the securities in the probability space, can also be used to determine relative risk. We use the prices that are obtained from the price distribution. One would expect that the price variation for the less risky securities be smaller (as a percent of the security's price) than for the more risky securities. This is generally the case. In Exhibits 25, 26, and 27 we show the price distribution resulting from the model assuming NOI volatility of 15%. To focus on the credit risk we held interest rates constant. Notice how much tighter the price range is for the AAA bond than for the collateral; look how wide the range is for the unrated class.

Exhibit 23: Effect of Loan Quality Dispersion: AAA CMBS Bond Class

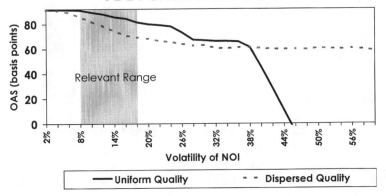

Exhibit 24: Effect of Loan Quality Dispersion: Unrated CMBS Bond Class

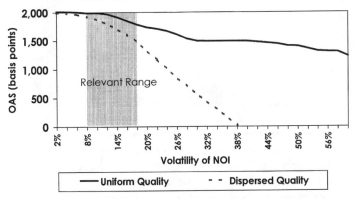

Exhibit 25: Price Distribution of Loan

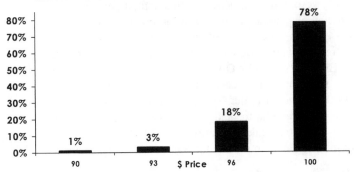

Exhibit 26: Price Distribution of CMBS — AAA

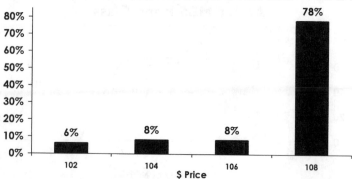

Exhibit 27: Price Distribution of CMBS — Unrated Class.

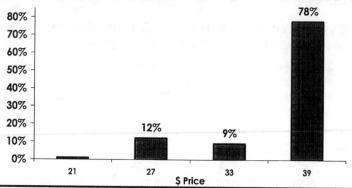

In Exhibit 28 we summarize the statistics of the distributions for each of the bond classes. In general, the lower rated classes have the highest risk as measured by the coefficient of variation.[24] However, since the recoveries from default negatively impact the senior bonds which are priced at a premium, the standard deviation for the AAA is higher than the AA, and similarly for the A. The BBB shows a standard deviation of nearly zero, which indicates from a default perspective it is well protected and it is also not impacted by recoveries from foreclosures.

If we use the coefficient of variation as our risk measure, and OAS as our measure of relative value, we can construct the "efficient frontier" for investment analysis. In Exhibit 29, we plot OAS versus the coefficient of variation for each of the bond classes. One can see how clearly the BBB bonds and the unrated class lie on the boundary of the efficient frontier. This suggests that portfolios consisting of BBB and unrated class bonds can be formed to outperform combinations of the other bonds. Perhaps investors should take the ratio of OAS to the coefficient of variation as the measure of relative value, much like the Sharpe ratio in stock analysis.[25]

---

[24] The coefficient of variation normalizes the risk by looking at the ratio of standard deviation to the mean.
[25] William F. Sharpe, "Mutual Fund Performance," *Journal of Business* (January 1966).

Exhibit 28: CMBS Summary Statistics

	Mean*	OAS	Standard Deviation	Coefficient of Variation	Range
AAA	106.41	71	1.45	1.37%	4.65
AA	104.86	120	1.13	1.07%	3.61
A	103.00	150	0.69	0.67%	2.21
BBB	100.00	200	0.00	0.00%	0
BB	89.03	400	2.52	2.86%	17.82
B	77.95	590	8.43	10.81%	59.34
UR	36.38	1610	4.36	13.24%	14.69
Loan	98.63	163	2.64	2.69%	10.46

* This data are for the single loan case. The standard deviations will be significantly lower for the ten loan case.

Exhibit 29: OAS versus Coefficient of Variation — CMBS bond classes and Loan

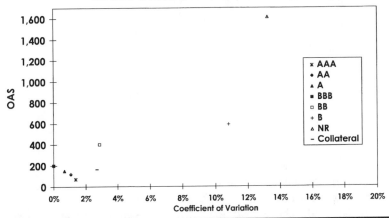

CONCLUSION

In this chapter we introduced a model which uses the borrower's behavior to construct a decision payoff matrix for exercising default and prepayment options and utilizes option theory to value these options. The model employs interest rates and the net operating income of the mortgaged property as the two underlying factors. Based upon the model, the option values can be assessed. We then derived an option-adjusted spread (OAS) to measure the relative value of commercial mortgages and commercial mortgage-backed securities. Given a market price, the OAS decreases as the risk exposure increases. The model serves as a unifying framework, bringing real estate valuation, fixed-income pricing, and option theory together. Factors affecting the real estate, mortgages, and structure are evaluated simultaneously across a wide range of scenarios. This sort of analysis helps reveal hidden weaknesses in the structure and enables the analyst to compare deals.

Appendix: Model Specification

The embedded options of commercial mortgages are American options which can be exercised at any time prior to expiration. Given state variables — interest rate and net operating income — we denote the rest of the variables as follows:

r = default-free one-period spot rate
N = net operating income
S = the expected present value of the future promised payments
C = the value of the prepayment option
D = the value of the default option
H = the total embedded option value which is equal to C plus D
G = the expected present value of the next period H
W = the market value of the underlying loan which is equal to S minus G
B = the market value of the collateral property
M = the scheduled mortgage payment
M^* = the potential refinancing scheduled mortgage payment
U = the face amount of mortgage remaining balance
Δ_d = foreclosure expense
Δ_c = prepayment penalty

We assume the process of r and N in discrete time as follows:

$$\log r_t = \alpha_t + \log r_{t-1} + \varepsilon_t$$

$$\log N_t = a_t + \log N_{t-1} + \zeta_t$$

where t is time index and, for any given t, ε and ζ have constant variances, σ^2 and s^2 respectively, and is correlated with correlation coefficient ρ.

To satisfy the above conditions, instead of generating ε and ζ directly, we generate ε and ζ and assume a relationship between ζ, ε, and ξ as follows:

$$E\left[\varepsilon^2\right] = \sigma^2$$

$$E\left[\xi^2\right] = (1-\rho)s^2$$

$$\zeta = b\varepsilon + \xi$$

where

$$E[\xi] = E[\varepsilon\xi] = 0,$$

$$b = (\rho s)/\sigma$$

Then we have

$$E[\varepsilon] = E[\zeta] = 0$$

$$E[\varepsilon\zeta] = \rho s \sigma$$

$$E\left[\zeta^2\right] = s^2$$

To obtain property value B, we assume B=N/(r–rg) where g is a content along time. The property value B can be interpreted as the present value of an infinite series of prevailing net operating income with a growth rate r multiplied by g and discounted by the prevailing interest rate r. Since r, B, and N are known initially, g can be obtained through the equation. The value of (r–rg), in essence, is the capitalization rate of the property.

Triggering Conditions

The prepayment triggering conditions:

(i) N > M*
(ii) $G + \Delta_c < S - U$

The default triggering conditions:

(i) N < M
(ii) G < S + M – B

The default-as-a-method-of-prepayment triggering conditions:

(i) N > M*
(ii) $G + \Delta_d < S - U$

Exhibit 30 provides an arbitrage table for decision support.

Implementation of the Options Calculation

Based on the stochastic processes of N and r, as well as generic mortgage debt information, we are able to generate r, N, B, M, M*, U, and S to span the whole solid binomial pyramid.

Starting from the maturity date of the mortgage debt, the option value G can be calculated backward in time.

At maturity date of period T:
Given r, N, B, M, and S=U, based on the default and prepayment trigger condition:

$$H = \begin{cases} U + M - B \text{ (default)} \\ 0 \text{ (otherwise) and } G = 0 \end{cases}$$

Exhibit 30: Arbitrage Table for Decision Support

Triggering Condition				Action Code	H value t < T	H value T
I	II	III	IV			
$B-M = Min[B-M, U+\Delta_d, U+\Delta_c] < S-G$	N<M			1	S+M−B	U+M−B
	N>M	$U+\Delta_d = Min[U+\Delta_d, U+\Delta_c] < S-G$	N>M*	2	S−U−Δ_d	0
			N<M*	0	G	0
		$U+\Delta_c = Min[U+\Delta_d, U+\Delta_c] < S-G$	N>M*	3	S−U−Δ_c	0
			N<M*	0	G	0
$U+\Delta_d = Min[B-M, U+\Delta_d, U+\Delta_c] < S-G$	N>M*			2	S−U−Δ_d	0
	N<M*	B>S+M-G		0	G	0
		B< S+M−G	N>M	0	G	0
			N<M	1	S+M−B	U+M−B
$U+\Delta_c = Min[B-M, U+\Delta_d, U+\Delta_c] < S-G$	N>M*			3	S−U−Δ_c	0
	N<M*	B> S+M-G		0	G	0
		B< S+M−G	N>M	0	G	0
			N<M	1	S+M−B	U+M−B
$Min[B-M, U+\Delta_d, U+\Delta_c] \geq S-G$				0	G	0

Note: numbers 0,1,2, and 3 in Action column denote to "no action," "default," "default-as-a-method-of-pre-payment," and "prepay" respectively.

At time t where t < T:
Given r, N, B, M, M*, U and S, based on the default and prepayment trigger condition:

$$H = \begin{cases} S + M - B & \text{(default)} \\ S - U - \Delta_d & \text{(default as involuntary prepayment)} \\ S - U - \Delta_c & \text{(prepay)} \\ G & \text{(otherwise)} \end{cases}$$

and then G can be calculated from next-step H by discounting the interest rates with weighted probabilities.

Chapter **18**

Performing Financial Due Diligence Associated with Commercial Mortgage Securitizations

David Baranick, C.P.A.
Director
Real Estate Industry Services Group
Price Waterhouse LLP

Shahid H. Quraishi
Principal Consultant
Asset Securitization Group
Price Waterhouse LLP

INTRODUCTION

The term "due diligence" has become a common term in the vocabulary of those involved in the securitization of commercial mortgage loans. However, the term means different things to different people. Due diligence is used here to describe verification procedures performed on information which, in some form or another, will be provided to potential investors, rating agencies or other interested parties. Such procedures may be performed by third party contractors such as accountants, attorneys, engineers and others. Other procedures may be performed by issuers and underwriters to satisfy their fiduciary responsibilities. We will explore some of the most common applications of due diligence on the financial information relative to a securitization transaction.

Due diligence can be performed on behalf of buyers or sellers of securities. The primary motivating factors in sellers (or their agents) hiring a third party, such as an accounting firm, to perform due diligence on the financial information includes satisfying fiduciary responsibilities of the issuer and underwriter, enhancing the marketability of the securities, and providing expertise in the analysis of collateral to enhance the asset underwriting. Other factors include the ability of third parties to provide a critical mass of professionals to analyze massive amounts of information in a relatively short time frame and the need to create a centralized repository of information obtained relative to the assets. The primary motivating factor in buyers contracting for due diligence services is to obtain independent comfort on the accuracy of the information supplied as well as to conduct a more exhaustive analysis of the value of the securities than is generally supplied by the seller.

The three main areas of financial due diligence that will be explored here include analysis performed on loan collateral, property security, and structure modeling.

LOAN COLLATERAL AND PROPERTY INFORMATION DUE DILIGENCE

Analysis of the loans which represent the collateral for the securities is performed to assess the collectibility of the scheduled principal and interest payments inherent in the loans. Very often the ability of the borrower to pay the debt service on the loan is directly related to the cash flow generated from the property securing the loan. In fact, most such loans are originated on a non- recourse basis. The cash flow of the property reflects the net cash available from rents received after paying normal operating costs such as utilities, property taxes, repairs and maintenance and other capital expenditures. Therefore, the due diligence must not only focus on the borrowers' payment history but should also involve analysis of the underlying property.

Summarization of Key Loan Terms

Most important to the asset due diligence in a securitization is to obtain a thorough understanding of the collateral itself. Commercial mortgage loan terms can vary from straightforward fixed rate fully amortizing loans to the more complicated variable rate balloon loans with stringent yield maintenance provisions. Properly capturing salient loan terms is imperative in properly modeling the cash flow which will eventually pass through to the bonds. The cash flow depends on much more information than just the loan balance, rate and maturity. Other loan terms such as interest-only periods, prepayment and yield maintenance provisions, guarantees, frequency of adjustments, extension options, default terms and other key note and mortgage provisions need to be considered and understood. Exhibit 1 illustrates a reporting format for some of the more common loan provisions that are necessary to capture when underwriting the collateral included in a mortgage pool being securitized.

Exhibit I: Mortgage Loan Schedule

Loan	Original Balance ($)	Origination Date	First Payment Date	Cut-off Date Balance ($)	Amortization	Maturity	Loan Type	Rate Type	Index	Spread (%)	Mortgage Rate (%)	Monthly Payment ($)	Rate Cap	Rate Floor
1	400,000	12/4/95	1/1/96	397,200	300	12/1/00	Balloon	Fixed	N/A	N/A	7.20	2,858.21	N/A	N/A
2	500,000	9/12/95	11/1/95	496,500	IO	10/1/05	Balloon	Variable	1-Year T-Bill	2.50	9.30	3,847.88	5.093	4.907
3	820,000	6/30/95	8/1/95	814,260	240	7/1/15	Fully Amortizing	Variable	15-year T-Bill	3.00	7.50	6,559.62	5.075	4.925
4	600,000	12/30/95	2/1/96	595,800	360	1/1/03	Balloon	Fixed	N/A	N/A	10.10	5,272.65	N/A	N/A
5	1,050,000	1/14/95	3/1/95	1,042,650	300	2/1/20	Fully Amortizing	Fixed	N/A	N/A	5.80	6,590.92	N/A	N/A

Exhibit 2: Definition of Key Operating Statistics

Net Operating Income (NOI) The excess of revenues over certain operating expenses excluding interest, income tax, amortization and depreciation expense.

Debt Service Coverage Ratio (DSCR) The ratio of the Net Operating Income to the scheduled debt service for the same period.

Loan-to-Value Ratio (LTV) The ratio of the outstanding principal balance of a loan to the appraised value of the underlying property.

Occupancy The percentage of the property occupied on a per square foot or per unit basis.

Rent per square foot (or unit) The ratio of the rental revenue for a period to the occupied square feet (or number of units) during that period.

Expense per square foot (or unit) The ratio of operating expenses for a period to the occupied square feet (or number of units) during that period.

Lease Rollover Schedule Summary of the total occupied leased space scheduled to expire by year in which the leases expire.

Verification of Underlying Loan Information

Verification of the loan terms described above is not an overly complex process, however, it does require a strong understanding of real estate lending. Most important is an ability to read, decipher and understand the legal documents which represent the collateral. The loan documents can include, but are not limited to, notes, mortgages, security agreements, modifications, loan servicing history and similar information associated with any senior or junior liens. Ensuring that all the relevant documents have been made available is critical and often difficult. Performing loan terms due diligence can span a number of weeks.

As a consequence, it is important to remember during the process some of the terms may have changed. Balances amortize, variable loan rates adjust, loans get modified or are paid off, and remaining term to maturity moves. Keeping current with any such changes helps in maintaining control over the process.

Summarization of Key Operating Statistics

The due diligence on the collateral should start with the accumulation of key statistics. These statistics provide the basis for an initial assessment of the viability of the loan as a securitizable asset. These ratios, calculations and percentages are usually obtained from borrower provided information which is later subject to further scrutiny. Some of the more significant statistics include net operating income, debt service coverage ratios, loan-to-value ratios, occupancy percentages, rent and operating expense per square foot, lease expiration years and others. Exhibit 2 summarizes the definitions of the more key operating statistics. This list is by no means exhaustive and will vary depending on the property types involved in the transaction.

Verification of Underlying Property Financial Information

Once the key operating statistics have been accumulated, the verification process begins. Financial statement information used to derive NOI and other revenue and expense information can be examined in many different ways. One of the most common ways to check the financial statements is to subject them to an audit by independent certified public accountants. However, for a securitization of a large pool of small to medium size loans, auditing each property would be cost prohibitive. Instead, specific procedures could be designed to obtain the desired level of comfort that the borrower's numbers are reliable. Revenues can be examined by comparing amounts to annualized rent rolls. Rent rolls in turn would be compared to actual lease agreements. In some cases, such as large retail centers or office buildings, all leases may need to be modeled using one of many off-the-shelf lease modeling software packages. This would allow a greater level of detail in checking any expense recoveries or percentage rents. Operating expenses can be compared to actual utility bills, property tax bills, insurance policies, management and other contractual arrangements.

Underwriting of the Asset's Cash Flow

Once there is satisfaction that the borrower's information is reliable, an assessment is made as to whether the results are "market." Rating agencies, such as Standard & Poor's, Fitch, Duff & Phelps, and Moody's, have a significant impact on the profitability of the securitization transaction. Each of the agencies have their own underwriting criteria and will look at assets differently. It is important to understand the criteria used by the agencies and assess the conformity of the information obtained from the borrower with these criteria. A standardized underwritten cash flow should be derived for presentation to rating agencies as well as for prospective investors. NOI should be adjusted for market rates related to such items as management fees, capital reserves, non-recurring revenues and expenses, leasing commissions, and tenant improvements. Rental revenues should be adjusted to reflect leases in place at the time of the transaction. The underwritten cash flow which will be derived from these adjustments will be the basis for determining the credit quality of the loan collateral.

Data Capture

The information obtained during the due diligence process can be maintained in a variety of formats. Ultimately a database which captures all of the relevant information must be compiled. Such a database may be constructed from asset level due diligence forms. These forms, commonly referred to as "asset data sheets," include all the information necessary to populate the database. Exhibit 3 provides an illustration of what an asset data sheet might look like. This database is used to provide the empirical analysis and collateral table information presented in the offering documents. Examples of some typical tables that would be included in an offering circular are presented in Exhibits 4-7.

Exhibit 3: Sample Asset Data Sheet

COMPANY X SECURITIZATION
Loan Data Extract Sheet

Cut-off Date

		Response
1.	Asset Number	
2.	Pool Number	
3.	Property Name	

COLLATERAL INFORMATION

4.	Collateral Type	
5.	Borrower Name	
6.	Insurance and Tax Escrow Required (Y/N)	
7.	Current Monthly Escrow Required (Tax and Insurance)	
8.	Positive Escrow Balances	
9.	Appraised Value	
10.	Appraisal Date	
11.	Source of Appraised Value	
12.	Original LTV	
13.	Current LTV	
14.	City	
15.	State	
16.	County	
17.	Address (1)	
18.	Address (2)	
19.	Units	
20.	Unit Mix	
21.	Gross Building Square Feet	
22.	Net Rentable Square Feet	
23.	Number of Stories	
24.	Land Area	
25.	Year Built	
26.	Year Renovated	
27.	Block	
28.	Lot	
29.	Elevators/ Walk Up	
30.	Property Manager	
31.	Property Manager Contact	
32.	Property Manager Phone #	
33.	Last Property Inspection Date	
34.	Occupancy	
35.	Occupancy as of Date	
36.	Environmental Phase I Report (Y/N)	
37.	Environmental Phase I Date	
38.	Environmental Phase II Report (Y/N)	
39.	Environmental Phase II Date	
40.	Structural Report (Y/N)	
41.	Structural Report Date2	
42.	Monthly Cap Ex Reserve Funds Required	

Collateral Information Comments:

Exhibit 3 (Continued)

MORTGAGE INFORMATION

43. Lien Position (First, Second, etc.)	
44. Senior Liens Amount	
45. Junior Liens Amount	
46. Senior/Junior Lien Loan Terms	
47. Recourse (Y/N)	
48. Recourse Provisions / Guarantees	
49. Cross-Collateralized (Related Loans)	
50. Cross-Defaulted (Related Loans)	

Mortgage Information Comments:

NOTE INFORMATION

51. Accrual Rate (Current)	
52. Pay Rate (Current)	
53. Current Monthly Debt Service	
54. Variable or Fixed	
55. Variable Rate Index	
56. Variable Rate Spread	
57. Variable Rate Cap	
58. Variable Rate Floor	
59. IO Period	
60. Future step(s) or change in rate(s)/ payment(s) (Y/N)	
61. Next Monthly Debt Service Change Amount	
62. Next Monthly Debt Service Change Date	
63. Original Amortization Term	
64. Remaining Amortization Term	
65. Amortization Type (IO, Balloon, Fully Amortizing)	
66. Negative Amortization Allowed (Y/N)	
67. Negative Amortization Caps	
68. Cash Flow Note (Y/N)	
69. Grace Periods (# of days)	
70. Default Interest Rate	
71. Calculation of Interest (30/360, Actual/365, Actual/360,etc.)	
72. Origination Date	
73. Closing Date	
74. Loan Originator	
75. Loan Acquired From	
76. Date Loan Acquired	
77. First Payment Date	
78. First P&I Payment Date	
79. Maturity Date	
80. Pay Due Date (day of month)	
81. Original Term	
82. Seasoning	
83. Remaining Term	
84. Prepayment Provisions (Y/N)	
85. Evidence of Modified Loan (Y/N)	
86. Modification Date	
87. Terms of Modification	

Exhibit 3 (Continued)

88.	Evidence of Loan under Repayment Plan (Y/N)	
89.	Terms of Repayment Plan	

Note Information Comments:

COLLATERAL FINANCIAL INFORMATION

90.	Month of Most Recent Fiscal Year-End	
91.	Year of Most Recent Fiscal Year-End	
92.	Fiscal Rental Income	
93.	Fiscal Sales	
94.	Fiscal Other Income	
95.	Fiscal Disposition Income	
96.	Fiscal Total Income	
97.	Fiscal Cost of Sales	
98.	Fiscal Repairs & Maintenance	
99.	Fiscal Utilities	
100.	Fiscal Management Fees	
101.	Fiscal Appraisal/Environmental Fees	
102.	Fiscal Taxes	
103.	Fiscal Insurance Expense	
104.	Fiscal Legal Expense	
105.	Fiscal Other Expenses	
106.	Fiscal Depreciation Expense	
107.	Fiscal Interest Expense	
108.	Fiscal Total Expenses	
109.	Fiscal Net Income	
110.	Fiscal Net Operating Income	
111.	DSCR Using Fiscal NOI	
112.	DSCR Using Fiscal NOI (including senior notes)	
113.	Month of Most Recent YTD Information	
114.	Year of Most Recent YTD Information	
115.	YTD Rental Income	
116.	YTD Sales	
117.	YTD Other Income	
118.	YTD Disposition Income	
119.	YTD Total Income	
120.	YTD Cost of Sales	
121.	YTD Repairs & Maintenance	
122.	YTD Utilities	
123.	YTD Management Fees	
124.	YTD Appraisal/Environmental Fees	
125.	YTD Taxes	
126.	YTD Insurance Expense	
127.	YTD Legal Expense	
128.	YTD Other Expenses	
129.	YTD Depreciation Expense	
130.	YTD Interest Expense	
131.	YTD Total Expenses	
132.	YTD Net Income	
133.	YTD Net Operating Income	
133a.	Annualized YTD NOI	

Exhibit 3 (Continued)

133b.	DSCR (using annualized NOI)	
133c.	DSCR (using annualized NOI including senior notes)	

Financial Information Comments:

SERVICING

134.	Cut off date Principal Balance
135.	Current Legal Balance
136.	Arrears ($)
137.	Original Approved Principal Balance
138.	Date of Last Payment
139.	Days Delinquent
140.	Date Interest Paid Through
141.	Next Payment Date
142.	Payment Frequency (Monthly, Quarterly, Etc.)
143.	Length of Servicing (in months)
144.	Number of Times 30-59 Days Late in Past 12 Months
145.	Number of Times 60-89 Days Late in Past 12 Months
146.	Number of Times Over 90 Days Late in Past 12 Months

Servicing Comments:

GROUND LEASE

147.	Evidence of Ground Lease (Y/N)
148.	Evidence of Ground Lease Payment Schedule
149.	Ground Lease Expiration

Other Comments:

Exhibit 4: Loan Characteristics by Range of Cut-off Date Balance

Range ($ 000s)	Number of Loans	Percent of Total	Cut-off Date Balance ($)	Percent of Total
400-600	4	20.00	2,100,000	10.50
701-800	2	10.00	1,550,000	7.75
801-1,000	4	20.00	3,570,000	17.85
1,001-1,200	3	15.00	3,350,000	16.75
1,201-1,400	6	30.00	7,980,000	39.90
1,401-1,500	1	5.00	1,450,000	7.25
Totals	20	100.00	20,000,000	100.00

Exhibit 5: Loan Characteristics by Range of Interest Rate

Range (%)	Number of Loans	Percent of Total	Cut-off Date Balance ($)	Percent of Total
5.00-5.999	3	15.00	3,500,000	17.50
6.00-6.999	3	15.00	3,060,000	15.30
7.00-7.999	4	20.00	3,590,000	17.95
8.00-8.999	5	25.00	5,450,000	27.25
9.00-9.999	3	15.00	2,650,000	13.25
10.00-10.999	1	5.00	600,000	3.00
11.00-11.999	1	5.00	1,150,000	5.75
Totals	20	100.00	20,000,000	100.00

Exhibit 6: Loan Characteristics by State

State	Number of Loans	Percent of Total	Cut-off Date Balance ($)	Percent of Total
CA	5	25.00	5,150,000	25.75
FL	3	15.00	3,800,000	19.00
NJ	3	15.00	2,150,000	10.75
NY	5	25.00	6,280,000	31.40
TX	2	10.00	1,420,000	7.10
VA	1	5.00	400,000	2.00
WA	1	5.00	800,000	4.00
Totals	20	100.00	20,000,000	100.00

Exhibit 7: Loan Characteristics by Range of Loan-to-Value Ratios

Range (%)	Number of Loans	Percent of Total	Cut-off Date Balance ($)	Percent of Total
50-60	1	5.00	400,000	2.00
60.01-65	2	10.00	1,320,000	6.60
65.01-70	6	30.00	7,020,000	35.10
70.01-75	8	40.00	8,560,000	42.80
75.01-80	2	10.00	1,800,000	9.00
80.01-85	1	5.00	900,000	4.50
Totals	20	100.00	20,000,000	100.00

Exhibit 8: Percent of Principal Balance Outstanding

Certificate	Prepayment Scenarios				
Balance as of Date	1	2	3	4	5
December 31, 1996	100	100	100	98	98
December 31, 1997	78	78	72	68	68
December 31, 1998	64	64	52	44	38
December 31, 1999	52	52	30	25	22
December 31, 2000	32	32	18	6	6
December 31, 2001	21	21	0	0	0
December 31, 2002	8	8	0	0	0
December 31, 2003	0	0	0	0	0
December 31, 2004	0	0	0	0	0
Weighted Average Life	4.22619	4.22619	3.238095	2.869048	2.761905

STRUCTURE MODELING

Investment banks in the commercial mortgage-backed securities market have created exotic securities designed to meet the needs of investors regarding credit quality, liquidity, and rate of return comparable to treasuries of similar duration. During recent years in the evolution of the commercial securitization market, the role of the accounting firm providing structure modeling expertise has created added value to investment banks and additional integrity in the calculations being printed in the offering documents, including in the Prospectus Supplements and Private Placement Memoranda. Investment bankers, investors, and rating agencies have relied upon accountants to provide modeling expertise on tax assumptions that may affect REMIC qualification issues, residual valuations, esoteric collateral amortization and bond pay down rules.

Structure modeling involves reverse-engineering the securitization structure and verifying the computational information found in the Prospectus Supplement and Private Placement Memorandum. Reverse-engineering is the process of re-modeling the proposed structure by projecting the collateral amortization on each of the underlying loans, modeling the bond pay down rules found in the Pooling and Servicing Agreement, calculating the yield to maturity on the senior and subordinate bonds, modeling defaults and recoveries, calculating the value of the residual and creating a bond OID (original issue discount) legend to determine the estimated tax liability to an investor. Structure modeling is needed in the due diligence process because certain information cannot be verified in the Prospectus Supplement and Private Placement Memorandum without the complex modeling of the securitization structure. Such items include certificate decrement tables and yield to maturity tables based upon different prepayment scenarios. The prepayment scenarios reflect the prepayment penalties on the loans as well as the associated yield maintenance premiums on the tranches. Examples of such tables are illustrated in Exhibits 8 and 9.

Exhibit 9: Yield to Maturity: Class X Certificate

Assumed Purchase Price	Prepayment Scenarios				
as a Percentage of Par	1	2	3	4	5
100%	7.02	6.88	6.82	6.91	6.74
90%	7.63	7.45	7.38	7.51	7.25
85%	7.81	7.65	7.60	7.72	7.47
80%	7.89	7.71	7.68	7.79	7.59

The offered certificates must be verified by the accountant against the information found in the Prospectus Supplement. These certificates are usually the most senior certificates in the deal, such as the 'A' class certificates. The subordinate certificates, such as the 'B' class certificates, are often sold through private placements. These certificates are verified when the Private Placement Memorandum is given comfort.

The process of modeling a deal is based upon the timing of the transaction, specifically the closing and the settlement dates. The modelers will work with the investment bank structuring group to get the initial modeling assumptions on the collateral and deal structure on the bonds. The loan amortization, prepayment penalty formulas, and number of loans that go into the deal will change as property level and loan level due diligence are performed. The modeling process is continual and may take place up to closing.

Structure modeling provides the investment bank underwriting the transaction with a higher degree of comfort that the structure and all the calculations and information marketed to an investor are correct. The investor has greater confidence that the investment bank has correctly calculated the information that the investor is relying upon in purchasing a senior tranche, subordinate tranche, or residual interest. The investor may also require calculations of the deal based upon specifically requested scenarios.

Collateral Modeling

The first step in securitization modeling is to amortize each loan and generate the total net interest and total available principal to the bonds, including prepayment penalties on each loan, assuming different prepayment scenarios. Modeling the collateral cash flows involves amortizing each loan that goes into the issuing entity based upon the underlying property amortization schedules. Each month, the gross interest is determined based on the loan terms. The remainder of the payment is scheduled principal. The securitization model will amortize each loan based upon the modeling assumptions which include the cut-off date balance, the mortgage rate, the remaining weighted average maturity, the balloon term and the interest accrual method (e.g., 30/ 360, actual/360, etc.) The modeler generates a report that shows remaining balance, net interest, unscheduled principal, scheduled principal, net cash flow and gross cash flow on a loan by loan basis or on an aggregate collateral basis.

Bond Modeling

The second step in the securitization modeling process is to model the bond waterfall rules based upon the payment priorities found in the pooling and servicing agreement.

The collateral model has already amortized the loans to determine the total principal and net interest available to pay the bonds. The first step in bond modeling is to allocate the net interest and total principal to the various bond classes based upon the payment priorities outlined in the pooling and servicing agreement.

The next step is to calculate the interest that is due on each bond. Some bond interest is based upon the weighted average net rate minus a spread. The total principal distribution amount is the difference between the prior period collateral balance minus the current period collateral balance. In some deals, the collateral needs to be separated into different sub-pools. In these cases, the various sub-pools are allocated to specific classes.

Once the initial bond structure is set up, the next step is to calculate the bond cash flows and decrement table based upon any number of scenarios. One scenario may assume no prepayments, in which case there is no yield maintenance calculation. Another scenario may require the yield maintenance calculation based upon the percentage allocation rules. The modeler would then re-run each scenario and verify the decrement table and any yield sensitivity table.

After the cash flows are run for each of the scenarios, the yield to maturity will be calculated based on the bond cash flows and the price paid for the certificates.

Bond OID Legend

The tax rules require that bonds issued with OID contain the following "OID Legend" information on the face of the certificates: (1) the aggregate amount of OID, (2) the issue date, (3) the initial interest rate, (4) the prepayment assumption to be used in accruing OID (5) the yield to maturity, and (6) if the instrument has short accrual period, the method used to determine the yield to maturity and OID for the short period. All of this information is compiled and calculated as a result of the information obtained during the due diligence and modeling process.

Residual After-Tax Analysis

The final step in the structure modeling due diligence process is to determine the value of the residual interest. Commercial securitization transactions are usually structured using REMICs (real estate mortgage instrument conduits). A REMIC is an entity created by the Internal Revenue Code which, for state law purposes, can be a corporation, partnership, trust, or separate pool of assets. A REMIC is required to have an ownership class known as a "residual interest."

A residual interest is often structured so that it will not receive any cash flow (i.e., there is no economic income). However, due to the interrelationships of the collateral, bond structure, yield on the collateral and yield curve on the bonds, timing of respective cash flows, and the OID rules, a residual interest may have phantom taxable income in the initial years followed by phantom taxable losses in later years. (Note that phantom income (loss) is created where taxable income (loss) exceeds economic income (loss)).

Although taxable income will generally equal taxable loss over the life of the REMIC, the residual interest has a negative value due to the fact the present value of the taxes required to be paid on the phantom income in the early years of the REMIC exceeds the lesser present value of the tax benefits on the phantom losses in the later years. In most securitizations, this result is caused by the sequential pay structure where the senior tranches have lower passthrough rates than the subordinated tranches. Thus, while the collateral yield may be constant over the life of the REMIC, the weighted average bond yield will increase over time due to the impact of the yield curve, causing phantom income in early years and phantom losses in later years.

USE OF TECHNOLOGY

Technology has always played an integral role in the structuring of commercial mortgage securitization transactions as well as the ongoing monitoring, reporting, and servicing of commercial mortgage loans. We are now seeing the due diligence attestation process being significantly enhanced through the use of technology and proprietary and vendor licensed analytical tools. Sophistication of the technology used in the due diligence process is dependent upon the nature and complexity of the technology utilized by the issuer with respect to the data capture analysis and preliminary aggregation of loan information. However, there is little dependence on the issuer's system in structuring the securitization transaction.

During the securitization process, technology can help streamline an otherwise segmented process. The flow of data and reconciliation between each point in the process is critical. One of the key issues concerning the technology used to perform due diligence involves the type of host systems that are in place. These systems can range from being fully integrated, where the loan origination through securitization modules are connected on an integrated system, to a disjointed system, where data is interfaced between different sub-systems for origination, structuring, securitizing and ongoing management reporting. For example, if a centralized system is used to originate a loan, service that loan, and provide management reporting, then the data is usually contained since there are fewer interfaces with fewer data manipulation processes. On the other hand, a decentralized system is constantly passing data from one sub-system to another, which usually leads to excessive computer time, manpower, and, depending upon how the data is transferred, data integrity errors.

A centralized database is often the best mechanism to ensure consistent data, whether it is used for preliminary structuring, presentation to rating agencies, loan due diligence, or prospectus reporting. A centralized database virtually guarantees that all groups involved in the securitization process use the same data. The advantage of using a non-centralized database, however, is that each group, using their own data and often their own software application, should reconcile to one anothers' databases, and this process of reconciliation can offer greater assurance as to the accuracy of the information.

Exhibit 10 illustrates a typical processing flow for a securitized transaction. The process has been divided into five phases which a typical securitized transaction would go through.

Exhibit 10: Typical Processing Flow for a Securitized Transaction

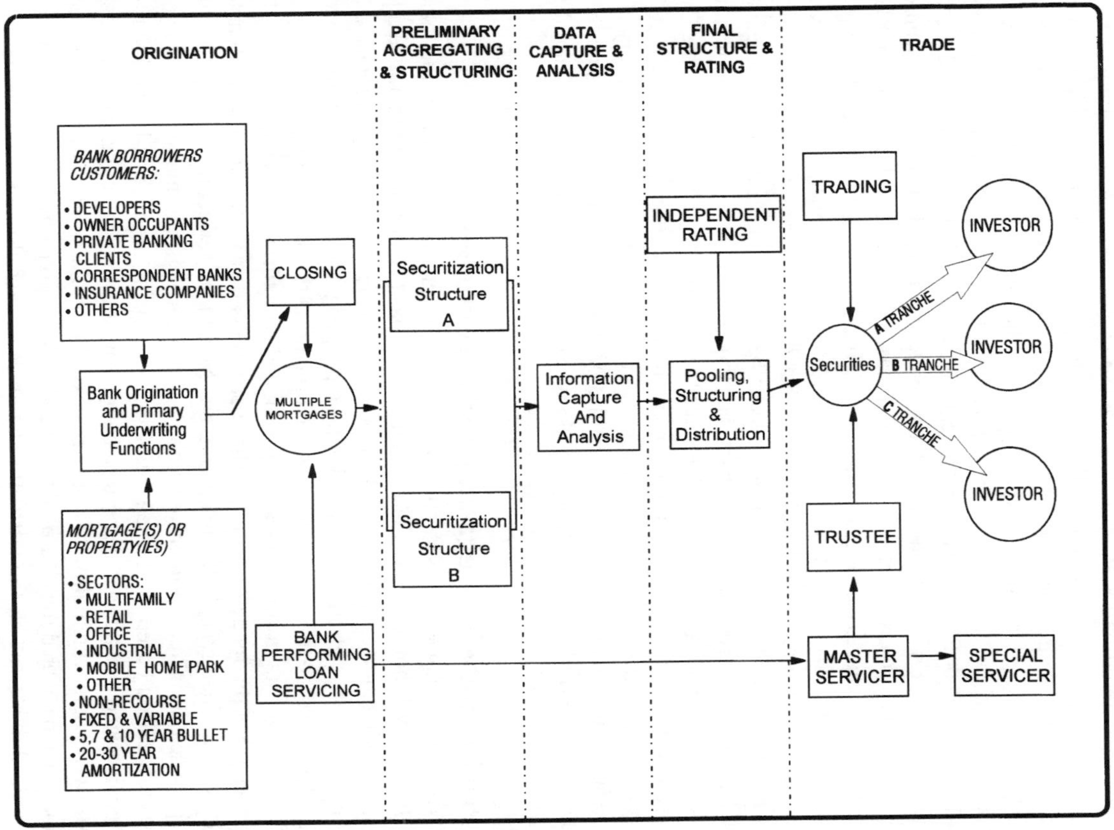

Origination

The origination phase primarily involves the underwriting of the commercial mortgage loan and the distribution of proceeds from the lender. The underwriting process consists of analyzing collateral and loan information. Ideally, this information can be directly entered into a distributed database using a Wide Area Network or remote access. As people in the field collect data, they can feed it into a central repository, thereby eliminating the need for re-entering the collected information at later stages into different systems with varying formats. If the infrastructure is not in place to support this method, spreadsheets or other types of templates, which can be developed in almost all major PC-based databases, can be used as long as strict standards are maintained. These templates can be sent via an electronic feed or by diskette where they are directly imported into a central database. Both of the above methods ensure greater data integrity and less manual work. In addition, many new technologies permit storage of loan documents with even greater ease. An emerging technology in this market is the compact disk (CD), which has developed from a read-only device to a write and read device. Loan documents can be scanned into a PC, downloaded onto a CD, and then stored for easy retrieval. The functionality for searching and finding key fields is still under development, but once this feature becomes available, the CD will become an extremely powerful instrument in the underwriting process.

The elimination of paper assists in reducing the number of purely clerical errors in the transfer of information. Third party due diligence can focus on the market worthiness of the consistency checks and flags can be built into the due diligence software to further reduce the risk of error.

Preliminary Aggregating and Structuring

Whether the loans to be securitized are newly originated or acquired, the loans are typically warehoused until a large enough pool has been created to facilitate a possible securitization execution. The loans in the pool are preliminarily aggregated based on a variety of criteria such as collateral type, geographic distribution, loan size, etc. as a precursor to the strategic process of structuring the transaction.

During preliminary aggregation and structuring, loans are selected based upon a specific range of criteria. These criteria can be restrictions on loan amount, LTV, term, loan type, balloon amount, etc. Many loan servicing systems now offer a "pool selection" component, whereby a set of loans is automatically extracted for securitization based upon the size of the pool or the number of loans. Even more sophisticated analysis can be performed by downloading loan information to database software tools which allow for greater flexibility in the process of pool selection. A loan may be tagged for a particular tranche and functionality. "What-if" scenarios can be used to stress test the portfolio and analyze cash flow projections based upon numerous variables, such as fluctuations in interest rates, prepayments, or default rates. Analysis can also be performed using spreadsheets; however, a database-type application is usually more suited to this type of analysis, given the complexity and volume of loans usually analyzed.

Data Capture and Analysis

It is very common to have an abundance of information about each loan at the time of its origination. Such information will have been gathered during the underwriting process. However, the loans continue to earn interest and make payments which require ongoing servicing until the actual closing of the securitization. In addition, new information such as updated operating statements, rent rolls, new lease agreements, etc. may become available during the period subsequent to origination but prior to issuance of securities. Such information will be accumulated by the issuer for use in offering materials.

A number of sources provide the central database with information. Although electronic feeds are usually faster, more efficient, and less costly and should be utilized whenever possible, manual feeds into central databases are still prevalent. Lack of standardization inhibits the complete computerization of data capture. Third party appraisals, for example, are usually in a non-standard format, since different appraisal companies use different forms and methods. Thus input from third party appraisals is inevitably manual. Financial statements usually follow the same course, as well as market studies and source documents. External market data is now currently available electronically and can be fed directly from one system to another, with minor manipulation.

Final Structure and Rating

Once the initial pool characteristics have been determined, the pool statistics and structuring alternatives can be developed in order to present the transaction to rating agencies. Such preliminary structural alternatives will allow the issuer, underwriter, and rating agency to better assess the economics of the transaction by optimizing the proceeds from the sale of securities.

Presentation of due diligence collateral data table preparation in a prospectus (or other type of offering circular) and to rating agencies has also improved tremendously as data manipulation tools have become easier to use. Currently, Excel, for example, allows for a variety of database type development activities, such as their new "pivot table" utilities which allow for dragging and dropping fields onto the x and y axis to create sophisticated stratifications of data. Spreadsheet technology has certain limitations, particularly when the portfolio is large. Database technology provides an opportunity for the more complex presentation of data for investor and rating agency reporting. Database software such as Paradox, Dbase, and Microsoft Access are off-the-shelf tools that are commonly used. Data collection and manipulation can be made in such a database software while spreadsheets can be linked for table generation. Currently there are query engines (such as Microsoft Query) that allow for seamless integration between databases and spreadsheets.

Utilizing leading edge technology is essential when modeling a complex securitization transaction.

There are numerous ways to model a securitization structure using different securitization modeling technology. For example, the prevalent tool used to model securitizations has been through the use of spreadsheet software such as Excel or proprietary C++ based models using a scripting language format to model complicated bond structures and prepayment penalty and yield maintenance formulas. It is important to use a model that is robust, user friendly, and flexible to handle complicated modeling assumptions. Models which are not flexible typically result in the securitization process becoming tedious and lacking integrity in the results.

The securitization cash flow model should be integrated in terms of the collateral amortization cash flows being linked to the bond structure and price/yield module to create vectors of default and yield tables. It is important for the model to calculate residual valuation and OID legending once the securitization structure has been finalized using settlement prices on the certificates. The residual valuation analytical tool should be linked to the cash flow model to increase efficiency and integrity of the results. Many times spreadsheet residual models fail to account for the REMIC and residual tax law and therefore the result simply becomes an inaccurate estimate.

Trade

Once the securitization transaction is closed on the settlement date, there is a Trustee, Master Servicer and Special Servicer in place responsible for ensuring the monthly reporting and processing to investors and residual holders. These parties provide on-going information in order to monitor the performance of the securities. Subordinate investors desire more analysis on the defaults on particular properties and stress testing prepayment lockout scenarios. It is important for these investors to have the analytical tools to make a smart investment decision in purchasing a security and in monitoring the future performance of the security. A senior bondholder will worry less about potential losses, since the subordination creates a substantial credit enhancement. The senior holder may be concerned about prepayments if there are no lockout restrictions. Therefore, the need to have sophisticated analytical tools to monitor the performance of the securities is more critical to the subordinate bondholders.

The trustee is responsible for calculating the monthly bond payment to certificateholders. Industry practice is for the trustee to model the bond payment priorities in a spreadsheet. The loan level information is then downloaded into the spreadsheet and the cash flows are passed on to the certificates based upon the bond paydown structure. A more sophisticated approach is to model the transaction in a C++ based scripting language incorporating all trigger events, lockouts, defaults, and yield maintenance formulas so there is no manipulating of the system in mid-stream.

The servicer is responsible for tracking all property performance information on a particular loan. A problem occurs when there are multiple sub-servicers using different report layouts and different software. Having a common reporting system for tracking and reporting property and loan performance information helps to minimize any problems related to the consolidation of information.

COMFORT LETTER

Issuers and underwriters typically require third party due diligence contractors to issue a written report in order to fully document the degree of due diligence that was performed. This report is retained along with other information to show that the issuer has made a responsible effort to establish the accuracy of the information being provided to investors. This report is typically referred to as a "comfort letter," but more specifically this letter describes the procedures which were performed and the results therefrom. The comfort letter will typically be addressed to the issuer and the underwriter to support their work. While the comfort letter is intended to be made available to investors, they are not included in the offering materials.

Chapter **19**

Legal Perspectives on Disclosure Issues for CMBS Investors

Michael R. Pfeifer, J.D.
Senior Litigation Partner
Wolf & Pfeifer, A Law Corporation

INTRODUCTION

In 1975, mortgage-backed securities did not exist. By 1995, Wall Street and the federally related agencies had created a huge market in mortgage-backed securities. According to most estimates, there are over $2.2 trillion in mortgage securities outstanding, with issuance of publicly rated residential mortgage pass-through securities reaching $542 billion by the end of 1994, and an additional $123 billion by the end of the first six months of 1995. By December 31, 1994, 64% of all residential mortgage originations, and over 40% of the existing residential mortgage stock, had moved into securities.[1]

In contrast, while the market in existing commercial mortgages has been estimated at over $800 billion, it has remained relatively untouched by securitization, with no more than 5% of the value of outstanding commercial mortgages having been securitized. The Mortgage Bankers Association of America estimates, however, that during 1994 and 1995, the volume of commercial mortgage securitization averaged about $20 billion per year, and that, even with the securitization activities of the Resolution Trust Corporation winding down, those levels are likely to continue.[2] Some market analysts believe the volume of commercial mortgage-backed securities ("CMBS") issued over the next four years is likely to double, with growth based on increased investor comfort and acceptance in the high yield sector.[3] With amendment

---

[1] Kenneth G. Lore, *Mortgage-Backed Securities* (Illinois: Clark Boardman Callahan, 1996), pp.1-7, 15.
[2] David Lereah, "Steady Growth in Commercial Sector," *Real Estate Finance Today* (December 18, 1995), p. 4.
[3] Lore, *Mortgage-Backed Securities*, pp. 2-58.

of the Secondary Mortgage Market Enhancement Act[4] ("SMMEA") in 1994 to include commercial and multifamily mortgages, the CMBS market appears poised to take off.

In this environment, it is important for Wall Street investors to understand that, although many (albeit wrongly) view the real estate collateral pooled for a residential MBS as homogeneous and similar in certain respects to corporate bonds, the same assumptions cannot be made for CMBS in light of the unique and diverse nature of commercial real estate. There are major differences in underwriting, appraisals, and loan documentation, as opposed to existing "Fannie Mae" or "Freddie Mac" standardized residential loan programs and market guidance. There are a host of different legal and regulatory issues involving investment authority, borrower structure and credit, and property zoning; the existence of leases and tenants as well as other interested third parties; greater insurance requirements; and a variety of different permissible prepayment risks.[5] Successful CMBS investment requires vast quantities of detailed information about these and many other matters. And while this fact is well understood by most CMBS investors (who are frequently large and sophisticated institutions), many are only dimly aware of the complicated legal mechanisms that generate this information, or the degree to which the rating agencies rely on those mechanisms to grant an "investment grade" label to a particular issue.

The purpose of this chapter is to provide some insight into those mechanisms by introducing the reader to the applicable securities laws, explaining how the disclosure requirements of those laws affect the conclusions of the various rating agencies, and outlining some of the legal issues with respect to information disclosure that investors face, not only in the purchase and sale of CMBS, but as existing certificateholders. The chapter concludes with an effort to identify some of the emerging CMBS disclosure issues that are even now beginning to impact investment decisions, and that will take on even greater importance over the next few years.

DISCLOSURE REQUIREMENTS OF THE SECURITIES LAWS

The Federal Securities Statutes of 1933 and 1934

The basic federal securities statutes were enacted as part of a whole system of reform legislation in the depression years immediately following the market crash of 1929-

---

[4] The Secondary Mortgage Market Enhancement Act of 1984 ("SMMEA") contains numerous provisions designed to increase participation by the private sector in the secondary market for mortgages. It provides for preemption of state securities laws and legal investment restrictions, changes to margin and borrowing requirements, use of mortgage-backed securities as collateral, and investment in "mortgage related securities" by depository institutions.

[5] See Joseph Philip Forte, "From Main Street to Wall Street: Commercial Mortgage-Backed Securities," *Property & Probate* (American Bar Association, January/February 1996), pp. 8,12; Joseph Philip Forte, "Commercial Mortgages in the Secondary Market," *Mortgage Banking* (October 1985) p. 37. See also, Michael R. Pfeifer, "Are Your Documents 'Standard'?" *Servicing Management* (February 1995), p. 70.

30. Following the crash, Congressional hearings were held to inquire into securities market practices, and several key pieces of reform legislation were enacted. The dominant theme of this legislation was the so-called "disclosure philosophy": that fully informed markets would be fairer markets. This philosophy was implemented in two seminal statutes: (1) *The Securities Act of 1933* (the "1933 Act") 15 U.S.C. §§ 77a-77aa, which regulates the distribution of securities by requiring comprehensive disclosures in connection with public offerings through registration statements filed with the Securities and Exchange Commission ("SEC"), and by requiring that a detailed prospectus be furnished to all investors; and (2) *The Securities Exchange Act of 1934* (the "1934 Act"), 15 U.S.C. §§ 78a-78ll, which deals primarily with trading of securities following initial distribution by regulating stock exchanges and other securities markets (as well as brokers and dealers), and by establishing broad anti-fraud and anti-manipulation standards. An integrated reporting system links disclosures made under the 1933 and 1934 Acts.

Applicability of these provisions depends on whether the instrument involved is a "security," which is defined basically the same in both Acts. Section 2(1) of the 1933 Act defines a security as follows:

"...unless the context otherwise requires — the term 'security' means any note..., bond..., evidence of indebtedness..., collateral trust certificate..., investment contract..., or, in general, any interest or instrument commonly known as a 'security,' or any certificate of interest or participation in...any of the foregoing."

Due to the nature of the instrument and the circumstances in which it is purchased, a certificate evidencing an ownership interest in a pool of mortgages almost always constitutes an "investment transaction," requiring the mortgage-backed certificate issued in the transaction to be treated as a "security" under federal securities laws. Thus, most CMBS investment vehicles, including "pass-through" securities, mortgage-backed bonds, collateralized mortgage obligations (CMOs), and real estate mortgage investment conduits (REMICs), are probably governed by the provisions of the 1933 and 1934 Acts.

Requirements of the 1933 Act Section 5(a) of the 1933 Act requires an effective registration statement before a security may be sold through instruments of interstate commerce, unless the security is exempt or sold in an exempt transaction. In addition, purchasers of a security in a registered offering must receive a prospectus that meets the requirements of the 1933 Act. The SEC must declare the registration statement effective before a security may be sold, but the Act does not provide for an SEC evaluation of the merits of securities offerings. Under "Regulation C," certain types of securities may be registered for an offering to be made on a continuous or delayed basis in the future. Such registration is often referred to as "Rule 415" or "Shelf" registration. "Exempt" securities include government, bank, and savings and loan offerings (but not those of their subsidiaries), certain promissory notes (and participation interests therein) originated by government regulated banking institutions and secured by a first lien on a single parcel of real estate, and so-called "private offerings" (defined in detail in "Regulation D") which may only be made on a limited basis to certain sophisticated and fully informed persons, usually a small number of wealthy or institutional investors. A "safe harbor" exception to the registration requirement has also been created under Rule 144A of the 1933 Act for "resales" by persons other than the issuer to institutional investors that meet certain criteria. And an additional exemption exists under Section 4(6) for offers or sales by an issuer solely to one or more accredited investors. This so-called "small offering" exemption is conditioned upon certain criteria, including a statutorily prescribed maximum purchase price of $5 million for the offering, the absence of public advertising, and the filing of certain specified notices with the SEC.

Section 11 of the 1933 Act imposes *absolute liability* on the issuer in a registered public offering of securities and, subject only to a "due diligence" defense, on all officers and directors of the issuer who sign the registration statement. Such liability is in favor of purchasers of the registered securities for any *untrue statement of a material fact or omission to state a material fact* in the registration statement. By way of damages, the plaintiff purchaser can recover the total amount he has invested, less any distributions received or value retained. Section 12(1) imposes such liability on those who offer or sell securities without the registration required by Section 5 of the Act, and Section 12(2) extends liability to offerors and sellers for false or misleading statements in prospectuses or other registration documents.

The standard of what is *"material"* has been defined by the SEC, in Rule 405, as those facts as *"to which there is a substantial likelihood that a reasonable investor would attach importance in determining whether to purchase the security registered."* The Supreme Court has applied the so-called *Northway* standard in determining materiality under several provisions of the securities laws and has held that this standard, originally adopted under Section 14 of the 1934 Act in a proxy solicitation context, is an appropriate uniform definition of materiality for other antifraud provisions of the federal securities laws. Under that test, a fact is material if there is "a substantial likelihood" that a reasonable shareholder would consider it important in making an investment (or voting) decision or "put another way," as the Supreme Court said, if the unknown or misstated fact, if correctly known, would have "significantly altered" the "total mix" of available information about the issuer and the security in question.

Requirements of the 1934 Act The 1934 Act requires public companies — generally defined as those with assets in excess of $5 million with equity securities held by at least 500 shareholders — to register with the SEC and to provide ongoing disclosure about their financial condition and other significant activities through filing with the SEC of quarterly and annual (10Q and 10K) reports, and in connection with specific events. As amended by the SMMEA, the 1934 Act also establishes margin requirements, determines whether CMBS must be registered under state securities laws, and whether the securities will be legal investments for certain institutional investors. But the most important provision of the 1934 Act for CMBS investors may be Section 10(b). That section makes it unlawful for any person, directly or indirectly, to use or employ any manipulative or deceptive device in connection with the purchase or sale of any security. Although Section 10(b) does not specifically provide for a private right of action, the courts have implied one.

Rule 10b-5 was adopted by the SEC pursuant to Section 10(b) of the 1934 Act. It prohibits, in connection with the purchase or sale of any security, the employment of any scheme or device to defraud; the engagement in any act, practice, or course of business that operates or would operate as a fraud or deceit, and more specifically, the making of any material misrepresentation or omission of a material fact "necessary in order to make the statements made, in the light of the circumstances under which they were made, not misleading."

Although elements of a Rule 10b-5 violation vary slightly from court to court, the following items must generally be established:

- The Defendant must have used an instrumentality of interstate commerce or of the mails or of any facility of interstate commerce;
- A material misrepresentation or omission, or other deceptive or manipulative device;
- In connection with the purchase or sale of any security;
- With deliberate or reckless intent on the part of the defendant;
- On which the plaintiff relied, to the extent that reliance is not presumed under the circumstances;
- Which caused injury to the plaintiff.

This Rule has been interpreted to create a federal civil private right of action in favor of any plaintiff defrauded in the purchase or sale of securities, and can also be the basis for criminal securities fraud prosecutions and injunctive action brought by the SEC to enforce future compliance and disgorge "ill-gotten" gains or otherwise "do equity" for past intentional or reckless noncompliance. Because of the broad impact of a Section 10(b) violation, these provisions have spawned a proliferation of class action lawsuits for fraud and alleged misuse of insider information.

Minimum SEC Disclosure Requirements In public offerings of securities, various forms adopted by the SEC establish minimum disclosure requirements. Issuers of mortgage-backed securities have been permitted to use Form S-11, which is used to register the securities of issuers whose primary business is acquiring or holding for investment interests in real estate or real estate companies. Usually, issuers of mortgage-backed securities choose to include in their registration statements additional information not required by SEC guidelines. And even for those securities that do not fall within the registration requirements of the 1933 and 1934 Acts, the required disclosures of Form S-11, derived from Regulations S-K and S-X, are instructive. These include: a description of the investment policies of the registrant and the underlying real estate collateral, the outstanding principal amounts, weighted average, remaining term to maturity, and interest rates of all mortgages in the pool, material aspects of the tax treatment of the registrant and the security holders, the arrangements made by the registrant with respect to the management of its real estate, purchase, sale and servicing of mortgages and investment advisory services, including detailed information about all companies retained to perform servicing functions, and financial statements and related information of the issuer.

Obviously, detailed information about the nature and performance characteristics of the underlying mortgage collateral is required. Disclosures regarding prepayment and credit characteristics of the collateral are the most important. The information provided commonly includes aggregate and average unpaid principal balance of certificates and loans, pool numbers where applicable, ranges of and weighted average coupon rates and remaining terms to maturity, weighted average life, and prepayment experience. For residential mortgages, it is not uncommon for issuers to use certain standard prepayment models and charts, but this is ordinarily not feasible for CMBS issues, where the mortgages may contain varying "lock out" provisions. Information from which the likelihood of repayment can be inferred, as opposed to the timing of such repayment, can include the terms of the mortgages, geographic location, loan to value ratios, delinquency and foreclosure information, to the extent available, state law limitations on enforcement, including redemption considerations and anti-deficiency statutes, number of loans and geographic dispersion, range of loan size, largest loan and largest loan as a percentage of the pool. Hazard and other insurance information is commonly included, and a variety of other more specialized items of information unique to commercial real estate, including methods of interest rate calculation and accrual, different adjustment and payment dates, caps and floors, cash flow structures and debt service coverage ratios, tenant and lease information and net operating income for the underlying projects, and environmental considerations. The issuer's goal should be to provide both accuracy and clarity in the prospectus disclosure, and investors should look for hypothetical examples as hallmarks of more meaningful disclosure.

The Trust Indenture Act of 1939

The Trust Indenture of 1939 (the "1939 Act") applies to the offering and sale of debt securities, and requires that all debt securities not subject to enumerated exceptions be supported by trust indentures that comply with detailed requirements specified in the Act. Commercial mortgage-backed securities that are issued as debt securities, such as collateralized mortgage obligations ("CMOs") must be issued under a qualified indenture. The provisions required for an indenture to be qualified originally had to be set forth in the indenture itself. Under the Trust Indenture Reform Act of 1990 ("Indenture Reform Act"), however, these provisions are now part of federal statutory law.

The 1939 Act also prescribes certain standards for trustees and additional disclosure requirements for a prospectus concerning the trustee and trust indenture. In order to secure approval of an indenture for a security that is required to be registered under the 1933 Act, the issuer of the debt security must file with the SEC a statement of eligibility and qualification of the trustee in addition to a registration statement. Under Section 305(b) of the Act, the SEC must refuse to permit a registration statement to become effective if it finds that a security subject to the 1939 Act to which the registration statement relates is not issued under a qualified indenture or the trustee is ineligible. Indentures must be qualified at the time the registration statement becomes effective but, under the Indenture Reform Act, the issuer may delay naming a trustee until the initial issuance of securities. Virtually all debt securities exempt under the 1933 Act are also exempt under the 1939 Act, although industry standards have generally adopted the requirements of the 1939 Act without regard to its applicability to a particular transaction.

The Investment Company Act of 1940

The Investment Company Act of 1940 (the "1940 Act") regulates "investment companies" (essentially defined as any issuer that "holds itself out as being engaged primarily...in the business of investing, reinvesting or trading in securities"). Most issuers of CMBS fall within this definition and must comply with the Act's provisions unless they meet the requirements of a few narrowly drawn exceptions, obtain a special exemption under Section 6(c) of the Act, or sell the securities in a private placement or "offshore" beyond the SEC's jurisdiction. The 1940 Act requires all nonexempt investment companies to file a detailed registration statement with the SEC containing extensive information about the issuer, its investment objectives, and its policies. The Act also contains various provisions which seek to regulate the management practices and capital adequacy of the issuer, the soundness of its accounting practices and financial statements, and its advertising and selling practices. What is most important for investors to know is that, because compliance with the Act is expensive and time consuming, and the Act's substantive review of related transactions may *prevent* typical structured finance transactions altogether, CMBS issuers often try to structure their transactions in such a way that the actual issuer will be either an exempt investment company or not an investment company at all.

The Secondary Mortgage Market Enhancement Act of 1984

The Secondary Mortgage Market Enhancement Act of 1984 ("SMMEA") was enacted for the purpose of increasing participation by the private sector in the secondary market for mortgages. It provides for preemption of state securities laws and legal investment restrictions, changes to margin and borrowing requirements, use of mortgage-backed securities as collateral, and investment in "mortgage related securities" by depository institutions. SMMEA was expanded in 1994 to include within the definition of "mortgage related securities" mortgages secured by property on which is located one or more commercial structures.

State Blue Sky Laws

In addition to the federal securities laws, most states have enacted their own laws regulating the offer and sale of securities. Often referred to as "blue sky laws" from an early Supreme Court case that recognized their attempt to control offerings that had "no more substance than so many feet of blue sky," these statutes usually contain requirements for state registration of nonexempt securities and various antifraud provisions. While most states have adopted the Uniform Securities Act, state by state variance necessitates careful planning by CMBS issuers and the additional administrative compliance burden can be quite expensive. That is why the SMMEA preemption of state securities laws is so important to many issuers. Under SMMEA, states were given 7 years to override this preemption, and a surprising number have done so. At least 10 have overridden the preemption of state registration provisions for "mortgage related securities." And no less than 17 have overridden the "legality of investment" provisions, all with respect to insurance companies only, however, limiting the amount of their assets that can be invested in mortgage related securities. A few states have also limited legal investment authority for other entities such as state chartered banks and savings associations. In each instance, CMBS investors may wish to investigate the extent to which their own state's laws have been preempted by SMMEA.

Insider Trading and Securities Fraud Enforcement Act of 1988

Although Rule 10b-5 under the 1934 Act does not expressly address trading on the basis of material non-public information, the courts have found such activity to be in fact a violation. In the leading case of *SEC v. Texas Gulf Sulfur Co*, the Court of Appeals for the Second Circuit found that certain officers, directors and employees of "TGS" had violated Rule 10b-5 by purchasing TGS stock or facilitating the purchase by others through "tipping," without disclosing to the general public material information concerning the company's discovery of a possible ore strike. The Court held that an "insider," who possessed material inside information, "must either disclose it to the investing public, or, if he is disabled from disclosing it in order to protect a corporate confidence, or chooses not to do so, must abstain from trading in or recommending the securities concerned while such information remains undisclosed." The Insider Trading and Securities Fraud Enforcement Act of 1988, enacted in response to various well publicized scandals in the second half of the decade, expanded the civil penalty exposure for insider trading liability by authorizing the SEC to seek such penalties against "controlling persons" of up to three times the profit gained or loss avoided by the unlawful trading or tipping.

The Private Securities Litigation Reform Act of 1995

In late December of 1995, Congress overrode a Presidential veto to pass the Private Securities Litigation Reform Act of 1995 (the "1995 Act"), for the stated purpose of "reforming Federal securities litigation." Characterized by some as "the most far reaching change in five decades in laws affecting the liability of Wall Street," the 1995 Act amends the 1933 and 1934 Acts by creating a "safe harbor" to issuers for certain predictions about the future performance of their securities, tightens the pleading requirements for private securities fraud cases to mandate more specific allegations, and limits the liabilities of accounting firms and underwriters to a percentage of blame for any alleged fraud. The Act also limits recoverable damages in private securities fraud cases, severely restricts securities law class action suits, imposes "mandatory" sanctions on attorneys who bring frivolous lawsuits, and permits defendants to be held "jointly and severally liable" only when they "knowingly" commit a securities law violation. And while the Act provides for further study and a report by the SEC on whether senior citizens or qualified retirement plans require greater protection against securities fraud, the Act also amends the Racketeer Influenced and Corrupt Organizations Act ("RICO") to eliminate reliance on any conduct that would have been actionable as civil fraud in the purchase or sale of securities to establish a violation of the statute. The degree to which the changes made by the 1995 Act will affect CMBS investors, many of whom are institutions rather than individuals, remains to be seen.

ROLE OF THE RATING AGENCIES

Under SMMEA, a security must, among other things, be rated in one of the two highest rating categories by at least one nationally recognized rating organization to qualify as a "mortgage related security," and thereby reap the benefits of the statute's federal preemption of state securities laws and other provisions. Beyond this statutory requirement, capital market investors generally place enormous reliance on the rating that the credit rating agencies assign to a particular security issue. Investors rely on the rating because the agencies perform their own tests on the mortgage pool, including analysis of the mortgage documents, mortgaged property, tax structure, loan servicing and administration issues, as well as the likelihood of timely repayment using historical loan experience for the collateral type and its own statistical databases.[6] This relieves the investor of the tremendous burden and expense of independent investigation of basic disclosure information.

    The four credit rating agencies are Standard and Poor's, Moody's Investors Service, Fitch Investors Service, and Duff and Phelps. Each company has developed its own criteria and methodology for rating transactions. These are quite elaborate and a detailed discussion is impossible here. Their focus, however, is on the two primary risks associated with long term obligations: the risk of nonpayment or partial payment and the risk of late payment of the securities. Normally, the agencies pursue a multi-level analysis which includes (1) a review of the legal structure of the security offering; (2) a review of the credit risks to the investor; and (3) an analysis of the sufficiency of credit protection for the investor based on the credit risks in the transaction. These, in turn, determine the type and degree of credit support required by the transaction, which may include over col-

---

[6] Forte, "From Main Street to Wall Street: Commercial Mortgage-Backed Securities," pp. 12.

lateralization, pool insurance, mortgage insurance, guarantees, reserve funds or required cash advances.[7]

What some investors fail to realize, however, is that the agency ratings are only as good as the accuracy and currency of the data given to them by the issuer, supplemented of course by their own research. The fact, however, that each rating agency uses different modes of analysis to arrive at a given rating is clear evidence that there is no objective certainty in the process. This is why many sophisticated CMBS investors want to perform their own analysis on the raw data, and why an understanding of the disclosure obligations of issuers under the securities laws will always remain important.

DISCLOSURE ISSUES
FOR EXISTING CERTIFICATE HOLDERS

It is not enough for investors to be concerned with disclosure of information merely at the security issuance stage. As investments mature, the underlying mortgages securing the investment are also maturing. In CMBS, the complexity and dynamic nature of income property mortgages make the collateral pool subject to a vast array of subtle changes which may materially affect the viability of the investment. Many investors who recognize this are creating a tremendous demand for loan level, collateral level, and even borrower level information from commercial mortgage servicers. This is creating a host of dilemmas for servicers.[8]

In almost every instance, the relationship between the investor and servicer is one of "agency," in which the servicer as agent owes to its principal, the investor, the highest duty of loyalty and fidelity. This basic agency relationship is the source of a "fiduciary" duty" — to place the investor's interests above those of the servicer. The terms of this relationship are almost always defined by a written contract. In the commercial context, this is the Correspondent Agreement or Pooling and Servicing Agreement. In the residential context, the relationship is most often with one of the secondary market agencies, Fannie Mae, Freddie Mac or Ginnie Mae. In the residential MBS market, lengthy and detailed Seller/Servicer Guides define the duties a servicer has with respect to the handling of information it obtains. Whether commercial or residential, however, the written requirement is usually for total and complete disclosure on demand of every bit of information in the servicer's possession at any reasonable time and in whatever format requested by the investor. (See e.g., Freddie Mac Guide, Vol. 2, Ch. 51.9; Fannie Mae Servicing Guide, Vol.I, 403)

The fiduciary duties created by a relationship of agency give rise to the potential liability of servicers for what is known as "constructive fraud," in the event

---

[7] Lore, *Mortgage-Backed Securities*, pp. 9-3, 4.
[8] See Michael R. Pfeifer, "Sharing Secrets: Emerging Legal Risks In the Handling of "Non-Public" Mortgage Servicing Information," *Mortgage Banking* (December 1995) p. 67.

any information transmitted to the investor is inaccurate or misleading and the investor relies on it to its detriment. The existence of a fiduciary relationship eliminates the normal requirement for a fraud claim that the party responsible for misinformation have intended to deceive or mislead. In such a context, intent is presumed. This opens up the possibility of punitive damages against a servicer for "fraud" in connection with the disclosure of erroneous information, even if there is no "self-dealing," and even if there is no actual intent to deceive.

The situation is difficult enough in a straightforward servicer/investor relationship. The real difficulties occur, however, when a loan portfolio is securitized and a trustee is interposed between the servicer and investor/certificate holder. The purpose of a trustee in structured finance is to provide only one master for the servicer. But trustees are often reluctant or ill equipped to answer certificate holder "after-issue" questions about the status of the whole portfolio or individual loans. So certificate holders increasingly find themselves in the position of being able to get answers from no one. From a CMBS Buyers Meeting in Boston, that occurred in April, 1995, and was attended by many of the largest institutional investors in the country, the following comment appears in the minutes: "Many in the group would like to see servicers work directly for the certificate holders. In most cases, servicers report to trustees. A number of CMBS buyers are not satisfied with the answers (or lack of answers) they receive from trustees and want direct access to servicers."

But there are grave problems for servicers in dealing directly with certificate holders. While the ultimate fiduciary duties of agency are likely to remain the same, the servicer/agent becomes accountable to a potentially far larger group of principals, whose various interests may be quite diverse. Does the servicer's fiduciary duty extend only to the trustee or to the individual certificate holders? When there is a conflict, who does the servicer answer to? And what about the nightmare situation for the servicer where there are multiple tranched classes of certificate holders? Are some more equal than others? These issues are only now beginning to be addressed by the courts and there are certainly no clear or reliable guidelines anywhere in the law.

Another problem with having servicers provide information directly to certificate holders in the mortgage-backed securities context is the issue of "insider trading." Where there are multiple certificate holders, or multiple classes of certificate holders, and otherwise non-public information is given only to some — or only to those who ask for it — and the information is then used or relied on for the purpose of making decisions about holding or selling securities, servicers find themselves in the strange position of owing a fiduciary duty of disclosure to existing investors, while at the same time potentially violating the securities laws' prohibitions against "tipping" to someone in a position to trade on the information. The conflict of interest is made even more vexing by the new industry trend — at least in the commercial sector — of *requiring* servicers to purchase for their own account the subordinate or "First Loss" position in a new security issue, as a condition precedent for "appointment" as servicer on the transaction. How can a careful servicer avoid liability for breach of its fiduciary duties when the CMBS market actually *requires* the servicer to purchase for its own account an interest in the security it is to service?   Again, since there is little or no case law on this issue, servicers have good reason to be concerned about their potential liability, while investors are likely to remain frustrated by servicers' reluctance to talk to them.

EMERGING CMBS DISCLOSURE ISSUES

Wall Street's demands on issuers and servicers for more detailed and current information are such that many of larger issuers and servicers are developing elaborate computerized "mortgage information warehouses" from which investors and rating agencies can withdraw current information about CMBS portfolio assets. These systems offer on-line access to investors to examine collateral characteristics and ongoing after-issue performance on some kind of "real time" basis. In some, certificate holders of CMBS transactions and the general public are restricted to portfolio level information updated monthly, weekly, or even daily, while loan and property level information is available to market participants who sign a confidentiality agreement. Many issuers and servicers consider implementation of such systems to be a competitive necessity and, accordingly, there is no additional cost to investors. Responding to the same competitive pressures, some servicers have begun setting up electronic "bulletin boards" on the Internet accessible with a password which expires when the investor's interest is transferred. The legal issues associated with implementation of such systems have only just begun to be explored.

Another intriguing development, because of the apparent conflicts of interest involved, is the joint venture recently formed by REIS Reports Inc. and Standard & Poor's Corp. as reported in the June 19, 1995 issue of *Commercial Mortgage Alert,* to provide investors with an "early warning" about the likelihood of losses on CMBS. Responding to what they claim are strong investor demands for timely delinquency and remittance data, updated rent rolls, borrower financial statements, and improved cash-flow forecasting, REIS and S&P have apparently decided to "fill a void" in the market *themselves* rather than waiting for servicers to do so. In offering the service, REIS is supposed to be tapping its own database, although the published report on the venture states that "information on property financial statements and rent rolls...can be plugged in if servicers make it available." Problems can arise, however, if servicers are asked to provide such non-public information on a "confidential basis," like other information is usually provided. The motivation for servicers' to comply with such requests, even when they are not on a confidential basis, are obvious when the servicer itself is being rated by the very agency urgently requesting the information, and that rating is essential for the servicer's survival. The prevalence of "rated servicing" in the CMBS market now makes such conflicts much more likely.

Another source of emerging developments are the various trade industry initiatives underway to help streamline the information disclosure process and formulate solutions to the various conflict of interest problems outlined above. These include the development of standardized data collection and reporting formats such as the Commercial Real Estate Asset Management ("CREAM") database developed by the MBA's Commercial Real Estate Finance Committee, and the Sample Certificate holder/Rating Agency Report, and standardized loan document formats being developed separately by the Making the Market Work group, a committee of a joint industry group called the "Capital Consortium" composed of representatives from the MBA, the National Realty Committee and the National Association of Realtors®. In an effort to provide more concrete guidelines for servicers in the management and disclosure of non-public servicing information, the Real Estate Capital Resources Association ("RECRA"), with the participation of the some of the industry's leading commercial servicers and trustees, has developed an elaborate data element matrix with specific suggestions for what data should be disclosed to whom, along with sample clauses for insertion into a complete model Pooling and Servicing Agreement. Input was solicited from investors, trustees, other servicers, and rating agencies, and refinements based on that input, including extensive annotations, are presently underway to both the matrix and sample Agreement.

Finally, the most dynamic source of emerging CMBS disclosure issues in the next few years is likely to be the inherent conflict between the federal securities statutes and the multiplicity of state laws and regulations pertaining to the underlying commercial real estate mortgage collateral. These include differences in state laws affecting the validity and enforceability of mortgages generally, usury restrictions, foreclosure requirements and timeframes, hazardous waste and environmental liability laws, zoning and land use laws, and a host of other statutes and regulations too numerous to mention that make commercial real estate collateral anything but simple and homogeneous.

CONCLUSION

As the CMBS market continues to expand, investors are likely to confront ever more complex challenges in their attempts to understand and evaluate the exotic investment vehicles that Wall Street has devised to provide greater liquidity in the financing of commercial real estate. So far, there are real questions about the ability of the disclosure laws to keep up with what investors are being asked to sink their money into. While it is possible that this situation could change, past history teaches that remedial changes to the securities laws normally do not occur until after a considerable number of investors have been "burned." In the CMBS market, the stakes are high and only if investors pay the utmost attention to disclosure issues are they likely to escape the flames.

Chapter **20**

€volving Generally Accepted Accounting Principles for Issuers of and Investors in CMBS

David Baranick, C.P.A.
Director
Real Estate Industry Services Group
Price Waterhouse LLP

Israel Snow, C.P.A.
Manager
Real Estate Industry Services Group
Price Waterhouse LLP

INTRODUCTION

Ideally, corporate financial statements should provide relevant and reliable financial information to the users of those statements. Certainly, one would assume that for all companies similar transactions would be reflected in a comparable manner. Generally Accepted Accounting Principles (GAAP), the conventions, rules and procedures that define accepted accounting practice at a particular time, places a premium on comparability and consistency of financial reporting and strives to ensure "representational faithfulness" — the validity of the representation of transactions and events in the financial statements. However, in determining the appropriate accounting for eco-

383

nomic events, GAAP concedes a large role to "estimation" and "reasonableness of presentation." Consequently, there is often a wide range of subjectivity inherent to financial reporting. This is particularly true for new and emerging business areas. As transactions become more complex and new products enter the financial markets, the accountant is often left without authoritative guidance governing the appropriate manner in which to reflect a specific transaction. The proliferation of securitizations in the capital markets and the multitude of different instruments that are currently trading provides a primary example of the difficulties that accountants encounter as they try to apply static GAAP rules while still ensuring the representational faithfulness of the financial report.

There are several broad theoretical questions that underlie the determination of the appropriate accounting associated with the issuance and sale of commercial mortgage-backed securities (CMBS). How significant a role should the legal form of the transaction play in determining the accounting treatment? Should there be symmetry between the accounting of the issuer and the accounting of the investor — that is, must we ensure that the same asset not be recorded in the accounts of two entities? What are the fundamental characteristics of ownership that would trigger the recording of a sale or purchase and the resultant transference of an asset from one entity to another for accounting purposes? One may argue that legal title would be a reasonable starting point of this discussion. However, we must clearly consider other factors including (i) which entity enjoys the economic benefits of ownership, (ii) which entity bears the risks associated with ownership of the asset and (iii) where a "seller" retains continuing "involvement" with an asset, at what point does the involvement really amount to continued ownership? Finally, once ownership of an asset is determined, on what basis should the resultant asset be recorded — historical cost, fair market value or some other valuation methodology? These conceptual questions form the foundation underlying the evolving GAAP accounting for both issuers of and investors in CMBS.

During June 1996, the Financial Accounting Standards Board (FASB) approved Statement of Financial Accounting Standards No. 125, "Accounting for Transfers and Servicing of Financial Assets and Extinguishments of Liabilities" (SFAS No. 125). The goal of the FASB in issuing SFAS No. 125 was to address some of the theoretical deficiencies in the accounting that arose as a result of the complexity of the transactions that have evolved since the issuance of the pre-1997 accounting literature. SFAS No. 125 is effective for transactions that take place after December 31, 1996 and is to be adopted only prospectively. Companies will not be permitted to elect early adoption, and transactions occurring before December 31, 1996, will continue to be recorded in accordance with the previous pronouncements (hereafter referred to as "pre-1997 accounting"). As a result, the user of financial statements will be required to understand the provisions of both the pre-1997 accounting and SFAS No. 125.

Prior to analyzing the provisions of SFAS No. 125, we will examine how the pre-1997 accounting standards addressed the above questions from the perspectives of both the issuer and the investor. We will discuss the pre-1997 accounting and analyze certain aspects of these transactions for which the pre-1997 accounting provides no specific guidance due to the inability of these standards to anticipate the multitude of permutations of these transactions that have entered the capital markets. With this background we will be able to summarize and examine the provisions of SFAS No. 125 as it modifies and addresses the shortcomings of the pre-1997 accounting standards.

PRE-1997 ACCOUNTING GUIDANCE: ISSUER PERSPECTIVE

From the perspective of the issuer of CMBS, the primary authoritative pre-1997 accounting pronouncements are Statement of Financial Accounting Standards No. 77, "Reporting by Transferors for Transfers of Receivables with Recourse" (SFAS No. 77), issued by the FASB in December 1983 and FASB Technical Bulletin No. 85-2, "Accounting for Collateralized Mortgage Obligations" (TB 85-2), issued in 1985. What is perhaps most unique about this pair of pronouncements is their emphasis on the legal form of the transaction. SFAS No. 77 applies only to "transfers of receivables with recourse that purport to be sales of receivables." To apply SFAS No. 77 to a transaction, the transaction must take the legal form of a sale. After this prerequisite is met, three criteria must be met to enable the transferor to account for the transfer as a sale. Similarly, TB 85-2 presumes that all collateralized mortgage obligations (CMOs) are borrowings that should be recorded as liabilities in the issuer's financial statements — since in legal form, such transactions are collateralized loans. This presumptive borrowing can be overcome but only in the circumstances stipulated by TB 85-2. Of particular note is that the SFAS No. 77 criteria and the TB 85-2 criteria are not substantively the same.

For transfers of receivables that purport to be sales, SFAS No. 77 stipulates that there are three general conditions that must be met for the issuer to record a sale of the receivables, remove the asset from the accounts and record any gain or loss resulting from the transaction: (i) the transferor must surrender control of the future benefits of the assets, (ii) the transferor's obligations under the recourse provisions can be reasonably estimated and (iii) the transferee cannot require the transferor to repurchase the assets sold.

Surrender of Control

The first criteria for sale treatment is that the seller/transferor must surrender control of the future economic benefits embodied in the receivables. This implies that while one entity may have title to the mortgages, the entity that owns the mortgage in substance is the entity that will benefit from the asset in the future and can deny or regulate access to that benefit by others. This criteria has several implications. Firstly, in certain instances the sponsor will retain servicing rights. Generally, service contracts do not leave control in the hands of the sponsor. However, if the purchaser cannot unilaterally replace the sponsor, it is then essential to determine what the underlying substance of the transaction is to determine whether control over the mortgages has really passed to the purchaser. Secondly, if the transferor retains an option to repurchase the receivables, this will generally imply that control has not passed. On the other hand, if the transferor retains a right of first refusal, this does not preclude a conclusion that control has passed. In this case, the transferor cannot act unilaterally — he can exercise his right only after an independent offer from an unrelated third party has been tendered.

Special Purpose Entities Some of the most difficult issues that result from the requirement that control is relinquished relate to complexities in the nature of securitization transactions that were not anticipated by the FASB in 1983. At that time, special purpose entities (SPEs), such as trusts issuing undivided interests in a pool of mortgages or minimally capitalized corporations issuing debt, had not yet been developed. While the form of the transfer of the mortgages to an SPE may comply with the SFAS No. 77 sales criteria, it is often difficult to determine who substantively controls the SPE. The Securities and Exchange Commission (SEC) believes that the mere insertion of an SPE should not change the underlying accounting for the transaction. The view of the SEC is that the key question regarding SPEs is whether they should be consolidated in the sponsor's financial statements (i.e., whether they are, in fact, a direct part of the sponsor). The SEC's position as stated in the FASB's Emerging Issues Task Force (EITF) Topic D-14, "Transactions Involving Special Purpose Entities," is as follows:

> Generally, the SEC staff believes that for nonconsolidation and sales recognition by the sponsor or transferor to be appropriate, the majority owner (or owners) of the SPE must be an independent third party who has made a substantive capital investment in the SPE, has control of the SPE, and has substantive risks and rewards of ownership of the assets of the SPE (including residuals). Conversely, the SEC staff believes that nonconsolidation and sales recognition are not appropriate by the sponsor or transferor when the majority owner of the SPE makes only a nominal capital investment, the activities of the SPE are virtually all on the sponsor's or transferor's behalf, and the substantive risks and rewards of the assets or the debt of the SPE rest directly or indirectly with the sponsor or transferor.

It is important to note here that the FASB has issued a separate exposure draft, entitled "Consolidated Financial Statements: Policies and Procedures," addressing consolidation issues. In this proposed standard, the FASB takes the position that a company must consolidate all entities that it controls. The proposed standard defines control and provides detailed guidance for its application. With respect to SPEs, the proposed standard states that "the activities and use of assets of special-purpose entities established to transfer interests in financial assets often are strictly limited by their creating instruments, and some may be examples where sponsors have effective control." REMIC structures, however, typically relieve issuers of control over the financial assets.

The Tax Reform Act of 1986 (the Act) established the Real Estate Mortgage Investment Conduit (REMIC) as a passthrough vehicle for the purpose of issuing multiple-class real estate mortgage-backed securities. The Act permitted the use of tranche structures as a credit enhancement feature for private label passthroughs. As a result, most transactions that qualify are structured as a REMIC and incorporate the use of an SPE.

Risks and Benefits of Ownership From a theoretical perspective, there are those who argue that the degree of risk retained by the sponsor should be evaluated as an element of determining whether a sale should be recognized. They believe that the benefits and risks of ownership are inseparable. However, the approach taken by SFAS No. 77 is that the benefits and risks of ownership can indeed be separated. As outlined above, the second criteria for sales recognition is that the recourse provisions can be reasonably estimated. Thus, the degree of risk inherent in the retention of recourse does not preclude sales treatment -- it must merely be quantified. We record a sale and simply provide a reserve or allowance for the expected loss under the recourse provisions. It is important to note that while the Office of Thrift Supervision follows GAAP as established by SFAS No. 77, other agencies permit banks and certain other financial institutions for regulatory purposes to record transfers of receivables with recourse as a sale only when the transferor (a) retains *no risk* of loss from the assets transferred and (b) has no obligation for the payment of principal or interest on the assets transferred. These regulatory bodies are reluctant to segregate the benefits and the risks of ownership. Also of note is that insurance company regulations are substantially consistent with GAAP. This chapter is focusing solely on GAAP reporting requirements and does not address conventions applicable to regulated entities.

Credit Enhancement Features and Recourse

The nature of the credit enhancement features that accompany many issues of CMBS are such that they could not have been anticipated by the authors of SFAS No. 77 in 1983. Consequently, the interpretation of whether these features constitute mere recourse provisions and thus do not preclude sales treatment or are something other than mere recourse is quite complex.

SFAS No. 77 defines recourse as "the right of a transferee of receivables to receive payment from the transferor of those receivables for (a) failure of the debtors to pay when due, (b) the effect of prepayments, or (c) adjustments resulting from defects in the eligibility of the transferred receivables." While failure of debtors to pay when due is a fairly straightforward concept, the "effect of prepayments" is not as simple. For instance, if the seller guarantees a prescribed timing for the collection of receivables to minimize the investor's prepayment risk, this provision may be construed as a form of payment resulting from the effects of prepayment. However, while sellers can guarantee yields or rates of return and still record a sale, the mortgage (receivable) must be sold for its entire contractual payment schedule.

Over Collateralization Another credit enhancement feature not addressed by SFAS No. 77 is over collateralization. This is a form of recourse that provides the purchaser with protection if the purchaser doubts the financial stability of the seller. The question arises, however, as to how the seller should account for the excess mortgages serving as the collateral. In this case, although there is no authoritative guidance, these assets are sometimes classified in the balance sheet of the seller with a caption similar to "sold under agreement to repurchase."

Indemnification As the markets have evolved, transferors now provide indemnification for many matters beyond those outlined in SFAS No. 77. These items include subordinated participations, put options, holdback reserves, deposits of excess servicing fees in escrow accounts, and indemnifications against risks of certain events occurring including possible denial of REMIC status or changes in tax laws. SFAS No. 77 appears to preclude some of these circumstances from employing sale treatment. Some practitioners argue that the possibility of such events happening are remote and, accordingly, such indemnifications should not preclude sales treatment. Such remote possibilities may be provided for in a contractual agreement in order to make a purchaser/investor more comfortable with their investment at a minimal potential cost to the issuer. However, in most instances, the indemnification provisions may indicate too much continuing involvement on the part of the transferor.

Estimation

This leads us to the intricacies of the estimation process. If the seller's obligations under the recourse provisions cannot be reasonably estimated, sales treatment will be denied. Consequently, the ability to estimate the obligation is of great significance. For instance, if the pool of mortgages includes a substantial amount of mortgages from one entity, it may be necessary for the sponsor to provide additional guarantees relative to the default risk associated with the entity. The issuer may then agree to buy back that entity's mortgages in the event of a ratings drop. However, this would be difficult to estimate since the probability of a company being downgraded is difficult to assess. If the seller desired sales treatment, he may as an alternative agree to only provide additional collateral in the event of a ratings downgrade. The requirement to provide additional collateral would then only require the seller to update loss estimation — sales treatment would be preserved.

Another complication that arises in the estimation process relates to the timing of the expected payments under the recourse provisions. In certain cases, the transferor's expected payout may not be expected to occur for a number of years. In these cases, then, it may be appropriate to record initially only the "present value" of the expected recourse payments with interest expense to accrue periodically on the balance outstanding under the recourse provisions. In cases where the timing of the future cash flows could be reasonably estimated, the EITF accepted this approach in

EITF Issue No. 92-2, "Measuring Loss Accruals by Transferors for Transfers of Receivables with Recourse."

The guidelines for estimating the seller's loss relating to the recourse provisions are outlined in EITF Issue No. 92-2. From a theoretical perspective, the objective is to measure the fair value of the retained recourse obligation at the date of the transaction. The liability should include all probable credit losses over the life of the receivables. Such obligations may be recognized on a present value basis if the timing of the estimated cash flows can be reasonably estimated. If the undiscounted amount of the recourse obligation differs materially from the discounted amount, then the undiscounted amount should be disclosed in the notes to the financial statements.

As with all accounting estimates, certain qualitative judgements will need to be made by the management of the company in determining a probable future cost to the seller of the recourse provisions. Management will have to consider factors including the type and number of loans included in the underlying asset pool, the servicing history and overall quality of the mortgages, the age of the loans, the extent of portfolio diversification (such as geographic, number of different borrowers, industry of borrowers, etc.) as well as the general credit risk with respect to the commercial mortgages.

Repurchase Provisions

If there are clauses requiring a transferor to repurchase assets sold, sales treatment is generally denied under SFAS No. 77. An exception to this is where there is a cleanup call. A cleanup call is an option held by the servicer, who may be the transferor, to repurchase the remaining mortgages when the outstanding balance falls to a level at which the cost of servicing those receivables becomes unreasonable. If such interests are not significant to the transferor, SFAS No. 77 does not preclude sales treatment. However, EITF Issue No. 89-2, "Maximum Maturity Guarantees on Transfers of Receivables with Recourse," clarifies this by requiring that the determination of whether such interests are significant to the transferor must be based upon the contractual payment schedule and not on the seller's expectations of future outstanding balances based on estimates of prepayments.

Collateralized Mortgage Obligations

As noted above, TB 85-2 establishes the presumption that all CMOs are borrowings that should be reported as liabilities in the issuer's financial statements. CMOs are recorded as a liability and the related mortgages remain as assets unless all of the following conditions are met:

- Neither the issuer nor its affiliates have the right or obligation to substitute collateral or obtain it by calling the obligation. An exception is made for cleanup calls of small amounts.
- The expected residual interest is nominal.
- The investor can look solely to the issuer's assets or third parties (such as insurers or guarantors) for repayment of both principal and interest on the

obligation, and neither the sponsor of the issuer nor its affiliates are secondarily liable.

• Neither the issuer nor its affiliates can be required to redeem the obligation prior to its stated maturity other than through normal paythrough of the collections.

If the above conditions are met, then the presumption of the CMO as a borrowing can be overcome since (1) all but a nominal portion of the future economic benefits from the underlying mortgage loans are irrevocably passed to the investors and (2) no affiliate of the issuer can be obligated to make future payments with respect to the CMO obligation. These criteria differ substantially from the SFAS No. 77 criteria outlined above. Exhibit 1 is a comparison of SFAS No. 77 and TB 85-2.

CURRENT AUTHORITATIVE ACCOUNTING GUIDANCE: INVESTOR PERSPECTIVE

Until this point, the discussion has focused on the pre-1997 accounting treatment for transactions in CMBS from the perspective of the seller. All the issues relating to whether a sale has occurred are relevant only to the seller. Clearly, if an investor invests in trust certificates or in passthrough bonds, it would be inappropriate for this investor to record a loan to the trust or corporation. Thus, based upon the pre-1997 accounting literature, there is no symmetry between the investor and sponsor accounting for these transactions. The issues relating to the accounting from the investor's perspective are issues that apply globally to any investment in debt securities of a third party entity (in this case the SPE). With reference to such investments, the FASB issued Statement No. 115, "Accounting for Certain Investments in Debt and Equity Securities" (SFAS No. 115). SFAS No. 115 applies to all entities including banks and other financial institutions except for qualified not-for-profit organizations. SFAS No. 115 specifically states that from the perspective of the investor, CMOs and REMICS are always debt securities (regardless of whether the issuer classifies them as debt or equity). However, it is important to note that SFAS No. 115 provides a precise definition of debt securities. Consequently, any complex structure should be reviewed for conformity to the required legal form of the transaction before SFAS No. 115 is applied. The issuance of SFAS No. 125 has not substantially modified the accounting for CMBS from the investor's perspective.

Classifications of SFAS No. 115

In general, the financial statement classification of an investment in debt securities is not determined by the nature of the instrument invested in. Thus, two companies, or for that matter even one company, can own two trust certificates or bonds in the same pool and still classify them differently. This arises because the focal point of determining the accounting treatment rests in management's plans for holding the assets. SFAS No. 115 divides investments into three broad classifications: (i) held-to-maturity securities, (ii) trading securities and (iii) available-for-sale securities.

Exhibit 1: Comparison of SFAS No. 77 and TB 85-2

	SFAS No. 77	TB 85-2
Primary factor considered for determination of accounting.	Transaction purports to be a sale.	Transaction structured as a collateralized borrowing.
Impact of recourse provisions to seller for credit losses and effect of changing interest rates.	Does not preclude sales treatment.	Even if no such recourse provision, may still be construed as a borrowing.
Impact of the retention of an interest in the receivables by the seller.	Even retention of a substantial interest does not preclude sales treatment of the remaining interests.	More than a nominal interest retained precludes sales treatment.
Recording of residual interests (resulting from rate spread).	Permitted.	Not permitted.
Application to CMBS structured as debt securities, in practice.	Generally, not applied.	Applied when the sponsor retains any interest, however minor, in the pool.
Application to CMBS structured as participations, in practice.	Applied even if the seller retained recourse on some of the participations.	Generally, not applied.

Held-to-Maturity Securities When an investor has the positive intent to hold an investment to its maturity (a mere absence of intent to sell is insufficient) and has the financial ability to do so, then the asset is classified as a "held-to-maturity" security. If the investor would sell the investment in response to changes in market interest rates, changes in the security's prepayment risk, changes in the availability of and yield on alternative investments, changes in the foreign currency risk or change in the entity's own needs for liquidity, its funding sources and terms, then the investment cannot be classified as held to maturity. As implied by the classification, sales out of this account should be rare; however, sales of the "tail portion" of CMBS may not be a violation of the investment's status as held-to-maturity. SFAS No. 115 stipulates that if 85% of the principal balance outstanding at the acquisition has been collected due either to prepayments on the security or to scheduled payments on a debt security in equal installments (both principal and interest), then the sale of the remainder is permitted. This 85% rule applies to debt securities that are payable in equal installments that comprise both principal and interest including level payment CMBS. It also applies to variable rate debt securities where scheduled payments would be payable in equal installments absent a change in interest rates.

Trading Securities and Available-for-Sale Securities "Trading securities" are purchased and held for precisely that purpose — to be sold in the near term. "Available-for-sale securities" are those investment securities that do not meet the criteria for classification as either "held-to-maturity" or "trading." The financial accounting and reporting of investments in CMBS depends upon which of the above classifications the investment falls under. Exhibit 2 summarizes the fundamental accounting for CMBS under each possible classification.

Interest Yield Computations

Certain complexities arise with respect to the accounting for investments in CMBS in accordance with SFAS No. 115. While the interest yield calculation for a typical investment can be established at the time of investment based upon the purchase price, terms of the issue and loan origination and other fees, this computation is complicated in the case of CMBS by the prepayment or call features relating to the underlying mortgages. Certainly, in some cases, prepayments and the exercise of calls can be reasonably estimated and computed. However, the difficulty with such an approach arises as time passes and actual experience differs from the initial estimates. What, then, is the appropriate way to adjust the expected yield to the actual yield? Furthermore, how can we account for such prepayment features in cases where the effect of such features is not subject to reasonable estimation? To deal with this complexity, it is necessary to follow the guidance in Statement of Financial Accounting Standards No. 91, "Accounting for Nonrefundable Fees and Costs Associated with Originating or Acquiring Loans and Initial Direct Costs of Leases" (SFAS No. 91).

Estimation Method SFAS No. 91 permits, but does not require, estimation of expected prepayments for purposes of computing the effective yield when the pool includes a large number of loans that have sufficiently similar characteristics that the prepayment experience of the loans can be expected to be similar in a variety of interest rate environments. The FASB stipulates that for estimation to be permitted, the prepayments must be probable and the timing and amount of prepayments must be reasonably estimated. If, as time passes, actual prepayment experience differs from that initially expected, the investor should then recalculate a new yield based upon the best available current information (including actual prepayment experience and anticipated future payments). This newly calculated effective yield is then used to compute the current loan carrying value as if the yield was applied from the initial investment. The difference in value that arises from this recalculation must then be charged to interest expense.

Contractual Method When an entity cannot, or elects not to, employ the estimation method, then it employs what is often referred to as the contractual method. The effects of future prepayments are disregarded in the initial computation of the effective yield. As prepayments arise, the book discount or premium related to such prepaid amounts are written off to interest expense.

For floating interest rate deals, an additional complication is introduced into the effective yield calculation. As the index changes, we are faced with determining whether the related amortization schedule must change. With respect to this point, the FASB is flexible and allows an investor the option of either leaving the amortization schedule unchanged or adjusting it prospectively based upon the interest rates now in effect.

Exhibit 2: Summary of Basic Accounting by an Investor in CMBS

	Held-to-Maturity Securities	Trading Securities	Available-for-Sale Securities
Asset Valuation	• Carried at historical cost net of amortization of purchase discounts or premiums, as applicable. • Loan origination fees are deferred and amortized over the life of the loan. • Market value is only of significance if the investment value is other than temporarily impaired.	• Carried at market value. • Loan origination fees are not deferred.	• Carried at market value. • Loan origination fees are deferred and amortized over the life of the loan.
Income Statement	• Interest income on investment is recorded as adjusted for any periodic amortization of purchase discounts or premiums, as applicable, and amortization of loan origination fees in accordance with the effective interest method.	• Interest income on investments is recorded as adjusted for any periodic amortization of purchase discounts or premiums, as applicable, in accordance with the effective interest method. • Loan origination fees are recorded as an expense as incurred. • Unrealized gains and losses resulting from fluctuations in the investment's market value are included in current earnings.	• Interest income on investment is recorded as adjusted for any periodic amortization of purchase discounts or premiums, as applicable, and amortization of loan origination fees in accordance with the effective interest method. • Unrealized gains and losses are not recorded on the income statement. The difference between market value and the historical cost net of amortization of purchase discounts or premiums, as applicable, is reported separately as a component of stockholder's equity.

At this point, it should be fairly obvious that the investor's selection from the above methods could have a substantial impact on the reported return from the investment.

CMO Residual Interests and Interest-Only Certificates

Certain unique and rather complex accounting issues arise relative to investments in CMO residual interests and interest-only certificates. These were addressed in detail by EITF Issue No. 89-4, "Accounting for a Purchased Investment in a Collateralized Mortgage Obligation Instrument or in a Mortgage-Backed Interest-Only Certificate," and EITF Issue No. 93-18, "Recognition of Impairment for an Investment in a Collateralized Mortgage Obligation Instrument or in a Mortgage-Backed Interest-Only Certificate."

Interest Yield Computations Initially, interest income is accrued based on an effective yield computed using the purchase price and anticipated future cash flows. Cash received reduces the accrued interest balance. When accrued interest is reduced to zero, any additional cash received reduces the recorded investment balance. At each reporting period, this process is repeated based on the then-current estimate of future cash flows. The assumptions incorporated in these calculations regarding prepayment estimates and future interest rates should be consistent with the assumptions used by marketplace participants for similar instruments.

Sometimes, changes in interest rates may affect the determination of future cash flows. For example, interest paid to variable-rate tranche holders may affect the holders of the CMO residual interests or interest-only certificates. Additionally, the level of reinvestment earnings will be affected by changes in interest rates. In such cases, current interest rates (using the prevailing yield curve) should be used to estimate these cash flows.

Classification These high-risk instruments usually require active management. As a result, they will usually be classified as trading securities or available-for-sale securities and will be carried at market value. This is of particular interest to financial institutions who, in the existing regulatory environment of risk-based capital, must determine whether they have the ability to hold these instruments to maturity.

Applicability EITF Issue No. 89-4 and EITF Issue No. 93-8 apply when the prepayments are probable and can be reasonably estimated (i.e., a pool of high-credit-quality assets). If the underlying collateral is of lesser quality, these methodologies do not apply. The SEC staff indicated that such instruments should be accounted for conservatively in a manner that adequately reflects the nature of the high-risk structure.

SFAS NO. 125

The goal of the FASB in issuing SFAS No. 125 is to address some of the theoretical deficiencies in the pre-1997 accounting that are outlined above and to directly address the issues that arise as a result of the complexity of the transactions that have evolved since the issuance of the current authoritative literature. The following sections summarize the provisions of this new pronouncement.

Financial Components Approach

SFAS No. 125 is based upon an approach referred to as the "financial-components approach." From a theoretical perspective, this approach to CMBS is new in several ways. In the past, when a pool of assets was transferred, the guidance under SFAS No. 77 and TB 85-2 essentially took an "all or none" approach. That is, the transaction was viewed as one transaction and, based upon an assessment of certain key characteristics of the transaction, the entire transaction, as one inseparable unit, was viewed either as a sale or a collateralized borrowing from the transferor's perspective. (This approach was often referred to as a "predominant characteristics approach.") This resulted, in certain cases, in asymmetry in the accounting as the same assets can reside on the accounting records of the transferor and the investors in the pool. SFAS is based upon the belief that financial assets can be divided into a variety of component assets, and that, for each component, an assessment can be made as to who controls the asset. Indeed, from the perspective of the parties to CMBS transactions, the very nature of these transactions from an economic perspective is the disaggregation of financial assets into separate component interests that often reflect multiple participations, or tranches. SFAS No. 125 is designed to reflect this reality.

Another substantial theoretical change to the accounting, as outlined in SFAS No. 125, is that the sequence of transactions is irrelevant. It will no longer be necessary to ask the question — did enough events occur that are condition precedent for a sale? Rather, after the transaction occurs, the accountant will simply look at each component and determine who is currently the "owner." If the investor "owns" the assets, then, we conclude, that the transferor has sold the assets, simply because he does not have the characteristics of an owner. Thus, if a transferor sells financial assets it owns and simultaneously writes a put option (such as a guarantee or recourse obligation) on those assets, it should recognize the put option in the same manner as an entity that writes an identical put option on assets it never owned.

The key to the financial components approach is that the "owner" of an asset is the entity that "controls" the assets. For CMBS, SFAS No. 125 reverts to an old definition of asset, that outlined in FASB Concept Statement No. 6, "Elements of Financial Statements:"

> To have an asset, an entity must control future economic benefit to the extent that it can benefit from the asset and generally can deny or regulate access to that benefit by others... Many physical things and other agents are in effect bundles of future economic benefits that can be unbundled in various ways, and two or more entities may have different future economic benefits from the same agent at the same time or the same continuing future economic benefit at different times.

SFAS No. 125 rejects a "risks and rewards" approach to establishing owner-ship. Essentially, the FASB feels that such an approach has potential for inconsistencies in interpretation of facts to arise and involves detailed identification, measuring and weighing of numerous and varied risks and rewards that comprise a financial asset.

Determination of Asset Ownership

SFAS No. 125 outlines three conditions that must be met to determine that a transf-eror has surrendered control and a transferee has received control over components of financial assets.

First, the transferred assets must be isolated from the transferor. Specifically, they must be beyond the reach of a transferor and its creditors even in bankruptcy or other receivership. Consequently, the same transaction may have different accounting based upon the applicable jurisdiction and the resultant laws regarding the nature of limited recourse provisions. While this provision may sound legalistic, the FASB was sensitive to the cost-benefit implications of this rule and does not require that a legal opinion be obtained to determine whether the provision has been complied with. The accountants must merely have reasonable assurance that the assets have been isolated from the transferor. Some of the basic questions that must be addressed to facilitate the accountant's analysis are:

- Can the transferor revoke the transfer?
- What type of bankruptcy or receivership can the transferor or SPE be placed into?
- Are the transferor and transferee affiliated?
- Is the transfer a true sale at law?

The next two conditions are that (i) the transferee must obtain the right, free of condi-tion that effectively constrain it from taking advantage of that right, to pledge or exchange the transferred assets and (ii) the transferor cannot effectively maintain con-trol over the transferred assets through (1) an agreement that both entitles and obli-gates the transferor to repurchase or redeem them before their maturity or, (2) an agreement that entitles the transferor to repurchase or redeem transferred assets that are not obtainable elsewhere. Clearly, if any of these conditions are not met, the trans-feree does not really control the assets.

Isolation of Assets To clarify this concept, SFAS No. 125 focuses on beneficial inter-ests retained by an initial transferor of assets to a SPE. Often, a transferor retains a junior interest in the SPE which will be reduced by any credit losses on the financial assets in the SPE. As a result of the retention of this interest, the interests issued by the SPE receive favorable credit ratings deriving from the transferor's credit standing. Such securitization do not isolate the transferred assets from the transferor because it cannot be reasonably assured that the transfer would be construed to be a true sale at law. On the other hand, if the transferor received only cash in exchange for the assets, then it could be concluded that the transferred assets are isolated from the transferor.

Some securitizations use two transfers to isolate assets from the transferor. That is, a transferor transfers assets to a SPE and provides no credit or yield protection. The charter of this SPE establishes it as a single purpose entity and thus it cannot undertake any other business or incur any liabilities. The SPE then transfers the assets to a trust and retains a junior interest in the assets. Based on the principles outlined above, the first transfer is a true sale at law while the second transfer is not designed as a true sale at law. In this situation, it is unlikely that the first SPE can ever enter bankruptcy. Furthermore, even if the SPE did somehow enter bankruptcy, it is unlikely that a receiver could reclaim the transferred assets. Consequently, in this two-step transaction, the assets are effectively isolated beyond the reach of the transferor or its creditors, even in bankruptcy.

The discussion above relates solely to transferor entities that are subject to the U.S. Bankruptcy Code. If a transferor is subject to bankruptcy procedures different from the U.S. Bankruptcy Code, it may be possible for a transferor to provide credit or yield protection in a one step securitization and still effectively isolate the transferred assets from the transferor. For example, the FDIC has limited powers over assets transferred by a U.S. bank to a SPE. Specifically, such assets could only be obtained by the receiver if it makes the investors completely whole. That is, the FDIC cannot obtain the assets until the investors are paid all the economic benefits contained in the transferred assets, including any bargained for yield. Thus, the jurisdiction over an entity's bankruptcy proceedings will impact whether a given transaction meets this criterion of isolating the assets from the transferor in bankruptcy or receivership.

Transferee's Right to Pledge or Exchange Transferred Assets SFAS No. 125 provides examples of conditions that constrain the transferee from taking advantage of its right to transfer assets and conditions that do not constrain that right. Most conditions imposed by a transferor would preclude sales treatment. For example, a call option or forward contract to repurchase transferred assets not readily obtainable elsewhere constrain the transferee from selling the assets. On the other hand, a clean-up call does not preclude sales treatment. Furthermore, a transferor's right of first refusal, a requirement that the transferor's permission (not to be reasonably withheld) be obtained and a prohibition on the sale of the assets to the transferor's competitor (provided there are other willing buyers) do not preclude sales treatment.

Treatment of SPEs

SFAS No. 125 directly addresses the issues inherent in the widespread existence of SPEs. Specifically, to be accorded sales treatment, a transfer to an SPE is a sale only if the SPE is a qualified SPE. An SPE is "qualified" if it is a trust, corporation or other vehicle limited to (i) holding title to the transferred financial assets, (ii) issuing beneficial interests, (iii) collecting cash proceeds from assets held, reinvesting proceeds in financial instruments specified in the legal documents establishing the SPE pending distribution to holders of beneficial interests and otherwise servicing the assets held and (iv) distributing proceeds to holders of its beneficial interests. Furthermore, the SPE must have standing at law distinct from the transferor. If a transferor controls the SPE, then a sale has not occurred. Clearly, if the transferor has the ability to unilaterally dissolve the SPE, the transferor has still retained control over the assets contributed to the SPE.

The holders of beneficial interests in the SPE must have the right to pledge or exchange those interests and the SPE must be shielded from the transferor and its creditors in bankruptcy and receivership. The rules outlined in SFAS No. 125 try to mirror the real world view of securitization transactions. While the beneficial interest holders in an SPE do not own the underlying assets held by the SPE, their rights and interests in the pool clearly represent a form of asset ownership. It is these rights that determine ownership of the reconstituted assets. This is what led to the development of the financial-components approach. The emphasis of isolation in bankruptcy was driven by securitization transactions. Investors and, moreover, credit rating agencies, analyze the possibility, however remote, that the transferor, its affiliates or the SPE will enter bankruptcy or receivership and what the implication of such a proceeding might be. Often, legal letters are obtained, detailing these possibilities. Transaction structures contemplate these possibilities and are often designed to minimize the chance of bankruptcy. Thus, it seems quite intuitive that the accounting should follow an analogous logic.

After the consummation of a securitization transaction, the owners of beneficial interests (new asset holders) must be identified, their interests measured for financial reporting purposes and the transferor must then record a gain or loss on the transfer. Any undivided beneficial interests that the transferor retains or any servicing assets retained continue to be carried on the transferor's books.

Asset Valuation and Measurement of Gain or Loss

SFAS No. 125 draws a distinction in the measurement basis between the continuing interests held by the transferor and the newly created interests held by the holders of the beneficial interests. Interests retained by a transferor should be recorded at an allocated carryover basis. The previous carrying value should be allocated to interests sold and retained based upon their relative fair values at the date of the transfer. Newly created interests are to be recorded initially at fair value. Fair value is defined as "the amount at which the asset could be bought or sold in a current transaction between willing parties, that is, other than in a forced liquidation sale." While quoted market prices typically provide the best evidence of fair value, often such values are not available. In these instances, an estimate of fair value shall consider prices for similar assets and the results of valuation techniques including: (i) present value of estimated future cash flows using a discount rate commensurate with the risks involved, (ii) options-pricing models, (iii) matrix pricing, (iv) option-adjusted spread models and (v) fundamental analysis. Techniques shall incorporate assumptions that market participants would use in their estimates of values, future revenues and future expenses, including assumptions about interest rates, default, prepayment and volatility. Estimates of future cash flows shall be the best estimate based on reasonable and supportable assumptions and projections and should consider the likelihood of all possible outcomes. Note that if an estimate of fair value is not practicable, the assets should be recorded at zero.

A transfer of financial assets in which the transferor surrenders control over the financial assets would be accounted for as a sale to the extent that consideration other than beneficial interests in the transferred assets is received in exchange. To measure gain or loss, the transferor compares the basis of the assets transferred to the proceeds. Proceeds include cash, put or call options held or written (for example, guarantee or recourse obligations), forward commitments, swaps (for example, a provision that converts interest rates from fixed to floating) and servicing liabilities.

Occasionally, it may be impracticable to estimate the fair value of assets obtained or liabilities assumed. In the case of assets, they should be recorded at zero. In the case of liabilities, no gain should be recognized on the transaction and liabilities must be estimated and accrued at the greater of the (a) amount that would be recorded in accordance with Statement of Financial Accounting Standards No. 5, "Accounting for Contingencies" (SFAS No. 5), or (b) the excess, if any, of (1) the fair values of assets obtained less the fair value of other liabilities assumed, over (2) the sum of the carrying values of the assets transferred.

Amendment to SFAS No. 115

SFAS No. 115 is the primary standard governing an investor's accounting. SFAS No. 125 amends SFAS No. 115 to provide that interest only strips or any other loans or receivables that can be prepaid or otherwise settled in such a way that the holder of the security would not recover substantially all of its investment cannot be recorded as held-to-maturity securities. Thus, these must be classified as debt securities that are either available-for-sale or trading.

ACCOUNTING FOR MORTGAGE SERVICING RIGHTS

Authoritative Literature

In May 1995, the FASB issued Statement of Financial Accounting Standards No. 122, "Accounting for Mortgage Servicing Rights - An amendment of FASB Statement No. 65" (SFAS No. 122). This standard modified Statement of Financial Accounting Standards No. 65, "Accounting for Certain Mortgage Banking Activities" (SFAS No. 65). SFAS No. 65, as modified by SFAS No. 122, addresses the accounting for mortgage servicing rights when they are separated from the underlying assets as a result of the sale or securitization of the assets with servicing retained by the seller. SFAS No. 125 includes some additional modifications to the accounting for mortgage servicing rights. The following addresses the pre-1997 accounting for such rights and how such accounting is modified by the adoption of SFAS No. 125.

Balance Sheet Recognition and Initial Measurement

Pre-1997 Guidance Certain entities purchase or originate mortgage loans with a "definitive plan" to securitize those loans and retain the mortgage servicing rights. A "definitive plan" exists when investors have committed to purchase the CMBS before the purchase or origination date, the entity makes a commitment to sell the CMBS to an investor or underwriter within a reasonable period (usually 30 days) after the purchase or origination date or has made a commitment before the purchase or origination to deliver the mortgage loans for consideration and estimates of the selling price have been made.

Where the entity has a definitive plan, the cost of the mortgage loans should be allocated to the servicing rights and the mortgage loans (without the servicing rights) based upon the relative fair value as of the date of purchase or origination. In performing this allocation, it is assumed that there is a normal servicing fee and that the rights to the remaining cash flow from the underlying mortgages will be securitized.

If the servicing fee differs from a normal servicing fee, then the entity recognizes an excess servicing receivable or liability which will approximate the present value of the difference between the normal and stated servicing fee rates over the term of the mortgages.

If an entity securitizes loans, although there was initially no definitive plan to do so, then the above-mentioned allocation methodology is applied to the amortized loan cost as of the date of the securitization.

For purposes of the allocations, fair value is defined in the same manner as discussed previously. Certainly, the valuation techniques for mortgage servicing rights should incorporate assumptions that market participants would use in their estimates of future servicing income and expense, including assumptions about prepayments, defaults and interest rates.

SFAS No. 125 SFAS No. 125 changes the pre-1997 accounting in a number of ways. First, it eliminates the separate accounting for the excess servicing receivable. This proposed change arose due to the practical difficulties associated with establishing benchmarks for the normal servicing fees in relatively illiquid markets (i.e., all markets other than residential mortgages). Second, if the entity does not service assets for others, then no allocation is made to a servicing receivable account.

Additionally, the FASB has decided to view servicing liabilities differently than servicing assets. Servicing assets arise in situations where the estimated future revenues from the service contract, including stated servicing fees, late charges and other ancillary revenues, are expected to exceed the servicer's costs of performing the servicing. Servicing liabilities arise when the expected costs to the servicer are expected to exceed the estimated future revenues. While servicing assets retained are initially measured at allocated carrying cost, servicing liabilities are initially measured at fair value. From a theoretical perspective, the FASB is essentially considering servicing liabilities to be new obligations arising from the securitization.

SFAS No. 125 stipulates that rights, held by a servicer, to future interest income from the serviced assets in amounts that exceed contractually specified servicing fees are, in substance, interest-only strips. Consequently, these must be accounted for in accordance with SFAS No. 115, as discussed previously. Furthermore, if an entity securitizes assets, retains all of the resulting securities, and classifies them as held-to-maturity securities, the entity is not required to separately record a servicing asset or liability.

Amortization of Servicing Assets and Liabilities

Pre-1997 Guidance Mortgage servicing rights are currently amortized in proportion to and over the period of net servicing income. Excess servicing receivables are amortized using the interest method as outlined in EITF Issue No. 86-38, "Implications of Mortgage Payments on Amortization of Servicing Rights."

SFAS No. 125 As noted above, excess servicing receivables are not separately accounted for under SFAS No. 125. Furthermore, the above amortization methodology now applies to servicing assets and liabilities separately as opposed to merely applying it to net servicing rights.

Impairment and Other Subsequent Loss Recognition

Here too, the changes in the accounting relate to the elimination of the excess servicing receivable and the separate statement of servicing liabilities.

Excess Servicing Receivable Under pre-1997 accounting, impairment is recognized based on the present value of the estimated remaining future excess servicing fee revenue discounted at the same discount factor used to calculate the original excess servicing fee receivable (see EITF Issue No. 86-38). This accounting does not apply under SFAS No. 125.

Mortgage Servicing Rights, Assets and Liabilities Under pre-1997 accounting, impairment of mortgage servicing rights is recognized based upon the fair value of each impaired stratum through a valuation allowance. That is, an entity must stratify all the mortgage servicing rights it owns based upon the predominant risk characteristics of the underlying loans. These characteristics include loan type (for example, adjustable rate vs. fixed rate, conventional vs. government guaranteed or insured loans), size, note rate, date of origination, term and geographic location. The fair value of each stratum is determined and the carrying amount is written down to such fair value through a valuation allowance. However, fair value in excess of the carrying value is not recognized. SFAS No. 125 applies this accounting to servicing assets. The distinction made by SFAS No. 125 for servicing liabilities is that if the liability increases, this increase is recognized immediately as a loss in earnings.

Exhibit 3: Illustration of Carrying Cost Allocation to Retained Interests

Assumed Data	
Carrying value of mortgage loans transferred to the SPE	$1,000,000
Fair value of mortgage loans transferred to the SPE	1,250,000
Cash received for fair value of beneficial interests sold to unrelated third parties (90%)	1,125,000
Fair value of beneficial interests retained by the sponsor (10%)	125,000

Journal Entry	Debit	Credit
Cash (net cash received)	$1,125,000	
Mortgage loans (90% of carrying cost)		900,000
Gain or transfer		225,000

The bonds purchased by the sponsor remain on the accounts at $100,000, the allocated carrying amount of the underlying mortgage loans receivable.

Transition For excess servicing receivables and servicing rights recognized prior to January 1, 1997, receivables that do not exceed contractually specified servicing fees shall be combined, net of any previously recognized service obligations under that contract, as a servicing asset or liability. If such receivables exceed the contractually specified servicing fees, they should then be reclassified and accounted for as interest-only strips receivable.

ILLUSTRATIONS OF PROVISIONS OF SFAS NO. 125

The following examples will illustrate the sponsor's accounting for simple securitizations. In these cases, the sponsor establishes a trust for the purpose of issuing paythrough bonds. The trust is a qualifying SPE. Exhibit 3 illustrates the methodology for allocating the previous carrying amount between the assets sold and the retained interests based on the relative fair values at the date of the transfer.

The next example expands on Exhibit 3. In this case, the sponsor retains a recourse obligation to repurchase delinquent loans and obtains a call option to purchase loans similar to those transferred to the SPE. Exhibit 4 illustrates the accounting for proceeds from a securitization other than cash.

Prior to this point, we have implicitly assumed that no servicing asset or liability arose from the securitization. Exhibit 5 expands on Exhibit 3 by adding in the complexities that arise when there is a servicing asset. The servicing asset is recorded at the allocated previous carrying amount.

The example illustrated in Exhibit 5 did not clarify whether the servicing fee was normal or excessive since this no longer has relevance under SFAS No. 125. However, it is important to point out an important ramification of this. An excess servicing fee resembles, from an economic perspective, the beneficial interests retained by holding interest-only strips. However, if they are structured as servicing fees, a servicing asset is recorded as illustrated and this asset is amortized as previously discussed. If, however, the item was structured as an interest-only strip, the investment would be recorded in accordance with SFAS No. 115 as previously discussed.

Exhibit 4: Recourse Obligation Retained and Call Option Obtained by the Servicer

Assumed Data	
Same as in Exhibit 3 except:	
Cash received	$1,100,000
Fair value of recourse obligation	100,000
Fair value of call option	125,000

Net Proceeds of Securitization	
Cash received	$1,100,000
Plus: call option	125,000
Less: recourse obligation	-100,000
Net proceeds	$1,125,000

Gain on Transfer	
Net proceeds	$1,125,000
Carrying amount of mortgage loans transferred (90%)	900,000
Gain on transfer	$225,000

Journal Entry	Debit	Credit
Cash	$1,100,000	
Call option	125,000	
Mortgage loans		900,000
Recourse obligation		100,000
Gain on transfer		225,000

Exhibit 5: Accounting for Servicing Asset

Assumed Data	
Same as in Exhibit 3 except:	
Cash received	$1,075,000
Fair value of the servicing asset resulting from the retention by the servicer/issuer of part of the interest income as compensation for performing the servicing	50,000

Allocation of Carrying Amount Based on Relative Fair Value			
	Fair Value	Percentage of Total Fair Value	Allocated Carrying Amount
Interest transferred	$1,075,000	86	$860,000
Servicing asset	50,000	4	40,000
10% interest retained	125,000	10	100,000
Total	$1,250,000	100	$1,000,000

Journal Entry	Debit	Credit
Cash	$1,075,000	
Servicing asset	40,000	
Mortgage loans		900,000
Gain on transfer		215,000

At this time, the beneficial interests retained are recorded at their allocated carrying amount of $100,000. The gain on transfer represents the difference between the cash proceeds ($1,075,000) and the allocated carrying value of the assets transferred ($860,000).

Exhibit 6: Impracticable to Estimate Fair Value of a Servicing Asset

Assumed Data			
Same as in Exhibit 4. Additionally, there is a servicing asset whose fair value cannot be practicably estimated.			

Net Proceeds of Securitization	
Cash received	$1,100,000
Plus: call option	125,000
Less: recourse obligation	-100,000
Net proceeds	$1,125,000

Allocation of Carrying Amount Based on Relative Fair Value			
	Fair Value	Percentage of Total Fair Value	Allocated Carrying Amount
Interest transferred	$1,125,000	90	$900,000
Servicing asset	0	0	0
10% interest retained	125,000	10	100,000
Total	$1,250,000	100	$1,000,000

Gain on Transfer	
Net proceeds	$1,125,000
Carrying amount of loans transferred	900,000
Gain on transfer	$225,000

Journal Entry		
	Debit	Credit
Cash	$1,100,000	
Servicing asset	0	
Call option	125,000	
Mortgage loans		900,000
Recourse obligation		100,000
Gain on transfer		225,000

Note that this case assumes that we are confident that the servicing revenues are adequate for performing the services.

The next two examples outlined in Exhibits 6 and 7 illustrate the implementation of the recommendation of SFAS No. 125 where it is not practicable to estimate the fair value of either assets obtained or liabilities assumed.

Summary

SFAS No. 125 is the FASB's attempt to accommodate recent innovations in the financial markets. It recognizes the fact that assets can be broken into components. Ownership is determined by control over the assets and SFAS No. 115 guidelines apply to the investments in such assets. Recourse provisions, indemnifications and credit enhancement features are considered only inasmuch as they have an impact on the legal isolation of the asset from the transferor and are components which need to be valued and recorded. Estimation no longer plays a role in determining whether a sale has been consummated. Finally, consistent standards are established to distinguish between transfers of assets that are sales and those that are secured borrowings.

Adoption and Effective Date

SFAS No. 125 is effective for transactions that take place after December 31, 1996 and is only to be applied prospectively. Companies will not be permitted to elect early adoption, and transactions occurring before December 31, 1996 will continue to be recorded in accordance with the previous pronouncements. As a result, the user of financial statements will then be required to understand the provisions of both the currently existing standards and the new standard (if and when adopted) to have a full appreciation of the recording of these transactions.

Exhibit 7: Impracticable to Estimate Fair Value of a Recourse Obligation

Assumed Data			
Same as in Exhibit 6 except:			
Cash received			$1,000,000
Fair value of servicing asset			50,000
Impracticable to estimate the fair value of the recourse obligation			

Net Proceeds of Securitization			
Cash received		$1,000,000	
Plus: call option		125,000	
Less: recourse obligation		unknown	
Net proceeds		$1,125,000	

Allocation of Carrying Amount Based on Relative Fair Value			
	Fair Value	Percentage of Total Fair Value	Allocated Carrying Amount
Interest transferred	$1,125,000	90	$900,000
Servicing asset	50,000	4	40,000
10% interest retained	75,000	10	60,000
Total	$1,250,000	100	$1,000,000

Journal Entry		
	Debit	Credit
Cash	$1,000,000	
Servicing asset	40,000	
Call option	125,000	
Mortgage loans		900,000
Recourse obligation		265,000
Gain on sale		0

Note that the recourse obligation is recorded in the amount necessary to ensure that no gain is recognized on the transaction.

Chapter *21*

Federal Income Taxation of REMICs and CMBS

John W. Alexander, C.P.A.
Partner and National Tax Director of
Mortgage Banking and Asset Securitization
Price Waterhouse LLP

Joseph L. Ferst, C.P.A.
Director
Real Estate Industry Services Group
Price Waterhouse LLP

Gregory S. McCauley, C.P.A.
Manager
Financial Services Industry Practice
Price Waterhouse LLP

INTRODUCTION

This chapter summarizes the tax rules applicable to REMICs (real estate mortgage investment conduits), their sponsors, and interest holders with particular attention paid to issues that arise when a REMIC is used to securitize commercial mortgages. Although this chapter focuses on the federal taxation of REMICs, several related topics are discussed including taxable mortgage pools, passthrough certificates, and paythrough bonds. Additionally, there is a brief discussion of the recently proposed FASIT (financial asset securitization investment trust) legislation. If enacted, the FASIT legislation will provide statutory rules for the securitization of any debt instrument (e.g., automobile loans and credit cards), as well as provide an alternative vehicle for the securitization of commercial and residential mortgages.

BACKGROUND

There are a variety of reasons for securitizing assets. For example, a holder can convert relatively illiquid receivables into actively traded property (e.g., securitizing commercial loans into commercial mortgage-backed securities) and, for regulated entities such as banks, simultaneously reduce risk-based capital requirements. Structured as a sale for financial reporting, the issuer can reduce concentrations in certain types of loans thus transferring credit and interest rate risks to third parties. By "selling" assets it may be possible to reduce debt ratios and improve capital and operating ratios. It may be possible for issuers to gain access to new and more diverse sources of funding such as individual investors or pension funds. Issuers also may use securitizations as a means of increasing fee income by using the funds from the securitization to make new loans for which origination or commitment fees can be earned, entering into servicing contracts on securitized debt, earning structuring fees or retaining arbitrage gains flowing from the securitization.

Another primary goal of any securitization is to maximize the price received for the assets being securitized. To maximize the price, the specific needs of a variety of investors must be met. Often this entails channeling cash flows to investors in a specific order, thus providing a degree of call protection and better matching the maturity needs of the investor based on the sequential pay and yield maintenance characteristics. Tranching of cash flows also may be used to provide credit support by creating credit support tranches that receive cash flows only after tranches with a higher priority are paid in full. While many commercial securitizations involve sequential pay arrangements, some recent securitizations have a pro rata structure than can isolate the fast-pay loans from the longer maturity loans to better match maturity requirements.

It is imperative in most securitizations that the issuing entity not be subject to an entity level tax. Other tax issues that must be addressed include determining whether the assets have been sold to investors or whether the investors are acting more like collateralized lenders; whether the instruments issued should be treated as debt or equity of the issuing entity; and whether the form of the transaction should control over its substance (e.g., a transaction that purports to be a sale for financial reporting but which may be more properly treated as a financing for tax purposes).

REMICs were created as part of the Tax Reform Act of 1986 to facilitate the securitization of mortgage loans. In fact, through the simultaneous introduction of the taxable mortgage pool rules, Congress intended REMICs to be the preferred, if not sole, vehicle for issuing multiple classes of debt secured by mortgages. If a REMIC election is made and the requisite requirements are satisfied, the REMIC, its sponsor, and REMIC interest holders are assured that, generally, there will be no tax imposed on the REMIC and the regular interests issued by the REMIC will be treated as debt for all federal income tax purposes. The parties to the securitization no longer are subject to the uncertainties inherent in the tax law. Accordingly, many inefficient features, such as overcollateralization and mismatching of cash flows, common with past securitizations, no longer are necessary solely to ensure the desired tax treatment.

FORMATION

A REMIC is intended to function as a cash flow conduit with no tax levied at the conduit level. The REMIC holds assets, substantially all of which must be mortgage loans, and generally issues one or more classes of debt known as *regular interests*. The REMIC also issues an ownership interest referred to as the *residual interest*, or simply, the *residual*. However, for each REMIC there must be one and only one class of residual interest, although that one class may have multiple owners.[1] The cash flows from the REMIC assets are passed through to the regular and residual interests.

For tax purposes, a sponsor[2] is treated as receiving the REMIC regular and residual interests in exchange for the assets contributed regardless of the actual sequence of steps.[3] The sponsor allocates its basis in the assets contributed, increased by organizational expenses,[4] to the regular and residual interests actually or deemed received in proportion to the fair market value of those interests as of the pricing date,[5] if any or, if none, the startup day.[6] If the interests are sold, gain or loss is computed by comparing the sale price to the allocated basis in the interest disposed. If the sponsor retains an interest in the REMIC, any difference between the fair market value of the interest and its allocated basis (i.e., deferred gain or loss) is deferred and recognized over the life of the REMIC for residual

---

[1] In practice, many REMIC securitizations use back-to-back REMICs, referred to as "multi-tiered REMICs," to accomplish various structuring objectives that may not be possible using a single REMIC. For example, to meet the specified portion rules applicable to interest-only strips when the strip relates only to certain loans in the REMIC, a multi-tier REMIC may be required. The assets of the lower-tier REMIC generally are the mortgages being securitized while the assets of the upper-tier REMIC generally are the lower-tier REMIC regular interests. Each of the entities in a multi-tier REMIC generally is treated as a separate REMIC for federal income tax purposes and must separately satisfy the qualification tests even though they may have been created under a single legal document.

[2] A sponsor is defined as a person who directly or indirectly transfers qualified mortgages and related assets for regular and residual interests in a REMIC.

[3] For example, the sponsor might contribute assets to the REMIC, and receive the cash from the sale of the REMIC regular interests. Alternatively, this transaction might be structured as an issuance of the REMIC regular interests for cash and a purchase from the sponsor of qualified mortgages. Regardless of the form, the sponsor is treated as having contributed assets in exchange for the REMIC regular and residual interests and then having sold the regular interests for cash.

[4] Organizational expenses are those incurred by the sponsor or by the REMIC and that are directly related to the creation of the REMIC. The expense must be incurred during a period beginning a reasonable time before the startup day and ending before the date prescribed by law for filing the first REMIC tax return. Examples include legal fees for services related to the formation of the REMIC, such as preparation of a pooling and servicing agreement and trust indenture; accounting fees related to the formation of the REMIC; and other administrative costs related to the formation of the REMIC.

[5] The pricing date means the date on which the terms of the regular and residual interests are fixed and the prices at which a substantial portion of the regular interests will be sold are fixed.

[6] The startup day means the day on which the REMIC issues all of its regular and residual interests. A sponsor may, however, contribute the property to a REMIC in exchange for regular and residual interests over any period of 10 consecutive days and the REMIC may designate any one of those 10 days as its startup day. The day so designated is then the startup day, and all interests are treated as issued on that day.

interests or as a yield adjustment for regular interests.[7] The REMIC itself recognizes no gain or loss on formation.

Syndication expenses incurred by the sponsor or other person to market the interests in a REMIC are applied to reduce the amount realized on the sale of the interests. Examples of syndication expenses are brokerage fees, registration fees, fees of an underwriter or placement agent, and printing costs of the prospectus or placement memorandum and other selling or promotional material.

REMIC QUALIFICATION

Qualification as a REMIC is not automatic, and certain conditions must be satisfied both at formation and on an ongoing basis to obtain and retain REMIC status. The qualifications relate to the election to be treated as a REMIC, the types of interests that may be issued, the composition of the REMIC assets, the REMIC taxable year, and provisions restricting who may hold residual interests.

Any entity (regardless of whether the entity is a partnership, trust, or corporation under state law), or a segregated pool of assets within an entity,[8] may elect REMIC status. If a REMIC election is made and the REMIC meets certain qualifications it will not be subject to federal income tax except on certain enumerated transactions. The election is made by timely filing a Form 1066, U.S. Real Estate Mortgage Investment Conduit Income Tax Return, for the first year of the entity's existence. The due date of the required calendar year return is April 15 following the end of the preceding calendar year; however, under appropriate circumstances, extensions of time to file may be requested.

The REMIC return must be signed by a person who could sign the return absent the REMIC election. Thus for a REMIC that is a corporation or a trust under applicable state law, the REMIC return must be signed by a corporate officer or trustee, respectively. The return of a REMIC that is a segregated pool of assets must be signed by a person who could sign the return of the entity that owns the assets under applicable state law.[9] In addition, the REMIC may designate a Tax Matters

---

[7] The deferred gain or loss on regular interests is recognized as if the amounts were market discount and bond premium, respectively, and the sponsor is treated as having made an election to accrue the market discount and amortize the bond premium. These deemed elections are not treated as actual elections and do not bind the sponsor with respect to the accrual of discount on other debt obligations under section 1278 or serve as an actual election to amortize bond premium under section 171.

[8] To qualify for REMIC status, the assets identified as part of the segregated pool must be treated for all federal income tax purposes as assets of the REMIC and interests in the REMIC must be supported solely by assets of the REMIC. For credit rating purposes, however, it may be necessary to transfer the assets to a separate bankruptcy remote entity.

[9] These rules generally apply to REMICs whose startup day is after November 10, 1988. With limited exceptions, for REMICs whose startup day is before November 10, 1988, the REMIC tax return may be signed by any person who held a residual interest during the taxable year to which the return relates or by a fiduciary acting for the REMIC and who has furnished the required notice.

Person in the same manner as a partnership may designate a Tax Matters Partner under the federal tax rules pertaining to partnerships.[10]

Once made, the election is irrevocable for that taxable year and subsequent years. In addition, the entity must keep sufficient records to demonstrate compliance with the REMIC provisions. Certain disclosures regarding the terms and conditions of the regular and residual interests, a description of prepayment and reinvestment assumptions, and the legal form of the entity under applicable state law, and other disclosures are required on the REMIC initial return.

The Asset Test

As of the close of the third month beginning after the startup day and at all times thereafter, "substantially all" of the assets of the REMIC must consist of qualified mortgages and permitted investments. This allows time for the REMIC to accumulate the required mortgages and effectively allows time for the sponsor to substitute any assets during the initial grace period as long as substantially all of the assets of the REMIC consist of qualified mortgages and permitted investments as of the end of that period.[11] As a practical matter, since the startup day is the date on which the regular and residual interests are issued, generally the collateral for the issuance would have been identified.

The "substantially all" test is met if the REMIC owns no more than a "de minimis" amount of assets other than qualified mortgages and permitted investments. "De minimis" is not defined in the code or regulations;[12] however, if the adjusted basis of the other assets is less than 1% of the aggregate adjusted basis of all of the REMIC assets, then the substantially all test will be satisfied. A REMIC failing the 1% safe harbor may nevertheless demonstrate on a facts and circumstances basis that it owns no more than a de minimis amount of other assets.

Qualified Mortgages A qualified mortgage is any obligation "principally secured by an interest in real property" that was either transferred to the REMIC on the startup day in exchange for regular or residual interests in the REMIC, or was purchased by the REMIC within the three-month period beginning on the startup day provided the purchase was pursuant to a fixed price contract in effect on the startup day. Qualified mortgages include participation certificates or other certificates of beneficial interest in an obligation principally secured by an interest in real property, such as a mortgage passthrough certificate or a stripped mortgage passthrough certificate.[13] The conversion feature of a convertible mortgage is not treated as a separate asset,

---

[10] For this purpose, all holders of residual interests are treated as general partners.

[11] The language in the statute effectively permits a grace period in excess of three months and up to almost four months under certain circumstances. For example, if the startup day was March 1, the close of the third month after the startup day would be June 30.

[12] All references to code, section, and regulations refer to the Internal Revenue Code of 1986, as amended, and the regulations thereunder.

[13] Although stripped mortgage passthrough certificates are specified in this text, tax regulations provide that any stripped bond or coupon may be considered a qualified mortgage if the obligation that was stripped would have been considered a qualified mortgage.

but is treated as incidental to, and therefore a part of, the mortgage or pool of mortgages to which it relates. Certain instruments that call for contingent payments may be qualified mortgages provided that total noncontingent principal payments at least equal the instrument's issue price. Qualified mortgages also include any regular interest in another REMIC that was transferred to the REMIC on the startup day in exchange for regular or residual interests in the REMIC. Residual interests in other REMICs are not qualified mortgages even though residuals may qualify as real estate assets for thrifts and REITs (real estate investment trusts).

In certain limited circumstances it is possible to substitute one qualified mortgage for another. A "qualified replacement mortgage" is one that would have been a qualified mortgage if it had been transferred to the REMIC on the startup day. Additionally, it must be received in exchange for another obligation within the three-month period beginning on the startup day, or must be received for a "defective obligation" within the two-year period beginning on the startup day.[14]

"Defective obligations" generally are not considered qualified mortgages. A "defective obligation" is any mortgage that is in default, or default is reasonably foreseeable. Additionally, a defective obligation includes one that was fraudulently procured by the mortgagor, was not principally secured by an interest in real property, or does not conform to a customary representation or warranty given by the sponsor or prior owner of the mortgage regarding the characteristics of the mortgage (or the characteristics of the pool of mortgages of which the mortgage is a part). The defect must be one that affects the mortgage's status as a qualified mortgage had the defect been discovered before the startup day,[15] otherwise the defective obligation is nonetheless considered a qualified mortgage.[16] If a mortgage is defective, several remedies exist. Within 90 days of discovery of the defect, the REMIC must either cause the defect to be cured or must dispose of the defective mortgage. Even if the defect is not cured, the mortgage is still considered to be a qualified mortgage from the startup day through the end of the 90-day period. If the defect is neither cured nor disposed of within the 90-day time period, the obligation ceases to be a qualified mortgage for purposes of the REMIC asset qualification test.

An alternative available to the REMIC is to substitute the defective mortgage with a "qualified replacement mortgage." Although, as discussed earlier, substitution of mortgages is discouraged, the replacement of a defective obligation is allowed. If the substitution was made after the expiration of the two-year window, the substituted mortgage would not be considered a qualified mortgage and could

---

[14] The code provides for Treasury to issue regulations to effectively distinguish between mortgage "replacements" and mortgage "swaps" with the objective that only the former would be considered a qualified replacement mortgage. To date, no such regulations have been issued.

[15] The language in the regulations speaks to the *discovery* of the defect, not its occurrence.

[16] The regulations provide an example wherein the sponsor represents that all mortgages transferred to a REMIC have a 10% interest rate, and it is later discovered that one of the mortgages has a 9% interest rate. The 9% mortgage is considered to be defective, but the defect does not affect the status of that mortgage as a qualified mortgage. Accordingly, there is no mandate to cure the defect or to dispose of or substitute the mortgage for REMIC qualification purposes.

possibly disqualify the REMIC. Therefore, after the expiration of the two-year window the only viable alternatives would be to cure the defect or dispose of the defective mortgage within the 90-day period.

The entire issue of resolving a defective mortgage problem is effectively bypassed if the adjusted basis of the defective mortgage(s) comprises less than 1% of the aggregate adjusted basis of all of the REMIC assets, or could otherwise be shown to be de minimis in amount. Because commercial mortgage securitizations often comprise a limited number of mortgages, the prospects of relying on the de minimis exception are limited.

Principally Secured by an Interest in Real Property As noted, qualified mortgages must be principally secured by an interest in real property. "Real property" is defined by reference to the REIT rules. Under these rules, real property generally includes land and any improvements thereon of an inherently permanent nature such as buildings, and their structural components such as wiring, heating and cooling systems, and plumbing. Items not of a permanent nature such as window air conditioners, business machinery, and office furnishings generally fall outside of this definition. State or local law definitions of real property generally are not controlling.

"Interests in real property" include fee ownership, co-ownership, or options to acquire land or leaseholds of land or improvements thereon. The definition also includes ownership shares in cooperative housing corporations and time-shares, but does not include certain oil and gas interests. The REMIC regulations provide examples of "obligations secured by an interest in real property." These include mortgages, deeds of trust, and installment land contracts; mortgage pass-through certificates guaranteed by GNMA, FNMA, FHLMC, or CMHC (Canada Mortgage and Housing Corporation); other investment trust interests that would be considered to be permitted investments if the investment trust were a REMIC; and certain obligations secured by manufactured housing. However, obligations that are secured by obligations secured by real property (e.g., collateralized mortgage obligations issued by a non-REMIC) are not qualified mortgages since they are not principally secured by an interest in real property. A REMIC regular interest is always considered an obligation principally secured by an interest in real property; a residual interest is not.

For an obligation to be principally secured it must meet one of two tests. Under the first test, an obligation is principally secured by an interest in real property if the fair market value of the interest in real property securing the obligation was at least 80% of the adjusted issue price[17] of the obligation either at the date

---

[17] "Adjusted issue price" used in this context is generally presumed to draw from the rules related to debt instruments with original issue discount (OID). In a lending transaction, the adjusted issue price generally is the amount loaned. With respect to any other debt instrument that might otherwise fall under the OID rules (e.g., a REMIC regular interest held as an asset of another REMIC), the adjusted issue price generally represents the original issue price of the debt adjusted for payments of principal and amortization of OID.

4

the obligation was originated,[18] or at the time the sponsor contributes the obligation to the REMIC.[19]

The determination of whether an obligation is principally secured by real property under the above definition presents practical issues in commercial mortgage securitizations. As noted above, the definition of real property generally excludes items not of a permanent nature. However, appraisals of real property often look to the earnings potential of the facility, which may include personal property used in conjunction with the property and, furthermore, the personal property may in part be security for the loan. For example, the value of a congregate care facility may be based on its potential to attract residents. This attraction is based in part on the living accommodations, including furnishings and medical equipment owned by the facility. An appraisal based on capitalizing the earnings of the property or an appraisal based on comparable sales generally would not be concerned specifically with the value of the personal property attached thereto other than in its usefulness in the overall revenue generating potential of the entire structure. For REMIC qualification purposes, however, this distinction is important and the value of the personalty must be separated from the value of the realty.

Under the second test, if at the date the obligation was originated, substantially all of the proceeds of the obligation were used to acquire, protect, or improve an interest in real property and the real property was the only security for the obligation, then the obligation will be considered principally secured by an interest in real property.[20]

Sponsor's Reasonable Belief If the sponsor reasonably believes an obligation is principally secured by an interest in real property at the time of contribution to the REMIC, the obligation will be considered as principally secured by an interest in real property. However, if the sponsor knows or has reason to know that the obligation fails both of the qualification tests described above, the obligation will not be considered principally secured by an interest in real property.

Basis for reasonable belief may be established based on representations and warranties made by the originator of the obligation. In addition, if evidence exists that the originator of the obligation typically made mortgage loans within an established set of guidelines, and that any mortgage loan issued within those guidelines would satisfy at least one of the qualification tests, then basis for reasonable belief exists.

---

[18] If an obligation is significantly modified prior to the time the obligation is contributed to the REMIC, the obligation will be considered as originated on the date the modification occurred. As discussed later, the concept of "significant modification" also is relevant in determining whether a prohibited transaction has occurred.

[19] The fair market value of the real property interest must be reduced first by any liens that are senior to the obligation being tested, and then must be reduced by a proportionate amount of any lien that is of equal priority with the obligation being tested.

[20] For purposes of this test, third party credit enhancements, including state or federal loan guarantees, are not considered additional security for the loan. In addition, the fact that the obligor may carry personal liability for the obligation is of no consequence for this test.

Notwithstanding the sponsor's reasonable belief that an obligation is principally secured by an interest in real property, if the REMIC later discovers that the obligation is not principally secured by an interest in real property, the obligation is a defective obligation.[21] Significantly, the obligation loses its status as a qualified mortgage 90 days after the discovery of the defect by the REMIC. This is consistent with the rules pertaining to defective obligations generally.

Defeasance Particularly with commercial loan securitization, situations may arise when it is necessary to release a particular property. If a REMIC releases its lien on real property that secures a qualified mortgage, that mortgage generally ceases to be a qualified mortgage on the date the lien is released. However, the obligation will continue to be treated as a qualified mortgage if the mortgagor pledges substitute collateral that consists solely of certain government securities; the mortgage documents permit such a substitution; the lien is released to facilitate the disposition of the property or any other customary commercial transaction, and not as part of an arrangement to collateralize the REMIC offering with obligations that are not real estate mortgages; and the release occurs later than two years after the startup day.

Mortgage Modifications and Assumptions Extensive case law and published IRS rulings deal with the issue of whether a debt obligation has been modified so significantly as to amount to the reissuance of the obligation. In response to uncertainty in this area, the IRS has issued final regulations that set forth "bright-line" tests for determining when a modification is significant. These bright-line tests apply to alterations of a debt instrument on or after September 24, 1996. Taxpayers may rely on these rules for alterations of a debt instrument after December 2, 1992, and before September 24, 1996.

If a mortgage is "significantly modified," the unmodified mortgage is treated as disposed of in exchange for a new mortgage (i.e., the mortgage as modified).[22] If the modification occurs after the mortgage is contributed to the REMIC, but not within the initial three-month window, it is important that the modified mortgage meet the definition of a qualified replacement mortgage. Otherwise, the modified mortgage will not be a qualified mortgage and may jeopardize the REMIC qualification. Additionally the "disposition" of the original mortgage (i.e., before modification) would be a prohibited transaction, as discussed later.

If the modification occurred before the mortgage was contributed to the REMIC, the mortgage is treated as originated on the date of the modification. The modification date (i.e., the new origination date) may be important in determining whether the mortgage is principally secured by an interest in real property under the 80% tests discussed previously.

---

[21] Interestingly, the reasonable belief test is applied at the sponsor level; whereas the discovery of the defect is left to the REMIC.

[22] In addition to being relevant to the asset qualification test, if a mortgage is "significantly modified," it will be considered as a disposition of the mortgage and may represent a prohibited transaction. Accordingly, any net income from the disposition could be subject to a 100% tax.

Under the regulations,[23] taxpayers must first determine whether a debt instrument has been modified. Generally, an alteration of a legal right or obligation of the holder or the issuer whether evidenced by an express agreement (oral or written), conduct of the parties, or otherwise, is a modification. Generally excepted from the definition of a modification is an alteration that occurs by operation of the terms of the debt instrument. These alterations may occur automatically (e.g., a periodic resetting of the interest rate based on an index) or may occur as a result of the exercise of an option provided to the issuer or holder. There are, however, important "exceptions to the exception" that cause certain alterations to be considered modification, even if the alterations occur by operation of the instrument's terms. For example, even though allowed by the terms of the instrument, the substitution of a new obligor would be a modification. However, a temporary failure of the issuer to perform its obligations under the debt instrument, including a delay in payment, is not a modification. Absent a written or oral agreement to alter *other* terms of an instrument, an agreement by the holder to stay collection or temporarily waive an acceleration clause or similar default right is *not* a modification *unless and until* the forbearance remains in effect for a period exceeding two years following the issuer's initial failure to perform, and any additional period during which the parties conduct good faith negotiations, or during which the issuer is in bankruptcy proceedings.

Once a modification has occurred, it is tested to determine whether it is significant. A "significant modification" of a debt instrument would be treated as an exchange of the original debt instrument for a new debt instrument. The regulations provide specific rules for determining the significance of certain types of modifications. The bright-line tests cover changes in:

- yield;
- timing and/or amounts of payments;
- the nature of the instrument; or
- accounting or financial covenants.

Modifications of a type not described above are significant only if, based on the facts and circumstances, the legal rights or obligations that are altered and the degree to which they are altered are economically significant.

Generally, a change in the annual yield over the remaining life of an instrument would be a significant modification if the change exceeds the greater of 25 basis points or 5% of the annual yield of the unmodified instrument.

A change in the timing or amounts of payments would be a significant modification if it materially defers payments due under an instrument. The deferral may occur through an extension of the final maturity date, or through deferral of payments due prior to maturity. The materiality of the deferral depends on the facts and circumstances (e.g., length of the deferral). A deferral of payments

---

[23] Treasury Regulation 1.1001-3(c).

within a safe-harbor period will not be considered material if the deferred payments are unconditionally payable by the end of the safe-harbor period. The duration of the safe-harbor period is the lesser of five years or 50% of the original term of the debt. Payment of a portion of a debt instrument would generally not be a significant modification.

In general, changing the obligor on a recourse debt instrument is significant; exceptions (subject to conditions) are provided for changes in obligors occurring as part of tax-free reorganization and other tax-free transactions, and transactions in which the new obligor acquires substantially all of the assets of the original obligor. The substitution of a new obligor on a nonrecourse instrument is not a significant modification. The addition or deletion of a co-obligor, or a change in the priority of the instrument relative to other debt of the issuer, is significant if the change results in a change in "payment expectations."

For recourse instruments, a modification that releases, substitutes, adds, or otherwise alters the collateral, guarantee, or other form of credit enhancement is significant if the modification results in a change in payment expectations. For nonrecourse instruments, in general, such a change is significant. A substitution of collateral is not significant, however, if the collateral is fungible. In addition, a substitution of a similar commercially-available credit enhancement contract is not significant, and improvement to property securing a nonrecourse debt is not a significant modification.

A change from substantially all recourse to substantially all nonrecourse, or vice versa, is a significant modification, subject to two exceptions. A modification that changes a recourse debt to a nonrecourse debt is not significant if the instrument continues to be secured only by the original collateral. If a modification results in an instrument or property right that is not debt for tax purposes, the modification is significant.

A modification that adds, deletes, or alters customary accounting or financial covenants is not a significant modification.

If more than one of the above specific terms of an instrument is modified, each modification would be tested separately and, if no single modification would be a significant modification, there would be no significant modification of the instrument. Multiple changes to a single term would be treated as a single modification and tested for significance.

The REMIC tax regulations list several modifications that will not be treated as significant modifications notwithstanding the general rules stated above. These exceptions are:

- changes in the terms of the obligation caused by default or default that is reasonably foreseeable;
- an assumption of the obligation as described below;
- the waiver of a due-on-sale clause or due-on-encumbrance clause; and,
- conversion of an interest rate by a mortgagor pursuant to the terms of a convertible mortgage.

Assumptions that fall within the exception above are those when (i) the buyer of the mortgaged property acquires the property subject to the mortgage without assuming any personal liability; (ii) the buyer becomes liable for the debt, but the seller also remains liable; or (iii) the buyer becomes liable for the debt, and the seller is released by the lender.

The modification of a mortgage which backs a passthrough certificate or an investment trust which is, in turn, held as an asset in the REMIC, generally will not be considered a modification of the passthrough certificate or the investment trust.

Permitted Investments In addition to qualified mortgages, a REMIC may hold "permitted assets." Included in this category are cash flow investments, qualified reserve assets, and foreclosure property.

Cash Flow Investments Cash flow investments are temporary investments of cash received from qualified mortgages prior to their regularly scheduled distribution to regular and residual interest holders in the REMIC. Cash flow investments must be passive investments earning a return in the nature of interest. Cash received from qualified mortgages includes payments of principal and interest as well as principal prepayments and prepayment penalties, if any. In addition, cash received from qualified mortgages includes payments made under credit enhancement contracts (discussed at the end of this section). It also includes cash received as proceeds from the disposition of qualified mortgages and proceeds from the repurchase of defective mortgages by the sponsor or prior owner where the defective mortgage was transferred to the REMIC in breach of a customary warranty. Finally, cash received from qualified mortgages includes cash flows from foreclosure property and the proceeds from the disposition of such property.

The tax regulations describe a temporary period as the period between the time the REMIC receives the cash and the time the REMIC distributes the cash to the regular and residual interest holders. However, the tax regulations also state that this temporary period may not exceed 13 months.[24] Consequently, any investment held for a longer period is not considered a "cash flow investment" and therefore is not considered a permitted investment for the REMIC asset qualification test.

Qualified Reserve Assets Historically, reserve funds have not been popular forms of credit enhancement in commercial securitizations because of their increased costs when compared to providing credit enhancement structurally through the use of subordinated tranches. The REMIC rules, nevertheless, provide rules for the treatment of reserve funds established either inside or outside the REMIC.

A qualified reserve fund is any "reasonably required reserve" to provide for full payment of expenses on qualified mortgages; amounts due to regular interests in the event of default on qualified mortgages, lower than expected returns on

[24] If the REMIC holds investments in a commingled account, the REMIC may use any reasonable method of accounting, such as first-in/first-out, to determine the holding period applicable to its cash flow investments.

cash flow investments, or prepayment interest shortfalls;[25] or any other contingency that could be addressed under a credit enhancement contract. A qualified reserve asset is any intangible property held for investment as part of a qualified reserve fund and is treated as a permitted investment.

Not only must the funds held in reserve be used for the purposes discussed above, but, in order to qualify as a qualified reserve fund, the reserve must be "reasonably required."

Several factors must be considered in determining whether the amount held as a reserve is reasonably required. The credit quality of the qualified mortgages, the extent and nature of any guarantees pertaining to the qualified mortgages or the regular and residual interests, and the expected amount of expenses of the REMIC and the expected availability of proceeds from the qualified mortgages to meet those expenses. Although these are considerations in determining whether the amount of a reserve is reasonably required, the regulations do not set specific parameters around any of them.

The determination of whether a reserve is reasonably required is ongoing, and the considerations mentioned above should be presumed to apply continuously. Accordingly, the tax rules require that a reserve must be "promptly and appropriately" reduced to the extent it exceeds an amount that is reasonably required. This reduction is generally presumed to be required as payments are received on the qualified mortgages. However, it is possible that a reserve may become excessive notwithstanding payments on qualified mortgages. In this case, too, the reserve must be promptly and appropriately reduced. On the other hand, if at any time the amount held in reserve is less than is reasonably required, the reserve may be increased with cash received from payments from qualified mortgages or with contributions by the residual interest holder.

The amount held in reserve will be presumed to be reasonably required and the reserve "promptly and appropriately reduced" in one of two circumstances. The first case is when the amount in the reserve does not exceed the amount required by a nationally recognized independent rating agency as a condition for providing the rating for REMIC interests desired by the sponsor. The latter instance is when the amount in the reserve does not exceed the amount required by a third party insurer or guarantor as a condition of providing credit enhancement.[26] Even so, the presumption may be rebutted by the IRS (Internal Revenue Service) if the amounts required under either of these circumstances are not "commercially reasonable" when taking into account the factors discussed earlier.

Assets held in a qualified reserve fund need not generate any income. However, if assets held in a qualified reserve fund generate income, no more than 30 percent of the gross income from the assets in such fund may be derived from the sale or other disposition of property held for less than three months. This pro-

---

[25] A prepaid interest shortfall is the difference between the amount of interest that would have accrued during the accrual period and the interest that did accrue up to the date the mortgage prepaid.

[26] The insurer or guarantor cannot own, either directly or indirectly, either a regular or residual interest in the REMIC. Indirect ownership is generally determined under the rules regarding related taxpayers under section 267(c) of the code.

hibition does not apply if the disposition is necessary to prevent default on a regular interest. The pending default on the regular interest, however, must be the result of a default on a qualified mortgage.

The consequence of violating the income rule is especially severe insofar as the reserve fund risks losing its status as a qualified reserve fund not only for the taxable year in which the violation occurs, but for all subsequent taxable years as well.

Under certain circumstances, reserve funds may be maintained outside the REMIC and not be subject to the limits on qualified reserve funds under the asset qualification test. These so-called "outside reserve funds" must be maintained to pay the expenses of the REMIC or to make payments to the regular and residual interest holders. In addition, the REMIC organizational documents must "clearly and expressly" state that the reserve fund is an outside reserve fund and not an asset of the REMIC. Those documents must also clearly identify the owners of the reserve fund and state that, for all federal income tax purposes, amounts transferred by the REMIC to the fund are treated as amounts distributed directly to those owners or their transferees. If all of these conditions are not satisfied, the reserve fund will be presumed to be an asset of the REMIC and therefore subject to the permitted investment rules pertaining to reserve funds.

Foreclosure Property To qualify as foreclosure property, the property must be acquired in connection with the default or imminent default of a qualified mortgage. As in the case of foreclosure property acquired by a REIT, property is allowed to remain in foreclosure property status for up to two years before it ceases to qualify as such. However, the Secretary of the Treasury may grant additional time (up to six years in total from the date the property was acquired by the REMIC) to provide for the orderly liquidation of the REMIC interest in such property.

Credit Enhancement Contracts In general, for purposes of the REMIC asset qualification test, neither credit enhancements nor collateral supporting such credit enhancements are treated as separate assets of the REMIC. Rather, payments made under credit enhancement agreements are generally considered payments made with respect to the qualified mortgages they support.

Examples of credit enhancement contracts given in the tax regulations include letters of credit, pool insurance contracts, and guaranteed insurance contracts designed to guarantee full or partial payment of principal and interest with respect to qualified mortgages or to make full or partial payment to regular or residual interests. Typical causes for the activation of credit enhancement features include delinquent principal and interest payments on qualified mortgages or defaults on qualified mortgages, unanticipated losses or expenses incurred by the REMIC, or lower than expected returns on temporary investments of payments on qualified mortgages.

In addition, credit enhancement contracts include other arrangements whereby either the sponsor, servicer, or some other third party agrees to make advances of (1) delinquent principal and interest on qualified mortgages; (2) taxes, hazard insurance premiums, and certain other expenses to protect the REMIC security interest in the qualified mortgage; and (3) temporary advances to facilitate REMIC administration.

If a qualified mortgage defaults and the REMIC is supported by a credit enhancement from a guarantor, the fact that the guarantor may have an option of paying the entire amount of principal due on the defaulted mortgage, or continuing to make principal and interest payments (whether in accordance with the original amortization schedule or some other schedule), does not affect the arrangements status as a credit enhancement contract treated as a qualified mortgage asset.[27]

Like a credit enhancement contract, an agreement by a servicer or a third party to make up prepayment interest shortfalls is not considered a separate asset of the REMIC. Rather, payments made under such an agreement are treated as payments on the qualified mortgages to which they relate.

The Interests Tests

To qualify as a REMIC, all of the entity's interests must be regular or residual interests. In addition, there must be one (and only one) class of residual interest and distributions, if any, with respect to such interest must be pro rata.[28]

REMIC Regular Interests A REMIC may have one or more classes of regular interests. A regular interest must be issued on the startup day, must have fixed terms, and must be designated by the REMIC as a regular interest in the REMIC initial tax return.[29] A regular interest may be issued in the form of debt, stock, an interest in a partnership or trust, or any other form permitted under applicable state law. As noted previously, however, regular interests in the REMIC are debt obligations of the REMIC for all federal income tax purposes.

The holder of a regular interest must be unconditionally entitled to receive a specified principal amount. If the form of the regular interest is not debt, the holder must nonetheless be entitled to a specified amount that would otherwise represent the principal amount of the debt had the interest been issued in debt form (e.g., preferred stock).

Regular interests will not fail to qualify if the timing, but not the amount of or the right to the principal payments, is contingent on prepayments of qualified mortgages and income from permitted investments. Neither will an interest fail to qualify as a regular interest simply because the amount or timing of payments of principal or interest with respect to a regular interest is affected by defaults on qual-

---

[27] This holds true even in the case wherein the guarantor is entitled immediately to proceed with foreclosure yet continues to support the REMIC with scheduled payments.

[28] An interest is defined as de minimis if the interest is not specifically designated as an interest, and, as of the startup day, the fair market value of that interest is less than either $1,000 or 1/1,000 of 1% of the aggregate fair value of all of the regular and residual interests in the REMIC, whichever is less.

[29] A regular interest has fixed terms on the startup day if, on the startup day, the REMIC organizational documents irrevocably specify (1) the principal amount of the regular interest, (2) the interest rate or rates used to compute interest payments, if any, with respect to that interest, and (3) the latest possible maturity date of the interest.

ified mortgages and permitted investments, unanticipated expenses incurred by the REMIC, or lower than expected returns on permitted investments.

A regular interest may be subordinated. That is, a regular interest may bear all or a disproportionate share of losses due to cash flow shortfalls arising from defaults or delinquencies on qualified mortgages and permitted investments, unexpected expenses incurred by the REMIC, lower than expected returns on permitted investments, or prepayment interest shortfalls. A regular interest by its terms also may call for the deferral of interest payments.

Finally, contingencies with a remote probability of occurrence do not affect the qualification of a regular interest. In no event, however, may the latest possible maturity date as specified in the organizational documents be contingent.

Interest Payments on Regular Interests Interest payments, if any, must be made at either a fixed rate, a qualified variable rate, or must consist of a specified portion of the interest payments on the qualified mortgages. Except in the case of an interest that entitles the holder to a specified portion of interest payments on qualified mortgages, such as an interest-only strip, an interest in a REMIC will not qualify as a regular interest if the amount of the interest payment is disproportionately high to the principal amount.[30]

REMIC Qualified Variable Rates[31]
Current Value Variable Rates A REMIC regular interest issued on or after April 4, 1994,[32] may bear interest at a variable rate whose variations can reasonably be expected to measure contemporaneous borrowing costs. In addition, the rate must be set at a "current value." That is, the rate in effect at any time during the term of the instrument must equal the value of the rate on any day that is no earlier than three months prior to and no later than one year after the first day on which the value is in effect.[33] In addition, a rate equal to the highest, lowest, or average of two or more qualified floating rates is a variable rate.

---

[30] The tax regulations define disproportionately high as any class where the issue price of the class is greater than 125% of its "specified principal amount," generally the outstanding principal at issuance. However, the tax regulations make an exception for de minimis beneficial interests necessary to facilitate the formation of the REMIC.

[31] The tax regulations pertaining to OID contain certain interest rate qualification tests to which the REMIC regulations refer. However, the rules in the OID regulations exist for the general purpose of determining whether stated interest on a debt obligation should be treated as "qualified" interest or as OID. The variable rate test in the REMIC regulations, on the other hand, tests the interest rate solely for the purpose of determining whether the beneficial interest in the REMIC qualifies as a regular interest for the purpose of satisfying overall REMIC qualification. The OID and REMIC rules are not the same in all instances.

[32] Generally, for interests issued after November 12, 1991, but before April 4, 1994, the current value rule was not applicable. The precursor to this rule allowed a REMIC regular interest generally to have a variable rate determined by reference to the OID rules. For example, a rate based on the average cost of funds of one or more financial institutions or a rate equal to the average of two or more objective interest indices would constitute acceptable variable rates.

[33] If a debt instrument provides for two or more qualified floating rates that can reasonably be expected to have approximately the same values throughout the term of the instrument, the two rates together constitute a single qualified floating rate for REMIC regular interest qualification purposes.

Weighted Average Variable Rates A rate based on the weighted average interest rates on some or all of the qualified mortgages qualifies as a variable rate even if the interest rate on some or all of the qualified mortgages on which it is based are subject to a cap or floor, or are otherwise reduced by a number of basis points or a fixed percentage. The weighted average rate, however, must be derived from qualified mortgages that bear either a fixed rate of interest or a qualified variable rate of interest (as that term is used herein for REMIC qualification purposes).

Additions to, subtractions from, and multiples of current value or weighted average rates are permitted. The stated rates may be expressed as (1) the product of the current value or weighted average rate and a fixed factor, (2) a constant number of basis points more or less than the current value or weighted average rate, or (3) the product, plus or minus a fixed number of basis points, of the current value or weighted average rate and a fixed factor.

Caps and Floors Any of the variable rates described above may be subject to a cap or a floor and still qualify as a variable rate. The cap or floor may specify a maximum rate or a maximum number of basis points by which a rate may be increased or decreased from one payment period to the next or over the term of the regular interest. In addition, a rate subject to a funds-available cap may qualify as an acceptable variable rate as long as the cap is based only on amounts available for distribution (including both principal and interest received on some or all of the qualified mortgages as well as amounts held in a reserve fund), and is not simply a device to bypass the REMIC qualification restrictions on variable rates.[34]

Combination of Rates During the term of a REMIC regular interest, the interest rate may shift from one fixed rate to another, or from one qualified variable rate to another. Additionally, the rate may be fixed in one period and variable in another or *vice versa*.

Specified Portions If interest payments on a regular interest are a specified portion of the interest payments on the qualified mortgages of the REMIC, two general tests must be satisfied. First, the portion specified must be expressed either as (1) a fixed percentage of the interest that is payable at a fixed rate or a qualified variable rate on some or all of the qualified mortgages, (2) a fixed number of basis points of the interest payable on some or all of the qualified mortgages, or (3) the interest payable at either a fixed rate or qualified variable rate on some or all of the qualified mortgages in excess of a fixed number of basis points or in excess of a qualified variable rate.

---

[34] The test for a "device" is based on facts and circumstances including whether the rate payable to the regular interest holders is below the rate payable on the qualified mortgages on the startup day, and whether, historically, the rate of interest payable to the regular interest holders has been consistently below that payable on the qualified mortgages.

Second, the specified portion must be established as of the startup day. Once established, it may not vary from the startup day until the time the regular interest is no longer entitled to receive payments.[35]

Call Premiums An interest does not qualify as a regular interest if the interest is entitled to prepayment penalties determined by reference to the length of time the regular interest is outstanding. For example, if the terms of an interest provide that a premium will be paid if the interest is repaid early, either as a result of unanticipated prepayments on qualified mortgages or as a result of a "clean-up call," the interest will not qualify as a regular interest.

However, an interest will not fail to qualify as a regular interest if the organizational documents provide that the REMIC must allocate among and pay to its regular interest holders any customary prepayment penalties received with respect to qualified mortgages. Additionally, prepayment penalties may be allocated among the REMIC classes in any manner specified in the organizational documents. For example, because of the disproportionate risk borne by interest-only classes, the REMIC may allocate all prepayment penalties to one or more interest-only classes.

The Residual Interest To qualify as a REMIC the entity must have one and only one class of residual interest. A residual interest is an interest in a REMIC that is issued on the startup day, is not a regular interest, and is designated as a residual interest in the REMIC initial federal income tax return. Distributions, if any, to holders of a residual interests must be pro rata. However, a residual interest is not required to make any distributions whatsoever.

Payments by the REMIC for services rendered to the REMIC in the ordinary course of business, e.g., a normal servicing fee paid to a mortgage banker, are not considered interests in the REMIC. Likewise, stripped bonds or stripped coupons held outside the REMIC are not considered interests in the REMIC (either regular or residual) even if created in a transaction preceding or contemporaneous with the formation of the REMIC and created from the same qualified mortgages transferred to the REMIC, such as "excess servicing."[36] While the IRS has published safe harbor rates for establishing the demarcation between normal and excess servicing on one-to-four family residential loans, no guidance has been issued for determining normal servicing on commercial loans. However, because the IRS's position is that excess servicing is not a separate interest in the REMIC, it should not affect the qualification.

Other rights not treated as interests in the REMIC are rights of a credit enhancer to be reimbursed for amounts advanced to a REMIC under a credit

---

[35] A specified portion is not treated as varying over time simply because the interest holder's entitlement to the interest on some or all of the qualified mortgages depends on the absence of delinquencies or defaults with respect to those mortgages.

[36] The IRS has taken the position that amounts paid to a mortgage servicer in excess of reasonable compensation for the services to be provided should be treated as a retained interest in the underlying mortgage. In substance, the servicer is treated as retaining an interest-only strip, i.e., engaging in a coupon stripping transaction, to which basis must be allocated.

enhancement contract even if interest is to be paid on the amount, and rights to acquire or obligations to purchase mortgages and other assets from the REMIC pursuant to a clean-up call or a qualified liquidation. Similarly, the right to acquire convertible mortgages upon their conversion is not considered an interest in the REMIC. The regulations also provide that the retention of contingent rights, such as a percentage of mortgagor profits rights, in certain circumstances, will not be treated as an interest in the REMIC.

The Arrangements Test

The tax regulations impose certain penalties on transfers of a REMIC residual interest to a "disqualified organization."[37] The objective of the rule generally is to prevent certain "excess inclusion" income (discussed later in the chapter) attributable to the residual interest holder from escaping taxation by discouraging the transfer of the residual interest to an organization not subject to federal income tax.

To meet this objective, the regulations require that, to qualify as a REMIC, the entity or segregated group of assets must have reasonable arrangements in place to ensure that the residual interest is not held by a disqualified organization. Reasonable arrangements are deemed to exist if the residual interest is issued in registered form, and the REMIC organizational documents expressly prohibit ownership of a residual interest by a disqualified organization. Additionally, the prohibition on transfers to prohibited persons must be noted on the face of the registered certificate or in some other conspicuous document such as an offering circular or private placement memorandum. Further, the REMIC must have reasonable arrangements to ensure that, in the event that the residual interest is held by a disqualified organization, the REMIC will provide to the IRS, transferrers, or agents of the disqualified organization information needed to compute the tax on the transfer upon request.

If the residual is transferred to a disqualified organization,[38] the transferrer is liable for a tax equal to the highest corporate tax rate times the present value of the total anticipated excess inclusions with respect to the transferred residual for periods after the transfer.[39] The tax is considered an excise tax and must be

---

[37] A disqualified organization means the United States, any state or political subdivision thereof, any foreign government, any international organization, or any agency or instrumentality of any of the foregoing, or any organization (other than certain farmers' cooperatives) that is exempt from the income tax unless the organization is subject to tax on unrelated business income.

[38] The tax rules contain an exception for disqualified organizations that temporarily hold a residual interest when the REMIC is formed. The rules exempt the disqualified organization from the tax as long as the disqualified organization has a binding contract to sell the residual interest and the sale actually occurs within seven days (before or after) of the REMIC startup day.

[39] The present value of the anticipated excess inclusions is computed by discounting the anticipated excess inclusions from the end of each remaining calendar quarter (or portion thereof) in which those excess inclusions are expected to occur back to the date of the transfer. The discount rate to be used is the quarterly long-term applicable federal rate in effect on the date of the transfer. In addition, anticipated payments take into account events that have already occurred up to the date of the transfer and must be based upon the prepayment and reinvestment assumptions that would have been used under the "PAC" (prepayment assumption catch-up) method (discussed later in the text) had all regular interests been issued with OID. In addition, any required or permitted clean-up calls are to be taken into account, as well as any qualified liquidations provided for in the REMIC organizational documents.

paid no later than April 15 of the calendar year following the calendar year of the transfer. If the transfer is through an agent of the disqualified organization (such as a broker or nominee), then the agent will be held liable for the tax. The transferrer will be relieved of liability for the tax if the transferee furnishes the transferrer an affidavit[40] that the transferee is not a disqualified organization and the transferrer, at the time of the transfer, does not have actual knowledge that the affidavit is false.

"Pass-thru" Entities with Disqualified Organizations as Beneficial Owners If the owner of the residual interest is a "pass-thru" entity of which a disqualified organization is a member, a tax is imposed on the pass-thru entity. A "pass-thru" entity is any regulated investment company, real estate investment trust, common trust fund, partnership, trust or estate, and certain cooperatives.[41] The tax is equal to the product of the amount of excess inclusion income allocable to the disqualified organization for the taxable year and the highest corporate tax rate. In effect, the pass-thru entity is held liable for the tax on the excess inclusion income that would otherwise escape taxation. This tax also is in the nature of an excise tax and is due no later than the fifteenth day of the fourth month following the close of the taxable year of the pass-thru entity. In addition, the residual income that would otherwise be included in the gross income of the pass-thru entity is reduced by the amount of the tax.

If the record holder of the interest in the pass-thru entity furnishes an affidavit to the pass-thru entity that the record holder is not a disqualified organization,[42] and for any period the pass-thru entity does not have actual knowledge that the affidavit is false, the tax will not be imposed.

Waiver of Tax The tax on transfers to disqualified organizations may be waived if, within a reasonable time after discovery that the transfer was to a disqualified organization, steps are taken so that the residual interest is no longer held by the disqualified organization.[43] However, tax still may be assessed on the transferrer during the period the residual interest was held by the disqualified organization.

---

[40] An acceptable affidavit would include the transferee's social security number with a statement under penalties of perjury that the social security number is the transferee's; or a statement by the transferee under penalties of perjury that the transferee is not a disqualified organization.

[41] If a person holds an interest in a pass-thru entity as a nominee for another person, then the nominee is treated as a pass-thru entity with respect to the interest that it holds in the pass-thru entity.

[42] The affidavit should include either (1) a social security number with a statement under penalties of perjury that the social security number is that of the record holder, or (2) a statement under penalties of perjury that the record holder is not a disqualified organization.

[43] With respect to the tax on pass-thru entities, the wording of the statute implies that either the pass-thru entity may dispose of the residual interest or that the disqualified organization may cease to be affiliated with the pass-thru entity. Either solution would satisfy the requirement of the statue that the residual interest no longer be held by a disqualified organization.

Discovery and Obligation to Furnish Information There is, in fact, no obligation *per se* on the part of the REMIC to determine if an interest in its residual class has been transferred to a disqualified organization. However, upon request from the transferrer, or, if applicable, the agent of the disqualified organization, the REMIC must furnish information sufficient to allow the computation of the present value of the anticipated excess inclusion income. The information must be furnished to the requesting party and to the IRS within sixty days of the request. The REMIC may charge a fee for providing this service and the fee will not be considered income from a prohibited transaction.

REMIC Disqualification

If an entity or segregated pool of assets fails to qualify as a REMIC at any time during the tax year, the loss of REMIC status is considered effective as of the beginning of the tax year.[44] If the IRS determines that the loss of status was inadvertent, REMIC status may be continued or the loss of status disregarded, whichever the IRS deems appropriate. In addition, the REMIC as well as any beneficial interest holders must make any adjustments the IRS may specifically require. To help demonstrate that the failure was inadvertent, within a reasonable time after discovery of the event or events that caused the loss of REMIC status steps should be taken to cure the defect.

TAXATION OF THE REMIC

The REMIC recognizes no gain or loss on formation. Prospectively, REMIC taxable income generally is computed in the same manner as for an individual; however, the code and regulations provide specific rules for certain items as noted below:

- Accrual method accounting must be used and a calendar year must be adopted.
- Original issue discount on qualified mortgages held by a REMIC (including regular interests in other REMICs) are computed using statutory rules that require the REMIC to estimate prepayments on the obligations[45] and make adjustments in each accrual period to account for differences between actual payment experience and the estimated payment experi-

---

[44] After 1991, an unincorporated entity that loses its REMIC status risks being classified as association taxable as a corporation under the taxable mortgage pool rules discussed later in the text.

[45] Residential mortgage securitizations generally estimate prepayments using the Public Securities Association (PSA) prepayment model. Because of "lockout periods" and associated prepayment penalties for early payment, many REMIC securitizations of commercial mortgages assume the mortgages will pay according to their stated terms (i.e., no prepayments).

ence. This methodology often is referred to as the prepayment assumption catch-up method, or PAC method.[46]

- Gain or loss on any asset held by the REMIC is treated as ordinary (not capital) gain or loss.
- Market discount on any market discount bond is included in income currently on a constant yield basis.
- The limits on deducting investment interest do not apply.
- Bad debts are not treated as nonbusiness bad debts. Accordingly, the bad debt loss will not be treated as short-term capital loss.
- Deductions for foreign taxes, charitable contributions, medical and moving expenses, personal exemptions, net operating loss carryovers, and certain other items are not allowed.
- Expenses incurred in forming the REMIC are not treated as expenses of the REMIC. Instead, the sponsor's basis in assets contributed to the REMIC are increased for organizational expenses.
- Gains, losses, income or deductions attributable to prohibited transactions are excluded from taxable income.
- Finally, to the extent income from foreclosure property is separately taxed under the REMIC rules, only the after-tax income is included in the computation of REMIC taxable income.

While accrual of market discount is required, a REMIC holding debt obligations acquired with bond premium must make an affirmative election if it desires to amortize the bond premium.

---

[46] Section 1272(a)(6) provides that the daily portion of original issue discount is determined by allocating to each day in an accrual period a ratable share of the excess (if any) of the present value of future payments determined at the end of the accrual period plus payments applied to stated redemption price at maturity during the period, over the adjusted issue price of the debt obligation at the beginning of the accrual period. In determining the present value of future payments, the original yield to maturity, events which have occurred before the close of the accrual period, and a prepayment assumption determined as specified in regulations must be used.

The general formula for computing OID for an accrual period can be expressed as follows:

$$OID_n \text{(must be positive)} = AIP_{n+1} + P_n - AIP_n$$

where OID_n is the amount of OID for the accrual period. AIP_{n+1} represents the adjusted issue price of the instrument at the end of the accrual period, and P_n represents the payments received during the period (other than qualified stated interest). AIP_n represents the adjusted issue price of the instrument at the beginning of the accrual period. The adjusted issue price of an instrument at the end of an accrual period is the present value of the remaining payments on the instrument determined by discounting those remaining payments at the instrument's assumed yield to maturity. An instrument's yield to maturity is the discount rate that on the instrument's issue date, when applied to the projected stream of payments to be made on the instrument, causes the present value of the stream of payments to equal the instrument's issue price.

Nonaccrual of Interest

For tax purposes, an accrual method taxpayer generally must recognize income when the right to the income is fixed and the amount can be determined with reasonable accuracy. Under this principle, interest on a loan (performing or nonperforming) must be accrued as income unless the taxpayer has a reasonable expectation that the interest is uncollectible at the time of the accrual. This depends on the facts and circumstances of each nonaccrual loan, with the taxpayer carrying the burden of proof to establish that the interest is not collectible.

The collectibility of interest income with respect to nonaccrual loans has been a source of controversy between some taxpayers and the IRS. Being largely a factual (rather than legal) issue, such controversies are usually resolved on a facts-and-circumstances basis, either with the IRS directly or through the courts. The IRS may, however, seek to force the recognition of interest income on legal grounds as well. For example, the IRS has taken an administrative position that original issue discount (OID) must be accrued notwithstanding that the holder of the obligation had a reasonable expectation that the amount would not be collected; such a position seeks to differentiate OID from "stated" interest, thus denying taxpayers the right to rely on existing regulations and case law.

Bad Debts

For REMICs, bad debts are deductible under the specific charge-off method under rules applicable to most nonbank taxpayers. A deduction for wholly worthless debt must be taken in the year of the worthlessness. A deduction for partially worthless debt generally is available in the year the amount that is partially worthless is "charged off." The total or partial worthlessness of a debt is a facts-and-circumstances, loan-by-loan determination. As a factual issue, whether a loan is wholly or partially worthless, often is a source of controversy between taxpayers and the IRS.

Foreclosed Property

Upon a default by the borrower, the holder of a mortgage will probably have several alternatives available for attempting recovery, in whole or in part, of its investment. The range of a holder's alternatives depends on a variety of factors, including: the terms of the note; the nature of the mortgaged property; the applicable state law; and the existence of any guarantee or insurance. For a REMIC, there are the additional considerations of rules related to permitted investments and prohibited transactions (discussed elsewhere in this text).

Generally, the following alternatives will be available to a REMIC:

Deed in lieu of foreclosure. The lender can accept the borrower's voluntary conveyance of the property in settlement of the obligation. Such conveyances are frequently utilized to avoid the cost, delay and administrative complexities associated with foreclosure sales.

Foreclosure sale. The lender can force a foreclosure sale, in which it acquires the property securing the debt. Foreclosure sales also may result in a third party acquiring the property, with the sales proceeds remitted to the lender. Foreclosure sometimes involves the lender's right to a deficiency judgement (when the value of the property is less than the outstanding debt) and the borrower's right of redemption (allowing the borrower to reacquire the property by paying the debt and related charges within a specified time).

Under general tax principles, the receipt of property is considered to be the receipt of payment on the obligation. In an "in lieu of" conveyance, the mortgaged property is treated as transferred in consideration of the cancellation of the debt. Any excess of the lender's adjusted basis in the debt over the fair market value of the property received generally is treated as a bad debt deductible under the specific charge-off method.

In a foreclosure sale, the REMIC recognizes a bad debt for the excess of the basis in the loan over the bid price of the property. The tax rules generally provide that, absent clear and convincing evidence to the contrary, the bid price will be presumed to be the fair market value of the property. However, the IRS has successfully argued, and won in the courts, that to the extent the fair market value of the property is in excess of the bid price, the lender (in this case the REMIC) must recognize a gain.

Cancellation of Indebtedness Income

Because of defaults on collateral held by a REMIC, or for other reasons, situations may arise when a REMIC will be unable to repay regular interest classes according to their terms. Therefore, it is possible for a REMIC to default on its regular interests.

Under general tax principles, income from the discharge of indebtedness is includible in gross income unless it is excluded under one of four specific provisions, two of which may be relevant to a REMIC: a debt discharge in a Title 11 bankruptcy action, or a discharge when the taxpayer is insolvent outside bankruptcy. The term "insolvent" refers to an excess of liabilities over the fair market value of assets immediately prior to the discharge. The exclusion from taxation is limited to the amount of the insolvency.

When an amount is excluded from gross income through one of the above provisions, a taxpayer is required to reduce its tax attributes, in a specified order. For a REMIC, any such attribute reduction will fall largely on the basis of its property (e.g., mortgages or securities). The dollar-for-dollar reduction in such basis essentially represents a deferral of the cancellation of debt income until the reduced-basis property is paid off, paid down, sold, or exchanged.

Taxes Imposed on the REMIC

Prohibited Transactions A 100% tax is imposed on the net income from "prohibited transactions." Net income is generally determined by subtracting from the gross income attributable to a prohibited transaction the deductions permitted under the tax statute that are directly associated with the transaction. If a prohibited transaction results in a loss, neither the gross income attributable to that transaction nor any deduction associated therewith is taken into account in determining net income from prohibited transactions.

A prohibited transaction includes the disposition of a qualified mortgage other than a disposition pursuant to the substitution of a qualified mortgage with a qualified replacement mortgage, or the repurchase of a defective mortgage; the default or foreclosure of a mortgage; the bankruptcy or insolvency of the REMIC; or a qualified liquidation. Other prohibited transactions include the receipt of any income attributable to any asset of the REMIC that is neither a qualified mortgage nor a permitted investment; the receipt of fees or other compensation for services; and gain (but not loss) from the disposition of any cash flow investment other than pursuant to a qualified liquidation. However, the disposition of a qualified mortgage or the realization of gain from the disposition of a cash flow investment will not be considered a prohibited transaction if the disposition is required to prevent default on a regular interest (due to a default on qualified mortgages) or to facilitate a clean-up call.

Tax on Contributions after the Startup Day A 100% tax is levied on contributions to the REMIC after the startup day. The tax is not levied on contributions of cash made to facilitate a clean-up call or a qualified liquidation, any guarantee payments, any contribution during the three-month window beginning on the start-up day, any contribution to a qualified reserve fund by the holder of a residual interest in the REMIC, and any other cash contributions that may be permitted by future regulations.

Tax on Net Income from Foreclosure Property A tax equal to the highest corporate rate in effect for the year is imposed on certain foreclosed property net income. The net income subject to tax is determined by reference to the real estate investment trust rules and generally includes income such as gains from subdividing and selling property, certain rents contingent on profits of a party related to the REMIC, or rents from property that might be considered to be, in effect, compensation to the REMIC for other than customary services.[47]

Each of the three REMIC-level taxes — the prohibited transactions tax, the tax on contributions after the startup day, and the tax on net income from certain foreclosure property — is computed and reported on the REMIC annual income tax return, Form 1066, Schedule J.

---

[47] Once property ceases to be foreclosure property (i.e., generally after it has been held two years, unless permission is received from the IRS, pursuant to the REIT rules, to extend the foreclosure period), in theory any income derived thereafter would no longer be subject to the tax on net income from foreclosure property. However, *any* income earned after the property no longer qualifies as foreclosure property would presumably be income from nonpermitted assets subject to the 100% tax on prohibited transactions. Additionally, the qualification of the REMIC would be jeopardized if the amount of nonpermitted assets exceeded a de minimis amount.

Clean-up Calls and Qualified Liquidations — Overview

For administrative reasons, such as when the costs of servicing a class outweigh the benefits associated with maintaining the class, the REMIC may exercise a so-called "clean-up call" on a regular interest class prior to maturity. In lieu of clean-up calls on individual classes, the organizational documents generally provide for "optional terminations" with respect to the securitization as a whole. A decision to liquidate a REMIC may be made for a myriad of reasons including administrative convenience. Most organizational documents typically permit an optional termination when the outstanding aggregate balance of the mortgage assets falls below a certain percentage of the original aggregate balance.[48]

The prohibited transaction rules, discussed previously, generally impose taxes on the REMIC for certain enumerated transactions. However, certain dispositions to facilitate clean-up calls and qualified liquidations will not be prohibited transactions. For example, the net income from the dispositions of qualified mortgages, or from the disposition of cash flow investments, to facilitate a clean-up call, or as part of a qualified liquidation, will not be subject to the 100% tax on net income from those transactions. Additionally, contributions to the REMIC that are made in cash will not be subject to the 100% tax on contributions made after the startup day, if the contribution is made to facilitate a clean-up call or qualified liquidation.

Clean-up Calls A clean-up call, as defined in the regulations, is the "redemption of a class of regular interest, when, by reason of prior payments with respect to those interests, the administrative costs associated with servicing that class outweigh the benefits of maintaining the class." Various factors may be taken into account to determine whether the redemption of a regular interest class qualifies as a clean-up call for tax purposes. Such factors include the number of holders of the class, the frequency of payments to those holders, the effect a redemption will have on the yield of the class, and the proportion of current principal outstanding at the time of the liquidation to the total original principal of the class. However, a safe-harbor provision provides that the redemption of a class will be considered a clean-up call for tax purposes when the outstanding principal balance of that class is no more than ten percent of its original balance, regardless of the other factors.[49]

Liquidations A "qualified liquidation" is a transaction in which the REMIC adopts a plan of complete liquidation and, within a 90-day period starting with the date of adoption of the plan, sells all of its assets and distributes the proceeds to the regular and residual interest holders. The liquidation does not need to be in any special

---

[48] For example, a recent CMBS prospectus provided that the servicer will repurchase all of the mortgages once their aggregate principal balance is equal to or less than five percent of the aggregate original principal balance.

[49] As a condition of qualifying as a regular interest, there can be no call premium associated with the right to exercise a call. In addition, the redemption of a class of regular interests undertaken to profit from interest rate changes does not qualify for tax purposes as a clean-up call.

form. The REMIC needs only to attach a statement to its final tax return stating the first date of the liquidation period.

A liquidation generally is treated as the sale of the REMIC assets and the distribution of the proceeds from such sale to the regular and residual interests holders. The legislative history of the REMIC provisions suggests that no gain or loss on the sale is recognized at the REMIC level. However, it appears this language may have been erroneously included in the legislative history and may not be reliable. Whether or not the REMIC recognizes gain on the liquidation of assets may be important to the holder of the residual interest. While this does not change the residual holder's total income, it may have an effect on the character (ordinary versus capital) and timing of the income or loss that will be recognized.

TAXATION OF RESIDUAL INTEREST HOLDER[50]

The residual interest holder retains the ownership rights in the net assets of the REMIC and, consequently, is taxed on the net income of the REMIC. The income of the REMIC must be determined for each calendar quarter and then prorated to each day in the quarter. The residual interest holder must report income based on the number of days the residual interest was held in the quarter, prorated for the proportion of the total residual class owned. The annual taxable income is the sum of the quarterly amounts.

REMIC taxable income or loss passed through to the residual interest holder is treated as ordinary income or loss. However, any gain or loss on the disposition of a residual may be ordinary or capital, depending on the character of the residual in the hands of the holder.

The basis of the residual interest generally is its cost if purchased in a secondary market transaction. If acquired upon the formation of the REMIC, the basis generally represents an allocation of the sponsor's basis in the property contributed to the REMIC. For residuals with no economic value or whose acquisition was accompanied by the receipt of an inducement payment, this basis generally will be zero. Basis is increased for REMIC net taxable income and decreased (but not below zero) for net tax losses and distributions. Unused losses may be carried forward indefinitely by the residual holder and may be used to offset income from the same residual interest. Any distribution by the REMIC to the residual interest holder will not be included in that holder's income to the extent the distribution does not exceed the holder's tax basis. Any distributions in excess of the holder's basis are treated as gain from the sale or exchange of the residual interest.[51]

---

[50] For a thorough discussion of tax issues peculiar to residual interests, see Kirk Van Brunt, "Tax Aspects of REMIC Residual Interests," 2 *Florida Tax Review 152* (1994).

[51] Gain or loss on residual interests held by a bank or thrift subject to section 582(c) is treated as ordinary income (not capital gain). Regular interests are afforded the same treatment.

Excess Inclusion Income

Most commercial REMIC residual interests have minimal or no economic value and may be entitled only to nominal distributions, if any. Regardless of economic value, residual interest holders are taxed on the net income or loss of the REMIC. The net income of a REMIC in early years often greatly exceeds economic income (which often is zero). This excess of taxable income over economic income generally is referred to as "phantom income." The "excess inclusion income" rules seek to assure that the phantom income is subject to tax. Accordingly, the taxable income of a residual interest holder generally cannot be less than the excess inclusion income and cannot be offset by net operating losses whether from the current year or from prior or subsequent years. If the holder of the residual interest is a member of an affiliated group filing a consolidated income tax return, the taxable income of the group cannot be less than the sum of the excess inclusions attributable to all residual interests held by all members of the group.

Excess inclusion income is determined quarterly and is the excess (if any) of the calendar quarter taxable income of the REMIC over the sum of the "daily accruals" for the quarter attributable to the residual interest. In simplified terms, the daily accruals are intended to represent a reasonable economic return to the residual interest holder. For the REMIC first quarter, the daily accrual is equal to the issue price of the residual interest times 120% of the long-term applicable federal rate (AFR).[52] For the purpose of computing daily accruals on a particular REMIC, the AFR for the first period remains constant throughout the life of the REMIC. For subsequent quarters, the issue price of the residual interest is increased for daily accruals (if any), as computed above, and decreased for any distributions made to the residual interest holder.[53] The calculation of excess inclusion income is made by the REMIC and reported to the residual interest holder. The calculation is not adjusted to reflect the price paid by subsequent purchasers; therefore, regardless of the price paid by a subsequent purchaser, if the original issue price was zero, excess inclusion income generally will equal the entire quarterly taxable income of the REMIC. Considering that many residual interests are issued with no value, i.e., the issue price is zero, the calculation above is simplified. In substance, all taxable income of the REMIC is excess inclusion for all quarters.

Because excess inclusion income is determined quarterly, taxable income for the quarter cannot be less than the excess inclusion income for the quarter. Additionally, taxable income for the year *cannot* be less than the sum of the excess

---

[52] In general, the long-term AFR is based on the average market yields during a calendar month on outstanding marketable obligations of the United States with remaining periods to maturity of greater than nine years. The AFRs are published monthly in a revenue procedure.

[53] The original issue price increased for daily accruals from prior periods and reduced by distributions is referred to as the adjusted issue price and is the amount used for purposes of computing excess inclusions for subsequent periods. This amount does not represent the residual interest holder's basis in the interest but is used solely for computing the amount of excess inclusion income for ensuing quarters. Subsequent contributions to the REMIC by residual interest holders (for example, pursuant to a clean-up call) may increase the adjusted issue price.

inclusion income for each quarter in the year. Losses in any quarter within the same taxable year cannot offset excess inclusion income from prior or subsequent quarters. For example, assume the excess inclusion income in the first three quarters of the year is $200 per quarter ($600 in total). In the fourth quarter the REMIC reported a net loss of ($800). Regardless of what other losses or deductions the residual interest holder might have, taxable income of the residual interest holder for the year cannot be less than $600.

Thrift Exception Thrifts,[54] and certain special purpose subsidiaries of those thrifts, holding residual interests with "significant value" may be exempt from the general rule that taxable income cannot be less than excess inclusion income. That is, under certain circumstances the thrift and its qualified subsidiaries may offset their excess inclusion income with their deductions and net operating losses but not losses or net operating losses of other members of the consolidated group.

A residual interest has significant value if the residual interest is issued at an aggregate issue price that is equal to or greater than two percent of the aggregate of the issue prices of all regular and residual interests in the REMIC. In addition, the anticipated weighted average life of the residual interest must be at least 20% of the weighted average life of the REMIC.[55]

Tax Exempt Holders The excess inclusion income of a tax-exempt organization is treated as unrelated business taxable income.

Transfers of "Noneconomic" Residuals If a "noneconomic" residual interest is transferred, the transfer will be ignored for all federal tax purposes if a significant purpose of the transfer was for the transferor to avoid or impede the assessment or collection of tax. A significant purpose to avoid or impede the assessment or collection of tax exists if, at the time of the transfer, the transferor knew or had reason to know that the transferee would be unwilling or unable to satisfy the tax liability with respect to its share of the future taxable income of the REMIC.

The regulations provide a safe harbor for establishing that the transferor does not have this "improper knowledge." Under the safe harbor, two requirements must be met. First, the transferor must conduct a reasonable investigation of the financial condition of the transferee and conclude that the transferee has historically paid its debts as they came due and there is no significant evidence to indicate that the transferee will not continue to do so in the future. Second, the transferee must represent to the transferor that it understands that, as the holder of a noneconomic

---

[54] For this purpose, a thrift means an organization to which section 593 applies. Generally, this would include the following entities as defined in the tax law: domestic building and loan associations, mutual savings banks, and cooperative banks.

[55] The anticipated weighted average life of a REMIC is the anticipated weighted average lives of all classes of interests in the REMIC. In determining the weighted average life of the REMIC, payments on each of the classes are aggregated as if one payment were being made on a single regular interest. The regulations provide specific rules for making this computation.

residual interest, it may incur tax liabilities in excess of cash flows due the holder, and that the transferee intends to pay taxes associated with holding the residual when due.

A residual interest is "noneconomic" for this purpose unless at the time of the transfer, the present value of the expected future distributions to the residual interest equals or exceeds the projected tax liability computed at the highest corporate tax rate on the present value of expected excess inclusion income.[56] In addition, at the time of the transfer, the transferor must reasonably expect the REMIC to make distributions to the transferee sufficient to satisfy the tax liability with respect to future excess inclusion income on or after the time such tax liability accrues.

Transfers to Foreign Persons A transfer to a foreign person of a residual interest with "tax avoidance potential" is disregarded for all federal tax purposes. A residual interest has tax avoidance potential unless, at the time of the transfer, the transferor reasonably expects that, for *each* excess inclusion, the REMIC will make a distribution at least equal to 30% of such excess inclusion amount, and that such distribution will be made when the excess inclusion accrues, but no later than the close of the calendar year following the year of the accrual. Unlike the rules pertaining to noneconomic residuals, there is no discounting of anticipated excess inclusion amounts.

Under a safe harbor provision, a reasonable expectation exists if the 30% test would be satisfied if the mortgage collateral were projected to prepay at rates from 50% to 200% of the rate assumed in the pricing of the instruments and used for purposes of computing income under the PAC method.[57]

The above rules do not apply if the excess inclusion income is income effectively connected with a trade or business in the United States.

Transfers by Foreign Persons To further ensure that excess inclusion income is taxed, transfers of residual interests by foreign holders to a U.S. person, or to a foreign holder in whose hands the residual income would constitute income effectively connected with a U.S. trade or business, is disregarded if the transfer has the effect of permitting the transferrer to avoid tax on excess inclusion income. However, the transfer is disregarded only with respect to those sections of the tax statute and regulations dealing with the taxation of foreign persons on U.S. source income and the accompanying rules on foreign withholding taxes.

Pass-thru Entities If a residual interest is held by a REIT, regulated investment company (e.g., mutual fund), common trust fund, or certain cooperatives, excess

---

[56] The present value of the anticipated excess inclusions is computed by discounting the anticipated excess inclusions from the end of each remaining calendar quarter in which those excess inclusions are expected to occur back to the date of the transfer. The discount rate to be used is the quarterly long-term applicable federal rate in effect on the date of the transfer.

[57] Or the rate that would have been assumed had the mortgages been issued with original issue discount

inclusion income generally is treated as a separate item that passes through to the beneficial owner, with the general excess inclusion rules applying to the beneficial owner.[58]

Wash Sales

Under a general rule, a loss realized from the sale or other disposition of stock or securities will not be recognized for tax purposes if substantially identical stock or securities are acquired, or a contract or option to acquire has been entered into within a period of 30 days before and 30 days after a sale or disposition. Rather, the loss is deferred and the basis of the acquired stock or security is increased. Additionally, limited guidance is provided that takes into account differences in the amounts disposed as compared to the amounts acquired, and *vice versa*.[59] If the loss was sustained by a dealer in stock or securities and the loss arose from a transaction made in the ordinary course of that business, the dealer will not be subject to these "wash sale" rules.

While the term "security" is not well defined, REMIC regular interests likely will qualify as securities. Taxpayers will be able to look to relevant case law and rulings in determining whether one regular interest is substantially identical to another. However, the wash sale rules are statutorily applicable to REMIC residual interests. Further, with respect to residual interests, the 30-day window is extended to six months both before and after the sale. More importantly, any residual interest is automatically considered to be substantially identical to any other residual interest.[60] Because guidance has not been issued, it also is unclear how holders of residual interests would apply the general rules that allow taxpayers to account for differences in amounts acquired and sold. Consequently, if a holder sells a residual interest at a loss and within six months, either before or after the sale, buys another residual interest, some portion, if not all of the loss, will be deferred.

The application of the wash sale rules to sponsors also is not totally resolved. Under the REMIC rules, the acquisition of a residual interest upon formation of the REMIC is not "by purchase or by an exchange on which the entire amount of gain or loss was recognized by law." In fact, the REMIC rules specifically state that gain or loss is not recognized on the formation of the REMIC. Arguably, therefore, the acquisition of a residual interest at formation should not result in the deferral of losses from sales of other residual interests. Additionally, if the sponsor can be viewed as a dealer in securities under existing rules, and the disposition of the residual is in the ordinary course of the dealer's trade or business of dealing in residuals, the wash sale rules would not apply.

---

[58] In addition, certain rules require that reserves related to certain variable life insurance contracts not be adjusted for excess inclusion income attributable to a residual interest owned by a life insurance company.

[59] For example, it is unclear whether the test is made based on the original issue price of the residual, the dollar amount of collateral held by the REMIC, the dollar amount of bonds issued by the REMIC, or some other measure. Obviously, there are arguments both for and against any of the listed benchmarks.

[60] As well as to similar ownership interests in taxable mortgage pools (discussed later).

It is unclear whether an inducement payment (discussed in the next section) made to dispose of a noneconomic residual interest would be allowed as an ordinary deduction, deferred under the wash sale rules, or treated in some other manner (e.g., a loan to the recipient of the payment).

Inducement Payments

Most residual interests in recent securitizations have no economic value. For example, the residual may not be entitled to any distributions but must report taxable income in the early years and will report offsetting taxable losses in the later years. Therefore, the holder of the residual interest will have to pay income taxes in the early years and then hope to receive refunds in later years. Consequently, it is common to have the sponsor of the REMIC make a payment to the "purchaser" of the residual as an inducement to make the acquisition. Payments also are commonly made by holders desiring to retransfer residuals to subsequent holders. The "inducement payment" typically represents the net present value of the anticipated future tax payments, net of tax benefits and cash distributions (if any), expected by the residual holder, plus a risk premium.

There are numerous unanswered questions related to inducement payments both from the payor's and recipient's perspective, a full discussion of which is beyond the scope of this chapter. However, some of the unresolved issues are: (i) the proper treatment of inducement payments by a sponsor, e.g., is the payment deductible as an ordinary expense or should it be treated as a loss from the sale or exchange of the residual interest; and (ii) the proper treatment by the recipient of an inducement payment; e.g., is the amount taxable in the year received or may the amount be deferred and amortized on some basis (e.g., straight-line or using time value of money principles) over the period to which it relates,[61] and what is the character of the income when recognized (ordinary or capital).

Mark-to-Market and Inventory Rules

Final regulations under the section 475 mark-to-market rules provide that residual interests are not securities for purposes of those rules, with the result that section 475 dealers may not mark residual interests to market.[62] The IRS also has taken the position in a published ruling that residual interests may not be marked to market or carried at the lower of cost or market by holders that qualify as dealers. The IRS was concerned that dealers would be able to effectively avoid the intended purpose of the excess inclusion rules and effectively avoid phantom income problems if they were allowed to use inventory methods for residual interests. However, the regulations do not affect the character of any gain or loss ultimately recognized by a dealer in residuals.

---

[61] Similar issues existed when notional principal contracts were being structured with significant up-front payments. The IRS ultimately issued rules providing for the deferral of most payments by the recipient and the payor. In the area of prepaid loan points, the IRS decided that, economically, points represented a reduction in the amount loaned even though significant case law would have supported a contrary view.

[62] Earlier proposed regulations had exempted only noneconomic residuals.

TAX REPORTING ISSUES

Regular Interest Holder

A regular interest holder must use the accrual method of accounting to report income from that instrument. Items that the holder may have to consider include OID, coupon interest (referred to as qualified stated interest or QSI), market discount, bond premium or acquisition premium. Because investors generally will not be able to model a REMIC securitization to determine the taxable income for a single bond,[63] REMICs are required to provide investors information sufficient to compute taxable income. Information on an investor's SIS (Supplemental Information Statement)[64] for each quarter includes the adjusted issue price,[65] qualified stated interest paid, OID accrued (also included in daily OID accruals), and the market discount fraction.[66]

The SIS is prepared quarterly and is available to investors on request. IRS Publication 938, updated annually, provides investors with the names, addresses, and phone numbers of REMIC issuers from whom they may request copies of the SIS. If requested, the SIS must be provided no later than the earlier of two weeks from the date of the request or 30 days following the close of the calendar quarter. At the end of the year, for persons entitled to an IRS Form 1099-INT or 1099-OID, the supplemental statement must be included with the Form 1099. Unlike most other Form 1099 reporting which is due January 31, Form 1099 reporting for REMIC regular interests must be made by March 15.

Disposition Gain on REMIC Regular Interests If a REMIC regular interest is sold or otherwise disposed of at a gain, a portion of that gain must be treated as ordinary income, notwithstanding the character of the instrument as capital or ordinary in the hands of the investor. The portion of the gain that is to be treated as ordinary is the excess, if any, of the amount that would have been includible in the gross income of the investor if the yield on the instrument were 110% of the applicable federal rate at the beginning of the investor's holding period over the amount actually includible in gross income with respect to the instrument.

---

[63] Computation of taxable income by a regular interest holder would require the holder to have perfect information regarding the mortgage prepayment assumptions, the paydown rules for the other REMIC classes, and other complex elements of the securitization.

[64] Because this supplemental data is generally released in factor format, the supplemental information statements often are referred to as "tax factors" or "factor sheets."

[65] The adjusted issue price reported is computed as if the regular interest had been held continuously by the first purchaser of the instrument.

[66] The market discount fraction can be used for a variety of purposes including computing market discount earned, bond premium amortized, and is used to assist the holder in determining the fixed fraction necessary to amortize acquisition premium. The market discount fraction represents either OID for the period over remaining OID, or qualified stated interest for the period over remaining qualified stated interest.

Residual Interests

Each calendar quarter the REMIC must furnish a Form 1066 Schedule Q to each person who held the residual interest during the quarter. The Schedule Q must be delivered or mailed no later than the last day of the month following the close of the calendar quarter.[67] If the residual interest was held by a nominee, the nominee must furnish the Schedule Q to the person for whom it is acting no later than 30 days after receiving it.

The Schedule Q must report the holder's share of taxable income or net loss for the calendar quarter, the holder's share of daily accruals and excess inclusion income for the quarter and, if the holder is an individual or similar person subject to limitation on investment expense deductions, the holder's share of the REMIC investment expenses (generally servicing and administrative fees).

Although quarterly notice to the IRS is not required, the REMIC must attach to its annual income tax return a copy of each Schedule Q for each person or nominee who held the residual interest at any time during the REMIC taxable year.

Thrift Qualifying Asset Percentage   Thrift institutions are one of the few remaining taxpayers eligible to maintain a reserve for bad debts. To qualify as a thrift, among other things, at least 60% of the thrift's assets must fall into any one of several categories of assets. These categories generally consist of residential real property loans,[68] REMIC regular and residual interests to the extent backed by qualified assets (as discussed in this section), cash, and certain government securities,[69] but not commercial mortgages.

A regular or residual interest in the REMIC will be considered to be a qualifying asset in the proportion that the underlying assets of the REMIC are themselves qualifying assets. If that percentage is at least 95%, the entire interest is considered to qualify. Accordingly, the reporting requirements for the quarterly Schedule Q require that the REMIC disclose the percentage of the REMIC assets that satisfy the thrift qualifying asset test. The reported percentage is based on the ratio of the average adjusted basis of the REMIC thrift qualified assets to the average adjusted basis of all of the REMIC assets for the calendar quarter.

Unlike residential mortgage securitizations, commercial securitizations often combine multifamily residential loans with loans secured by office buildings, hotels, shopping centers, congregate care, and other real property. Additionally, since the collateral is often viewed as a bundle of cash flows, the total issue price of the deal often is not allocated to individual loans being securitized; thus, it is diffi-

---

[67] Under proposed regulations, the REMIC would have up to 41 days to issue the Schedule Q.

[68] Multifamily residential mortgages often are securitized with mortgages on commercial properties, but generally qualify as residential loans for purposes of this test. Generally a multifamily residential mortgage secured by property, used in part for nonresidential purposes, will be considered to be a residential real property loan if at least 80% of the property's planned use at the time the loan was made was residential.

[69] The determination of whether 60% of a thrift's total assets fall into one of these categories is generally made either at the end of the year or is based on the average assets outstanding during the year.

cult to determine the adjusted issue price of residential and nonresidential loans for purposes of the above disclosures. Accordingly, thrifts contemplating investing in commercial securitizations should consider whether the regular or residual interest will represent a qualifying asset for purposes of the 60% test.[70]

Thrift Qualifying Real Property Loan Percentage Thrifts using the bad debt reserve method are required to maintain a reserve for qualifying real property loans and nonqualified loans (i.e., loans not secured by real property). Because residual and regular interests are considered loans, the REMIC must report the percentage of its assets that are qualifying real property loans. Qualifying real property loans generally include most loans secured by real property, *including* loans secured by commercial real estate. Similar to the thrift qualifying asset test, a regular or residual interest in the REMIC will be considered to be a qualifying real property loan in the proportion that the underlying assets of the REMIC are themselves qualifying real property loans. If that percentage is at least 95%, the entire interest is considered a qualifying real property loan.

Accordingly, the reporting requirements accompanying Schedule Q require the disclosure of the percentage of the REMIC assets that meet the definition of qualifying real property loans. The reported percentage is based on the ratio of the average adjusted basis of the REMIC qualifying real property loans to average adjusted basis of the REMIC total assets for the calendar quarter.[71] If the percentage is at least 95%, the entire interest is considered to qualify.

REIT Qualifying Asset Percentage To qualify as a REIT, an entity must satisfy a number of asset and income tests which depend on the definition of the term "real estate assets." A regular or residual interest in a REMIC is treated as a "real estate asset," and any income attributable thereto is treated as qualifying REIT income if 95% or more of the REMIC assets are "real estate assets." If less than 95% of a REMIC assets are "real estate assets," a REIT is treated as holding and receiving directly its proportionate share of the REMIC assets and income.

The reporting requirements accompanying Schedule Q call for the disclosure of the percentage of the REMIC assets that satisfy the REIT asset requirement. The reported percentage is to be based on the ratio of the average adjusted basis of

---

[70] The budget reconciliation bill passed by Congress in December 1995, and subsequently vetoed by the President, contained a provision that would have repealed the special bad debt rules for thrift institutions under section 593. However, the bill did not repeal the 60% qualifying asset test applicable to institutions seeking to meet the definition of a domestic building and loan association or cooperative bank. If the bill ultimately is enacted, qualifying as a domestic building and loan association or cooperative bank will be almost irrelevant for federal income tax purposes, but may still have implications for state and regulatory purposes.

[71] Qualifying real property loans and nonqualifying loans generally are important only at year-end when the thrift's annual addition to the bad debt reserve is computed. However, most institutions project their annual additions for planning and estimated tax purposes; therefore, quarterly data is helpful. As noted, the qualifying asset test can be made at year-end or on the basis of averaging throughout the year.

the REMIC "real estate assets" to the average adjusted basis of the REMIC total assets for the calendar quarter. If the percentage is at least 95%, the entire interest is considered to qualify.[72]

For purposes of each of the three tests above, a REMIC holding a regular interest in another REMIC must take into account the other REMIC percentages of qualifying assets in reporting its own percentages. REMICs that are part of a tiered structure are treated as one REMIC for purposes of determining the REIT and thrift percentage disclosures.

Foreign Holders

Although payments of U.S. source interest and OID to non-U.S. investors generally are subject to a 30% withholding tax, no withholding tax applies to interest and OID that qualify as "portfolio" interest. In addition, U.S. source interest and OID are exempt from the 30% withholding tax if such payments are "effectively connected" to a foreign person's U.S. trade or business. Withholding relief also may be available under an income tax treaty.

In general, interest and OID qualify as portfolio interest if the following requirements are met:

- The beneficial owner of the obligation provides a Form W-8, which certifies the owner's foreign status. The Form W-8 is valid for only three calendar years.
- The obligation is issued after July 18, 1984.
- The obligation is issued in registered form (e.g., book entry). Bearer form obligations also may qualify, provided certain foreign-targeting requirements are satisfied.

Although portfolio interest is exempt from U.S. withholding, such payments must be reported on Form 1042-S (unless the obligation is in bearer form and targeted to foreign markets).

REMIC regular interests: REMIC regular interests are, by definition, issued after July 18, 1984, and regular interests typically are issued in registered form. Consequently, interest and OID paid on a REMIC regular interest usually will qualify as portfolio interest if the beneficial owner provides a Form W-8.

REMIC Residual Interests For residual holders, the underlying obligations held by the REMIC must be issued in registered form after July 18, 1984 in order to qualify for the portfolio interest exception. In addition, a 30% withholding rate applies to any excess inclusion income that is not effectively connected with a U.S. trade or business; excess inclusion income is not eligible for the portfolio interest exception or treaty relief.

---

[72] The REMIC regulations require that, if the percentage of REIT assets reported on the Schedule Q is less than 95%, the REMIC must report additional information on the Schedule Q regarding asset composition and certain items of income related to REIT qualification.

TAXABLE MORTGAGE POOLS

Congress intended that REMICs be the exclusive means of issuing multiple-class mortgage-backed bonds. Multiple-class mortgage securitizations issued after December 31, 1991, that do not make a REMIC election risk being classified as a taxable mortgage pool (TMP). An entity classified as a TMP will be treated as an association taxable as a corporation,[73] thus subject to an entity level tax, and will not be allowed to join in filing a consolidated return.

An entity will be classified as a TMP if substantially all of the entity's assets consist of debt obligations,[74] and more than 50% of those obligations are real estate mortgages or interests therein;[75] the entity is the obligor under debt obligations with two or more maturities;[76] and the payments on the debt obligations "bear a relationship to"[77] payments on the debt collateral.

PASSTHROUGH CERTIFICATES AND PAYTHROUGH BONDS

The nature of commercial mortgages and the commercial mortgage market obviates, as a practical matter, the need for any substantive discussion of passthrough certificates. Mortgage passthrough certificates are not an economic necessity to the commercial mortgage securities marketplace and would generally be less profitable to a sponsor. There is limited ability to use reserve funds, create effective credit support tranches, and vary the maturities of the bonds issued. Since any meaningful evolution in the commercial securitization marketplace has been fairly recent (post-REMIC enactment), nearly all commercial mortgage securitizations to date have been accomplished using a REMIC tax structure, other than those offered as beneficial interests in REITs.

Mortgage passthrough certificates generally are structured to qualify as fixed investment trusts for tax purposes, e.g., grantor trusts. Common examples of mortgage passthrough certificates are Freddie Mac PCs, Fannie Mae MBSs, and Ginnie Maes. In general, holders of the certificates are deemed to hold an undivided ownership interest in the mortgages in the trust. Payments received on the mortgages (generally net of servicing costs) are distributed proportionately to each of the certificate holders.

---

[73] The TMP rules apply to entities as well as portions of entities. However, a thrift generally will not be classified as a TMP.

[74] The "substantially all" test is based on facts and circumstances. However, the tax regulations provide that "substantially all" will *not* be satisfied if less than 80% of the assets are debt obligations.

[75] Excluded from this classification are single family mortgages more than 89 days delinquent, and multi-family and commercial mortgages more than 59 days delinquent.

[76] The regulations indicate that this test is satisfied if the stated maturities of the obligations are different.

[77] Payments on the debt obligations "bear a relationship to" payments on the collateral if, under the terms of the debt, the timing and amount of payments are in large part determined by the timing and amount of payments or projected payments on the collateral.

To qualify as a grantor trust, there generally must be only one class of ownership, and the trustee must not have the power to vary the investment. The regulations allowed multiple classes of ownership under limited circumstances. For example, multiple classes of ownership are allowed if there is no power to vary the investment, the trust was formed to facilitate direct investment in the assets of the trust, and the existence of multiple ownership interests is *incidental to that purpose*. Two examples given in the regulations are a senior subordinated structure when both classes share proportionately in receipts until a default occurs, and the issuance of stripped bonds or stripped coupons.

Paythrough bonds, or collateralized debt obligations, generally refer to debt instruments issued by an entity, such as a trust or corporation, that are backed by a pool of loans or other receivables (such as credit card loans) that comprise the assets of the issuer. While paythrough bonds still may be issued, they offer few advantages over a simple grantor trust structure (except the transaction might be structured as a financing as opposed to a sale), and will have to be tested under the taxable mortgage pool rules. Accordingly, few paythrough mortgage bonds have been issued since 1991.

FINANCIAL ASSET SECURITIZATION INVESTMENT TRUST (FASIT)

Currently under consideration in Congress is the financial asset securitization investment trust or FASIT — a new securitization vehicle that will accommodate a broad range of debt instruments including mortgages. The FASIT legislation will provide definitive rules for the securitization of any debt obligation, similar to what the REMIC provisions did for mortgage debt. FASIT legislation was passed by Congress in December 1995 but the bill was vetoed by the President. Prospects for enactment of the legislation currently are uncertain. Additionally, if enacted, the provisions may differ significantly from those passed by Congress in 1995. The following discussion highlights the major differences between the REMIC provisions and the FASIT provisions.

The FASIT provisions will be elective, and unless mortgages are being securitized, there is no provision similar to the taxable mortgage pool rules that will penalize an issuer that does not elect FASIT status. Any entity may elect FASIT status, and if it does, must use the accrual method of accounting and generally will not be subject to an entity level tax except on certain prohibited transactions similar to a REMIC. There can be only one class of ownership interest (comparable to a residual) but the ownership interest must be held by a single domestic corporation that is not exempt from tax.

The FASIT may issue regular interests that will be treated as debt of the FASIT. A regular interest can be issued at any time (not just at the inception of the FASIT thus, for example, facilitating the issuance of debt backed by revolving credit). Generally, a regular interest's issue price cannot exceed 125% of its stated principal amount, must have a yield to maturity that is less than the AFR plus 5%, and have a stated maturity that does not exceed 30 years. Additionally, similar to a REMIC, the regular interest must have a specified principal amount, fixed terms, be designated as a regular interest and is allowed to carry interest rates similar to those available to a REMIC. However, a "high yield" regular interest carries with it significant restrictions. A "high yield" interest is a regular interest that does not need a specified principal amount (e.g., it could be an interest-only bond), the issue price is not limited to 125% of the stated principal amount, and the yield to maturity may exceed the AFR plus 5%. However, a "high yield" regular interest may be held only by a domestic corporation not exempt from tax.

The FASIT rules provide that *none of the income* of the holder of the ownership interest or any "high yield" regular interest may be offset with deductions, losses, or net operating loss carryforwards. In substance, all the income from these instruments is treated in a manner similar to REMIC excess inclusion income.

When property is contributed to a FASIT, gain (but not loss) is recognized in an amount equal to the excess of the property's value over its adjusted basis. Also gain is recognized on property held outside the FASIT by the holder of the ownership interest if the property supports any regular interest. Special valuation rules are provided for determining the value of debt obligations contributed to the FASIT. Generally, the value will be the sum of the present values of the reasonably expected payments under the instruments discounted using a rate equal to 120% of the AFR. The cash flows should reflect expected prepayments and nonpayments (i.e., credit losses) but not the cost of servicing the loans or administrative costs. Additional guidance is provided for valuing revolving credits.

The FASIT may hold any debt obligation; cash or cash equivalents; foreclosure property (similar to the REMIC rules); certain guarantee or hedge contracts; contract rights to acquire debt instruments, or guarantee or hedge instruments. Additionally, the asset test must be met at the end of the third month beginning after the date of formation and all times thereafter, but the FASIT may acquire additional permitted assets at any time.

Taxable income of the FASIT will be computed under the PAC method and will apply to all interest, OID, market discount, acquisition premium, and bond premium on all debt obligations held by the FASIT. Also, it is expected that the FASIT will have information reporting requirements similar to a REMIC.

At this point it is too early to determine whether FASITs might supplant REMICs. Obviously there are features of each structure that issuers will find attractive.

STATE TAX CONSIDERATIONS

Sponsors, trustees, investors, and return preparers must consider the state tax ramifications associated with commercial mortgage REMICs. While not all states have adopted specific provisions to address issues raised by the federal REMIC election, most that have generally follow the federal rules and do not impose a tax at the REMIC level. In addition, information reporting requirements, if any, may vary from state to state. Accordingly, the various state filing requirements should be reviewed.

SUMMARY

CMBS are, to a very great degree, dependent on the tax law. Borrowers, lenders, sponsors, investors, analysts, and others all must have a thorough understanding of the complex tax rules that govern REMICs, including the various time value of money rules for accounting for income and deductions. Failure to do so could result in loss of REMIC status and entity level taxation, or a 100% tax on certain REMIC transactions. New terms such as regular interests, residual interests, excess inclusion income, inducement payments, phantom income and others have found their way into today's lexicon of structured finance. The future for commercial mortgage securitization looks just as exciting with FASIT just over the horizon and other new entities, structures, and products that are on the drawing board and those that have yet to be imagined.

INDEX

Disclosure, 222
Discount bonds, 339
Discounters, 20
Discovery, 427
Dispersion, 255. See also Coupon dispersion; Loan-to-value dispersion; Loan-to-value ratio dispersion; Principal dispersion
Disposition gain. See Real estate mortgage investment conduits, 20
Disqualified organizations, 425-427
Distribution channels, 18
Distribution date, 95
DIV. See Derived investment value
Diversification, 295, 301. See also Geographic diversification; Income source; Pool diversification
Diversified-borrower mortgage pools, 189-195
Dollar duration, 271
Dollar-for-dollar reduction, 430
Downtown office markets, 29-31
DSC. See Debt service coverage
DSCR. See Debt service coverage ratio, 20
Due diligence, 245, 301. See also Commercial mortgage securitizations; Property information due diligence; Third-party due diligence; Underlying properties
process, 204
reports, 189, 202
Due on sale, 233
Due-on-encumbrance clause, 417
Due-on-sale clause, 417
Duration benefits, 314-315
Duration bond, 314

E

Earthquake risk, 245
Economic stress, 242
Edge cities, 31
Effective date, 405
Effective supply, 12
Effective yield calculation, 392
Efficient frontier, 344
EITF. See Emerging Issues Task Force
Eligibility, 66-68

Emerging Issues Task Force (EITF), 386, 388, 389, 394, 401
Empirical default model, 252-257
factors, 256-257
relationships, 253-256
Enforceability, 198-199
Engineering report, 207, 211
Entry barriers, 194
Environmental compliance, 230
Environmental indemnification, 202
Environmental liability, 90
Environmental policy, 218-220
items, response, 219
proper responses, 220
Environmental problems, 218
Environmental reports, 212, 230
Environmental studies, 207
EPA, 218
Equity dollars, 154
Equity investor, 316
ERISA guidelines, 102
Escalation provisions, 185
Escrow deposits, 233
Estimation, 388-389
Estimation method, 392
Estoppel certificate, 202, 229
Excess inclusion, 425
income, 434-437
Excess servicing, 424
receivable, 401
Excise tax, 425
Existence, 222
Expected performance profiles, 308-312
Expenses, 224-225
Expense-to-revenue ratios, 187
Extended stay hotels, 37-38
Extended-stay properties, 38
Extension feature, 278
Extension options, 350
Extension period, 120
Extension risk, 60-61, 278
External tail, 127

F

Face value, 324
Face-to-face meeting, 184
Fair market value, 409, 413, 430

$13,000,000,000

Commercial Real Estate Financing

Permanent Loans, Mezzanine Financing, Acquisition Lines

$6,000,000,000

Commercial Mortgage-Backed Securities

Zero Payment Default
As of July 31, 1996

...and we've only just begun.

NOMURA
SIZE MATTERS

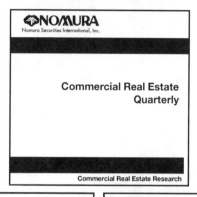

Due Diligence &
Portfolio Valuation

Portfolio & Exit
Strategies

For Information Call:
Phoebe Moreo -
National Director of Real
Estate Securitization Services
(212) 773-2475

E&Y KENNETH LEVENTHAL
REAL ESTATE GROUP
ERNST & YOUNG LLP

CMBS Issuance
& Investor
Analytics

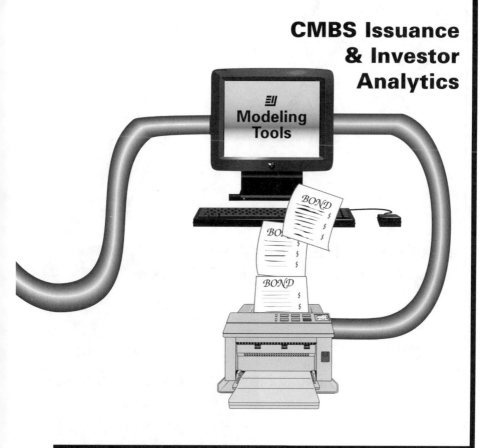

PRECISION MORTGAGE ANALYTICS YOU CAN TRADE ON

MorgVal- The precision, arbitrage-free system for analyzing individual commercial-mortgage-backed securities. MorgVal incorporates the refunding provisions of these securities, including both premium call and yield maintenance, in determining their fair values or option adjusted spreads.

- Analysis of individual mortgages and CMBS pools
- OAS and fair value determination
- Components of value, including prepayment and refunding provisions
- User-specified sector-specific origination expenses and non-economic prepayment rates
- Duration and convexity interest rate risk measures
- Total return analysis, including scenario-dependent cash flows
- Determination of forward yield curves and volatility term structure

With MorgVal, your analysis of a commercial mortgage instrument has never been more precise.

ArmVal- The precision, market-tested OAS calculator for adjustable rate mortgages. ArmVal is the ideal tool for hedging and secondary market trading.

- Fair value/ OAS calculation
- Prepayment rate model provided by Andrew Davidson & Co.
- Fast, arbitrage-free recursive valuation
- Risk characteristics, duration drift, and prepayment sensitivity
- Breakdown of total optionality into sequential periodic collars and life-time caps and floors

ArmVal is available in batch and interactive modes, as a subroutine library, and by subscription on the Bloomberg.

If you're looking for help with Real Estate Capital Markets Transactions...

Deloitte & Touche LLP and Univest Financial Services LLC have just made your choices much easier.

Twice the experience

Our new team brings powerful resources and experience to work for you.

We have the **experience** of working together on some of the largest bulk sales and securitizations to date. Knowing each members strengths and capabilities allows us to **function** together to achieve **maximum efficiency**.

We currently serve many of the leading issuers and other partici- pants in the real estate capital markets, and are the only team to offer a full range of consulting and technology services.

working for you.

We're there from start to finish, and then some.

- ✔ Because of our **unmatched knowledge** of the market, we can help you identify potential problems faster and recommend better solutions.

- ✔ Our commitment to the real estate capital markets doesn't stop with the transaction closing. We offer **consulting support** at every phase of the process, and our **market presence** allows us to respond quickly and effectively to your needs.

- ✔ We're with you for **the long run**. The systems and processes we've developed to serve our clients reflect our market knowledge and are designed to meet your needs in the future as well as the present.

Teamwork.

With it, you can win.

UNIVEST
Univest Financial Services LLC

Deloitte &
Touche LLP

Accounting, Tax and Consulting Services

Asset Securitization
At Your Fingertips...

The new **Structured Financing Workstation for Windows** by Wall Street Analytics, Inc. now allows virtually all assets to be easily securitized or reverse-engineered from within a powerful Windows environment:

- **Commercial Loans**
- **Auto Loans**
- **Credit Cards**
- **Re-Remics**
- **Whole Loans**
- **CMO/REMICs**

Over the past seven years, twenty–five major investment banks have used Wall Street Analytics, Inc. software to design and price over $70 billion in highly complex derivative securities. **The Structured Financing Workstation for Windows** now provides an off-the-shelf securitization system for a one-time fee as low as $75,000.

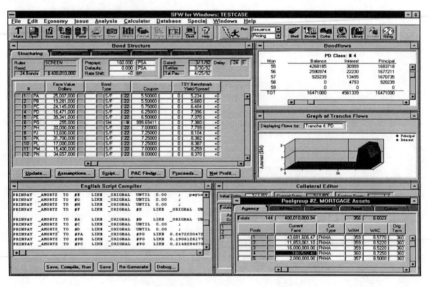

The SFW for Windows is part of a comprehensive and integrated financial product line that is soon to include a **Portfolio Risk Manager** on both Windows and Unix platforms, and a Unix-based version of the SFW. For more information or to receive a demonstration disk, call (415) 390-8730.

 **Wall Street Analytics, Inc.**

Announcing the two best securitization models on the Street:

SFW on Unix/Sparcstation

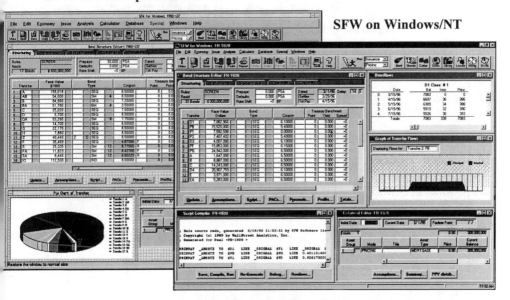

SFW on Windows/NT

And also announcing the fully-integrated Real Estate Finance Module for the property asset/leasing analysis of CMBS issues.

- Sizing of bond credit classes based on underlying asset information and rating agency criteria.
- Allows automatic loan default/recovery triggers based on projected LTVs and DSCRs.
- Fully supports NOI/NPCF property balance sheet projections based on rent rolls, vacancy rates, and expense projections.
- Leasing model allows an unlimited number of individual tenant leases, with rent-rolls, step-ups, tenant improvement costs, and leasing commissions.
- Allows scenarios with time and geographical variations in rent cost and occupancy rates.

A single press of the button will calculate how projected changes in Georgia rents impact the duration of your "B" piece. For more information or to receive a demonstration disk, call (415) 390-8730.

 Wall Street Analytics, Inc.

Is asset securitization right for our real estate interests'

That's a question we've been hearing frequently in recent months from real est
companies and institutional investors looking for opportunities in an uncertain
estate financial marketplace.

The answer depends largely on what you want to accomplish.

Consider Your Long-term Goals

If you're a real estate company, perhaps you're looking to refinance an exis
portfolio. Or, maybe you need additional capital growth and expansion. If you're
institutional investor, you also may be looking for a promising investment. Or eve
hedge. Or, maybe your concern is risk-based capital rules or other regulatory iss
Maybe diversification of your investment portfolio is driving your interest.

At Price Waterhouse, our real estate finance professionals will work with you to help you analyze your objectives and determine whether or not asset securitization is an appropriate strategy for achieving them.

Evaluate the Marketplace

Judging the current environment will be crucial. Currently, the public marketplace for REITs has ebbed, but there may be opportunities to create a private REIT. If securitization does not appear appropriate, perhaps a private partnership between a real estate company and an appropriate investment fund or international investor is the answer. The optimum structure will vary from deal to deal. In each case, the answer will address the objectives of the parties involved and meet the needs of the marketplace.

Determine the Best Way to Structure the Transaction

Our real estate capital markets team, led by Bruce Kiley, Joe Ferst, Dave Baranick and Shahid Quraishi, has developed a portfolio analysis methodology to help our clients analyze and evaluate individual assets as well as entire portfolios. Our services encompass a broad range of procedures: portfolio due diligence, market research, asset valuation, property inspections, rating agency presentations, financial statement audits, reviews and agreed-upon procedures, lease modeling and analysis of the tax consequences of various alternatives. Price Waterhouse real estate information systems consultants can provide complete design and implementation services for systems and operations infrastructure to support a client's securitization or other transaction activity from tracking loan servicing operations and transaction reporting through modeling for alternative transaction structures and tax scenarios. In addition, Price Waterhouse proprietary software simplifies ongoing tax reporting and ensures that accurate returns are completed and filed in a timely manner.

To learn more about how our Real Estate Industry Services Group can help you address the challenges of the evolving real estate finance marketplace, contact the professionals at Price Waterhouse.

For more information, call:

Bruce Kiley (212) 596-8355, **Joe Ferst** (212) 596-8151,
David Baranick (212) 596-8273 or **Shahid Quraishi** (703) 741-2386.

Price Waterhouse LLP

Real Estate Industry Services Group
Strategies for your success[SM]

Turn to Intex for Accurate CMBS Cashflows

Intex Solutions has built its reputation by providing the most accurate residential CMO & Asset-Backed Security cashflows. Our extensive coverage, detailed modeling and timely updates have given our customers unparalleled access to the data they need. The Intex CMO and ABS databases are widely considered to be the "industry standards."

The CMBS market requires even more attention to detail. Not only does Intex provide the models and tools you need to generate accurate cashflows, but we also support the scenario assumptions that are unique to the Commercial world. For this reason, Intex also provides a cross-platform graphical interface specially designed for the Commercial trader.

Intex Solutions – the logical choice to become the standard source of CMBS cashflows.

INTEX SOLUTIONS, INC.

35 Highland Circle, Needham, MA 02194
Tel: (617) 449-6222; Fax: (617) 444-2318